Catholicism
in
Early Modern History

A Guide to Research

John W. O'Malley, S.J.
Editor

Volume 2
Reformation Guides to Research

Catholicism
in
Early Modern History

A Guide to Research

Catholicism
in
Early Modern History

A Guide to Research

Volume 2
of
Reformation Guides
to Research

ISBN: 0-910345-02-3

Printed by Edwards Brothers, Ann Arbor, Michigan
Text is set in Bembo II

This book has been brought to publication by the Center for
Reformation Research St. Louis, Missouri
and the generous support of
The Thomas Jefferson University Press
Northeast Missouri State University

The paper used in this publication meets the minimum requirements of the American National
Standard for Permanence of Paper for Printed Library Materials Z39.48, 1984.

Contents

Introduction

THIS COLLECTION OF STUDIES has from the beginning been intended as a kind of companion volume to Steven Ozment's *Reformation Europe,* published by the Center for Reformation Research in 1982, and the idea for it was occasioned, in fact, by my own contribution entitled "Catholic Reform." While writing the piece I became more aware than ever of the vastness of the subject assigned me and of the desirability of a more extended presentation for the same readership. If it is true, as some historians now maintain, that at a distance of four hundred years the similarities among the various "confessions" are as striking as the differences, two volumes conceived along these lines should serve to complement and correct each other.[1]

In designing this collection I borrowed the general format employed for Reformation Europe. The present volume, too, is meant as "a guide to research." While possibly having other uses as well, it hopes primarily to introduce teachers and students to the state of the art in fields not quite their own and to suggest to them where and how future research might be done. The authors were instructed accordingly, though each was given the freedom to develop his or her contribution as seemed best. Some diversity in presentation resulted, but with substantial accomplishment, I believe, of the original intent.

Both volumes look, therefore, to identical goals and audiences, deal with roughly the same period of history and are concerned with religious questions or materials that evince similar methodological problems. From those points onward, some significant differences begin to appear. These differences result for the most part from substantive differences in the phenomena under investigation–the historical realities themselves and the historiographical approaches and topics they have suggested or that historians have imposed upon them. No book dealing with the Reformation need much concern itself with religious orders, but one dealing with its Catholic counterpart cannot ignore them.

Several considerations have thus guided me in the selection of topics for inclusion in this volume. First among these has been the

---

[1]See, e.g., Ernst Walter Zeeden, *Die Entstehung der Konfessionen: Grundlagen und Formen der Konfessionsbildung im Zeitalter der Glaubenskämpfe* (Munich, 1965) and, most recently and from an entirely different perspective, John Bossy, *Christianity in the West 1400-1700* (Oxford, 1985).

importance conventionally attached to an issue and the amount of research it has received, for instance, the religious orders, the Council of Trent, and the Inquisition. Secondly, attention had to be directed as well to issues where new methodologies were especially operative and causing new fields or new configurations in scholarship to emerge, such as popular piety, education, preaching, the role of women. It also seemed appropriate to provide treatment of topics that are of great importance in themselves but have been slighted in most conventional presentations of modern Catholicism–the liturgy, foreign missions, developments in theology and spirituality, and the solidification of Catholicism in Eastern Europe. The last topic suggested that some attention needed to be given to Catholicism as it declined or revived within given political or cultural units because most research has been carried on within such purviews, and has thus raised questions that a strictly trans-national or less traditional approach does not.

In other words, the attempt has been made to give as comprehensive a sampling as seemed feasible within the confines of one volume. Without doubt it would have been easier and in some ways more satisfying to limit the volume to a single political entity, e.g., Spain and the Spanish Empire, or to have limited it to a single issue, e.g., popular religion. However, the general neglect that the study of Catholicism in the early modern period has suffered in English-language and especially American historiography persuaded me that a broader vista would be more helpful and enlightening.

As was anticipated, such an approach has resulted in a volume with lacunae. Although art, literature, and theater are touched upon in several contributions, they each might well have received separate discussion. The same is true for Jansenism, for the papacy, for economic factors, and for the impact of the printing press. Some important issues are hardly mentioned, and specialists will note for their own area victims that have fallen along the way.

It was particularly difficult to decide which territories to elect for inclusion, for there could be no question of covering even all the major ones. Lack of separate treatment of Latin America, New France, and the Italian States indicates the most glaring sins of omission, some of which are not the result of the original plan but of problems encountered later. *Habent sua fata libelli!* The guiding principle was, in any case, to choose a few political units that because of their recognized importance, their influence beyond their own borders or their sheer historiographical manageability would serve as soundings pertinent to the purposes of the book. I might add in this context that all of the sixteen contributors found that they had to suppress or excise valuable information due to the limitations of space that I imposed upon them.

No doubt, a different editor would have produced a different book, perhaps a more judicious one. On the other hand, I believe that the contributions as they stand do in fact complement one another and, when taken collectively, convey a sense of the whole. Certain figures whose importance has long been recognized emerge with a more detailed and broader grounding. Teresa of Avila is certainly one of these. Charles Borromeo is another, though even more emphasis needs to be placed on an influence that deeply affected realities as diverse as seminaries, catechetics, church furnishings, preaching style and practice, episcopal administration, synodal legislation that became normative far beyond Milan and the embodiment in his person of a new ideal of "heroic" sanctity.[2] As we might have expected, the Jesuits seem to be omnipresent, but the resurgence of the older orders might come somewhat as a surprise. So might the early establishment and firm organization of catechesis in some localities. In the end, the reader will arrive at a much fuller and more sophisticated understanding of phenomena that, for all their complexity and sprawling vastness, can validly be gathered under the general rubric of Catholicism in the early modern period.

In that very regard another difference emerges with the volume edited by Professor Ozment. His title is apposite; the volume deals with Reformation Europe, not Protestantism as such. This volume, on the other hand, is concerned more directly with Catholicism–as it manifested itself in Church, society and culture. Moreover, by the very nature of the case, it extends beyond Europe.

This brings me to the title of the volume. The fact that I wavered back and forth over several alternatives points to the debates over interpretation that such labels suggest. The origins of the term Counter Reformation in late eighteenth and early nineteenth-century German historiography and the interpretive problems it raises have been recognized since Hubert Jedin's famous essay in 1946.[3] The term, originally designating the military, diplomatic, and political actions of Catholics against the Reformation in Germany up to the Treaty of Westphalia, eventually came to be applied in a more generalized way

---

[2]See now John Headley, ed., *San Carlo Borromeo: Catholic Reform and Ecclesiastical Politics in the Second Half of the Sixteenth Century* (Washington, 1987).

[3]*Katholische Reformation oder Gegenreformation?* (Lucerne, 1946).

to Catholicism in the period even by von Ranke. To many scholars, however, it sounded too negative and restrictive to designate the full breadth of the reality under consideration. It could seem to imply that whatever happened in Catholicism was a reaction to the Reformation and was altogether animated by the campaign against Protestantism. Various alternatives were devised, reflecting Jedin's own distinction between "Catholic Reform," which was fundamentally a continuation of healthy impulses within the Church of the late Middle Ages, and "Counter Reformation," the new anti-Protestant institutions and mentality.

It remains easier, however, to criticize the original term than to settle on an alternative. "Catholic Reform" is perhaps the most satisfactory and widely accepted of those proposed, but it lacks outside a determined context a clear chronological designation; and it, too, insofar as it stems from Jedin, implies an interpretative stance. "Catholic Restoration" labors even more heavily under both these difficulties.

Morover, both of them would suggest as a title to a book with the broad scope of this one that everything treated in it relates in some identifiable way to "reform" or "counter reform." That is generally true, but not always. One great exception, for instance, is the foreign missions. In the long run fewer enterprises during the epoch would turn out to be more important for the future of Catholicism, yet only by stretching the term can we label those missions "reform."

In finally determining the present title, I took my cue from Jean Delumeau's *Catholicism between Luther and Voltaire*, while divesting it of what might seem to be a French perspective. The result, I admit, is somewhat labored, but it has the advantages of comprehensiveness and neutrality. It thus seems preferable to a close equivalent, "Catholicism in the Confessional Age," for that, too, might suggest a school of interpretation. As the attentive reader will conclude from the nomenclature employed in the contributions that follow, we are surely far from any standard and consistent usage in this regard. Although we are supposed to be on guard and know better, we even let Counter Reformation slip in through the back door. For all its supposed menace, it has a familiar ring, is not long-winded, and points to a surely important aspect of an admittedly larger reality.

The fact that the title of this volume must be discussed and justified does suggest, however, those broad questions concerning modern Catholicism that are still under debate. Some of these are explicitly addressed from time to time by the authors of this volume, but they perhaps need to be posed more formally and generally at this point, as a kind of orientation.

Many of the contributions substantiate, for instance, how widely operative the anti-Protestant impulses were (and often how ill informed), but what were their chronological stages within any given phenomenon, and how do we account for important elements within Catholicism that these impulses do not seem to have touched effectively? Even aside from the Protestant question, what were the forms of Catholic "Augustinianism," and what role did they play in theology, ministry, piety and politics? A. D. Wright has raised these questions effectively.[4] Along that same line, how burdened was Catholicism with fear and a sense of sin?[5] H. O. Evennett's now classic *The Spirit of the Counter-Reformation* (Cambridge, 1968) details, for example, aspects of that "spirit" that were quite optimistic about human nature and that provide a doctrinal base for the joy, activism and ecstasy of "the Baroque."

The term Counter Reformation implies repression, yet several contributors comment on the welcome from most strata of society that the new endeavors received in those territories where Catholicism finally triumphed. How explain the immense and long-lived spiritual energies, most dramatically evidenced by the burgeoning of "spiritualities" with an unprecedented vigor and diffusion, and, perhaps more intriguing, how explain the later stagnation, even "dechristianization" that some historians perceive in the eighteenth century?[6] Thus, the question arises: when does this period within Catholicism draw to a close? The traditional 1648 for the "end of the Counter Reformation" is from the content of this volume obviously no longer valid, at least not outside Germany.

For that matter, when did "modern Catholicism" begin? Was there a point when a number of uncoordinated reforming initiatives gained a sense of cohesion and direction?[7] Or, a related question: just how continuous was modern Catholicism with the traditions of the late medieval Church? A certain amount of institutional continuity can be granted hands down, as in the structure of the older religious orders or, as Barbara Hallman has recently shown, in the nepotistic practices

---

[4]*The Counter-Reformation: Catholic Europe and the Non-Christian World* (New York, 1982).

[5]See Jean Delumeau, *La peur en Occident, XIV*-XVIII* siècles* (Paris, 1978), and *Le péché et la peur: La culpabilisation en Occident, XIII*-XVIII* siècles* (Paris, 1983).

[6]See, e.g., Jean Delumeau, *Catholicism between Luther and Voltaire: A New View of the Counter-Reformation* (Philadelphia, 1977): 203-31.

[7]See Romeo De Maio, *Riforme e miti nella Chiesa del Cinquecento* (Naples, 1973): 11-29.

of the Roman Curia.[8] Was there as well, however, an across-the-board shift in spirit, so that even the old institutions functioned in a new way, as Gottfried Maron maintained in his attack on Jedin's distinction between "Catholic Reform" and "Counter Reformation"?[9]

Jedin's greatest achievement was his *Geschichte des Konzils von Trient,* a work that helped fix in our minds the idea of a "Tridentine Era" in Catholicism. We use the term facilely, and Giuseppe Alberigo indicates in his contribution in this volume the sense in which the term *tridentinismo* possesses a validity. Yet, years ago John Bossy interpreted Evennett as being hesitant to attribute to the Council decisive influence for the turn Catholicism took.[10]

Granted that it did take a turn, was that turn basically retrograde, or did the new structures and mentality reflect and promote certain features characteristic of the modern world, as Wolfgang Reinhard has argued[11] and as Paolo Prodi has tried to demonstrate in his important book on the Papacy?[12] The most radical challenge to the modernity thesis comes from Bossy.[13] He concedes the fact, but re-evaluates it by counting what was lost to religion in both the Reformation and Counter Reformation. He rejects, in effect, the assumption that either movement was reform in *melius.*

This recent book brings us sharply back to the questions of good and bad that have dogged the historiography of the religious controversies of the sixteenth century from the very beginning, for those questions are inseparable from what happened and why it happened. Reform has no meaning apart from the conviction that some evil must be eliminated, some good set in its place. Reform cannot happen, therefore, without "reform rhetoric," whose task is to name both the evil and the good.[14] That rhetoric almost perforce permeates into our historiographical categories.

---

[8] *Italian Cardinals, Reform, and the Church as Property, 1492-1563* (Berkeley and Los Angeles, 1985).

[9] "Das Schicksal der katholischen Reform im 16. Jahrhundert," *Zeitschrift für Kirchengeschichte* 88 (1977): 218-29.

[10] "Postscript" to *Spirit of the Counter-Reformation,* p. 133. See the balanced analysis of this issue by A. D. Wright, "The Significance of the Council of Trent," *The Journal of Ecclesiastical History* 26 (1975): 353-62.

[11] "Gegenreformation als Modernisierung? Prolegomena zu einer Theorie des konfessionellen Zeitalters," "Archiv für Reformationsgeschichte 68 (1977): 221-52.

[12] *Il sovrano pontefice: Un corpo e due anime; la monarchia papale nella prima età moderna* (Bologna, 1982).

[13] *Christianity in the West.*

[14] See my "Developments, Reforms, and Two Great Reformations: Towards a Historical Assessment of Vatican II," *Theological Studies* 44 (1983): 373-406, esp. 385-88, 395-98.

We thus return to labels–*tridentinismo,* the Tridentine Era, *Seicentismo, el siglo de oro, le grand siècle,* Mannerism, triumphalism, the Baroque–and, of course, *Reformation* and *Gegenreformation.* These and other designations have been applied to phenomena under consideration in this volume, and they have often been extended, at least by implication, to phenomena other than those like art and literature from which they sometimes derived. They all originally connoted value judgments, positive or negative, that depended at least in part on the national context of the historians who devised them. For all countries, much depended on the ideological stance of the historian.

The problems implicit in such labels, as well as those spelled out in the questions I posed above, are perhaps too large ever to be satisfactorily resolved, but they do graphically illustrate what I meant when I elsewhere described this area of scholarship as "rife with controversial issues."[15] Having thus briefly ascended to the dizzying heights of these issues, however, the reader should be ready to turn with some relief to the more finite matters proposed in the following pages.

In so doing he or she will encounter familiar names, institutions and scholars, but will also encounter others that, despite their importance, are scarcely known except to specialists. Men like Stanislaus Hosius, Juan de Avila, Luis de Granada and Alessandro Valignano, for instance, are given their due along with the much better known Peter Canisius, Robert Bellarmine, John of the Cross, Blaise Pascal, Matteo Ricci and Reginald Pole. Women like the Mesdames Acarie and Guyon, Maria Maddelena dei Pazzi, Jeanne-Françoise de Chantal and Marie de l'Incarnation of Quebec take their place in relationship to Teresa of Avila. Recent literature on the Inquisition is reviewed, but so is literature on the liturgy. The reader will move beyond the scholarship of the giants of earlier generations like Henri Bremond, Hubert Jedin, Marcel Bataillon and Gabriel Le Bras to others who are pursuing the same general materials with similar or new methodologies.

The volume reveals fields of scholarship in which documentation exists in almost overwhelming abundance, much of it raw and virtually unexamined–but not all of it, by any means. In fact, many of the phenomena under discussion have been pursued by scholars for generations, though often with the restricted outlook of basically local, apologetic, or amateur historians. The quality of the resulting

---

[15]"Catholic Reform," 310.

publication has varied considerably, but much of it is, within the limits just described, of merit, and can be of considerable help to others who are able to address the materials in a different way.

The volume also reveals just how broadly the professional techniques of contemporary scholarship are being applied and how satisfactorily they are yielding results. Peter Burke discusses aspects of this scholarship that are perhaps best known, but other contributors return to the issue of methodology. Much of what these latter deal with has aroused little interest in North America, which is less a commentary on the competence and importance of the scholarship than on the cultural isolation or particular focus that the two great oceans and our dominant heritage have helped produce in us. This volume should serve in a modest way as a corrective to that situation.

In any case, both older and more recent scholarship have far from exhausted the materials, as practically all the contributors assert. Comparative studies seem, for instance, especially to be lacking in most fields. The pace of change, different in different sectors, needs further consideration; conflict surely existed between the zealous aims of the reformers and *la longue durée* resistant to change of established institutions and mores. Major figures like Ignatius Loyola and Filippo Neri await contextualization. Unlike its Reformation analogue, the historiography of Catholicism has produced relatively few studies of "the Counter Reformation in the cities."

Certain realities in modern Catholicism of seemingly great significance have, moreover, so far practically escaped systematic study and, hence, escaped the nets thrown by this volume. Phenomena like "Forty hours" *(Quarant' ore)*, the *Tre ore* or *Siete Palabras* of Good Friday, the myriad of novenas that sprang up in the seventeenth century fall midway between "spirituality" and "popular piety." These were all accompanied by sermons or series of sermons, many still extant. In effect the period also created what have come to be known as "ministries of interiority" like retreats, spiritual direction and in some circles apparently a new understanding of the positive uses of the sacrament of Confession. Jerónimo Nadal, the most influential early Jesuit except Ignatius himself, commended the ministry of Confession to his brethren as entailing kind of personalized sermon.[16] These and other problems await their historians.

---

[16]See my "Unterwegs in alle Lände der Welt: Die Berufung des Jesuiten nach Jerónimo Nadal," *Geist und Leben* 59 (1986): 247-60, esp. 258.

To aid such enterprises a number of instruments of research now exist. Contributors name those most pertinent to their speciality, but those of a more general nature require some notice here, even at the risk of sometimes repeating titles discussed later and at the risk of stating the obvious. Among the latter is the *New Catholic Encyclopedia*, as well as the earlier edition of that same work. Also familiar to scholars are the *Dictionnaire de théologie catholique* and the *Lexikon für Theologie und Kirche*. In the same genre but less well known are *Catholicisme, Le dictionnaire de droit canonique* and especially the *Dictionnaire de spiritualité*. The latter series, now nearing completion, contains a wealth of information not otherwise easily available about matters that go far beyond what its title indicates. The same can be said of the *Dizionario degli Istituti di Perfezione*, also nearing completion.

The various dictionaries of national biography are always worth consulting, but a special word must be said about the *Dizionario biografico italiano*. Although still in course of publication, the score of volumes that have appeared especially commend themselves because of the high quality and detailed information of the entries and because of the special importance of Italians for our purposes. Both broader and narrower in scope are the volumes entitled *Contemporaries of Erasmus* published by the University of Toronto Press.

The bibliographical fascicules of the *Revue d'histoire ecclésiastique* are of wide coverage and provide an indispensable resource. The *Literaturberichte* of the *Archiv für Reformationsgeschichte* can be helpful. Again, the *Bibliographie internationale de l'Humanisme et Renaissance* ranges far beyond what one might expect and is particularly valuable for listing titles of publications related to religion as it intersects with culture.

* * *

I want to thank the contributors to the volume for their patience and, among them, especially Professor William S. Maltby, Executive Director of the Center for Reformation Research, for his advice and unfailing cooperation in this venture. I also want to acknowledge the translators for those contributions that had to be rendered into English: Marie-Claude Thompson (Blet), Debora Contrada (Marcocchi), Beth Holmgren (Kłoczowski) and Joseph Gladwin (Borromeo). I myself translated Giuseppe Alberigo's "The Council of Trent."

Early Modern Germany

Robert Bireley, S.J. *

TWO FEATURES GAVE GERMAN CATHOLICISM during the Early Modern Period a special character. More than any other country, Germany, or the Holy Roman Empire of the German Nation,[1] was the home of the Reformation. From 1517 onwards Catholicism there was on the frontline of the competition and conflict with the Protestants. This situation led at times to extreme militance, at times to recognition of the need for toleration. Secondly, the peculiarities of the imperial constitution meant that religion and politics were even more entangled here than elsewhere. As a result of Germany's political fragmentation the contest between Catholic and Protestant took place not only on the imperial level, where it was intertwined with the struggle between emperor and estates, but in a multitude of political jurisdictions from large territories through imperial cities to small principalities. The many ecclesiastical states whose origins were in the earlier Middle Ages and whose prince-(arch)bishops or prince-abbots held secular as well as ecclesiastical authority were peculiar to the Empire; only the Papal States supplied an analogy. Thus the history of Catholicism in Germany is of particular complexity.

Extremely fruitful for the study of Catholicism–and Protestantism–in Germany has been the work of Ernst Walter Zeeden and, more recently, Wolfgang Reinhard. In a seminal article in 1958, Zeeden called for a comparative study of the development of the principal Christian churches, or confessions, in the wake of the Reformation. He defined "confessionalization" (*Konfessionsbildung*) as "the intellectual and organizational hardening" of the diverging Christian confessions after the breakdown of religious unity into more or less stable church structures with their own doctrines, constitutions, and religious and moral styles. At the same time [this comprises] their active intervention

*I am grateful to Dieter Albrecht (Regensburg), Volker Press (Tübingen), Anton Schindling (Eichstätt), and Jared Wicks (Rome) for conversations that were most helpful in the preparation of this article. Responsibility for the contents, however, remains with me. Loyola University's Committee on Research generously provided me with a grant that made possible a trip to Germany for purposes of this article.
[1]The boundaries of the Empire remained somewhat unclear even after 1648. Included in this essay are the lands of the Bohemian Crown but not the Netherlands, Switzerland, or North Italy.

in the Christian world of Early Modern Europe, their defense against threats and attacks from outside, and the influences from non-ecclesiastical elements, especially the state, which helped in their formation."[2] Both Zeeden and Reinhard point up the interdisciplinary nature of the study required if we are to encompass all the forces at work in confessionalization. Both relate confessionalization in particular to the growth of the territorial state; this was the chief long-range political development in Germany in the sixteenth and seventeenth centuries. Reinhard (1982), moreover, has issued an impassioned plea for more cooperation between church historians and social and economic historians.

This approach focuses on the elements common to the growth of the three principal confessions or religious parties in the Empire: the Catholic, the Lutheran, and the Calvinist,[3] and thereby helps provide an avenue to ecumenical understanding. In addition, it places developments in the broad perspective of the church's interaction in history with different cultures and societies. The formation of the confessions is seen as three competing responses to the changes of the sixteenth century and the widespread demand for church reform. Reinhard (1977), building upon authors such as H. O. Evennett and Jean Delumeau, has argued that Catholicism as well as Protestantism contributed to the "modern world" through its promotion of rationalization, growing bureaucracy, social discipline, individualism, and an advance beyond European ethnocentrism. Subsequently (1983), he has proposed seven common procedures involved in the formation of confessional identity: the elaboration of clear theological positions; their promulgation and implementation through institutional forms such as nunciatures, synods, visitations; their internalization, especially through schools and seminaries; the use of the means of communication, especially the printing press, to propagandize and of censorship to hinder the propaganda of others; disciplinary measures, such as the visitation of parishes and other institutions; control of the nature of and access to rites; and the development of a peculiar confessional language, as in the predilection for certain saints' names.

Zeeden provided a conceptual framework in which to grasp the highly complex developments in Germany and into which research on

---

[2]Zeeden (1958): 251 (or 88 in the 1975 reprint); (1965): 9.
[3]The term confessions is used here to designate the Catholic and Protestant or Catholic, Lutheran, and Calvinist religious parties. The meaning should be clear from the context.

the Tridentine Reform can be fitted. He has also provided a much needed chronology that looks to the long term. The events of 1517 inaugurated an evangelical period, itself a response to the demand for church reform. Following the defeat of the Peasants Revolt in 1525 and the Diet of Speyer the next year, the beginnings of a Lutheran-style church started the process of confessionalization. For the Catholics, the process lagged twenty to forty years behind; it stretched out for over 150 years, and it proceeded at a different pace in different regions and states. For a substantial period there was a great deal of confusion, especially among the common people. Zeeden cites instances where the same individual functioned as a Catholic priest and Protestant pastor.[4] Only in the 1580s did a firm sense of Catholic identity begin to form, and in the early seventeenth century the Tridentine Reform began to show distinct successes. The Thirty Years' War interrupted this process drastically in many areas, but it picked up with new vigor after 1648 and continued into the early eighteenth century. Despite all imperfections and shortcomings, "the churches. . . (with considerable variation according to place, time, and confession) were actually reformed and stabilized in their new state."[5]

The Council of Trent was obviously a source of renewal and restoration for Catholicism in Germany. By the mid-1550s nearly eighty percent of the population was Protestant in some sense, and the church structure in many areas was a shambles.[6] Most of North Germany had been lost. Most resistant to the Protestant wave on the popular level were areas of the west and southwest including Habsburg Anterior Austria. In Wittelsbach Bavaria and in other Habsburg lands the commitment of the dynasty proved to be a bulwark against Protestantism. Many ecclesiastical princes, though not active reformers, were able to retain their states for the old Church, and these states later became springboards of reform. The *Acta Reformationis Catholicæ 1520-1570*, published by Georg Pfeilschifter, has thrown new light on the early reform efforts of the German bishops, to the point that it is necessary to revise the story of the early Catholic reform.[7] Another major documentary publication has been the *Correspondance* of Julius Pflug, Bishop of Merseburg and an influential figure with the emperor.

---

[4] Zeeden (1965): 74,77.

[5] Zeeden, Lang et al, 1, 16 (introduction). From this perspective, Gerald Strauss, *Luther's House of Learning* (Baltimore, 1978), does not carry his investigations far enough to see the results of the Reformation.

[6] Alois Schröer, "Das Tridentinum und Münster," in Schreiber (1951): 2, 311.

[7] The six volumes published to date take the story up to 1548. See also n10.

This masterful edition by J. V. Pollet, O.P., is rich in information on the period from 1530 into the 1560s, particularly on the fate of the Catholic Church in Saxony. The role of Rome in the implementation of Trent in Germany is more evident than ever from the important book of Josef Krasenbrink. The Papacy soon understood that it had to deal with the princes rather than the emperor. The Peace of Augsburg, which granted formal toleration to the Protestants in 1555, also provided the legal basis for the restoration of Catholicism in the lands of the Catholic princes. At the Diet of Augsburg in 1566, the legate, Giovanni Commendone, saw that he would never secure the acceptance of the Tridentine decrees for the Empire from either Emperor Maximilian II or the diet. He then gathered the Catholic members of the diet in his house where they declared verbally their unconditional acceptance of the dogmatic decrees but asked for indulgence regarding the reform decrees especially in the matter of provincial synods. The Curia came to see in the taking of the Tridentine Profession of Faith by German bishops, scarcely any of whom were present at Trent, the accceptance of the conciliar decrees. The general recognition of the legality of this demand in Catholic Germany was "a decisive step on the way to the implementation of Trent.[8] The German Congregation, founded under Pius V, was most effective under Gregory XIII. Its strategy was to secure good bishops and then to work from the top down. Of great value was the new style of nuncios introduced by Gregory. They were no longer chiefly political representatives with the emperor in Vienna or Prague but real instruments of church reform. Roving nuncios were employed in the south and northwest until permanent nunciatures were established in Graz (1580 until 1619) and Cologne (1584). The *Nuntiaturberichte aus Deutschland* remain an important source for the study of German Catholicism and especially its relations with Rome.[9] Georg Lutz and others have discussed their value as sources in the 1973 *Quellen und Forschungen aus italienischen Archiven und Bibliotheken,* and Reinhard (1971) has provided an overview of the early years of the nunciature in Cologne.

The best introduction to the implementation of Trent in the German dioceses remains the two-volume *Das Weltkonzil von Trient,* edited by Georg Schreiber, even though it has little on the Habsburg

---

[8]Krasenbrink (1972): 41.
[9]For series and volumes, see Baumgart, who, however, overlooks the recently begun series for the nunciature at Graz. See *Nuntiaturberichte,* Sonderreihe.

lands. Particularly helpful is Schreiber's lengthy introduction along with a subsequent article (1952); between them they touch on all the institutional problems confronting the Church in Germany. Tridentine decrees, rather than being accepted *in toto,* were usually worked into diocesan legislation. Provincial synods were rare, perhaps the two most important being those of Salzburg in 1569 and 1573. There was a vast discrepancy in the conduct of diocesan synods. Neither a diocesan nor a provincial synod was ever held in Mainz; five were held in Cologne between 1598 and 1627, then none until 1662, the last until the nineteenth century. For the synods, Schannat-Hartzheim (1759-1790) remains a valuable source.[10]

One instrument of church reform decreed by Trent was the renewal of an earlier institution, the regular visitation of his diocese by a bishop. Inspired by the French school of Gabriel Le Bras, Zeeden has focused new attention on the *Visitationsakten,* Protestant as well as Catholic. They include instructions for the visitors, questionnaires, minutes of interviews, final reports, subsequent decrees, and all the materials relating to the planning, execution, and follow-up of the visitations. They bring us down to basic church life as it was lived at the parish level and provide a special insight into the slow process of confessionalization. Methodological caution, however, must be observed. Marc Venard, the successor of Le Bras, has indicated the need to compare evidence from the *Visitationsakten* with other sources when this is possible, and he has suggested that they may tell us more of the mentality of the visitors than the religious life of those visited.[11] Zeeden envisions a *Repertorium,* in seven volumes, of all the *Visitationsakten* located in archives within the Federal Republic of Germany. Thus far the first volume and the first part of volume two have appeared.[12]

There is, then, a decided effort in Germany, largely through the *Visitationsakten,* to study the rural parish and to assess the effect of the Catholic Reform upon it. There is much to be done, and there is need to allow for broad regional differences. Peter Lang's two articles (1982,

---

[10]*Concilia Germaniæ.* Vol. 7 begins with 1564. Two studies in the series *Konziliengeschichte,* ed. Walter Brandmüller have been announced: Josef Leinweber, *Die Synoden in Italien, Deutschland und Frankreich von 1215 bis zum Tridentinum* and Gerhard B. Winkler, *Die nachtridentinischen Synoden in Deutschland.*

[11]"Die französischen Visitationsberichte des 16. bis 18. Jahrhundert" in Zeeden und Lang, eds., 64.

[12]One can only hope that current financial difficulties will not interfere with the completion of this project. Zeeden and Molitor, eds., 2d ed., includes a bibliography of published *Visitationsberichte* as well as of pieces relating or summarizing them in detail. The essays also discuss methodological issues.

1984)[13] make use of the *Visitationsakten* in different ways. In both he concludes that the reform began to take solid root after 1600. Earlier Alois Hahn produced a fine study of the reception of the Tridentine Reform from roughly 1565 to 1680 by the rural parish clergy in approximately three hundred parishes in Luxembourg and Lorraine under the jurisdiction of the Archbishop of Trier. For methodological soundness–Hahn uses many other sources to control evidence from visitations–, scope, and analysis the study is unequalled for the German-speaking lands. He finds improvement, especially in the personal residence of the pastor and the regular administration of the sacraments, but this is not so evident in the general Christian conduct of the pastor, despite many examples to the contrary, and in preaching and catechizing. Pastors were, Hahn concludes, relatively well off; poverty was not an obstacle to reform. Major hindrances were the failure to provide a Tridentine seminary, rights of patronage that underwent little change, and the persistence of a deeply rooted juridical concept of the pastorate.

Religion in the cities has been a focal point of research since the provocative work of Bernd Moeller in the early 1960s, but recent works have tended to look more at developments over the long haul. This is the case with two studies by non-German scholars who, from different methodological perspectives, show the increasing confessionalization in the second half of the sixteenth century. R. Po-chia Hsia's fine treatment of the untypical territorial city of Münster exhibits careful social analysis. Gerald Chaix offers a partial answer to the question why Cologne remained Catholic by pointing to the influence of the well-known Charter house there and especially to its literary production. But if Catholic Cologne seems to attract few German scholars, the opposite is true of Augsburg. Paul Warmbrunn has compared the evolution of practical toleration there and in three other imperial cities between 1555 and 1648, and Étienne François discusses Augsburg at length in an article that presents a highly nuanced picture of the practice of toleration in German cities from 1650 to 1800 and that anticipates what promises to be a highly significant *thèse d'état.* Three works analyzing the elite of Augsburg are nearing publication.[14] Kaspar von Greyerz's survey of research on religion and the city focuses

[13]"Reform in Wandel. Die katholischen Visitationsinterrogatorien des 16. und 17. Jahrhunderts," in Zeeden and Lang, 131-90.
[14]The *Habilitationsschrift* of Bernd Roeck and the dissertations of Katerina Sehr-Burens and Peter Steuer.

on the years before 1550 but includes much useful material for the period under discussion here.

Two institutions of the German Church remained relatively untouched by Trent: the prince-bishops and the cathedral chapters. They fell only with the secularization of 1803. After the secularizations of the Reformation, there remained twenty-four prince-bishops with seat and voice in the diet, apart from the territorial bishops of the Habsburg lands and the four bishops named by the Archbishop of Salzburg.[15] Since the late Middle Ages the prince-bishoprics and most cathedral canonries had been open only to nobility, thus giving the German Church increasingly the appearance of an "Adelskirche." Trent had taken no account of the German situation in its delineation of the ideal pastoral bishop. The governmental and administrative functions of the prince-bishop called for different qualities, and frequently he remained unordained. According to the Vienna Corcordat of 1448, which set out the procedures for the election of the prince-bishops, the chapters retained the right of election. This prevented either the emperor or the pope from controlling the episcopate. The Papacy did not hesitate to permit departure from Tridentine norms, especially regarding pluralism and ordination, when the possession of a bishopric by a powerful ruling house was thought necessary to prevent its secularization. The classic example was the bestowal of the Archbishopric of Cologne in 1583 on Ernest of Bavaria, a personally unworthy candidate who was to accumulate three other bishoprics in the northwest and establish a Wittelsbach secundogeniture there until 1761.

Yet there were outstanding prince-bishops imbued with the spirit of Trent. Alfred Wendehorst provides a rich treatment of the Bishops of Würzburg from 1455 to 1617 and especially Prince-Bishop Julius Echter von Mespelbrunn (1573-1617), a major and controversial figure of the Counter Reformation. Manfred Becker-Huberti has argued persuasively that Christoph Bernhard von Galen, Prince-Bishop of Münster from 1650-1678, who long suffered under his reputation as a "warrior bishop," deserves to be ranked among the great reform bishops of the seventeenth century. Others were Ferdinand of Bavaria (Cologne, Liège, Münster, Hildesheim, Paderborn), Dietrich von Fürstenberg (Paderborn), Ferdinand von Fürstenberg (Paderborn, Münster), Franz Wilhelm von Wartenberg (Osnabrück, Regensburg), and Johann Philipp von Schönborn (Würzburg, Mainz, Worms).

[15]Seckau, Gurk, Lavant, and Chiemsee.

The cathedral chapters saw themselves as "co-rulers" in the ecclesiastical states. Trent's efforts to restrict the power of these corporations met with only limited success. There were many ways in which they could limit the freedom of the prince-bishop, one being the electoral capitulation; the joint efforts of Pope Innocent XIII and Emperor Leopold I to disallow these in 1695 fell short of the goal. Georg Rauch concludes his exemplary study of the chapter in Mainz with the observation that the canons were, overall, men of average ability, little initiative, and easy life, but he cautions that each chapter was different and urges the need for comparative studies. These will greatly profit from the recently published three-volume opus of Peter Hersche. His impressive quantitative study of the 5725 cathedral canons from 1600-1800 reflects the growing interest in the social history of church institutions. It is obviously a major work, rich in data and interpretation and provocative of new lines of research.[16]

Princes fostered confessionalization, Reinhard (1983) suggests, to promote a sense of territorial identity, to encourage the social discipline necessary to create useful subjects, and to secure control of the Church and its material resources. For this reason there appeared what has been called "confessional absolutism," but he quickly adds that this was not a Machiavellian exploitation of the Church. Most princes took seriously their obligation to promote religion and honestly believed that the interest of the Church and the interest of the state overlapped. Furthermore, as Jürgen Bücking shows, princely promotion of religion did not always lead to more complete control of the Church. In the Tyrol the position of the bishops vis-à-vis the Habsburg rulers was stronger in the post-Tridentine period than it had been before the Reformation. In light of similar developments in neighboring states, Bücking concludes that one cannot speak in all cases of a growing "Staatskirchentum" prior to the middle of the seventeenth century. His point is that many scholars compare the position of the bishop to the Tridentine ideal rather than to the situation prior to the Reformation. This leads to a distorted picture of the way things were moving.

Volker Press, in a number of articles, has shown special interest in the social groups and networks that advanced confessionalization. He has suggested that the confessions developed with the help of humanistically educated laymen drawn from the cities, imperial and territorial, who held government positions at various levels in the

---

[16]This volume appeared in the outstanding *Germania Sacra* series. Most volumes published thus far focus on the Middle Ages.

territories. In the Catholic lands, Press sees this taking place especially in Bavaria, Anterior Austria, and the Tyrol. Initially, the process there lagged behind the Protestant lands, but by the end of the sixteenth century it caught up, largely because of the Jesuit schools. The explicit exception is the remaining Habsburg lands, where the nobility played the leading role in all the confessions.

The role of literature and language in the Counter Reformation and Baroque culture has been the subject of much recent stimulating interdisciplinary scholarship. Dieter Breuer's argument (1979) reflects the viewpoint of many: the study of German language and literature from the perspective of the evolution of a national tradition and a national state has long blocked the way to adequate appreciation of the particularist literary traditions associated with the Catholic states, especially Bavaria and Austria. Magisterial and indispensable for any interpretation of Catholicism in Early Modern Germany is Jean-Marie Valentin's three-volume study of the theater of the Jesuits in the German-speaking lands (1978), followed by a monumental bibliography listing 7,650 works, most in manuscript, that were written or produced from 1555 to 1775 (1983-84). For Valentin, the Jesuit drama was not interested so much in criticism of the Protestants as in putting forward positive Catholic values and stressing the importance of the active life as citizen.[17] He argues that the Counter Reformation in Germany was more open to the world, more optimistic, and less-divided than in France, where Gallicanism, Jansenism, and a pessimistic Augustinianism were salient strains. Another significant work is Geil van Gemert's exhaustive study of Aegidius Albertinus, a Belgian who came to Munich in 1590 as a court secretary and during the next thirty years produced a huge corpus of popular religious works. Many of his books were loose translations or adaptations from the Spanish, and they call our attention to the influence of popular religious literature from the Latin countries in Germany. Two series of essays edited by Valentin (1979) and Breuer (1984) and nearly a full issue of the *Zeitschrift für bayerische Landesgeschichte* (1984, 1) devoted to the literature of Upper Germany in the Baroque Age testify to the interest in this field in which, all agree, the surface has scarcely been touched.

Education was a means of Catholic Reform and of confessionalization. Several recent volumes have dealt with Jesuit activity,

[17]See also Valentin (1980).

especially in higher and seminary education.[18] Peter Schmidt, in a study similar to Hersche's in methodology, has analyzed the list of 5,228 alumni of the German College in Rome from 1552 to 1914 according to social, regional, and educational background, and subsequent career. He establishes that the goal of the college from the early seventeenth to the late eighteenth century was that set by the Papacy, the preparation of nobles for higher ecclesiastical positions in the German Church, and he assesses the degree to which this goal was met. A distinctive "seminary policy" of the Bavarian dukes that illustrated the expanding competence of the state and the role of the Jesuits in clerical education is the topic of Arno Seifert. No diocesan seminaries founded before 1600 in Germany survived, and few were successful before 1650. Karl Hengst has investigated from a largely juridical perspective the development of Jesuit activity in German Catholic universities until 1650, and Anton Schindling has looked at their humanist educational reforms at the universities in Dillingen, Dôle, Freiburg im Breisgau, and Molsheim. Earlier, Rudolph Reinhardt pointed to the decisive influence of Jesuit Dillingen on the Benedictine monasteries in Swabia, which led in particular to their heavier pastoral commitment.[19]

Thus far little has been said about the Habsburg lands. For them we have the masterful interpretation of R. J. W. Evans's *The Making of the Habsburg Monarchy 1550-1700*. The synthesis offered here is tentative, as Evans himself states, but it should be the starting point for research for some time to come. In the Habsburg lands too, one can speak of confessionalization, but with a different coloration. Evans devotes much less attention to the political, partly because he assumes knowledge of the principal events and partly because he considers it less important than the social, intellectual, cultural, and religious factors on which he concentrates. For Evans, what essentially created the Habsburg Monarchy was the establishment of the great magnate families and the implementation of the Counter Reformation, an arrangement that was merely confirmed by the government in the form of the dynasty. These three bonds—magnates, Church, dynasty—held together a monarchy distinctive for its size and ethnic diversity. The desire for social and intellectual order, a characteristic of seventeenth

---

[18]Duhr, though in many respects outdated, remains basic for the history of the Jesuits in Germany.

[19]As Schindling points out, the horizontal as well as the vertical study of religious orders, showing connections and mutual influences, can be an extremely fruitful approach.

century Europe emphasized by Evans, contributed to the growth of the monarchy and to the attractiveness of Catholicism, which contrasted with divided Protestantism. In addition, the international character of Catholicism was particularly suited to the dynasty with its imperial aura and its many subject nationalities.

The relationship between confessionalization and the increasing conflict, legal, political, and eventually military, between the confessions that culminated in the Thirty Years' War is a topic ripe for investigation. Van Gemert has recently argued that around 1600 in areas little touched by Protestantism, especially Bavaria, Catholic popular religious literature, reflecting a new self-confidence, became less polemical and more concerned with reform of the Catholic community.[20] Moreover, the process of confessionalization picked up renewed force after the long war and peaked only after 1700. According to François, confessional exclusivity grew more intense in many German cities after the Peace of Westphalia. Certainly, one cannot assume that confessionalization led inevitably to military confrontation.

Martin Heckel in his many studies has focused on an aspect of the struggle between the confessions that was highly prominent for contemporaries but is often overlooked today: its legal aspect. Heckel calls the Peace of Augsburg "the most important constitutional law of the First German Empire."[21] It broke with the medieval tradition by permitting the existence of two Christian confessions. It aided confessionalization by according control of religion to the territorial rulers, and it provided the individual with a modicum of religious freedom in the right of emigration, the first written constitutional right given Germans.[22] The main theme of Heckel's recent survey, *Deutschland im konfessionellen Zeitalter 1555-1648*, is the drawn-out conflict over the interpretation of the Peace, especially its provisions regarding the ecclesiastical states and church lands. The Peace of Westphalia concluding the Thirty Years' War in 1648 was considered the legitimate interpretation and a further development of the Peace of Augsburg. It recognized explicitly the parity of the two confessions and ushered in a body of imperial church law that was acknowledged to be superior to either Catholic or Protestant ecclesiastical law. Thus it provided a basic security to the religious parties that endured until

[20]"Zum Verhaltnis von Reformbestrebungen und Individualfrömmigkeit bei Tympius und Albertinus," in Breuer, ed., 108-9.
[21]Heckel (1975): 93.
[22]Heckel (1984): 48.

1803. The Peace froze the possession of ecclesiastical lands, rights, and privileges, including toleration, at the normative year 1624. Princes still enjoyed the right to regulate religion in their territories, but they were prohibited from changing the established religion. Thus subjects no longer had to fear a change. A prince could still force a dissident to emigrate (and the subject retained this right), but if the prince permitted him to stay, he had to grant him the right of "domestic devotion" thus subjects were not to be forced to attend services, much less to convert. This represented a significant gain for religious freedom. An exception was the Habsburg lands, where the ruler retained the full right of reformation. For the Catholics, in addition to stabilizing the religious situation, the normative year meant the survival of the ecclesiastical states and the Catholic majority in the electoral college that guaranteed the emperor would be Catholic. The result was increased confidence and reform activity that picked up quickly after the war. This was the significance of 1648 for the Catholic Reform.

The Thirty Years' War was an extremely involved European as well as German struggle with many and varied causes. Two major questions, perhaps ultimately unanswerable, are: at what point before 1618 did war between the confessions become virtually inevitable, if it ever did, and to what extent was the war a religious conflict? Heckel's survey implies ineluctable progression toward war as does much German historiography, but Evans (1973) has argued that Erasmian theology and Latin classicism with an accompanying spirit of toleration remained strong until the end of the century. As previously noted, van Gemert has pointed up the diminishing polemical character of much popular Catholic religious literature. Winfried Schulz's proposal that the weakened threat from the East following the conclusion of the Turkish War (1593-1606) resulted in increased militance in the Empire emphasizes a perspective often overlooked, and the religious nature of the war for Maximilian of Bavaria and Emperor Ferdinand II, the two leading Catholic princes, has been stressed by Robert Bireley. He has pointed up the many differences among the Catholics, the emperor, Maximilian, other German princes, Spain, and the Papacy, and has shown the tension at the Catholic courts between moderates and militants, groups roughly analgous to the contemporary French *bons français* and *devots.*

The study of the Thirty Years' War has been greatly enriched by the advance of two documentary collections. The *Briefe und Akten zur Geschichte des Dreissigjährigen Krieges* took the prewar story from the

1580s to 1613 in eleven volumes. The New Series, in two parts, now carries developments into the 1630s. The bridge between the two has been made by Hugo Altmann's *Die Reichspolitik Maximilians I von Bayern 1613-1618,* which is a thorough narrative as well as a collection of documents. Three further volumes now in progress will complete the years up to 1635 where the second documentary collection begins. This is the monumental *Acta Pacis Westphalicæ,* now edited by Konrad Repgen. Approximately forty-five volumes are foreseen, divided into three series, of which fourteen have this far been published.[23]

Toleration within the Empire was viewed differently by princes from toleration in their own states; for these they felt greater responsibility. Princes promoted confessionalization as we have seen. The ideal remained, for religious and political reasons, a state unified in faith. When they felt strong enough to do so, the princes often took measures to pressure people to convert. Where this was done systematically, it usually began with the expulsion of Protestant teachers and schoolteachers, continued with the imposition of civil disabilities, and proceeded to exile. Under Ferdinand II nearly one hundred thousand Protestants left the Habsburg lands rather than convert.[24] Others revolted, as in the Upper Austrian Peasants' Revolt of 1626. The well-known, late emigration of twenty thousand from the Archbishopric of Salzburg in 1731/32 is discussed at length by Franz Ortner. Generally, pressures to convert were accompanied by preaching and other pastoral efforts to win internal consent. Jesuit colleges were a favorite means to the recatholization of an area; they were often pastoral as well as educational centers, and they were obviously oriented toward the youth and the long-term conversion of a region.

But a Catholic theology of toleration of heretics had developed in the course of the sixteenth century, beginning in the Netherlands. It both reflected and influenced events on the imperial and territorial level. As Jean Lecler has shown, it was largely the extension to Protestant heretics of a position worked out by the medieval theologians for infidels. Private and even public exercise of their religion might be permitted in cases of necessity, by which was usually meant the preservation of public order from internal disruption or external attack. Such toleration did not imply that the ruler took religion less seriously; it meant that he recognized that the good of Catholicism and the state was better served by a degree of toleration. A principal reason for

[23]For individual volumes in these series, see Baumgart.
[24]Bireley, 46.

acceptance of the Peace of Augsburg by Catholic rulers, including Emperor Ferdinand I, had been the opportunity it gave them to exercise the right of reformation in their own lands. During the Thirty Years' War, Catholic moderates argued, eventually with success, for the greater good to be obtained for Church and Empire through peace with further toleration. On the territorial level, according to time and circumstances, there was a great variety of practical toleration enjoyed by Protestants in Catholic lands. Many ecclesiastical states were long too weak to enforce a rigid policy, and for many years the Habsburg rulers were compelled to make formal concessions to the Protestants. Klaus Jaitner has described the gradual process toward toleration of Duke Philipp Wilhelm of Neuburg in the lands of Jülich and Berg following the Peace of Westphalia. Toleration there was similar to that in the adjacent territories of the Great Elector.

Catholics lived outside Catholic states. Franz Schrader has studied the struggle of monasteries to stay alive in secularized territories, and Peter Lang has looked at the small Catholic community in the imperial city of Ulm. Important sources for Catholics living in the new "Diaspora" situation in the north, where the hierarchy no longer existed, are the nunciature reports and after 1622 the files of the Propaganda Fide, which assumed jurisdiction over them at that time.[25]

German suspicion of Rome had its roots in the Middle Ages, particularly in the Investiture Controversy. It grew in the fifteenth century into resentment expressed in the Grievances of the German Nation, and it nourished the virulent anti-papalism of Luther. But only with the decisive help of Rome had the Church in Germany survived and begun to grow strong again. Once it had recovered its health, and after 1648, felt secure, it began to grow impatient with practices that had appeared in the sixteenth century, such as extensive jurisdiction of the nuncios, that seemed to restrict its legitimate freedom of action. In addition, there was some unhappiness with papal policy during the Thirty Years' War, different aspects of which have been investigated by Dieter Albrecht and Konrad Repgen.

Johann Philipp von Schönborn, Archbishop of Mainz from 1647 to 1673, inaugurated the "Schönborn Era" in the German Church, so called because of the members of his family who held major ecclesiastical positions during the next century. The period began as a

---

[25]See Denzler, Tüchle (1962, 1972).

time of restoration, and the Schönborn Era, though certainly not without its shortcomings, saw the conclusion of the long process of confessionalization and reform in the German Church.[26] Johann Philipp represented a more self-conscious, postwar German hierarchy that intended to reassert traditional rights and privileges. His election to Mainz was a significant gain for the Catholic moderates in the Empire. He opposed the hardline policy of the nuncio at the Congress of Westphalia, Alessandro Chigi, later Pope Alexander VII, and he counselled against the well-known protest of the Peace. But as Friedhelm Jürgensmeier shows, Schönborn's policy was neither anti-Roman nor episcopalist. The German situation was different from that in France. The German episcopate had neither the sense of solidarity nor the theological resources for such a program. Febronianism was a much later development.

Bibliography

Acta Pacis Westphalicæ, eds. Max Braubach and Konrad Repgen (Münster, 1962-). (For series and volumes published and planned, see Baumgart, 163-64.)

Albrecht, Dieter, "Zur Finanzierung des Dreissigjährigen Krieges,"*Zeitschrift für bayerische Landesgeschichte* 19 (1956): 534-67. Rpt. in *Der Dreissigjährige Krieg: Perspektiven und Strukturen,* ed. Hans Ulrich Rudolf (Darmstadt, 1977): 368-412.

Altmann, Hugo, *Die Reichspolitik Maximilians I von Bayern 1613-1618* (Munich, 1978).(= *Briefe und Akten zur Geschichte des Dreissigjährigen Krieges,* Vol. 12.)

Baumgart, Winfried, *Bücherverzeichnis zur deutschen Geschichte. Hilfsmittel. Handbücher. Quellen.* 5th ed. (Munich, 1983).

Becker-Huberti, Manfred, *Die tridentinische Reform im Bistum Münster unter Fürstbischof Bernhard von Galen 1650 bis 1678* (Münster, 1978).

Bireley, Robert, *Religion and Politics in the Age of the Conterreformation: Emperor Ferdinand II, William Lamormaini, S.J., and the Formation of Imperial Policy* (Chapel Hill, 1981).

Bosl, Karl, ed. *Handbuch der Geschichte der böhmischen Lander,* vol. 2 (Stuttgart, 1974).

Breuer, Dieter, *Oberdeutsche Literatur 1565-1650. Deutsche Literaturgeschichte und Territorialgeschichte in frühabsolutistischer Zeit* (Munich, 1979).

————, ed., Frömmigkeit in der Frühen Neuzeit: Studien zur religiösen Literatur des 17 Jahrhunderts in Deutschland (Amsterdam, 1984).

[26]Jedin (1956).

Briefe und Akten zur Geschichte des Dreissigjährigen Krieges, eds. Moriz Ritter et al, 12 vols. (Munich, 1870-1978); New Series, eds. Dieter Albrecht, Kathrin Bierther et al, Part 1, 2 vols.: Part 2, Vols 1-5, 8 (Munich, 1907-). (For individual volumes and for those projected, see Baumgart, 162-63).

Bücking, Jürgen, *Frühabsolutismus und Kirchenreform in Tirol 1565-1665* (Wiesbaden, 1972).

Chaix, Gérald, *Reforme et Contre-Reforme Catholiques. Recherches sur la Chartreuse de Cologne au xvie siècle.* 3 vols. (Salzburg, 1981).

Concilia Germaniæ, eds. Johannes Schannat, Josef Hartzheim, et al, 11 vols. (Cologne, 1759-90).

Denzler, Georg, *Die Propagandakongregation in Rom und die Kirche in Deutschland im ersten Jahrzehnt nach dem Westfälischen Frieden. Mit Edition der Kongregationsprotokolle zur deutschen Angelegenheiten 1649-1657*(Paderborn, 1969).

Duhr, Bernhard, *Geschichte der Jesuiten in den Ländern deutscher Zunge*, 4 vols. (Freiberg/Regensburg, 1907-28).

Evans, R. J. W., *Rudolf II and His World (Oxford, 1973).*

————, *The Making of the Habsburg Monarchy 1550-1700: An Interpretation* (Oxford, 1979).

François, Étienne, "De l'uniformité à la tolerance: confession et société urbaine en Allemagne, 1650-1800," *Annales* 37 (July-August, 1982): 783-800.

Gemert, G. C. A. M. van, *Die Werke des Aegidus Albertinus (1560-1620). Ein Beitrag zur Erforschung des deutsch-sprachigen Schrifttums der katholischen Reformbewegung in Bayern um 1600* (Amsterdam), 1979.

Gebhardt, Bruno, *Handbuch der deutschen Geschichte*, Vol. 2, 9th ed. (Stuttgart, 1970).

Greyerz, Kaspar von, "Stadt und Reformation: Stand und Aufgabe der Forschung," *Archiv für Reformationsgeschichte*, 76 (1985): 6-63.

Hahn, Alois, *Die Rezeption des tridentinischen Pfarrerideals im westtrierischen Pfarrklerus des 16. und 17. Jahrhunderts* (Luxembourg, 1974).

Heckel, Martin, "*Autonomia und Pacis Compositio.* Der Augsburger Religionsfriede in der Deutung der Gegenreformation," *Zeitschrift für Rechtsgeschichte* 76 (1959), *kanonistische Abteilung,* 45: 141-248.

————, "Augsburger Religionsfriede. II. Juristisch," *Evangelisches Staatslexikon*, eds. H. Kunst et al, 2d ed. (1975): 93-97.

————, *Deutschland im konfessionellen Zeitalter* (Göttingen, 1983).

Hengst, Karl, *Jesuiten an Universitäten und Jesuitenuniversitäten: Zur Geschichte der Universitäten in der Oberdeutschen und Rheinischen Provinz der Gesellschaft Jesu im Zeitalter der konfessionellen Auseinandersetzung* (Paderborn, 1981).

Hersche, Peter, *Die deutschen Domkapitel im 17. und 18. Jahrhundert*, 3 vols. (Bern, 1984).

Höfer, Josef, and Karl Rahner, eds., *Lexikon für Theologie und Kirche*, 11 vols. (Freiburg, 1957-65).

Hsia, R. Po-chia, *Society and Religion in Münster 1535-1618* (New Haven, 1984).

Jahrbuch der historischen Forschung in der Bundesrepublik Deutschland, Berichtsjahr 1982 (Munich/New York, 1983).

Jaitner, Klaus, *Die Konfessionspolitik des Pfalzgrafens Philipp Wilhelm von Neuburg in Jülich-Berg von 1647 bis 1679* (Münster, 1973).

Jedin, Hubert, and John Dolan, eds., *History of the Church*, Vols. 5 and 6, trans. from the German (New York, 1980/81).

Jedin, Hubert, "Die Reichskirche der Schönbornzeit," *Trierer Theologische Zeitschrift*, 65 (1956): 202-16. Reprinted in H. Jedin, *Kirche des Glaubens, Kirche der Geschichte* (Freiburg, 1966) 1:455-69.

Jürgensmeier, Friedhelm, Johann Philipp von Schönborn (1605-1673) und die römische Kurie. Ein Beitrag zur Kirchengeschichte des 17. Jahrhunderts (Mainz, 1977).

Krasenbrink, Josef, *Die Congregatio Germanica und die katholische Reform in Deutschland nach dem Tridentinum* (Münster, 1972).

Lang, Peter, *Die Ulmer Katholiken im Zeitalter der Glaubenskämpfe: Lebensbedingungen einer konfessionellen Minderheit (Frankfurt, 1977).*

————, "Die tridentinische Reform im Landkapitel Mergentheim bis zum Einfall der Schweden 1631," *Rottenburger Jahrbuch für Kirchengeschichte*, 1 (1982): 143-67.

Lecler, Joseph, *Toleration and the Reformation*, trans. from the French, 2 vols. (New York, 1960).

Lutz, Georg, "Glaubwürdigkeit und Gehalt von Nuntiaturberichten," *Quellen und Forschungen aus italienischen Archiven und Bibliotheken* 53 (1973): 227-75.

Lutz, Heinrich, *Das Ringen um deutsche Einheit und kirchliche Erneuerung: von Maximilian I bis zum Westfälischen Frieden 1490 bis 1648* (Berlin, 1983).

Nuntiaturberichte aus Deutschland nebst ergänzenden Aktenstücken (1892-). (For Series and volumes published and planned, see Baumgart, 154-58.)

Nuntiaturberichte, Sonderreihe: Grazer Nuntiatur, Vol. 1, *Nuntiatur des Germanico Malaspina. Sendung des Antonio Possevino, 1580-1582 ;* Vol. 2, *Nuntiatur des Germanico Malaspina und des Giovanni Andrea Caligari, 1582-1587*, ed. Johann Rainer (Vienna, 1973/81).

Ortner, Franz, *Reformation, Katholische Reform und Gegenreformation in Salzburg* (Salzburg/Munich, 1981).

Pflug, Julius, *Correspondance recueilliée et éditée avec introduction et notes par J. V. Pollet, O.P.*, 5 vols. (Leiden, 1969-82).

Pfeilschifter, Georg, ed., *Acta Reformationis Catholicæ ecclesiam Germaniæ concernantia sæculi XVI. Die Reformationsverhandlungen des deutschen Episkopats von 1520-1570*, 6 vols. (Regensburg, 1959-).

Press, Volker, "Stadt und Territoriale Konfessionsbildung," *Kirche und Gesellschaftlicher Wandel in deutschen und niederländischen Städten der Werdenden Neuzeit*, ed. Franz Petri (Cologne/Vienna, 1980): 251-96.

Rauch, Gunter, "Das Mainzer Domkapitel in der Neuzeit. Zur Verfassung und Selbstverständnis einer adeligen geistlichen Gemeinschaft. (Mit einer Liste der Domprälaten seit 1500)," *Zeitschrift für Rechtsgeschichte* 92 (1975), 93 (1976), 94 (1977), kanonistische Abteilung 61: 161-227, 62: 194-278, 63: 132-79.

Reinhard, Wolfgang, "Katholische Reform und Gegenreformation in der Kölner Nuntiatur 1584-1641," *Römische Quartalschrift* 66 (1971): 8-65.

_____, "Gegenreformation als Modernisierung? Prolegomena zu einer Theorie des konfessionellen Zeitalters," *Archiv für Reformationsgeschichte* 68 (1977): 226-52.

_____, "Möglichkeiten und Grenzen der Verbindung von Kirchengeschichte mit Sozial- und Wirtschaftsgeschichte," *Wiener Beiträge zur Geschichte der Neuzeit* 8, *Spezialforschung und "Gesamtgeschichte:" Beispiele und Methodenfragen zur Geschichte der frühen Neuzeit,* ed. Grete Klingenstein and Heinrich Lutz (Munich, 1982): 243-78.

_____, "Zwang zur Konfessionalisierung? Prolegomena zu einer Theorie des konfessionellen Zeitalters," *Zeitschrift für historische Forschung* 10 (1983): 257-77.

Reinhardt, Rudolf, *Restauration, Visitation, Inspiration. Die Reformbestrebungen in der Benediktinerabtei Weingarten von 1567-1627* (Stuttgart, 1960).

Repgen, Konrad, *Die römische Kurie und der westfälische Friede. Idee und Wirklichkeit des Papsttums im 16. und 17. Jahrhundert, Vol. 1, Parts 1 and 2 (Tübingen, 1962/65).*

Schindling, Anton, "Die katholische Bildungsreform zwischen Humanismus und Barock," in *Vorderösterreich in der frühen Neuzeit,* ed. Hans Maier and Volker Press (Sigmaringen, forthcoming).

Schmidt, Peter, *Das Collegium Germanicum in Rom und die Germaniker. Zur Funktion eines römischen Ausländerseminars (1552-1914)* (Tübingen, 1984).

Schrader, Franz, *Ringen, Untergang und Überleben der katholischen Klöster in den Hochstiften Magdeburg und Halberstadt von der Reformation bis zum Westfälischen Frieden* (Münster, 1977).

Schreiber, Georg, ed., *Das Weltkonzil von Trient. Sein Werden und Wirken,* 2 vols. *(Freiburg, 1951).*

_____, "Tridentinische Reformdekrete in deutschen Bistümern," *Zeitschrift für Rechtsgeschichte* 69 (1952), *kanonistische Abteilung* 38: 395-452. Reprinted in *Concilium Tridentinum,* ed. Remigius Bäumer (Darmstadt, 1979): 462-521.

Schulze, Winfried, *Reich und Türkengefahr im späten 16. Jahrhundert. Studien zu den politischen und gesellschaftlichen Auswirkungen einer äusseren Bedrohung* (Munich, 1978).

Seifert, Arno, *Weltlicher Staat und Kirchenreform. Die Seminarpolitik Bayerns im 16. Jahrhundert* (Münster, 1978).

Spindler, Max, ed., *Handbuch der bayerischen Geschichte,* Vol. 2, *Das alte Bayern. Der Territorialstaat vom Ausgang des 12. Jahrhunderts bis zum Ausgang des 18. Jahrhunderts,* Vol 3, in 2 parts, *Franken, Schwaben, Oberpfalz. Bis zum Ausgang des 18. Jahrhunderts* (Munich, 1969/71). (Completely new editions are expected soon.)

Tüchle, Hermann, ed., *Acta SC de Propaganda Fide Germaniam spectantia. Die Protokolle der Propagandakongregation zu deutschen Angelegenheiten 1622-1649* (Paderborn, 1962).

—————, ed., *Die Protokolle der Propagandakongregation zu deutschen Angelegenheiten 1657-1667* (Paderborn, 1972).

Valentin, Jean-Marie, *Le Théâtre des Jésuites dans les pays de langue allemande (1554-1680), Salut des âmes et ordres des cités,* 3 vols. (Bern/Frankfurt/Las Vegas, 1978).

—————, ed., *Gegenreformation und Literatur: Beiträge zur interdisziplinären Erforschung der katholischen Reformbewegung* (Amsterdam, 1979).

—————, "Gegenreformation und Literatur: das Jesuitendrama im Dienste der religiösen und moralischen Erziehung," *Historisches Jahrbuch* 100 (1980): 240-56.

—————, Le Théâtre des Jésuites dans les pays de langue allemande. Répertoire chronologique des pièces représentées et des documents conservés (1553-1773), 2 vols. (Stuttgart, 1983/84).

Warmbrunn, Paul, *Zwei Konfessionen in einer Stadt. Das Zusammenleben von Katholiken und Protestanten in den paritätischen Reichstädten Augsburg, Biberach, Ravensburg und Dinkelsbühl von 1548-1648* (Wiesbaden, 1983).

Wendehorst, Alfred, *Das Bistum Würzburg*, Part 3, *Die Bischofsreihe von 1455 bis 1617* (Berlin/New York, 1978) (= Germania Sacra, New Series, 13).

Zeeden, Ernst Walter, "Grundlagen und Wege der Konfessionsbildung in Deutschland im Zeitalter der Glaubenskämpfe," *Historische Zeitschrift* 185 (1958): 249-99. Reprinted, except for pp. 276-86, in *Gegenreformation,* ed. E. W. Zeeden (Darmstadt, 1973): 85-134.

—————, *Die Entstehung der Konfessionen. Grundlagen und Formen der Konfessionsbildung im Zeitalter der Glaubenskämpfe* (Munich, 1965).

—————, und Hansgeorg Molitor, eds., *Die Visitation im Dienst der kirchlichen Reform,* 2d ed., (Münster, 1976).

—————, ed., with Peter Lang, Christa Reinhardt, Helga Schnabel-Schüle, *Repertorium der Kirchenvisitationsakten aus dem 16. und 17. Jahrhundert in Archiven der Bundesrepublik Deutschland,* Vol. 1, Hessen, Vol. 2, Baden-Württemberg, Part 1, *Der katholische Südwesten. Die Grafschaften Hohenlohe und Wertheim* (Stuttgart, 1982/84).

—————, and Peter Lang, eds., *Kirche und Visitation. Beiträge zur Erforschung des frühneuzeitlichen Visitationswesen in Europa* (Stuttgart, 1984).

For further literature, one should consult the handbooks listed above under Bosl, Gebhardt, Jedin and Dolan, and Spindler, the *Lexikon für Theologie und Kirche,* edited by Höfer and Rahner, and the surveys listed under Heckel and Heinrich Lutz. Works in progress are usually listed in the *Jahrbuch der historischen Forschung in der Bundesrepublik Deutschland,* the most recent available volume of which is for 1982. Invaluable for this or any period of German History is Baumgart, *Bücherverzeichnis zur deutschen Geschichte.* It includes all the major reference works, bibliographies, handbooks, *lexika,* dictionaries, as well as the principal documentary collections, with volumes published and projected, and the significant periodicals. It is now published by the Deutscher Taschenbuch Verlag (DTV) and is inexpensive.

Spain

William S. Maltby

THE IMPORTANCE OF RELIGION AND THE CHURCH in the life of early modern Spain is universally acknowledged. Few European governments matched the Spanish monarchy in its control over ecclesiastical institutions or in its willingness to allow religious considerations to influence foreign and domestic policy. There is also a widespread if largely undocumented conviction that ordinary Spaniards were influenced by Catholic attitudes and beliefs to a degree unparalleled elsewhere. Under ordinary circumstances the importance of the subject would virtually guarantee a well developed historiography, but except in certain rather limited areas this has not been the case.

In part this is because Spain in the past was unable to support historical studies on a northern-European scale. Its archives are uncommonly rich and, though individual scholars have made heroic contributions, all too often they were bound to their subjects by personal or corporate ties that left them open, perhaps unfairly, to charges of partisanship. In a more developed historical tradition this would mean little, but the absence of that critical mass of studies necessary to informed debate has made the problem far more serious. Foreign scholarship has not redeemed the situation. Drawn by an appreciation of Spain's influence on early modern Europe, French, Danish, German, English, and American historians have established a weighty presence in the literature. Unfortunately, they have not always dealt with Spanish religious history on its own terms. Given the cumulative weight of scholarship on the Protestant Reformation, this is perhaps inevitable, but it has led to distortions in the field as a whole. There is a persistent tendency to assume that movements important to the rest of Europe would have been equally interesting to Spaniards had they not been artificially suppressed. Conversely, phenomena that had few parallels elsewhere are likely to be ignored or to have their character obscured by false analogies. Underlying much of this is the often unspoken question, "how did Spain escape the Reformation?" If in asking this it is assumed that some form of Protestant revolt was the normative response to conditions within the late-medieval Church, other distortions will result, and they will be magnified according to the excellence of the works in which they are found.

31

It is far better to approach the religious history of early modern Spain as the outgrowth of conditions within the Peninsula before attempting to relate the Spanish experience to the rest of Europe. For those willing to do so, the best starting point is probably two recent and massive compendia: *La Historia de la iglesia en España*, volumes 3.1, 3.2, and 4 edited by R. García Villoslada, and *La teología española en el siglo XVI* (2v) by Melquiades Andrés Martín. The first is a cooperative effort, while the second is the product of a single hand, but both are useful surveys of current knowledge in their respective fields. As such they reveal the strengths and weaknesses of the literature as a whole, as well as some of the distortions in emphasis created by the interests of non-Spanish writers. It will immediately be apparent that among the most thoroughly studied of Spanish religious phenomena are the reforms undertaken at the beginning of the sixteenth century by Cardinal Francisco Jiménez de Cisneros and the various movements that arose from them. They not only figure prominently in the volumes mentioned above, but are the subjects of an impressive array of books and articles produced over the years by Spaniards and foreigners alike. Cisneros's efforts were directed at institutional reform as well as at spiritual and intellectual renewal. Characteristically, Spanish scholars have been most interested in the former. Demetrio Mansilla (1967-68) and Tarsicio de Azcona (1960) have placed the reorganization of the episcopate firmly where it belongs: as an extension of Ferdinand and Isabella's broader program of institutional reform. The temptation to see it through the refracting lense of the Reformation has been largely avoided. The diplomatic side of this process has, of course, been an object of attention since early in the last century. Negotiations with the papacy over episcopal appointments, the Inquisition, and the *patronato real* have always been recognized as landmarks in the development of the Spanish state, and studied accordingly.[1]

Reform of the religious orders, though equally important, has not been examined in the same depth. Little has been done in the past thirty years, and most of what was written before is the product of scholarship within the orders themselves. This is not necessarily a bad thing, but it is an example of one of those areas in which a single perspective has inevitably prevailed. The Dominicans have been well served by the works of Beltrán de Heredia, but Cisneros's own Franciscans would benefit from a new monograph that carries their history beyond the

---

[1]Serrano (1914, 1940), Sheels (1961), Aldea Vaquero (1961), Gutierrez Martín (1967), Lynch (1961).

pontificate of Sixtus IV. That one does not exist is hardly surprising. There is no modern scholarly biography of Cisneros himself. The quality and quantity of literature on other orders varies. Some fine work has been done on the monastery of San Benito de Valladolid and on the reforming abbot of Montserrat, García Jiménez de Cisneros,[2] but the only general study of the Benedictines is G. M. Colombás, *Corrientes espirituales entre los benedictinos observantes* (1963). There is a lengthy article on the Premonstratensians by J. Goñi Gaztambide.[3] The Capuchins, Jeronymites, and Augustinians were all the subject of early twentieth-century scholarship, but the Cistercians and several other orders have been almost entirely neglected, and all could benefit from new studies that incorporate modern methods and concerns. Some orders, of course, were not involved in the reform. The Jesuits, founded long after the death of Cisneros and always regarded with suspicion in Spain, have been studied by Astraín (1912-25), but the Trinitarians and Mercedarians were reformed only in the reign of Philip II and have not been studied at all. Under these circumstances José García Oro's *Cisneros y la reforma del clero español* (1971) must be seen as a guide to future research as well as a survey of existing knowledge.

The spiritual and intellectual aspects of reform have also received their share of attention. Cisneros like his royal master was deeply concerned with the education of the clergy and sought to revitalize learning through the support of scholars and by founding the university of Alcalá de Henares. His willingness to encourage the teaching of theology by the "three ways" (Scotism, Thomism, and nominalism) and his interest in biblical scholarship broadened the base of theological discourse and led to what some have described as a religious renaissance. It certainly paved the way for a brief efflorescence of Erasmian humanism and for other movements that were regarded with deep suspicion by the orthodox.

Some of these groups, though they never achieved wide acceptance, have fascinated historians and colored our interpretation of Spanish intellectual life as a whole. This is due in part, as J. H. Elliott said, to the influence of Bataillon's magisterial *Erasme en Espagne,*[4] but there are other reasons as well. Erasmianism is one of the points at which the distinctive academic culture of Spain made contact with the trans-Pyrenaean world. Like Erasmus himself, it exerts profound

---

[2]Colombás and Gost (1954), Zaragoza Pascual (1973-76), Suárez Fernández (1976).
[3]Colombás (1955).
[4]J. H. Elliott, *Imperial Spain* (New York, 1963): 389.

attraction for those moderns who are repelled by the grim orthodoxy of much sixteenth-century thought and who see the persecution of the Erasmians as the triumph of obscurantism. It is also linked to illuminism and to Protestantism. Illuminism has attracted considerable interest as a heterodox variation of that "interior" Christianity that later produced such spiritual giants as Saint Teresa and Saint John of the Cross. Protestants, however few they may have been, are of interest to Protestant scholars. The result has been a volume of work on all three phenomena, much of it produced by foreigners, that tends to obscure the truly dominant strains of Spanish religious thought. It is one of those rare cases in which history was written by the losers.

On the Erasmians, the work of Bataillon remains the best source. His verdict that most of these men were essentially orthodox victims of the friars whom they attacked stands. The illuminists have received more recent attention. The most recent survey by Antonio Márquez (1972) is based to some extent on Angela Selke's doctoral dissertation of 1954. Both argue that illuminism was an indigenous regional movement centered in New Castile, more specifically in the household of the Mendoza family, and that some of its tenets were genuinely heretical. Its character is summarized by Melquiades Andrés in his *Teología Española* and placed in the broader context of Spanish mysticism in his massive *Los Recogidos* (1975). The latter surveys the mystical tradition in Spain from 1500 to 1700 and provides a sober and valuable synthesis on this complex topic. In general, the illuminists or *alumbrados* are now seen as advocates of an interior Christianity who, in their search for a direct personal union with God, went too far. They differed from more orthodox mystics in their quietism and rejection of the sacraments and vocal prayer. Their theology, if they had one, is difficult to reconstruct on the basis of existing evidence, but it appears to have suffered from an exaggerated theocentrism that drastically limited human freedom and from their rejection of scholastic argument based in part on their motto, *no pensar nada.* Theological innocence may have contributed more to their difficulties with the Inquisition than any willful intent to break with orthodoxy.

The rejection of scholasticism, together with the desire to bypass the sacraments and liturgy of the Church, united the *alumbrados* in some minds with the Erasmists and Lutherans, though neither of these other movements was involved with mysticism, nor were the *alumbrados* unduly concerned with Scripture. There was, however, a certain amount of contact between individuals who might broadly be classified in one of these groups, as well as among those who were simply heterodox in a general way without adhering firmly to any particular school. The dangers of facile categorization are illustrated by the case of Juan de Valdés. The conclusions of Longhurst (1950) have been modified by José Nieto (1970), who argued that Valdés was more influenced by such indigenous currents as illuminism than by Erasmus, and that he arrived at a concept of *sole fide* without Luther. Real Protestants who consciously accepted Lutheran or other reformed teachings were few. In fact the inquisitors themselves were remarkably ignorant of reformed theology, but Spanish Protestantism has nevertheless attracted attention since the days of Ernst Schäfer (1902).[5]

In part this interest is tied to the perennial allure of the Inquisition. Few Spanish institutions have been so thoroughly studied, especially by foreigners, and books on the subject continue to be produced with some frequency.[6] This is not so much a manifestation of the Black Legend as a reflection of the volume, importance, and accessibility of inquisitorial records. Unfortunately, this very abundance has had a distorting effect comparable to that produced by Bataillon. Though the character of the institution is no longer the subject of much controversy, its study has provided historians with detailed, sometimes exhaustive, knowledge of what was regarded at the time as spiritually pathological. Much more is therefore known about intellectuals whose thought was the subject of inquisitorial concern than about those whose orthodoxy was not seriously questioned. The latter were, of course, in the majority, and it should not be assumed that their work was thereby unoriginal or even uncontroversial. Similarly, the rich harvest of popular errors uncovered by the inquisitors tells us little about the beliefs of ordinary Spaniards except through the hazardous and logically deficient procedure of defining the pious on the basis of what was or was not condemned.

It is perhaps fortunate that recent studies have led in a different direction, though the new emphasis is equally susceptible to distortion.

[5]A bibliography of this literature from 1940 to 1955 may be found in *Bibliographie de la Réforme, 1540-1648*, 3eme Fasc. (Leiden, 1961). It has been brought up to date by A. Gordon Kinder, *Spanish Protestants and Reformers in the Sixteenth Century* (London, 1983).
[6]The most recent general survey is Kamen (1985), which revises his earlier *The Spanish Inquisition* (London, 1965). See also the essay by J. L. Gonzalez Novalín in Villoslada, ed. *Historia de la iglesia en España* and the article by Agostino Borromeo in this volume, which contains additional references.

Inquisitorial records, especially those dealing with moral cases, are an unmatched source for the social historian. Led by Gustav Henningsen and Jaime Contreras, historians from several countries are using these as the basis for studies of sexuality, the family, and popular culture. They have also illuminated the problem of witchcraft, though this was a relatively minor concern in Spain, where official skepticism discouraged denunciations. A sampler of this material, taken largely from a symposium organized by Henningsen in 1979, has been assembled in French under the editorship of Bartolomé Bennassar.

The usefulness of inquisitional records is not, of course, limited to the periphery of Spanish religious life. Academic politics and inter-order rivalries ensured that even orthodox thinkers could be investigated, and the resulting documents are often useful for their minute dissection of certain aspects of the suspect's thought. The danger is that by relying too heavily on such sources the historian may lose the broader outlines of a writer's contribution and exaggerate his affinities with some heterodox group. A more productive approach would be to examine individuals within the context of Spanish theological development as a whole, working outward if necessary to the heretical manifestations of a particular movement.

Like many other countries sixteenth-century Spain was a battleground between two major forms of spirituality, though neither of them in this case falls outside the Catholic tradition. One, characterized by simplicity, interiority, moralism, systematic mental prayer, and sometimes a kind of biblicism, was largely an outgrowth of the Cisneran reforms and their observant Franciscan predecessors.[7] The other, which emphasized the sacraments, vocal prayer, and a revival of aristotelian rationalism, is usually seen as a reaction to the excesses of the reformers but in fact represents a different conception of religious life. Predictably, most thinkers fall somewhere along a line between the most extreme positions on either side. At this point few if any of them have been adequately studied.

Saint Teresa of Avila and her ally in the Discalced Carmelite reform, Saint John of the Cross, are perhaps the best known Spanish religious figures after Loyola, yet neither has been exhaustively studied. Saint Teresa has been victimized by scores of popular biographies, but the best surveys of her life and thought remain those published by members of her own order, *Santa Teresa y su Tiempo* by Efrén de la

---

[7]Andrés (1975): 22-23.

Madre de Dios and Otger Steggink (several editions of various sizes from 1968 to 1984) and the three-volume *Vida* by Silverio de Santa Teresa (1935-37). Saint John has always been more studied for his poetry than for his religious thought. José Nieto's *Mystic, Rebel, Saint* (1979) is a recent and welcome corrective, but on Saint Peter of Alcántara, one of the men who inspired both of them, there is little beyond a handful of articles in journals that are difficult to find outside Spain.

All three of these figures were both the instigators and the products of larger movements, but there has been little systematic study of these phenomena as a whole and little analysis of the ideas and forms of piety on which they rested. Some of these issues are raised by Otger Steggink's *La reforma del Carmelo* (1965), though his primary focus is on the meetings in 1566-67 between Saint Teresa and the General of the order, Giovanni Battista Rossi. There are also some major questions to be asked about the practical aspects of the movement. The two saints founded a number of convents and reformed many more. This was done only at considerable expense and in the face of determined opposition from powerful figures within the Church. At the same time their writings were regarded with the usual suspicion reserved for mystics, and their activities were carefully monitored by the Inquisition. Support and protection seem to have come primarily from the great nobles–Philip II did little on their behalf until 1579–but this raises some questions of its own. How did Saint Teresa gain the support of every faction in a notoriously divided court? What, in fact, inspired the *grandes* not only to support the Discalced Carmelites, but to undertake reforms of their own in the convents of other orders? The answer perhaps lies in a study of their relationship to the Church in general. The traditional emphasis on royal patronage has tended to obscure the fact that many benefices and even abbacies still lay within the gift of noblemen and that even when the right of direct nomination was not involved noble influence could be decisive. It is rather surprising, for example, to learn that in 1581 the Duke of Alba was able to reverse the appointment of the Dominican Provincial of Castile after the choice had already been announced by the King.[8] If little is known about the religious orders in earlier reigns even less is known about their activities after the accession of Philip II. Until these lacunae are filled such occurrences will remain impenetrable.

[8]The relevant documents are in *Documentos Inéditos para la historia de España* 35: 225-27, 243-44, 261-63.

The general shortage of studies on both mystics and reformers is even more marked outside the Discalced movement. Aside from the work of Melquiades Andrés and Beltrán de Heredia's *Las corrientes de espiritualidad entre los dominicos de Castilla* (1941), both of which are summaries rather than detailed analyses of individual thinkers, there is very little. This is doubly unfortunate because the devotional writings of some of these people–Luis de Granada comes to mind–were sufficiently well known to have influenced the piety of laymen.

None of this, however, compares with the neglect suffered by those who held opposing points of view. The historiography of Spanish intellectual life in the early modern period is not only sketchy, it is one-sided. Principled opposition to the reformers, mystics, and Erasmians came from a variety of sources. To characterize all of them as obscurantist, reactionary, or hopelessly unoriginal is both unfair and misleading. It is also profoundly unhistorical in that it tends to discourage analysis of those whose influence was the greatest.

To imply, for example, that the end of Erasmianism in Spain meant the end of humanism is to misunderstand both. Erasmianism was but one school within the larger movement, and in Spain, at least, it was by no means the most important. In contrast to modern opinion, many learned Spaniards found the Erasmians' suspicion of formal reason obscurantist and their political ideas naive. They much preferred the Italianate humanism imported from Bologna, because it combined philological and historical criticism with hard-headed Aristotelian rationalism. It was this humanism, exemplified in the early sixteenth century by Juan Ginés de Sepúlveda that, together with the neo-Thomism of Francisco de Vitoria and his followers, laid the groundwork for the political thought of the Salamanca School and the Jesuits, Suárez and Mariana.[9]

Neo-Thomism was, of course, the dominant system of thought in Spain after the 1530s. Though many of its advocates agreed with Melchor Cano that a theologian's highest calling was the defense of orthodoxy, its primary attraction was not conservatism but rigor, precision, and clarity. The inevitable association of Thomism with the Dominican order and particularly with the powerful convent of San Esteban de Salamanca has ensured that a sympathetic view would be presented in the various works of Beltrán de Heredia, but all too often

---

[9]For a discussion of this issue see J. A. Fernández Santamaria, *The State, War and Peace: Spanish Political Thought in the Renaissance 1516-1556* (Cambridge, 1977), and Muñoz Delgado (1978).

the neo-Thomists are known mainly through studies that focus on those whom they denounced to the Inquisition. The works of J. I. Tellechea Idígoras on Bartolomé Carranza, M. de la Pinta Llorente on Alonso Gudiel, and A. F. G. Bell on Luis de León and Francisco Sánchez's "El Brocense" are excellent examples. All were latter-day exemplars of the Cisneran tradition, and all deserve further study, but the energies of their opponents were not entirely consumed with these disputes.

The road to a more balanced assessment must start with a better understanding of Spanish academic life. F. Martín Hernández has made a beginning with his studies of clerical education (1961 and 1964), but something like Richard Kagan's work on the *collegios mayores* (which trained lawyers and administrators for the empire) is needed for the faculties of theology and philosophy.[10] This is not only a question of ideas, but of academic politics. The universities were a major battleground for inter-order rivalries as well as for a wide variety of other conflicts in both Church and state. Our understanding of the personal and institutional framework in which intellectual conflict took place remains inadequate. The next step is to examine or re-examine the contributions of such people as Vitoria, Melchor Cano, Domingo de Soto, Mancio, Alonso de Contreras, Laínez, and Salmerón. In spite of their importance some of them have received little systematic attention in forty years, though their influence on political theory has been more carefully examined.[11] The failure to study their thought as an organic whole ensures that only one half of the struggle for the Spanish mind will be understood and that even that half will be distorted.

It is clear, then, that a re-examination of theology, the academic environment, and the religious orders should be a high priority for scholars in the years to come. Other *desiderata* remain.

In 1970 Antonio Domínguez Ortiz, the dean of the seventeenth-century social historians, published the second volume of his *Sociedad española en el siglo XVII*. In it he summarized what was known about the Spanish clergy and suggested a program of study for the future. His concerns were largely secular. In his view the Spanish clergy constituted a powerful social class about which far too little was known. What were their origins? Where did their revenues come from, and

---

[10]Richard Kagan, *Students and Society in Early Modern Spain* (Baltimore, 1974).

[11]An important exception is Muñoz Delgado (1964, 1978). For political thought see Ramos et. al. (1984).

how were their estates managed? How were they related to other groups within Spanish society? To date, most of these questions remain unanswered.

The seventeenth century, however, may not be the best place to begin an investigation of the clergy. Church history, like its secular counterpart, flourishes in the presence of great issues. The reformers of the late fifteenth and early sixteenth centuries and the confrontation with the Enlightenment in the eighteenth have generated more interest than anything between. If too little is known about these epochs, the period from Trent to the Bourbon accession may be fairly described as a desert. Aside from some monographs on Molinism and probabilism—inspired largely by the impact of these movements outside Spain–there has been little written on any aspect of religious life in the Peninsula during these years.[12] The sixteenth century is not much better, at least from the perspective of someone like Domníguez Ortiz, but the relative familiarity of personalities and issues provide a toehold that is lacking a century later.

A model for such studies may be J. Bada's *Situació religiosa de Barcelona en el segle XVI* (1970). Writing in Catalan, Bada follows the history of the diocese through the post-Tridentine reforms without neglecting the political, social, or economic environment of the clergy.

Such works are rare. Without them it will be extremely difficult to heed Jedin's call for a study of the "application" and effects of the Council of Trent or to test in Spain Delumeau's contention that the masses were not "Christianized" until the Counter Reformation. The Spanish contribution to Trent has been widely studied, as have the diplomatic controversies between crown and papacy over the implementation of its decrees, but the actual results of all this in Spain are yet to be determined with any certainty.[13] A series of monographs on the implementation of Trent in various dioceses would be enormously useful, but the question must be approached in other ways as well.

It is known, for example, that the religious policies of Philip II were to some extent in conflict with those of the post-Tridentine papacy. In other respects they were the same. The most curious cases

---

[12]Carol (1978), Beltrán de Heredia (1968), Váquez (1961).

[13]Studies of the Spanish delegation at Trent include C. Gutierrez, *Españoles en Trento* (Valladolid, 1951), R. Burgos, *España en Trento* (Madrid, 1941), and F. Cereceda, *Diego Laínez* (Madrid, 1945). Goñi Gaztambide (1979) attempts to bridge the gap between theory and application.

were those in which Philip combined the two, as in his practice of suppressing mendicant convents, placing the friars under observant superiors, and using the money saved by these means to support newly cloistered orders of women. Unfortunately, no study summarizes these policies in any but the most general terms. His biographies have said little about his personal views, which may have been more complex than is generally assumed, and his ecclesiastical associates are less well known than comparable figures from his father's time. Even the formidable Quiroga, Inquisitor-general and Cardinal Archbishop of Toledo, has earned nothing more than a rather unreliable and now thoroughly outdated biography by Boyd (1934).

This lack of information on the spiritual leadership of the Church is paralleled in the post-Tridentine era by even greater lacunae in our understanding of actual practice. The manuals on moral theology produced after Trent have been studied in connection with the controversy over probabilism, and Hilary Smith has made an excellent start on the history of preaching, but more remains to be done. It is possible that the Tridentine emphasis on the pulpit (xxiii, can.1) could not overcome an engrained sacramentalism, but preaching manuals and printed sermons survive and deserve to be studied at greater length.

Education has been somewhat better served. If *Los Seminarios Españoles* by F. Martín Hernández (1964) did not fully satisfy the demands of social historians, it is nevertheless useful for its description of the founding of these institutions and for its introduction to the content and method of clerical education from 1563 to 1700. Catechisms, too, have been studied, especially in connection with the celebrated case of Archbishop Carranza,[14] but the spiritual education of the laity remains open to the investigator along with the whole field of lay education in general. A model might be the article by J.-P. Dedieu (1979) in which he discusses an improvement in catechization and attendance at the sacraments among males in the archdiocese of Toledo between 1540 and 1650.

Given the shortage of works on preaching, education, and even devotional literature, it is impossible to speak with confidence about the spirituality of literate Spaniards in the early modern era. The religion of the illiterate majority is even less accessible, thanks in part to the difficulty of the sources. Parochial archives were poorly maintained until long after Trent, and the records of confraternities

---

[14]Tellechea Idígoras (1972), Guerrero (1969, 1971).

and other lay groups tend to be formal and stereotypical. The best sources for the study of popular religion, aside from the documents of the Inquisition, are the records of diocesan synods, pastoral visits, and *relaciones "ad limina."* There is nothing particularly Spanish about this. Sources are a problem for students of popular religion in every country, and efforts to survey them are comparatively recent. V. Carcel Ortí 'and J. M. Marqués de Planaguma are examining *relaciones "ad limina"* and the proceedings of some diocesan synods have been published. At present the record of the sixteenth and seventeenth centuries is less complete than that of the fifteenth, but at least a beginning has been made.

Under these circumstances works of synthesis are predictably few. J. L. González Novalín has surveyed popular religion as a whole in *La Historia de la Iglesia de España* and made original contributions in the area of "superstitious" and votive masses (1975 and 1979). William A. Christian, Jr.'s *Local Religion in Sixteenth-century Spain* (1981) is somewhat narrower in scope than its title would indicate. It is nevertheless extremely useful, being a study of shrines in New Castile based largely on the *relaciones topográficas* collected by Philip II during the years 1575-80. The same author's *Apparitions in Late Medieval and Renaissance Spain* (1981) is drawn from parochial, diocesan, and inquisitorial investigations of visions reported by laymen between 1399 and 1523. Few were reported thereafter, because the impatience of the Inquisition with such manifestations became notorious.

Further evidence of popular practices, and of clerical efforts to control them, may be found in art and music. Here if anywhere material should be abundant. The culture of the Golden Age is much appreciated even outside Spain, but the professional orientation of art historians and musicologists was at one time an obstacle to its historical exploitation. They were until quite recently inactive in the field of religious art and reluctant to examine the religious issues or episcopal purposes that led to its commissioning. The iconographic methods of Panofsky, which made it possible to analyze the contents of works, met with considerable, sometimes unconscious, resistance from those trained in the older schools of formal criticism. New studies on specific artists, or projects, notably in Seville and Salamanca, have begun to correct this situation, but even they are not entirely satisfactory from the historian's point of view. This revival of interest in church art has been paralleled in musicology, where new editions of several major composers have been complemented by monographs on music at the cathedrals of Seville, Granada, Lérida, and Zaragoza.[15]

The remaining area in which substantial work has been done is that of missions. As this subject is directly related to the larger history of the Church in Spanish America, the two will be considered together. The golden age of American studies was the period between 1950 and 1970 when historians of various persuasions became interested in the transfer of European culture overseas. Much effort was devoted not only to the work of conversion, but to its institutional precedents, including the extension of the *patronato real* and the *encomienda* system to the New World. The controversies over jurisdiction between the regular and secular clergy were examined in some detail,[16] and the debate over the status of the Indians, begun by Las Casas, became the object of a minor scholarly industry.

The missions themselves, an integral part of imperial as well as religious expansion, were also studied intensively. Inspired in part by the work of Bolton, historians of several nations produced monographs on missionary activities in Chile, the La Plata region, the Brazilian frontier, and the northern borders of New Spain. In general, they were successful enough to discourage subsequent research. Other areas of study have been the Mexican Inquisition, where Richard Greenleaf (1961 and 1968) has gone far beyond the pioneering study of Henry Charles Lea (1922), and the arts, including music and architecture.[17]

Information on the secular clergy is far less complete. J. F. Schwaller has recently examined the origins of church wealth in colonial Mexico, but many parts of the empire never have been studied and little is known anywhere about the origins of the clergy, their political interests, or their education.[18] From the standpoint of church historians, studies on the education of secular priests should be given the highest priority. Without them it will be difficult to understand preaching, catechesis, liturgy, and other attempts to transmit religious culture outside the mission environment. As mission Indians were a minority, this project should also interest secular historians and anthropologists, but the fact that the intellectual history of the American Church before 1700 has yet to be written will be a major obstacle.

[15]Calahorra (1977-78), López Caló (1963), Mujal Eliás (1975).
[16]Bayle (1950), Ricard (1966).
[17]Keleman (1967), Stevenson (1960, 1968).
[18]Figuera (1965) is largely concerned with theories about the education of Indian clergy and is stronger on the eighteenth century than on earlier periods.

From the foregoing it would seem that if Spanish religious history is not exactly in its infancy, it still offers a substantial challenge to the researcher. Whether or not the challenge will be accepted is open to question. Clearly the problem is not one of inadequate sources. The Spanish empire and its Church were, by early modern standards, effective, well-organized bureaucracies. They preserved their records, and many have survived. Indeed, archival collections are so numerous as to preclude listing here. The most important is probably the Archivo Histórico Nacional in Madrid, which contains not only the papers of the Inquisition but those of monasteries and other religious institutions whose property was confiscated at the time of *desamortización.* The Archivo de Indias at Seville is the primary repository for the overseas empire, but virtually every national, municipal, diocesan, or monastic archive contains material of great value, as do the archives of at least some parishes. There is even something to be learned from papers preserved in the households of great families. Not all this material is adequately cataloged, and staffing problems sometimes result in irregular hours and other difficulties, but this is not unique to Spain.

The real obstacle to the development of a mature historiography lies not in the sources, but in the absence of support for historians. In Spain at least, this seems to be improving. The work of surveying archives and publishing documents continues, as does the production of monographs and general histories. The latter are of varying quality, with those devoted to the Americas being somewhat less satisfactory than those dealing with Spain itself. A few of the mongraphs continue to reflect partisanship, but a growing proportion of the most interesting work is now being published in Spain. This is appropriate and desirable, but it also reflects the decline of historical studies in the United States and northern Europe since 1970. That decline may have been more precipitous in Iberian history than in other fields. In America at least, many Iberian scholars have abandoned academic life, and few new ones are being trained.[19] The situation may change at some time in the future, but for now the impetus of the nineteen fifties and sixties has clearly been lost.

[19]Douglas L. Wheeler, "The Real Crisis in Iberian Historical Studies," *Bulletin, Society for Spanish and Portuguese Historical Studies* ix, 3 (October 1984): 7-12.

Bibliography

The quality of general histories varies widely. The best is *Historia de la iglesia en España,* R. García Villoslada ed. (Madrid, 1979), vols. 3.1, 3.2 and 4 (comprising volumes 18 and 19 of the Biblioteca de Autores Christianos series). Stanley G. Payne's *Spanish Catholicism: An Historical Overview* (Madison, Wis., 1984) is a brief survey, good, but not intended for the specialist in church history. Several works available in German are either too general or too dated to be of much use, but there are a number of excellent articles in the *Dictionnaire d'Histoire et Geographique Ecclésiastique* and in the *Diccionario de historia eclesiastica de España.* For Spanish America, two companion volumes, *Historia de la Iglesia en la America española* are of some value. The first, by León Lopateguí (Madrid, 1965) deals with Mexico, Central America, and the Antilles. The second, by Antonio de Egaña (Madrid, 1966) covers the southern hemisphere. H.-J. Prien, *Die Geschichte des Christentums in Lateinamerika* (Göttingen, 1978) is largely devoted to the modern period while Enrique Dussel's *Historia General* (Salamanca, 1983) surveys much the same material from the standpoint of liberation theology. Journals that sometimes contain pertinent articles are *Hispania Sacra, Revista Española de Teologia , Missionale Hispanica,* and *Studia Monastica.*

Aldea Vaquero, Quintin, "Iglesia y Estado en la España del siglo XVIII," *Miscelanías Comillas* (1961): 143-539.

Andrés Martín, Melquiades, *Los Recogidos. Nueva visión de la Mistica española de la Edad de Oro* (Madrid, 1975).

———, *La Teología española en el siglo XVI,* Biblioteca de Autores Christianos, 13, 14, (Madrid, 1976).

Astraín, A., *Historia de la Companía de Jesús en la Asistencia de España* 7 vols. (Madrid, 1912-25.)

Azcona, Tarsicio de, *La elección y reforma del episcopado* (Madrid, 1960).

Bada, J., *Situació religiosa de Barcelona en el segle XVI* (Barcelona, 1970).

Bataillon, M., *Erasme et Espagne* (Paris, 1937) rev. and enlarged ed. in Spanish, 2 vols. (Mexico, 1950).

Bayle, Constantino, *El clero secular y la evangelización de America* (Madrid, 1950).

———, "Los misiones, defensa de las fronteras," *Missionalia Hispanica* 8 (1951): 417-503.

Bell, A. F. G., *Francisco Sánchez El Brocense* (Oxford, 1925).

———, *Luis de León. A Study of the Spanish Renaissance* (Oxford, 1926).

Beltrán de Heredia, V., *Domingo de Soto* (Salamanca, 1960).

———, *Domingo Bañez y las controversias sobre la Gracia* (Madrid, 1968).

————, *Las corrientes de espiritualidad entre los domenicos de Castilla durante la premera mitad del siglo XVI* (Salamanca, 1941).

————, *Historia de la reforma de la Provincia de España (1450-1550)* (Rome, 1939).

Bennassar, Bartolomé, ed., *L'Inquisition espagnole* (Paris, 1979).

Bolton, H. E.., *Rim of Christendom* (New York, 1960, originally published 1936).

Boyd, M., *Cardinal Quiroga, Inquisitor General of Spain* (Dubuque, 1954).

Calahorra, Pedro, *La música en Zaragoza en los siglos XVI y XVII*, 2 vols. (Zaragoza, 1977-78).

Carcel Ortí, V., "'Relaciones ad limina' de trece diocesis del noroeste de Espana," *Archivos Leoneses* 66 (1979): 345-401.

Carol, J. B., *A History of the Controversy over the "debitum peccati"* (New York, 1978).

Colombás, G. M., *Corrientes espirituales entre los benedictinos observantes españoles del siglo XVI* (Barcelona, 1963).

————, and M. Gost, *Estudios sobre el primer siglo de San Benito de Valladolid* (Montserrat, 1954).

Colombás, Garcia M., *Un reformador benedictino en tiempo de los Reyes Catolicos: García Jiménez de Cisneros, Abad de Montserrat* (Montserrat, 1955).

Dedieu, Jean-Pierre, "'Christianisation' en Nouvelle Castille: catechisme, communion, messe et confirmation dans l'archevèché de Toledo, 1540-1650," *Mélanges de la Casa de Velasques* 15 (1979): 261-94.

Domníguez, Ortiz A., *Sociedad española en el siglo XVII*, vol. 2 (Madrid, 1970).

Efrén de la M. de Dios, and Otger Steggink, *Santa Teresa y su Tiempo* (Madrid, 1968).

Figuera, Guillermo, *La formación del clero indigena en la historia eclesiástica de America* (Caracas, 1965).

García Carcel, R., *Herejı́a y sociedad en el siglo XVI. La inquisición en Valencia* (Barcelona, 1980).

Goñi Gaztambide, José, *Los navarros en el concilio de Trento y la reforma tridentina en la diócesis de Pamplona*. 2d ed., 2 vols. (Pamplona, 1979).

————, "La reforma de los premonstratenses españoles en el siglo XVI," *Hispania Sacra* 13 (1960): 5-96.

Gonzalez Novalín, José Luis, *El Inquisidor General Fernando de Valdés (1483-1568)* (Oviedo, 1968).

————, "Las misas «artificiosamente» ordenadas," *Doce consideraciones sobre el mundo hispano-italiano* (Rome, 1979): 281-96.

————, "Misas supersticiosas y misas votivos en la piedad popular del tiempo de la Reforma," *Miscelánea José Zunzunegui* 2 (Vitoria, 1975): 1-40.

————, "La vida religiosa en Asturias durante la edad moderna" in *Historia de Asturias* 6. con. M. Fernández Alvarez, F. Tuero Bertrand (Oviedo, 1980).

Greenleaf, Richard E., *The Mexican Inquisition of the Sixteenth Century* (Albuquerque, N.M., 1969).

————, *Zumárraga and the Mexican Inquisition, 1536-1543* (Washington, D.C., 1961).

Guerrero, J. R., *Catecismos españoles del siglo XVI. La Obra catequética del Dr. Constantino Ponce de la Fuente* (Madrid, 1969).

_____, "Catecismos de autores españoles de la primera mitad del siglo XVI (1500-1559)," *Reportorio de las Ciencias Ecclesiásticas en España* 2 (Salamanca, 1971): 225-60.

Gutierrez Martín, L., *El privilegio de nombramiento de obispos en España* (Rome, 1967).

Hanke, Lewis, *The Spanish Struggle for Justice in the Conquest of America* (Boston, 1965).

Henningsen, G., *The Witches' Advocate: Basque Witchcraft and the Spanish Inquisition* (Reno, Nev., 1980).

_____, "El 'Banco de datos' del Santo Oficio. Las relaciones de causas de la inquisición española, 1550-1700," *Boletín de la real academia de la historia* 74 (1977): 547-70.

Kamen, Henry, *Inquisition and Society in Spain* (Bloomington, IN, 1985).

Keleman, Pal, *Baroque and Rococco in Latin America*, 2 vols. (New York, 1967).

Lea, Henry Charles, *A History of the Inquisition in Spain*, 4 vols. (New York, 1906-7).

_____, *The Inquisition in the Spanish Dependencies* (New York, 1922).

Longhurst, J. E., *Erasmus and the Spanish Inquisition: The case of Juan de Valdés* (Albuquerque, N.M., 1950).

López Calo, J., *La música en la catedral de Granada en el siglo XVI* (Granada, 1963).

Lynch, John, "Philip II and the Papacy," *Transactions of the Royal Historical Society* 11, 5th series, (1961): 23-42.

Mansilla, Demetrio, "La reorganización eclesiástica española del siglo XVI." *Anthologica Annua* 4 (1967): 97-238; 5 (1968): 91-216.

Márquez, Antonio, *Los Alumbrados* (Madrid, 1972).

Marqués de Planaguma. J. M., "'Relaciones ad limina' de la provincia ecclesiástica tarraconensis," *Analecta Sacra Tarraconensis* 47 (1974): 209-18.

Martín Hernández, F., *La formación clerical and los colegios universitario españoles, 1371-1560* (Vitoria, 1961).

_____, *Los Seminarios Españoles. Historia y pedagogía. 1563-1700* (Salamanca, 1964).

Mörner, Magnus, *The Political and Economic Activities of the Jesuits in the La Plata Region: The Habsburg Era* (Stockholm, 1953).

Mujal Eliás, J., *Lérida: Historía de la Música* (Lérida, 1975).

Muñoz Delgado, V., *La lógica nominalista en la Universidad de Salamanca 1510-1550* (Pontevedra, 1964).

_____, "Lógica, ciencia y humanismo en la renovación theólogica de Vitoria y Cano," *Revista española de teología* 38 (1978): 205-71.

Nieto, José C., *Juan de Valdés* (Geneva, 1970).

_____, *Mystic, Rebel, Saint: A Study of Saint John of the Cross* (Geneva, 1979).

Peers, E. Allison, *Handbook to the Life and Time of Saint Teresa and Saint John of the Cross* (London, 1954).

Phelan, John Leddy, *The Milennial Kingdom of the Franciscans in the New World,* 2d ed. (Berkeley, 1970).

Pinta Llorente, M. de la, *Causa Criminal contra el biblista Alonso Gudiel* (Madrid, 1942).

Ramos, Demetrio, et. al., *Francisco de Vitoria y la escuela de Salamanca. La ética en la conquista de America* (Madrid, 1984).

Redondo, Augustín, *Antonio de Guevara (1480-1545)* (Geneva, 1976).

Ricard, Robert, *The Spiritual Conquest of Mexico* trans. L. B. Simpson (Berkeley, 1966).

Schäfer, Ernst, *Beitrage zur Geschichte des spanischen Protestantismus und der Inquisition im sechzehnten Jahrhundert,* 3 vols. (Gütersloh, 1902).

Schwaller, John Frederick, *Origins of Church Wealth in Mexico. Ecclesiastical Revenues and Church Finances, 1523-1600* (Albuquerque, N.M., 1985).

Serrano, L., *Correspondencia diplomatica entre España y la Santa Sede durante el pontificado de San Pio V ,* 4 vols. (Rome, 1914).

Sheels, W. E., *King and Church: The Rise and Fall of the Patronato Real* (Chicago, 1961).

Silverio de Santa Teresa, *Vida de Santa Teresa,* 3 vols. (Burgos, 1935-37).

Smith, Hilary D., *Preaching in the Spanish Golden Age. A Study of Some Preachers of the Reign of Philip III* (Oxford, 1978).

Steggink, O., *La reforma del Carmelo español* (Rome, 1965).

Stevenson, Robert, *Music in Aztec and Inca Territory (Berkeley, 1968).*

_____, *Spanish Cathedral Music* (Berkeley, 1961).

_____, *The Music of Peru* (Washington, D.C., 1960).

Suárez Fernández, L., "Reflexiones en torno a la fundación de San Benito De Valladolid," *Homenage a Fray Justo Pérez de Urbel* (Silos, 1976).

Tellechea, Idígoras J. I., *El obispo ideal en el siglo de la reforma (Rome, 1963).*

_____, *El arzobispo Carranza y su tiempo,* 2 vols. (Madrid, 1968).

_____, ed., *Bartolomé de Carranza. Commentarios sobre el Catecismo (Madrid, 1972).*

Tibesar, Antonine, *Franciscan Beginnings in Colonial Peru* (Washington, D.C., 1953).

Vargas Ugarte, Rubén, *Concilios Limenses (1551-1722),* 3 vols. (Lima, 1951-54).

_____, *Historia de la Iglesia en el Perú* (Lima, 1953-1961).

_____, *Los Jesuitas del Peru,* 4 vols. (Lima, 1941).

Vázquez, I., *Fra Francisco Diáz de San Buenaventura, O.F.M. y las luchas contra el probabilismo en el siglo XVII* (Santiago de Compostela, 1961).

Zaragoza Pascual, E., "Documentos inéditos referentes a la reforma monástica en Cataluña durante la segunda mitad del siglo XVI," *Studia Monastica* 19 (1977): 93-205.

_____, *Los priores generales de la congregación de San Benito de Valladolid* 4 vols. (Silos, 1973-76).

France

Pierre Blet, S.J.

IN FRANCE THE IMPLEMENTATION OF THE TRIDENTINE reform was delayed for forty years by the Wars of Religion, the beginning of which practically coincided with the end of the Council. These efforts at reform that took place during the second half of the sixteenth century should not be underestimated, but they could not bear fruit until after the restoration of civil and religious peace in the very last years of the century. And while the first half of the seventeenth century was characterized by a flourishing of spiritual and religious life among an elite, the second half witnessed an institutional strengthening of the mystical élan found in those beginnings.

These religious movements and the figures associated with them have been the object of many studies. The persons themselves are, moreover, directly accessible through their writings, published in their own lifetime and reprinted many times afterwards. In fact, the religious (as well as the political and social) historiography of the seventeenth century has suffered from an overabundance of literary sources. The numerous memoirs, journals, letters, and works of oratory published in the period have oriented historians towards its most external and superficial aspects at the expense of the history of structures and institutions, which comes to light only through painstaking research in its archives. With a few exceptions, works in this latter category did not really appear before the second half of the present century.

General Bibliography

The history of the Church edited by Fliche and Martin devoted volume 18 to *La restauration catholique,* 1563 to 1648. The scope of the subjects presented in the volume is excessively limited, if one considers the character of the series. The volume provides, however, a particularly rich bibliography, and it includes aspects and viewpoints that can suggest new areas of research neglected in other manuals. The first part of the following volume on the political and doctrinal struggles of the seventeenth and eighteenth centuries corresponds better to what one expects from a general history, but it must be used with caution, for there are frequent inaccuracies.[1] The sixth volume of *Hubert Jedin's Handbook of Church History* pays considerable attention to Catholic reform in France.[2] The author of this section, L. Cognet, more theologian than historian, treats the history of spirituality with competence, but he obviously goes beyond his field when he addresses political and institutional questions.

Jean Delumeau's *Catholicism between Luther and Voltaire* (1977) provides a basic summary and essential bibliography on the Protestant and Catholic Reformation as a whole. It is now superseded for the period 1517-1620 by P. Chaunu's synthesis, *Eglise, culture et société* (1981) which well established information and judgments are combined with some suggestive interpretations and a rich bibliography. This study in fact goes beyond religious history and covers the entire cultural framework of the period. In the same way the double volume by R. Taveneaux, *Le catholicisme dans la France classique* (1980), offers a bibliographical point of departure for study, either general or specific, on various aspects of Catholic reform. A general overview, older and less documented but important for its balanced presentation of Catholicism in this period, can be found in the second volume the *Histoire du catholicisme en France* of A. Latreille (1960).

One hardly needs to stress that both the Reformation and Catholic Reformation must be situated in the context of political, economic and social history and in the general movement of the sciences, of the arts, and of the so-called collective mentality. Useful in this respect are P. Chaunu's *La civilisation de l'Europe classique* (1966) and R. Mousnier's *Les XVIe et XVIIe siècles* (1967).

Finally, religious history in general, but especially the religious history of France during the Ancien Regime, requires a precise knowledge of political institutions. For such knowledge, the two recently completed volumes by R. Mousnier, *Les institutions de la France sous la monarchie absolue* (1974-85), now constitute an indispensable synthesis.

Fundamental sources of the period can be consulted in old but reliable editions, e.g., *Loix ecclésiastiques de France* (1736), edited by the lawyer L. Héricourt, and the fourteen volumes of *Mémoires du clergé* (1768-71), which preserve collections of documents that the clergy of the seventeenth and eighteenth centuries consulted and cited in order to inspire or justify their proceedings–canons of early councils, letter

---

[1]Willaert (1960), Préclin and Jarry (1955-56).
[2]Jedin (1981), 6: 3-106.

of the popes, ordinances of kings, and other such documents. Similarly important are the three volumes of L. Thomassin, *Ancienne et nouvelle discipline de l'Eglise* (1679-81).

The Juridical Structure of the Concordat

Any study of the religious history of sixteenth-seventeenth century France must begin with the structures established by the Concordat of Bologna concluded in 1516 between Leo X and Francis I. This Concordat is sometimes subjected to strong criticism inspired most often by a confusion between the system of the Concordat and the much earlier system of benefices.[3] Volume 15 of the Fliche-Martin *Histoire de l'Eglise* gives a succinct account of the negotiations leading to the Concordat and of its content, with good bibliography.[4] The Concordat replaced not so much the freedom as the anarchy of canonical elections with nomination by the king to bishoprics and great abbeys. Without doubt the Valois kings had a tendency to consider ecclesiastical benefices as sources of revenue that could be used to pay for services rendered to the State, as for example to defray the expenses of an ambassadorship–a practice that was not the best means for enforcing the duty of residence[5]–but it is a mistake to think that all bishops nominated by the king did not care in the least for their flocks and that the kings were totally insensitive to their moral obligation in this matter. One must note that the *Assemblées du Clergé* at the end of the sixteenth century protested vigorously against abusive nominations and asked for a return to canonical elections.[6] The kings did not want to renounce their right acquired through the Concordat, but beginning with Henry IV they were ever more careful, with the advice of ecclesiastics from their *Conseils* such as Richelieu, Vincent de Paul, or their confessors, to designate prelates worthy of their office.[7]

An excellent assessment of the problem relative to the system of benefices and of the Concordat can be found in the article by Mme. Laurain-Portemer (1981) on the situation of Mazarin in the Church. Mazarin, a simple tonsured cleric, accumulated a series of rich benefices in the form of abbeys *in commendam*. This was in fact an improvement

---

[3]Willaert (1960): 66, 85; Broutin (1956).
[4]Aubenas and Ricard (1951): 171-82.
[5] E.g., Lestocquoy (1959): 25-40.
[6]See *Mémoires du Clergé*, 14: 11, 19, 38.
[7]See, e.g., my "Vincent de Paul et l'épiscopat de France,", in *Vincent de Paul* (Rome, 1983): 81-114.

on the situation in the preceding period when families held bishoprics and abbeys.[8] It is true that the system of *commenda* did not foster, with few exceptions, the reform of the monastic orders,[9] but at least one should avoid several current errors. In Canon Law one does not find bishoprics *in commendam*, for the system of *commenda* is by definition the attribution of a regular benefice to a secular cleric.[10] Neither does one find benefices given to lay people; only a cleric, at least tonsured, could receive an ecclesiastical benefice. In fact the *commendatories* were for the most part ecclesiastics constituted in sacred orders–bishops, doctors of law, or of theology and the like. It is through *la confidence,* an abuse condemned as a form of simony, or through pensions that lay people came to profit from ecclesiastical revenues.[11]

We need not dwell on the quarrel over benefices vacant *in curia,*[12] or on whether the right of nomination by the king was valid in the kingdom only according to the borders in 1516 or was extended to new borders. This latter question was settled by the indults that the kings requested in order to exercise their right of nomination in newly conquered provinces.[13] But one forgets too easily that the pope could and did refuse canonical investiture to some candidates of the king. This investiture was conceded only after examination of a dossier that the nuncio had to prepare on the king's candidates.[14] The nuncio might also dissuade the king in advance from inopportune nominations. M. Barbiche's editions of Del Bufalo's correspondence as nuncio and of Henry IV's letters to the Roman court[15]–as well as much of the documentations in the *Acta Nuntiaturae Gallicae*–reveal the extent of papal intervention in the nomination of bishops in France.

On the other hand, another aspect of the Concordat, given too little attention until now, is found in the clauses relative to law suits. Titles 23-25 forbade recourse to the Holy See *omisso medio,* and even in cases of such recourse they prescribed terminating the case in France by commissioners appointed there. Thus the Concordat of 1516 had

[8]See J. A. Bergin, "The Decline and Fall of the House of Guise as an Ecclesiastical Dynasty," *The Historical Journal* 25 (1982): 781-803.

[9]See Zakar (1966): 32-38.

[10]See Héricourt (1736): 222.

[11]Ibid., 387. By a *confidence* a cleric who had received canonical title to a benefice agreed to hand over part or all of the revenues to a third party, often a lay person.

[12]Evennett (1936).

[13]Darricau (1965).

[14]Blet (1974): 251-57.

[15]*Acta nuntiaturae gallicae,* vol. 4; Barbiche (1968).

imposed strict limits to the exercise of supreme jurisdiction by the Roman Pontiff.[16]

The Problem of Protestantism

King Francis I had just concluded the Concordat when he had to deal with the Protestant Reformation. True, he managed to find among the Lutheran princes useful assistance in his struggle against Charles V.[17] Without going so far as to say that the Concordat, by putting at the king's disposal the ecclesiastical revenues of his kingdom, dissuaded him from rallying to the Reformation, one can certainly recognize that the pact of Bologna sealed an alliance between the pope and the Most Christian King.[18]

French Protestantism, its political and intellectual origins, and its relationship with the State have been the object of many studies, not all of which have been distinguished for their objectivity. They have, however, assembled a great deal of information and documentation. The main lines of this history and the essential bibliography can be found in E. Léonard's *Histoire du protestantisme français* (1961), a fair and learned work. Confronted with the first Protestants, Francis I wavered between rigorism, promoted by the Parlements, and a certain tolerance. The French Protestants were harshly persecuted by his son, Henry II, and became a party to be dreaded by Henry's successors, thanks to the adherents they found among the lower and middle nobility. Catholics then regrouped around the house of Guise, while Catherine de Médicis attempted to maintain a balance between the two parties.[19] It was this weak policy that led to the Saint Bartholomew's Day massacres, whose political origins are confirmed in recent works, particularly in the edition by P. Hurtubise of the letters of the then nuncio, F. Salviati.[20] During almost half a century the kingdom of France was a prey to political calculations, personal ambitions, religious fanaticism, and the unleashing of the lowest human instincts; the State meanwhile sank into powerlessness.[21] Nevertheless, the idea of tolerance also had its supporters, and Henry IV's genius for conciliation succeeded in

---

[16]The text of the concordat is in Angelo Mercati, ed. *Raccolta di concordati (Rome, 1919): 233-51, esp. 241.*

[17]See, e.g., Henrich Lutz, *Christianitas afflicta (Göttingen, 1964).*

[18]See A. Levis-Mirepoix, et. al., *François Ier, (Paris, 1967): 189.*

[19]See Ivan Cloulas, *Catherine de Médicis (Paris, 1979).*

[20]*Acta nuntiaturae gallicae , vol. 11.*

[21]Chaunu (1967).

imposing it at the beginning of the seventeenth century. J. Lecler's well-known classic on the subject of tolerance can still be profitably consulted to follow the progress of the idea and its relative triumph with Henry IV.[22]

Many writers have been attracted by the personality and the accomplishments of this prince, but it is not sure that he has even yet revealed his secret. Léonard (1961) has explained well the meaning of the Edict of Nantes; it was not a charter of religious freedom but a compromise that made the Protestants, alongside the Catholics, a religious community, privileged and protected by the king. The king guaranteed them against the Catholic majority freedom of conscience and limited freedom of worship, schools, special tribunals, the right to assembly, and even forts with garrisons, one of which was the port of La Rochelle, open to the ocean and to Protestant England. By breaking the political power of the Huguenots while leaving them their religious freedom, Cardinal Richelieu did not renounce the idea of bringing them back to Catholicism through a policy of persuasion mixed with constraint.[23] The Thirty Years' War prevented Richelieu from realizing his great design. His successor, Mazarin, treated the Protestants leniently, a policy that accorded both with his temperament and political necessity. He did this to such an extent that he provoked vehement reproaches from the clergy, who saw the great social and economic power the Protestants still possessed in certain provinces.[24]

Louis XIV, though concerned about restoring religious unity, declared himself at first opposed to constraint in religious matters.[25] The solicitations of the clergy (whose major concern was then the return of the Protestants), the successes of the policy of conversion as well as its limitations, the influence of Le Tellier, and the favorable opportunity of peace restored at Nijmegen must all have later influenced the King towards revocation of the Edict. We cannot, however, determine which factor prevailed in his decision. The condition of his relationship with Rome might have played a role, but that could hardly have been the necessary and sufficient reason. It is important, on the other hand, to call attention to a factor often neglected. In 1598 the Parlement resisted the registration of the Edict of Nantes. In October, 1685, the registration of the revocation in the

---

[22]Lecler (1955), vol. 2.
[23]Blet (1967).
[24]Blet (1959), 2: 350-61.
[25]Orcibal (1951).

chambre des vacations did not present the slightest difficulty. A problem deserving more research, therefore, is the attitude of the Parlements toward the Protestants. Why would the magistrates, so disdainful of anything coming from Rome, be so harsh towards the Protestants? Was it the tradition of their social class, the material interests at play, or ambition for power threatened by a rich Protestant bourgeoisie? Meanwhile it will be advisable to consult the acts of the colloquium organized by the Société de l'Histoire du Protestantisme français in October 1985, where one may also find references to valuable studies of the question, published in the centenary year.[26]

The Parlements

In any case, research in the religious history of the Ancien Regime must reckon with the Parlements. These high courts of justice were composed of magistrates who owned their office. The magistrates formed a powerful body, feared by the king himself in whose name they rendered their judgments.[27] Their interventions in the life of the Church have not been ignored by historians, but many scholars have been deceived by the formulas and have interpreted their decrees as an execution of the king's orders. They assumed, if the Parlement suppressed a papal bull, an episcopal letter, or a thesis from the Sorbonne, that a minister of the king had set the judiciary system into motion.[28] This is to ignore the autonomy enjoyed by these courts, which proclaimed themselves "sovereign." Quick to intervene against the Protestants, the Parlements were also very distrustful towards Rome, which they set in opposition to the "rights and freedoms of the Gallican Church." Moreover, they remained constantly vigilant over the exercise of ecclesiastical jurisdiction, whether of the prelates of the kingdom or of the pope. By means of the *appel comme d'abus,* through which every subject of the king could have recourse to the Parlement against the decision of any tribunal, lay or ecclesiastical, the magistrates came to know the quarrels of a bishop with his chapter, with the religious of his diocese, or with his pastors. The Parlements did not refrain from dealing with spiritual matters; they intervened in marriage suits and were not afraid to send back to her monastery a nun who had been

---

[26]*La Révocation (1986).*
[27]Besides the fundamental work of Mousnier (1974-85) cited above, one should also consult his *La vénalité des offices sous Henri IV et Louis XIII,* 2d ed. (Paris, 1971).
[28]Gérin (1894).

declared free from her vows by a rescript of the Roman Chancery. The sessions of the *Assemblées du Clergé* were filled with complaints from prelates against these magistrates of the king, and the collections of the *Libertés de l'Église gallicane* contain a series of characteristic judgments of the Parlements.[29]

Finally, vested with the right to register royal edicts after verification and remonstrances, they claimed to share legislative power with the king. Louis XIV, it is true, compelled them for a time to moderate their pretensions, but they earlier dissuaded Henry III and Henry IV from officially publishing the decrees of Trent.[30] One would thus be tempted to see in these "sovereign courts" one of the main obstacles to the Catholic reform in France. However, the question must be asked whether their decisions were motivated by the desire to protect private interests and abuses or by respect for the law? There is, therefore, still need for research in the enormous mass of judiciary archives–the archives of the Parlements as well as those of the *Conseil d'Etat,* of the *Conseil Privé,* and of the *Grand Conseil*–to trace the judgments pronounced on ecclesiastical matters. It is already clear, however, that most of the encroachments upon the jurisdiction of the Church and of the Holy See were due to the Parlements, whereas the king and his *Conseils* generally intervened in favor of the clergy and its freedoms and of the authority of the Holy See.[31]

The Holy See and the Most Christian Kings

We must revise an old historiographical tradition that attributes the responsibility for all the tensions between France and Rome during this period to the kings and their ministers. As a matter of fact, the political interests of France were very often in harmony with the interests of the popes, who were anxious not to fall under the Emperor's tutelage. If Francis I had to reproach Paul III with his alliance with Charles V, his son Henry II made an alliance with Paul IV against Spain, the results of which were in fact not very glorious.[32] The end of the sixteenth century was dominated by the Wars of Religion. Pius

---

[29]See the editions of Pierre Dupuy, *Traitez des droits et libertés de l'Église gallicane,* 2: *Preuves des libertez de l'Église gallicane* (Paris, 1639), or by Durand de Maillane, *Les libertez de l'Église gallicane prouvées et commentées,* 5 vols. (Lyon,
[30]Martin (1919).
[31]Blet (1959), passim.
[32]Ancel (1909-11).

V sent his troops to help Charles IX against the Huguenot rebels.[33] When Gregory XIII set his hopes on Spain in order to confront the Reformation, Catherine de Médicis and Henry III tried to reconcile Catholic interests with French interests. One can follow in detail the relations between Gregory XIII and France in the *Acta Nuntiaturae Gallicae,* which cover the whole pontificate of this pope, whose archives are in an excellent state of conservation.[34]

The questions of the succession of Henry of Navarre to the throne, of the League, of the absolution of the prince by the French bishops and finally by Clement VIII have been the object, especially at the end of the last century, of many well documented studies that were utilized in V. Martin's thesis (1919). The editions of documents by M. Barbiche showed, moreover, how the former Huguenot knew how to assume without effort the style and the duties of the Most Christian King.[35] Nonetheless, an edition of the correspondence of Maffeo Barberini, nuncio to Henry IV and then to Marie de Médicis, the future Pope Urban VIII, would teach us a great deal more about the most ardent years of the French Counter Reformation at the time when the bishops, brought closer to Rome by the Protestant threat, clashed with the Parlements, the defenders of Gallican liberties.

The relations between Richelieu and the Holy See were the object of a gross caricature in Pastor's *History of the Popes,* which has unfortunately influenced French historiography.[36] The remarkable book by V.-L. Tapié (1952) on the France of Louis XIII and Richelieu presents a portrait of the minister that is more balanced and truer to the documents. Georg Lutz's study of the nuncio G. F. Bagno (1971), based on an exhaustive use of the Roman archives, shows the convergence between Richelieu's designs and the aspiration of the Barberini pope, who was concerned with the freedom of Italy. The correspondence of the nuncio F. Scotti shows also that the idea of a patriarchate of the Gauls, to which Richelieu aspired, was at most a scarecrow destined to extort concessions.[37] Some years after the death of the Cardinal, the advocate general at the Parlement of Paris reproached him with having made regrettable concessions to Rome.[38]

---

[33]Hirschauer (1922).
[34]*Acta nuntiaturae gallicae,* vols. 2, 7, 8, 12-13.
[35]Barbiche (1968), *Acta nuntiaturae gallicae,* vol. 4.
[36]*Geschichte der Papste* 13/1: 275 ff.
[37]*Acta nuntiaturae gallicae,* vol. 5.
[38]Blet (1959), 2: 70: "Il [Richelieu] a eu des complaisances préjudiciables à l'Etat dans les occasions qu'il a eues de traiter avec Rome."

Cardinal Richelieu was succeeded as head of the French government by Cardinal Mazarin, born a subject of the pope and gone over to the service of France. One must therefore be cautious before speaking of a secularization of the State and of the progress of nationalism in the seventeenth century. This cardinal minister had, it is true, bad personal relations with the new pope, Innocent X.[39] Yet this was the time when the French episcopacy requested a decision from Rome about the five propositions of Jansenius's *Augustinus* and received the bulls published against the book. As Georges Dethan (1981) has shown, Mazarin remained a man of peace, who in fact succeeded in signing the Treaty of Westphalia and the Peace of the Pyrenees, a man who did not hesitate to support the interventions of the popes against nascent Jansenism.[40]

When Mazarin died, the young Louis XIV took in hand the reins of power. The study of his relations with Rome was sent on a false trail by a saying attributed to Bossuet: "*Aussitôt que le roi avais pris le gouvernement de son royaume et surtout depuis M. Colbert, on avait eu cette politique d'humilier Rome et de s'affermir contre elle.*"[41] Works on this subject from the last century, especially those of Ch. Gérin (1870, 1894), who completely ignored the Roman archives, must be considered obsolete and can be used only for the sources cited. Perfectly well documented modern studies sometimes appear to confirm these earlier works, but they bear on the period of crisis during the pontificate of Innocent XI.[42] If one adds to these twelve years the crisis that had followed the incident of the Corsican Guard, it all adds up to only about fifteen years of tension out of the fifty-five of Louis XIV's personal government. R. Darricau (1969) has thrown light on the excellent relations of Clement IX with France. One should also take into account the constant efforts of the king for the conversion of the Protestants (efforts that obviously met Rome's desires), his pacifying interventions in the quarrel of the regulars, and finally his alliance with Clement XI against Jansenism in the last fifteen years of his reign, an alliance that

---

[39]See Henry Couville, *Etudes sur Mazarin et ses démêlés avec le pape Innocent X* (Paris, 1914).

[40]He did not first support the movement and then sacrifice it to his political interests as P. Jansen maintains without convincing proofs in her *Le cardinal Mazarin et le mouvement janséniste* (Paris, 1967).

[41]Abbé Ledieu, *Mémoires et journal sur la vie et les ouvrages de Bossuet* (Paris 1856), 2/1: 10. Historians have too often taken this passage and others from Ledieu, who was Bossuet's secretary, as if they came from the pen of Bossuet himself.

[42]Orcibal (1949), and *Acta nuntiaturae gallicae*, vols. 10 and 11.

Albert Le Roy (1892) treated in quite unilateral fashion and that I intend to discuss soon in a fourth volume on the *Assemblées du Clergé*. My book will demonstrate that, if Louis XIV was anxious to maintain the rights of his crown vis-à-vis Rome, the bishops of his kingdom were no less anxious to assert in that regard the rights of the episcopate.

The Episcopate

If it is an error to believe that each of the judgments of the Parlements was the consequence of an order of the royal court, it is a similar error to think that all the declarations or manifestations of the clergy published against Rome came from the prompting of the government. Even for the king the clergy represented a force to be respected. In the seventeenth-century society of "order," the clergy was the first order of the kingdom. The *assemblées generales,* held every five years, voted to the king a quota of the ecclesiastical revenues in the form of voluntary contribution and "dons gratuits" towards the expenses of the State.[43] Judiciary immunity, weak though it was for the lower clergy, ensured to the bishops practical untouchability, even more secure than that of the magistrates. It required the iron hand of Richelieu and the consent of Urban VIII to depose prelates accused of high treason.[44] In the absence of a national council of which they dreamt throughout the seventeenth century, the bishops of France became aware of their strength in their *assemblées.* The king had to reckon with them. They themselves thought that the pope should also respect their remonstrances. Classical historiography has misconstrued this, considering only the extraordinary *assemblée* of 1682. It has ignored, for example, the great *assemblée* of 1655-57 that prevented Pope Alexander VII from entrusting a bishop chosen by the king with the administration of the diocese of Paris, of which Mazarin wanted to deprive Cardinal de Retz. It has also ignored the warning given by the *assemblée* of 1655 to Louis XIV that the anointing at Reims indeed gave to the kings of France a higher status than other kings in the world, but that it "did not yet take them out of the flock to put them in the rank of pastors, to whom alone God has given the power to judge about the dogmas of faith."[45]

---

[43]Blet (1959). For the origins of the practice in the sixteenth century, see Louis Serbat, *Les assemblées du clergé de France . . , 1561-1615* (Paris, 1906), and Ivan Cloulas, "Les aliénations du temporal ecclésiastique sous Charles IX and Henri III," *Revue d'histoire de l'Eglise de France* 44 (1958): 5-56.

[44]Blet (1959), 2: 20-34.

[45]Ibid., 120-74, 332.

The Four Articles of 1682 on ecclesiastical power undoubtedly met the desires of the court, but they nonetheless corresponded to the opinion commonly held by most of the bishops and ardently championed by the most influential among them. Victor Martin (1929) showed that the first article on the independence of the temporal power from the spiritual power corresponded to the thinking of the clergy of France in the second half and even, according to him, in the second quarter of the seventeenth century. A. G. Martimort established in his study of Bossuet–a study whose great erudition reaches well beyond the person of the bishop of Meaux–that the Four Articles could be regarded as expressing the common doctrine of the French clergy at the end of the century. The same author did not take his thesis to its conclusion, however, and remained dependent upon earlier historiography when he attributed the publication of the Articles to the influence of Colbert, whereas the documents agree in emphasizing the role of the archbishop of Reims, Charles Maurice Le Tellier.[46]

When ten years later Louis XIV wanted to reestablish perfect harmony between Rome and Versailles, his ecclesiastical advisers, one of whom was the archbishop of Reims, consented to have a letter of apology sent to the pope, but made sure to avoid anything that could resemble a retraction of the doctrine.[47] Therefore when the Jansenist quarrel flared up again in the last years of Louis XIV's reign around the *Cas de conscience* and the *Nouveau Testament* by Quesnel, several prelates, following Cardinal de Noailles, the archbishop of Paris, wanted to keep for themselves the role attributed to them by the fourth article of 1682 concerning dogmatic decisions.[48] The religious agitation of the eighteenth century was to be the consequence of Louis XIV's failure to have the episcopate accept *pure et simpliciter* the constitutions of the popes; once more a small group of bishops was to hold its ground against papal authority with royal support.

In my three volumes on the Assemblies of the Clergy I described the main lines of that institution and of the relations between the clergy and the royal government. It would be possible again to go through the archives of the clergy to derive a clearer picture of the pastoral concerns that appear in the same *assemblées*.

Martin (1919) has shown how these prelates, as early as the end of the sixteenth century, wanted the reforms of Trent and joined their

---

[46]Blet (1972): 312-62.
[47]Ibid., 552-80.
[48]Le Roy (1892).

solicitations to those of the nuncios to obtain from the king the legal reception of the Tridentine decrees. When these solicitations proved fruitless, the prelates in 1615 declared themselves "obliged by duty and conscience to receive, as in fact they have received and do receive, the said council and promise to observe it as much as they can." Martin tends to overestimate the impact of this gesture. This "reception" did not have any of the juridical effects of a reception by letters of the king registered in the Parlement, a reception that would have turned the canons of Trent into the law of the kingdom, but it did have a highly significant symbolic and spiritual value.

This is all the more true because before 1615 the Tridentine canons had been doubly received. First, they had been accepted in a series of local councils–in Reims in 1564 and 1583, in Cambrai in 1565, in Rouen in 1581, in Bordeaux and Tours in 1583, in Bourges in 1584, in Aix in 1585, in Toulouse in 1590, in Narbonne in 1609.[49] Secondly, even if Henry III did not receive the Council, he published in 1580 his Ordonnance of Blois, which in its ecclesiastical section incorporated, sometimes in stricter forms, the Tridentine norms.[50] Not only were clandestine marriages declared invalid, for example, but the publication of bans became a condition of validity. Duly registered in the Parlements, the Ordonnance of Blois remained one of the bases of French ecclesiastical law. The Edict still deserves study, especially the effectiveness and mode of its application.

The spirit of the Tridentine reforms also penetrated the French episcopate as early as the beginning of the seventeenth century.[51] To be sure, there were shadowy areas in the general picture. We can perhaps pass over the accusations concerning the morality of some prelates, but when a Cardinal de La Valette or an Archbishop Henri de Sourdis headed the armies or the ships of the king, or when later Forbin de Janson, bishop of Marseille and then of Beauvais, undertook diplomatic missions for the Crown, they were surely less attentive to their pastoral duties as a result. Moreover, the bishops' very desire for reform induced them to control all religious forces in their dioceses. The regulars, also impelled by Tridentine zeal but asserting their papal privileges in order to undertake an autonomous ministry, often appeared to them as rivals or at best as inconvenient auxiliaries. This rivalry

---

[49]*Concilia novissima Galliae* (1646).
[50]Martin (1919). See the text of the Ordonnance de Blois in Isambert (1821-33), 14: 388 ff.
[51]Broutin (1956).

between regular and secular clergy was certainly one of the factors that slowed down an effective implementation of the Tridentine reform in France. C. Chesneau (1946) has given us a glimpse of this problem for a very brief period, but it lasted throughout the century.

On the more positive side, seventeenth-century France had a group of prelates who took Charles Borromeo and Francis de Sales as their models in ministry and as their masters in the spiritual life. They imitated more or less closely Borromeo's pastoral methods: visitations of the diocese, convocation of synods, appeals to the old and new orders, foundations of seminaries. All these prelates are not equally well known. Among those who have already found their historian one has to mention the holy bishop of Cahors, Alain de Solminihac,[52] as well as the bishops who succeeded each other in La Rochelle–Jacques Raoul, Henry de Laval, and Charles Frézot.[53] Bordeaux and its archbishops have been favored by historiography. Cardinal François de Sourdis was the object of a serius biography as early as the last century,[54] and Henry de Béthune at the beginning of the twentieth.[55] A study done with the rigors of modern criticism is available in the thesis of Bernard Peyrous on the diocese of Bordeaux in the seventeenth century.[56] One should not forget earlier studies on the dioceses of Clermont,[57] Paris,[58] and Limoges.[59]

Bossuet and Fénelon are preserved from oblivion by their place in literary history. Martimort's thesis (1953) points out aspects of Bossuet that were little known concerning his youth and the intellectual and spiritual milieu of his education, which was that not only of Bossuet but also of his colleagues. Jacques Lebrun's thesis on Bossuet's spirituality (1972) penetrated deeply into this essential aspect of the personality of the bishop of Meaux. Bossuet's rival in the literary arena, Fénelon, has lately enjoyed new favor.[60] One can expect above all from

---

[52]Sol (1928). See also Christian Dumoulin, *Alain de Solminihac* (Paris, 1981), and Raymond Darricau, *Alain de Solminihac évêque de Cahors* (Editions C.L.D., 1980).

[53]Pérouas (1964).

[54]L. W. Ravenez, *Histoire du cardinal François de Sourdis* (Bordeaux, 1867).

[55]Louis Bertrand, *La vie de Messire Henry de Béthune archevêque de Bordeaux*, 2 vols. (Paris, 1902).

[56]Bernard Peyrous, *La réforme catholique dans le diocèse de Bordeaux (1600-1715)*, 5 vols. (thèse d'Angers, 1982).

[57]Welter (1956).

[58]Ferté (1962).

[59]Aulagne (1906).

[60]The journal *XVIIᵉ siècle* dedicated to him a special number (1951-52), *Fénelon et le tricentenaire de sa naissance 1651-1951.*

the edition of his letters, now being prepared with great erudition by J. Orcibal,[61] a knowledge as complete as possible of a bishop who lived in a century so rich in documents.

Three monographs have further enlarged our knowledge of Catholic reform in three dioceses. R. Sauzet, referring in his work on the diocese of Nîmes (1970) to an article about the diocese of Nantes, points out that "contrary to the traditionally black picture of the Church of France at the beginning of the seventeenth century, everything is not just ruin and scandal in the diocese of Nîmes, just as it is not in the diocese of Nantes." The difficulties were nevertheless enormous in a diocese in which a number of parishes were ruled by a Protestant majority. In the second half of the century, Henry Arnauld tackled the intellectual and religious citadel of Protestantism in the west, Saumur.[62] Very diverse indeed are the characteristics of Arnauld, who confined himself more and more to his pastoral role, from those of Cohon of Nîmes, whose monarchical and French fervor was a component of this religious zeal. Each, however, wanted to be an imitator of Borromeo and showed himself as "visitor, caller of synods, founder of seminaries."[63]

A special case is the diocese of Strasbourg. In Alsace the Protestants, Lutheran by confession, were numerous. But until 1681 the bishop of the diocese was also the prince who had temporal authority and could use it directly in the service of Catholic reform. The success of the reform there was, if not complete, at least impressive. L. Châtellier (1981) does not hesitate to write that, in the end, fidelity to Rome prevailed over fidelity to the king; in the countryside the religion of the common people and the religion of the elite tended to converge. To these three studies must now be added P. Hoffman's book on Lyon (1984), a valuable American contribution to research on the Church in France.

Despite these studies, there are still bishops and dioceses that await their historian. It is thanks to studies like those I have mentioned, however, that we will be able to exorcise the hasty generalizations that have established as judgments of history the wit or the stylistic effect of a Marquise de Sévigné or a Duc de Saint-Simon and that will allow us to rediscover in the Church of France of the seventeenth century not only its pomp and its laws but also its profound life in all its diversity, dynamism, and mystery.

[61]*Correspondance de Fénelon* (1972-).
[62]Bonnot (1984).
[63]Sauzet (1979): 239.

Bibliography

Acta nuntiaturae gallicae, 16 vols. to date (Paris-Rome, 1961-).

Ancel, René, *Nonciatures de France. Nonciatures de Paul IV,* 2 vols. (Paris, 1909-11).

Aubenas, R., and R. Ricard, *L'Eglise de la Renaissance, 1449-1517* (Paris, 1951).

Aulagne, J., *La réforme catholique au dix-septième siècle dans le diocèse de Limoges (Paris-Limoges, 1906).*

Barbiche, Bernard, ed., *Lettres de Henri IV concernant les relations du Saint-Siège et de la France 1595-1609* (Vatican City, 1968).

Blet, Pierre, *Le clergé de France et la monarchie. Etude sur les assemblées générales du clergé de 1615 a 1666,* 2 vols. (Rome, 1959).

_____, "Le plan de Richelieu pour la réunion des protestants," *Gregorianum* 48 (1967): 100-29.

_____, *Les Assemblées du clergé et Louis XIV de 1670 à 1693* (Rome, 1972).

_____, "Le nonce en France au XVII siècle. Ambassadeur et délégué apostolique." *Revue d'histoire diplomatique* 88 (1974): 223-58.

Bonnot, Isabelle, *Hérétique ou saint? Henry Arnauld évêque janséniste d'Angers au XVII siècle* (Paris, 1984).

Bossuet, Jacques B., *Histoire des variations des Eglises protestantes* (Paris, 1688), also found in vol. 14 of *Oeuvres complètes, ed. F. Lachat (Paris, 1863).*

Broutin, Paul, La réforme pastorale en France au XVII siècle, 2 vols. (Paris, 1956).

Carrière, Victor, ed., *Introduction aux études d'histoire ecclésiastique locale,* 3 vols. (1934-40).

Cata, E., "Les évêques de Nantes du début de XVIᵉ siècle aux lendemain du concile de Trente et aux origines de la renaissance catholique." *Revue d'histoire de l'Eglise de France* 51 (1965): 23-70.

Châtellier, Louis, *Tradition crétienne et renouveau catholique dans l'ancien diocèse de Strasbourg* (Paris, 1981).

Chaunu, Pierre, *La civilisation de l'Europe classique* (Paris, 1966).

_____, "Le XVIIᵉ siècle religieux. Réflexions préables," *Annales. Economies. Société. Civilisations* 22 (1967): 279-302.

_____, *Eglise, culture et société. Essais sur réforme et contre-réforme 1517-1620* (Paris, 1981).

Chesneau, Charles, *Le Père Yves de Paris et son temps,* vol 1: *La querelle des évêques et des réguliers 1630-1638* (Paris, 1946).

Concilia novissima Galliae a tempore concilii tridentini celebrata, ed. Louis Odespun (Paris, 1646).

Darricau, Raymond, "Louis XIV et le Saint-Siège. La négociation du traité de Pise," *Annuaire-Bulletin de la société de l'histoire de France* (1965-66): 81-156.

_____, "Louis XIV et le Saint-Siège. Les indults de nominations aux bénéfices consistoriaux 1643-1670," *Bulletin de littérature ecclésiastique* 66 (1965): 16-34, 107-31.

_____, "Une heure mémorable dans les rapports entre la France et le Saint-Siège: le pontificat de Clément IX, 1667-1669," *Bolletino storico pistoese* 71 (1969): 73-98.

Delumeau, Jean, *Catholicism between Luther and Voltaire: A New View of the Counter Reformation* (London and Philadelphia, 1977, French ed. 1971).

Dethan, Georges, *Mazarin, un homme de paix à l'âge baroque 1602-1661* (Paris, 1981).

Dumoulin, Christian, *Alain de Solminihac au service de Dieu et de sa gloire* (Paris, 1981).

Evennett, H. O., "Pie IV et les bénéfices de Jean du Bellay. Etude sur les bénéfices français vacants en curie après le concordat de 1516," *Revue de l'histoire de l'Eglise de France* 22 (1936): 425-57.

Fénelon, François, *Correspondance de Fénelon*, ed. Jean Orcibal (Paris, 1972-).

Ferté, Jeanne, *La vie religieuse dans les campagnes parisiennes 1622-1695* (Paris, 1962).

Gaquère, François, *Le dialogue irénique Bossuet-Leibnitz: la réunion des Eglises en échec 1691-1702* (Paris, 1966).

Gérin, Charles, *Recherches historiques sur l'Assemblée du clergé de 1682,* 2d ed. (Paris, 1870).

_____, *Louis XIV et le Saint-Siège,* 2 vols. (Paris, 1894).

Godel, Jean, ed., *Le cardinal des montagnes. Etienne Le Camus évêque de Grenoble 1671-1707* (Grenoble, 1974).

Héricourt, Louis, *Les loix ecclésiastiques de France,* 11th ed. (Paris, 1736).

Hirschauer, Ch., *La politique de Pie V en France 1566-1572* (Paris, 1922).

Hoffman, Philip T., *Church and Community in the Diocese of Lyon, 1500-1789* (New Haven and London, 1984).

Imbart de La Tour, P., *Les origines de la réforme,* 4 vols. (Paris, 1905-14).

Isambert, Fr. A., *Recueil général des anciennes lois françaises,* 29 vols. (Paris, 1821-33).

Jedin, Hubert, ed., *Handbook of Church History,* vols. 5 and 6 (New York, 1980-81).

Judge, H. G., "Louis XIV and the Church," *Louis XIV and the Craft of Kingship,* ed. John C. Rule (Ohio State University Press, 1969)

La Révocation de l'Edit de Nantes et le protestantisme français en 1685, Actes du colloque de Paris (15-19 octobre 1985), réunis par Roger Zuber et Laurent Theis (Paris, 1986).

Latreille, André, *Histoire de catholicisme en France,* vol. 2: *Sous les rois très chrétiens* (Paris, 1960).

Laurain-Portemer, Madeleine, "Le statut de Mazarin dans l'Eglise," *Bibliothèque de L'Ecole des Chartres* 127 (1969): 355-419; 128 (1970): 5-80, reprinted in *Etudes Mazarines* (Paris, 1981): 19-153.

Le Brun, Jacques, *La spiritualité de Bossuet* (Paris, 1972).

Lecler, Joseph, "Qu'est-ce que les libertés de l'Eglise gallicane," *Recherches de science religieuse* 23 (1933): 385-410, 542-68; (1934): 47-85.

_____, *Tolerance and the Reformation*, 2 vols. (New York, 1960).

Léonard, Emile G., *Histoire générale du protestantisme*, 3 vols. (Paris, 1961-64). English translation of vols. 1 and 2, ed. H. H. Rowley (London, 1965-67).

L'Epinois, Henri de, *La Ligue et les papes* (Paris, 1886).

Le Roy, Albert, *Le gallicanisme au XVIIIe siècle. La France et Rome de 1700 à 1715* (Paris, 1892).

Lestocquoy, Jean, "Les évêques français au milieu du XVIe siècle," *Revue d'histoire de l'Eglise de France* 45 (1959): 25-40.

Lutz, Georg, *Kardinal Giovanni Francesco di Bagno* (Tübingen, 1971).

Martimort, Aimé Georges, *Le gallicanisme de Bossuet* (Paris, 1953).

Martin, Victor, *Le gallicanisme et la réforme catholique . . . 1563-1615* (Paris, 1919).

_____, *Le gallicanisme politique et le clergé de France* (Paris, 1929).

Mémoires du clergé ou recueil des actes, titres et mémoires concernant les affaires du clergé de France, 14 vols. (Paris, 1768-71).

Metz, R., "La paroisse en France à l'époque moderne et contemporaine," *Revue d'histoire de l'Eglise de France* 60 (1974): 269-95.

Meuvret, Jean, "La situation matérielle des membres du clergé séculier dans la France du XVIIe siècle. Possibilités et limites des recherches," *Revue d'histoire de l'Eglise de France* 54 (1968): 47-68.

Mousnier, Roland, *Les XVIe et XVIIe siècles. La grande mutation intellectuelle de l'humanité. L'avènement de la science moderne et l'expansion de l'Europe*, 5th ed. (Paris, 1967).

_____, *Les institutions de la France sous la monarchie absolue*, 2 vols. (Paris, 1974-85).

Moüy, Charles de, *L'ambassade du duc de Créquy 1662-1665*, 2 vols. (Paris, 1893).

Orcibal, Jean, *Louis XIV contre Innocent XI* (Paris, 1949).

_____, *Louis XIV et les protestants* (Paris, 1951).

Pérouas, Louis, *Le diocèse de La Rochelle de 1648 a 1724* (Paris, 1964).

Pignot, Henri, *Un évêque réformateur sous Louis XIV. Gabriel de Roquette évêque d'Autun*, 2 vols. (Paris-Autun, 1876).

Préclin, E., and E. Jarry, *Les luttes politiques et doctrinales aux XVIIe et XVIIIe siècles*, 2 vols. (Paris, 1955-56).

Prunel, Louis-N., *Sébastien Zamet évêque-duc de Langres, pair de France (1588-1655)*, 2 vols. (Paris, 1912).

Rocquain, F., *La France et Rome pendant les guerres de religion* (Paris, 1924).

Romier, Lucien, *Catholiques et huguenots à la cour de Charles IX* (Paris, 1924).

Sauzet, Robert, *Contre-réforme et réforme catholique en Bas-Languedoc. Le diocèse de Nîmes au XVIIe siècle* (Paris, 1979).

Sol, Eugène, *Le vénérable Alain de Solminihac abbé Chancelade et évêque de Cahors (Cahors, 1928)*.

Tapié, Victor-Lucien, *Le France de Louis XIII et de Richelieu* (Paris, 1952).

Taveneaux, R., *Le catholicisme dans la France classique 1610-1715*, 2 vols. (Paris, 1980).

Thomassin, Louis, *Ancienne et nouvelle discipline de l'Eglise,* 3 vols. (Paris, 1678-81).

Venard, Marc, *L'Eglise d'Avignon au XVIe siècle,* 5 vols. (Lille, 1981).

Welter, L., *La réforme ecclésiastique du diocèse de Clermont au XVIIe siècle* (Paris, 1956).

Willaert, Léopold, *Après le concile de Trente. La restauration catholique 1563-1648* (Paris, 1960).

The British Isles

Martin J. Havran

THE RECENT HISTORIOGRAPHY of Tridentine and seventeenth-century Catholicism in British Isles contrasts sharply in outlook and quality with most of the traditional literature. Ecclesiastical historians in both the Catholic and Protestant camps were slow to shake a habit of accommodating facts to suit their confessional convictions. Heightened standards of historicity, rather than a burst of charity and understanding, gradually weakened this tendency by the early twentieth century. The Protestant scholars who had long dominated historical writing and were themselves often guilty of bias, commonly disparaged the publications of their Catholic colleagues as little more than polemics or martyrology. There was something in this indictment. Catholic historians dwelled unduly on the heroic lives of missionaries and recusants who upheld the faith during the worst of penal times, and condemned the Protestant Reformation out of hand.[1] They earned greater respect as their interests broadened and the objectivity of their studies improved in response to this criticism. By World War II authors had pretty much laid their partisan loyalties aside.[2] The rapid development of Catholic Church history as a legitimate research field coincided with this fresh perspective.[3]

Two bibliographers at Oxford and the British Museum, David Rogers and Antony Allison, laid the foundation and set the tone of this presently expansive scholarship on post-Reformation Catholicism, particularly in England before c. 1700. In 1951 they launched *Recusant History,* which featured articles on Catholic life and thought with special emphasis on the gentry families whose homes sheltered priests and served as centers of clandestine worship. The editors insisted on strict honesty. "The Catholic historian," they warned, "must submit the view which, moved by feelings of loyalty to his Church, he would prefer to see vindicated, to the same objective scrutiny as every other, and if the facts warrant its rejection, he must reject it."[4] Scholars scoured

---

[1]The earlier publications by the Catholic Record Society, founded 1904, confirmed this emphasis.
[2]Dickens (1964): 339.
[3]Davidson (1971); Edwards (1972); Baker (1975).
[4]Allison and Rogers (1961): 10.

repositories for new sources, including the Westminster Cathedral Archives[5] and the Jesuit Archives,[6] both in London, the Borthwick Institute in York,[7] and the county record offices and private collections throughout England. This activity led to a substantially larger outflow of monographs and articles and in turn provided the basis for two authoritative general histories of English Catholicism since Elizabethan times.[8]

The momentum generated by this earlier work shows no signs of slackening. Today we have regional studies of the impact of the Counter Reformation,[9] syntheses of Elizabethan Catholicism,[10] a thorough historiographical essay on early Stuart Catholicism,[11] and an up-to-date analysis of the Church in 1558-1642, accompanied by documents and a full bibliography.[12] Meanwhile T. A. Birrell (Catholic University, Nijmegen) had founded in 1958 the *Newsletter for Students of Recusant History,* which put researchers round the world in touch with developments in the field.[13] It contained bibliographies, reported the activities of local Catholic history societies, some having their own periodicals (e.g. Essex, Worcestershire, and Staffordshire), traced the migration and accession of manuscripts, and abstracted postgraduate theses.[14] Another barometer of the growing interest in post-Reformation Catholicism is the annual conference held at St. Anne's College, Oxford, since the late 1950's.

The publication of the "Catalogue of Catholic Books . . . 1558-1640" equipped students with an essential tool for a systematic analysis of Catholic thought.[15] It lists by title and current repository nearly a thousand books and ascribes to their rightful presses those that appeared for security reasons with false imprints or none.

---

[5]They are especially useful on the seculars, whose history is yet to be fully written. But see Anstruther (1968-77), and Duffy (1983).

[6]Edwards (1966).

[7]Purvis (1967).

[8]See Bossy (1975), and Aveling (1976), discussed below.

[9]Two of the finest are by Manning (1969), and Haigh (1975).

[10]Bossy (1962); Prichard (1979); McGrath (1984).

[11]Hibbard (1980).

[12]Dures (1983).

[13]English Catholic literature needs more attention. For guidance, see Roberts (1966), and Tavard (1978).

[14]The Institute of Historical Research, London, annually publishes lists of theses completed in British universities.

[15]Allison and Rogers (1956); see Clancy (1974) for a comparable work on 1641-1700.

Several monographs have been built on this rich library.[16] The most recent, *Resistance & Compromise: The Political Thought of the Elizabethan Catholics* (Cambridge, 1982), by Peter Holmes, traces the theories of resistance and non-resistance that the clergy urged upon their co-religionists in response to changing circumstances. Non-resistance obtained in the 1560s before the religious issue had really been joined. The Northern Rising (1569) and the papal excommunication of the Queen (1570) at first encouraged resistance, and subsequently non-resistance as persecution mounted upon the arrival of the early missionaries. Resistance weakened during the Spanish War amid Protestant fears of Spanish imperialism,[17] and declined more rapidly towards the end of the reign as Catholics fell to quarrelling among themselves over control of the mission and over whether some accommodation with the national orthodoxy might not be the most prudent alternative to widespread proscription.

These varying responses illustrate the quandary that confronted Catholics during the Counter Reformation. Largely isolated from the Church on the continent and ostracized from the parochial structure of the nation unless they conformed at least minimally as church papists, they pondered how far they dared to go in satisfying the law while privately upholding their religion. Many came to realize that there was a difference between the pronouncements of the strenuous missionaries and what they could bring themselves to do in a practical way to save their lives and property. Some avoided trouble through casuistry (mainly equivocation and mental reservation) when confronted by the choice of accepting or rejecting the Oaths of Supremacy (1559) and Allegiance (1606).[18] Of the 314 English Catholic martyrs, 189 were executed between 1570 and 1603, twenty-five in James I's reign, and fewer than ten under Charles I.[19] The vast majority of the thirty- to sixty-thousand Catholics in England between 1570 and 1660[20] escaped penalty under the recusancy laws for all kinds of reasons, such as going underground, poor enforcement by local officials, the neighborliness of Protestants in communities where Catholic practices were shielded

---

[16]E.g., Clancy (1964); Milward (1977, 1978).

[17]Maltby (1971).

[18]Rose (1975) examines how honorable men, not cut out for martyrdom and otherwise loyal to the crown, coped with their consciences.

[19]Nuttall (1971).

[20]The figures are Bossy's (1975), Chap. 8. He defines a Catholic as one having regular access to the sacraments.

or ignored,[21] or just plain luck. The histories of more of these enclaves of Catholicism must be written before we can adequately explain how the old religion not only survived but grew modestly following the hard times of the 1580s.

The powerfully revisionist interpretation by John Bossy in *The English Catholic Community 1570-1850* (London, 1975) partly addresses this question. He advanced two controversial premises supported by a rich sociological exegesis of the Church's structural, intellectual, and ritualistic features. A new Catholic "community" emerged after 1570 from the shards of its shattered medieval past through the leadership of missionaries who successfully adapted the organization and administration of the mission to fit the needs of a persecuted minority. Secondly, by the seventeenth century Catholics had become a tiny sect exhibiting characteristics consistent with the English non-conforming pattern. The poorly distributed network of itinerant priests on which they depended gradually gave way to a system of resident chaplains at the gentry's estates. It is a pity that this highly original contribution has overshadowed another more conventional and in some ways more satisfying book on the same broad subject by Hugh Aveling, *The Handle and the Axe: The Catholic Recusants in England from the Reformation to Emancipation* (London, 1976), which contains one of the fullest bibliographies on English Catholicism and incorporates Aveling's earlier work on Yorkshire Catholics.[22]

Several scholars reacted sharply to Bossy's conclusions. In accordance with the current tendency to stress the role of the laity over that of the clergy or the government in bringing religious change,[23] J. J. Scarisbrick's *The Reformation and the English People* (Oxford, 1984), which concluded with Elizabeth's death, concentrates on the Catholic laity (without slighting women), rather than on the missionaries. He sees no break in the continuity between the pre-Reformation and mission Church, and no clear distinction between the traditional practice of Catholicism and the "hot clerical brand" of the militant Allen-Persons party after c. 1580. The discontinuity theme has also been challenged in a superb essay by Christopher Haigh (1981). He argues that Bossy's interpretation was invented by the Jesuit Robert

---

[21]On neighborliness, see Wrightson (1982), Chap. 2.
[22]Aveling (1960, 1963).
[23]A. G. Dickens pioneered this approach. See also Cross (1976) for a variation on this theme: religious conservatism delayed the wider acceptance of Protestantism in some areas, notably the North, until the 1590s.

Persons about 1600 to discredit the Marian clergy "who betrayed their faith to hold on to their livings" and to extol the sacrifices of the missionaries and gentry in rescuing the faith from annihilation. Against this "propagandist Jesuit version" of Elizabethan Catholicism Haigh places the origin of the Catholic revival in the 1560s, years before the arrival of the Jesuits, when under the leadership of the surviving Marian priests the incidence of recusancy was already heavy in the upland counties.

Although the literature is extensive, seventeenth-century Catholicism has not received the attention lavished on the Elizabethans as the standard-bearers of the Counter Reformation.[24] No Stuart historian, for instance, has successfully integrated Catholic life and thought into the framework of the nation's political, economic and social systems in a manner now common among students of Puritanism. Too often still, the Gunpowder Plot, James I's tolerance of recusancy while pursuing a supposedly disastrous pro-Spanish foreign policy, and the freedom and favors accorded Catholics by Charles I (abetted by his French Catholic wife and papal agents at court) take on a sinister meaning. The truth is that no matter how visible Catholics were at court, in government, or out in the provinces, they were for the most part loyal subjects quite disinterested in foreign-bred plots and incapable of overturning the political and ecclesiastical polities. They took full advantage of an easing of the recusancy laws under James I and Charles I to build a community that was more vital than at any other time between the reigns of Mary Tudor and Victoria.[25] In the end, however, the division between the Jesuits and the seculars and the entrenchment of manor-centered Catholicism, which served the needs of the Catholic commonalty poorly, undermined the English Counter Reformation.[26]

While the intensity and incidence of persecution declined following James I's succession, the legacy of virulent anti-Catholicism, especially in Parliament, ensured occasionally heavy interludes of proscription.[27] The King's abhorrence of violence, ecumenist outlook, and humane treatment of Scottish Catholics worked in the English Catholics's favor. Towards them he advocated tolerance, not toleration,

---

[24]Hibbard (1980), confirms the shortage of recent work on early Stuart Catholicism.
[25]Ibid. , 14.
[26]Aveling (1976): 64-67; Bossy (1975), Chap. 4.
[27]See Russell (1979) on parliamentary anti-Catholicism.

and his solution was "not the scaffold; it was Maryland."[28] He strove (fruitlessly) for fifteen years to arrange a marriage treaty with the foremost Catholic power, Spain, in hopes of ending a half-century of confessional wars.[29] In the years surrounding his succession he sought a better understanding with the papacy.[30] His convert wife, Queen Anne, was permitted to practice Catholicism privately at court,[31] and he seemed honestly sympathetic with the plight of peaceable Catholics. Neither the shock of the Gunpowder Plot[32] nor the demands of the episcopal bench, councilors and M.P.s persuaded James to revert to the stern policy of his predecessor. In his response to dissent, Catholic or Protestant, James wisely distinguished between moderates and radicals. He hoped through tolerance to induce moderates to reconcile themselves with the national orthodoxy, and he isolated and punished radicals who threatened it.[33]

Domestic and international circumstances during the reign of Charles I raised the longstanding popular fear of Catholics to something like national paranoia.[34] Calvinist diehards perceived the Thirty Years' War as a deadly confrontation between Popery and Protestantism. Even as the King and his ministers hounded conventiclers, they brushed off demands that England should rally behind the Protestant cause in the war. They preferred instead to court Spain and then France in a vain attempt to restore the Palatinate to the King's sister, Elizabeth. Charles appeared to be treating Catholics with unprecedented leniency: he pardoned condemned priests, periodically suspended the penal laws, appointed crypto-Catholics to the Privy Council, accepted Catholicism at court in deference to his wife, and conferred with papal agents. This seriously damaged his reputation with stern Protestants on the eve of the Civil War when, following John Pym's leadership in the House of Commons, they believed that a popish plot of vast dimensions, centered in the royal court, had been launched to overturn true religion and liberty in England. Charles had no such intention, we now realize, but a fresh appraisal of the putative plot, set appropriately in its international perspective, insists that if historians have often dismissed

---

[28]Wormald (1985): 147.
[29]Loomie (1973, 1978); Havran (1973).
[30]LaRocca (1984).
[31]Loomie (1971).
[32]Wormald (1985).
[33]Fincham and Lake (1985).
[34]Clifton (1971).

Pym's accusations as propaganda aimed at discrediting the regime, Protestants had solid reasons to entertain such fears.[35]

It has always been easier to criticize Charles I than to understand him. His personal religion, Arminianism, bore a superficial similarity to Catholic doctrine and practice and was considered for that specious reason a revolutionary departure from Anglican norms prevalent since the Elizabethan Settlement.[36] Notwithstanding his obduracy in other respects, he was remarkably tolerant of religious dissent. From an early age he identified himself psychologically and intellectually with traditional Christianity, shared his parents' ecumenical outlook, and admitted that the Catholic Church was a branch of the true, ancient Christian faith. This goes a long way towards explaining why he rejected persecution as a means of achieving conformity.[37] While he remained too isolated and aloof from affairs in the provinces to pay Catholics much mind–with the result that many continued to pay fines, go to prison, or compound for their lands in an irregular pattern of enforcement–the basic motive of his religious policy towards Catholics was to augment royal revenue at their expense at a time of mounting inflation and heavy crown debt, not to convert them.[38]

Catholics repaid the King's leniency by serving in the Royalist armies during the Civil War,[39] but as was the case with the nation generally, many tried to remain neutral.[40] How they fared during the Interregnum we know less thoroughly. The gentry served in the Royalist underground at home and abroad and some reaped the benefits after the Restoration. The Chapter of the English secular clergy reached an uneasy accommodation with the Cromwellian regime and passed for the administration of the mission until the appointment of a vicar-apostolic in 1685.[41] Little Counter Reformation spirit survived by the Restoration. The community settled down for more than a century thereafter as a tiny upper-class sect isolated in widely-scattered pockets of Catholic practice surrounded by a sea of Protestantism. Neither the dramatic consequences of the fictitious Popish Plot (1678-84)[42] nor the passing advantage (disadvantage?) of a Catholic monarchy immediately

---

[35]Hibbard (1983).
[36]Tyacke (1975).
[37]Havran (1983).
[38]Havran (1962); Lindley (1971).
[39] Mosler (1980); Newman (1981).
[40]Lindley (1973).
[41]Bossy (1975): 60-74.
[42]Miller (1975) is the only serious attempt to analyze Restoration anti-Catholicism.

before the Glorious Revolution affected this pattern of Catholic life.[43]

In Scotland, rationalization of the term Counter Reformation strains reason. Catholics in the northern kingdom failed to counter the Protestant establishment and, though the Reformation took firm root slowly in many localities, their number shrank by the early seventeenth century to an insignificant minority of perhaps three thousand. As is true of Scottish historical studies generally, which until a few years ago looked moribund, Scottish Catholicism has once again attracted considerable attention after a long interlude of near neglect.

Sources on the Scottish Catholic mission, whether printed or in manuscript, are thinner and generally less satisfactory than those for English Catholicism. Most of the available literature appeared fifty to a hundred years ago and falls short of decent scholarly standards. Monographs and biographies (even of John Ogilvie, d. 1615, the only Scottish Catholic executed for his faith during the Reformation) are comparatively scarce. Since 1950 articles in the *Innes Review* have adumbrated the dimensions of the subject, and serve importantly to counterbalance the heavily Protestant orientation of Scottish ecclesiastical history. Only a few primary sources can be mentioned in this necessarily brief essay: the Jesuit Archives in Rome; the Stonyhurst MSS (in the WCA, London); the Scottish Catholic Archives in Edinburgh,[44] which include the Blairs Papers (published in 1929) that are particularly useful for Scottish Jesuits and Scottish colleges abroad; and the Barbarini Latini MSS[45] that document the work of the Scottish secular clergy who first entered the mission in 1622 upon its reorganization under the supervision of *Congregation de Propaganda Fide*.[46]

Students of the Scottish Reformation lately have minimized the importance of 1560 as a critical turning point, notwithstanding the thundering impact of John Knox.[47] They have argued not altogether originally that Protestantism triumphed primarily for political and economic, rather than religious, reasons that were closely associated with the anti-francophone sentiments of the lairds (and their itinerant preachers), who aligned themselves with the reforming party in order to free the realm from foreign and papal influence.

[43]Williams (1968) has implications far beyond its regional concentration.
[44]McRoberts (1977).
[45]Also on film in the Pius XII Memorial Library, St. Louis.
[46]See Anson (1970): ix-xi, and Dilworth (1984).
[47]Wormald (1981) represents the widest departure from the confessional stereotype of reformation history.

The doyen of modern Scottish Reformation studies concluded a quarter-century ago that Protestantism advanced haltingly after 1560 without basically disrupting society or engaging in "that cold-blooded scaffold and faggot work" typical of Elizabethan England.[48] His foremost pupil–the finest scholar working today on early modern Scottish Catholicism–affirmed this view in his own analysis of the Reformation. But in closer harmony with the principal authority on the sixteenth-century mission,[49] he stressed the spiritual impact of religion in the localities. Mainly in the burghs he found that a combination of persecution, admonition and social pressure overwhelmed Catholic resistance, which had already been seriously weakened by the indifference of the papacy and the defection of many of the hierarchy, leaving them served poorly by a handful of priests.[50]

This much is clear in most accounts: by the 1590s Catholicism had nearly collapsed in Scotland. How this happened is not as apparent. More regional studies (comparable to those for England) are needed before any firm conclusions can be drawn on the complex pattern of acceptance and rejection of Protestantism. In the Western Highlands and the Islands, Catholicism consisted of "half-remembered beliefs and practices" bordering on paganism. But over much of the lowlands–in Midlothian, Renfrewshire, Ayrshire and elsewhere–the old religion showed surprising resilience.[51] This may be explained in part by the entry of Irish Franciscans, Dominicans, and larger numbers of seculars upon the Scottish mission.[52] Their hopes of recovering lost ground, however slim, were smashed by waves of Catholic phobia that swept the land from the outbreak of the Covenanter's rebellion against the Caroline regime in 1637 to the consolidation of Presbyterian hegemony two decades later as a result of the so-called Second Scottish Reformation.[53] Notwithstanding the reappearance of the Catholic liturgy at Holyrood Palace, Edinburgh, during the brief reign of James VII and the close relationship between Highland Catholicism and Jacobitism in the next century, it is nonsense to speak of any serious Counter Reformation in Scotland from at least the 1630s.

[48]Donaldson (1960): 75.
[49]Sanderson (1970).
[50]Cowan (1982); Durkan (1984).
[51]Cowan (1978): 30-36.
[52]Ross (1972); Stephenson (1979).
[53]Stephenson (1973); McCoy (1974).

The nature and paucity of sources for early modern Irish Catholicism have discouraged extensive research. Scholarship in this esoteric field, still the bailiwick of a few devotees championed by Monsignor Patrick J. Corish, has in no way matched the productivity on the English Church. The records of the (Protestant) Church of Ireland afford an unusual opportunity to study another side of the Counter Reformation, turned around, namely efforts by hierarchs such as Archbishop James Ussher of Armagh and Bishop William Beddell of Kilmore to convert the Irish through a carrot-and-stick policy of penal code enforcement and proselytization.[54] The patchy Catholic diocesan records and the published documents based on them are often in Gaelic. The history of several Irish continental colleges (eventually thirty-one) have been recovered.[55] A list of Irish Catholic prelates since 1534 has been published.[56] The Roman archives house some of the correspondence of Irish clergy–seculars, Dominicans, Franciscans, and Jesuits. There are few modern surveys on any aspect of Irish history for our period. Consequently, one must rely more heavily on articles in periodicals such as *Historical Studies, Studia Hibernica,* and *Archivium Hibernicum.*

Irish Catholicism raises questions quite different from those encountered in England or Scotland.[57] A conquered people, the Irish Catholics endured heavy political and financial pressure that tested their faith and led eventually to forced exile, expropriation, and bankruptcy of the landowning gentry.[58] The English regime failed to break the resistance of Catholics over most of the island, but by about 1700 as much as a third of the population was Protestant.[59] The ethnic diversity of the kingdom compounded problems of Church and State. Old Irish Catholicism, Gaelic and rural, emerged from its shrouded medieval past in many respects more pagan than Christian, fraught with superstition and prophecy that were inextricably bound with ancient custom. The more civilized Christianity of the Catholic Old English had little in common with such barbarous forms and folk culture.[60] In these circumstances the Counter Reformation priests bore a heavy responsibility: they tried with mixed success to reconcile Gaelic beliefs

---

[54]See Bradshaw (1978).
[55]Corish (1981): 142-43.
[56]Moody et al. (1984).
[57]Bossy (1971); Canny (1979): 58.
[58]See Simms (1976).
[59]Aveling (1976), 13.
[60]Clarke (1966).

and practices with Tridentine ideals; sustain the loyalty of the disaffected Anglo-Irish gentry; and combat the strenuous program of the government to make Catholics pay heavily for recusancy. The unique features of Irish Catholicism have been identified in a masterly book by Monsignor Corish.[61] These are his principal conclusions. The Irish Counter Reformation began in the 1590s– decades after its inception elsewhere in the British Isles–with the arrival of the Irish seminarians. Their labor brought swift results. By Jacobean times, despite the sizeable Protestant presence in some northern towns, the Established Church had already lost the struggle for religious allegiance. Ireland never constituted a mission outpost of the Catholic Church. It had a true Church in that the diocesan structure was maintained even when the political climate dictated the interim appointment of vicars-apostolic to some sees. By and large the English regime tolerated the hierarchy (except during the Cromwellian period) so long as they kept out of government affairs and winked at the proliferation of chapels in the Gaelic regions. An abundance of priests served the Irish Church, the Anglo-Irish rather better than the Gaels: by the 1630s there were about 800 seculars, 200 Franciscans, and 100 or so from the other orders. The Jesuits were not numerous in Ireland, perhaps no more than forty. The farther one moves from the towns into the countryside, the harder it becomes to unravel the mysteries of the Gaelic religion. Monsignor Corish's most important contribution is therefore his remarkable discussion of all that is presently known about Old Irish piety and practices.

Bibliography

A Critical Anthology of English Recusant Devotional Prose, 1558-1603, ed. John R. Roberts (Pittsburgh, 1966).

A New History of Ireland . Vol. 9, *Maps, Genealogies, Lists.* ed. T. W. Moody et al. (New York, 1984).

Allison, Antony F., and David M. Rogers, *A Catalogue of Catholic Books in English, Printed Abroad or Secretly in England 1558-1640,* (1956): 1-187.

———, "Ten Years of Recusant History," *Recusant History* 6 (1961): 2-11.

Anson, Peter F., *Underground Catholicism in Scotland 1622-1878* (Montrose, Scotland, 1970).

Anstruther, G., *The Seminary Priests. A Dictionary of the Secular Clergy of England and Wales, 1558-1850,* 4 vols. (Ware and Durham, 1968-77).

Aveling, J. C. H., *The Catholic Recusants of the West Riding of Yorkshire, 1558-1790* (Leeds, 1963).

---

[61]Chaps. 1-3, and pp. 140-45.

———, *The Handle and the Axe: The Catholic Recusants in England from Reformation to Emancipation* (London, 1976).

———, *Post-Reformation Catholicism in East Yorkshire, 1558-1790* (York, 1960).

Bibliography of the Reformation, 1450-1648, relating to the United Kingdom and Ireland for 1955-70, ed. Derek Baker (Oxford, 1975).

Bossy, John, "The Character of Elizabethan Catholicism," *Past & Present* 21 (1962): 39- 59.

———, "The Counter-Reformation and the People of Catholic Ireland, 1596-1641, *Historical Studies* 8 (1971): 155-69.

———, *The English Catholic Community 1570-1850* (London, 1975).

Bradshaw, Brendan, "Sword, Word and Strategy in the Reformation of Ireland," *Historical Journal* 21 (1978): 475-502.

Canny, Nicholas, "Why the Reformation failed in Ireland: *une question mal posée*," *Journal of Ecclesiastical History* 30 (1979): 1-28.

Clancy, T. H., *Papist Pamphleteers: The Allen-Persons Party and the Political Thought of the Counter-Reformation in England, 1572-1615* (Chicago, 1964).

———, *English Catholic Books, 1641-1700: A Bibliography* (Chicago, 1974).

Clarke, Aidan, *The Old English in Ireland 1625-42* (Ithaca, New York, 1966).

Clifton, Robin, "The Popular Fear of Catholics during the English Revolution," *Past & Present* 53 (1971): 23-55.

Corish, Patrick J., *The Catholic Community in the Seventeenth and Eighteenth Centuries*, Vol. 5, *Helicon History of Ireland* (Dublin, 1981).

Cowan, Ian B., *Regional Aspects of the Scottish Reformation*, Historical Association Pamphlet GS 92 (London, 1978).

———, *The Scottish Reformation. Church and Society in Sixteenth Century Scotland* (New York, 1982).

Cross, Claire, *Church and People 1450-1660. The Triumph of the Laity in the English Church* (Atlantic Highlands, New Jersey, 1976).

Davidson, Alan, "Sources for Church History: 4. Recusant History, A Bibliographical Article," *Local Historian* 9 (1971): 283-86.

Dickens, Arthur G., *The English Reformation* (London, 1964).

Dilworth, Mark, "The Counter-Reformation in Scotland: A Select Critical Bibliography," *Records of the Scottish Church History Society* 22 (1984): 85-100.

Donaldson, Gordon, *The Scottish Reformation* (London, 1960).

Duffy, Eamon, " The English Secular Clergy and the Counter-Reformation," *Journal of Ecclesiastical History* 34 (1983): 214-30.

Dures, Alan, *English Catholicism 1558-1642: Continuity and Change* (London, 1983).

Durkan, John, "William Murdock and the Early Jesuit Mission in Scotland, *Innes Review* 35 (1984): 3-11.

Edwards, Francis, "The Archives of the English Province of the Society of Jesus at Farm Street, London," *Journal of the Society of Archivists* 3 (1966): 107-15.

_____, "A Decade of Recusant History," *Clergy Review,* n.s. 57 (1972): 510-23.

Fincham, Kenneth, and Peter Lake, "The Ecclesiastical Policy of King James I," *Journal of British Studies* 24 (1985): 169-207.

Haigh, Christopher, *Reformation and Reaction in Tudor Lancashire* (London, 1975).

_____, "From Monopoly to Minority: Catholicism in Tudor England" *Transactions of the Royal Historical Society,* 5th ser., 31 (London, 1981): 129-47.

Havran, Martin J., *The Catholics in Caroline England* (London, 1962).

_____, *Caroline Courtier: The Life of Lord Cottington* (London, 1973).

_____, "The Character and Principles of an English King: The Case of Charles I," *Catholic Historical Review* 69 (1983): 169-208.

Hibbard, Caroline, "Early Stuart Catholicism: Revisions and Re-Revisions," *Journal of Modern History* 52 (1980): 1-34.

_____, *Charles I and the Popish Plot* (Chapel Hill, North Carolina, 1983).

LaRocca, J. L., "'Who Can't Pray with Me, Can't Love Me': Toleration and Early Jacobean Recusancy Policy," *Journal of British Studies* 23 (1984): 22-36.

Lindley, K. J., "Lay Catholics in the Reign of Charles I," *Journal of Ecclesiastical History* 22 (1971): 199-221.

_____, "The Part Played by Catholics," *Politics, Religion and the English Civil War,* ed. Brian Manning (London, 1973): 127-76.

Loomie, Albert J., "King James I's Catholic Consort," *Huntington Library Quarterly* 34 (1971): 303-16.

Maltby, William S., *The Black Legend in England: The Development of Anti-Spanish Sentiment* (Durham, North Carolina, 1971).

Manning, R. B., Religion and Society in Elizabethan Sussex (Leicester, 1969).

McCoy, F. N., *Robert Baillie and the Second Scots Reformation* (Berkeley, California, 1974).

McGrath, Patrick, "Elizabethan Catholicism: A Reconsideration," *Journal of Ecclesiastical History* 35 (1984): 414-28.

McRoberts, D., "The Scottish Catholic Archives, 1560-1978," *Innes Review* 28 (1977): 59-128.

Miller, John, *Popery and Politics in England 1660-1688* (New York, 1975).

Mosler, David F., "Warwickshire Catholics in the Civil War,:" *Recusant History* 15 (1980): 259-64.

Newman, P. R., "Roman Catholic Royalists: Papist Commanders under Charles I and Charles II, 1642-60," *Recusant History* 15 (1981): 396-405.

Nuttal, G. F., "The English Martyrs, 1535-1680: A Statistical Review," *Journal of Ecclesiastical History* 22 (1971): 191-97.

Prichard, Arnold, *Catholic Loyalism in Elizabethan England* (Chapel Hill, North Carolina, 1979).

Purvis, J. S., "The Archives of York," *Studies in Church History,* ed. G. J. Cuming (Leiden, 1967): 1-14.

Religious Controversies of the Elizabethan Age: A Survey of Printed Sources, ed. Peter Milward (London, 1977).

Religious Controversies of the Jacobean Age: A Survey of Printed Sources, ed. Peter Millward (Lincoln, Nebraska, 1978).

Rose, Elliott, *Cases of Conscience: Alternatives Open to Recusants and Puritans under Elizabeth I and James I* (London, 1975).

Ross, Anthony, "Dominicans and Scotland in the Seventeenth Century, *Innes Review* 23 (1972): 40-75.

Russell, Conrad, *Parliaments and English Politics 1621-1629* (Oxford, 1979).

Ryan, Conor, "Religion and State in Seventeenth-Century Ireland," *Archivium Hibernicum* 33 (1975): 122-32.

Sanderson, Margaret H. B., "Catholic Recusancy in Scotland in the Sixteenth Century," *Innes Review* 21 (1970): 87-107.

Scarisbrick, J. J., *The Reformation and the English People* (Oxford, 1984).

Simms, J. G., *Early Modern Ireland, 1534-1691,* Vol. 3, *A New History of Ireland* (London, 1976).

Spain and the Jacobean Catholics, Catholic Record Society Records Series, Vols. 64 and 68, ed. Albert J. Loomie (London, 1973, 1978).

Stephenson, David, *The Scottish Revolution 1637-44. The Triumph of the Covenanters* (New York, 1973).

_____, "The Irish Franciscan Mission to Scotland and the Irish Rebellion of 1641," *Innes Review* 30 (1979): 54-61.

Tavard, George, *The Seventeenth-Century Tradition: A Study in Recusant Thought* (Leiden, 1978).

Tyacke, Nicholas, "Puritanism, Arminianism, and Counter-Reformation," in *The Origins of the English Civil War,* ed. Conrad Russell (New York, 1973), 119-43.

Williams, J. Anthony, *Catholic Recusancy in Wiltshire, 1660-1791,* Catholic Record Society Monograph Series, Vol. I (London, 1968).

Wormald, Jenny, *Court, Kirk, and Community: Scotland 1470-1625* (London, 1981).

_____, "Gunpowder, Treason and Scots," *Journal of of British Studies, 24 (1985): 141-68.*

Wrightson, Keith, *English Society 1580-1680* (New Brunswick, New Jersey, 1982).

Catholic Reform in the Polish-Lithuanian Commonwealth
(Poland, Lithuania, the Ukraine, and Belorussia)

Jerzy Kloczowski

IN THE SIXTEENTH AND SEVENTEENTH CENTURIES, the Polish-Lithuanian Commonwealth comprised huge regions of central and eastern Europe–in some periods almost a million square kilometers with a population of eight to ten million.[1] Today almost a hundred million inhabitants live on its former territory in Poland, the Ukraine, Lithuania, and Belorussia. Vestiges of this great epoch and of the reform movements of the sixteenth through the eighteenth centuries are still evident in the culture of the peoples and even in the landscape with its characteristic baroque churches.[2] In examining the general historical context, at once similar to what we encounter in the rest of Europe and quite different from it, we must understand the changes that occurred in the religious life here in the very heart of Europe. The coexistence of different ethnic and religious groups is one of its most significant characteristics. Therefore, aside from the Poles, there are the Lithuanians, the Germans, the Jews, the Ruthenians, and to the east, the ancestors of the present-day Ukrainians and the Belorussians.

Roman Catholicism has been the faith of the vast majority of Poles since 966, and also of the Lithuanians, who finally and officially accepted Christianity only in 1386-87.[3] The Ruthenians belong to the Eastern Church, with their conversion dating back to the end of the tenth century. At the end of the sixteenth century, under the leadership of their bishops, a considerable percentage of the Ruthenians acknowledged the primacy of Rome; the Uniate (Greek Catholic)

---

[1] Good introductions to the history of Poland in English are Tazbir (1968) and Davies (1977, 1984). For a wider European context: Halecki (1952), Dvornik (1970). In the valuable series, *A History of East Central Europe,* announcement has been made of an important volume in preparation by Kaminski.

[2] The most comprehensive presentation of these religious changes is by Jobert (1974); Litak (1987) provides this in shorter form. *Bibliographie* (1965). For an attempt to assess Catholicism in the seventeenth century in a general way, Czaplinski (1969). See also Stasiewski (1960).

[3] For recent synthetic histories of Polish Christianity in the period, see Kloczowski (1970, 1980, 1987), Kumor and Obertynski (1974). An expanded edition of my work (1980) is in preparation in Polish at Lublin and in French at Paris, (Centurion Press, 1987). On cartography, see Bienkowski (1971).

Church from then on would have to live alongside the Orthodox Church. The tension between these two churches will weigh heavily on the complicated history of the Ukraine even today.[4]

In the very first years after Luther's Theses of 1517, Protestantism spread quickly in Poland–especially among the German population in the cities, with Gdańsk, a city on the Baltic growing rapidly in importance, at the fore.[5] In 1525 Poland officially recognized within its borders the first Protestant state in the World when it recognized the Prussian, Albrecht (Hohenzollern) of Brandenburg, former grand master of the Teutonic Order, as a vassal of the Polish king. Beginning in the 1550s, Protestantism, chiefly in the form of Calvinism, enjoyed great success among the rich Polish, Lithuanian, and, to some degree, even Ruthenian gentry.

Nevertheless, despite the efforts of Jan Łaski and the programmatic writings of Andrzej Frycz Modrzewski, a Polish national church was never created.[6] In the 1560s the emergence of the strong antitrinitarian movement of the Polish Brethren at the same time indicated the demise of Polish Protestantism.[7] (The Brethren would have great significance in Poland into the middle of the seventeenth century.) When, in response to growing Catholic opposition, the main Protestant churches came to an understanding in 1570 in Sandomierz, the "Consensus of Sandomir" firmly condemned the antitrinitarians.[8]

For its time, the religious tolerance of the Commonwealth, officially guaranteed by the constitutional statute in Warsaw in 1573 (the Warsaw Confederation)[9], was an exceptional phenomenon in Europe–along with the Siegmiograd of Hungary. We must add that in the sixteenth century and in the first half of the seventeenth, the ever-growing Jewish community enjoyed a far-reaching autonomy, complete with a parliament possessing a number of important powers.[10] In lesser proportions, there were also communities of Karaites,

---

[4]Ammann (1950).
[5]At present we lack a competent and comprehensive study of the Protestant Reformation in Poland, although Bartel (1966) provides a short outline up to 1556. For specific areas, see Kot (1953), Dworzaczkowa (1969), Ivinskis (1967), Kosman (1973), Williams (1978), Karzel (1979).
[6]Bałakier (1962), Kowalska (1969).
[7]Kot (1957), Williams (1980).
[8]Halecki (1915), Lehman (1937), Jörgensen (1942).
[9]Lecler (1955), Tazbir (1973), Weintraub (1971).
[10]Baron (1976), Hundert (1984).

Armenians, and Moslems who remained steadfast in their faith and yet maintained considerable allegiance to the state.[11]

The Parliament, Senate and Chamber of Deputies, all composed of representatives from the nobility of all ethnic groups, played a fundamental role in the Polish-Lithuanian Commonwealth. The nobility was a numerous class, about ten percent of the general population, and was socially and economically quite differentiated. In Poland the more absolute monarchy that was becoming so apparent in the rest of Europe did not exist, and attempts to strengthen the king's power met with the resolute opposition of the nobles. The Lithuanian and Ruthenian nobility were attracted to the model of a Polish nobility that possessed prior, legally established freedoms. In the seventeenth century especially, the Polonization of nobles of Lithuanian or Ruthenian background developed out of this cross-national solidarity among the nobility. For a long time historiography on this period found the key to understanding the defeat of the Protestant Reformation and the victory of Catholicism in the attitudes of the nobility.[12]

Historiography on the Counter Reformation has traditionally focused only on the struggle of the Catholic Church against the Protestants, and as a rule it judged the triumph of Catholicism negatively, even severely. Only later did an entirely different direction in research become defined that more clearly examined reform phenomena within Catholic society itself.[13] We are still far from concluding these investigations and arriving at a new, sweeping formulation of the changes and socio-religious movements in the Polish-Lithuanian state of the sixteenth and seventeenth centuries. It is important, however, to signal the direction in which these new orientations and proposals for research are moving.

II

Among the reasons that led to the failure of the Protestant Reformation in Poland was surely the inner dynamism and vitality of

---

[11]Szyszman (1980), Petrowicz (1971), Bogdanowicz (1942).

[12]For the general mood of the country and the role of the nobility, see the recent surveys: Bardach (1976), Maczak (1979), Fedorowicz (1982). On the nobility and religious changes, see Czarnowski (1933), with a thesis very controversial today; Schramm (1965).

[13]Krasiński (1838-40), aggressively anti-Catholic, long shaped the opinion of people reading English, as did Ljubović (1890) for those reading Russian. For discussions of the debate and state of research, see Wojtyska (1977).

the Catholic Church, a factor that has until now been insufficiently studied or stated. Moreover, the fact that Polish Protestantism gained momentum only in the fifth decade of the sixteenth century proved to be a disadvantage. By that time the reform forces in European Catholicism had already greatly increased and intensified, and their impact became even more pronounced in Central-Eastern Europe. It is also significant that Jan Łaski, Adrzej Frycz Modrzewski and Stanisław Hozjusz (Hosius), the three most prominent representatives of the various reform movements in Poland–men of European education and importance–belonged to exactly the same generation; they were born, respectively, in 1499, 1503 and 1504.

Hozjusz, nominated bishop of Chelmo in 1549 by King Zygmunt August, had by 1551 taken the lead in his episcopate with his decisive and energetic actions and his anti-Protestant writings. His treatise on Catholic doctrine, *Confessio fidei catholicae christiana,* published for the first time in 1553, saw thirty editions in different European languages during his lifetime. It therefore clearly answered the needs of the moment, and not only in Poland.[14]

All three of these men developed out of the same traditions of Erasmian reform, which had evoked a lively response among the Polish elite in the first decades of the century.[15] Even now the extent to which these Erasmian circles were the direct continuation of fifteenth-century reform traditions at Kraków University remains an open but important question for analyzing the character of religious reform in Poland in the sixteenth century. Recent studies emphasize the significance of these traditions.[16] In Poland, as in other parts of Europe, a polarization of religious positions occurred within Humanism over the course of the century, a parting of the ways for persons sometimes bound to one another by many ties, like Hozjusz and Modrzewski.

As is well known, earlier studies on the origins of Protestantism emphasized the decline of the Catholic Church and its clergy as one of the principal reasons for the birth of new churches. Today we are generally far from such a formulation of the issue and treat more

---

[14]On Hozjusz: Liedke and Gustaw (1971), with extensive bibliography; see also Williams (1981). An important edition of the oldest biography is by Rescius (1938), and in illustrated form by Treterus (1938); on the latter, see Chrzanowski (1984). On Modrzewski, Piwko (1969, 1979).

[15]Williams (1977). Cytowska (1965) has compiled the sources, along with a commentary; Schmydtowa (1972) brings sharply into relief the influence of Erasmus on the Protestant poet, Mikołaj Rej.

[16]Czartoryski (1970), Rechowicz (1974).

cautiously the assessments of the reformers of successive generations in the fifteenth and sixteenth centuries. Their reproaches often did not reflect specific problems, but were the expression of emerging needs and of a greater ecclesiastical and moral consciousness. In any case, in Poland, despite constant difficulties and crises in the fifteenth and early sixteenth centuries, the improvement rather than the decline of the Church's institutions must, generally speaking, be taken into account. Specialized studies on the Polish parish clergy generally show, among other things, that in the early sixteenth century the clergy resided in their parishes to a much greater degree that was generally true in the West. This of course assured the continuing functioning of the parish, especially since interdicts, which often paralyzed religious life in the West for years, were a much less frequent phenomenon. Throughout the period, despite evidence of crisis, there was a considerable and growing dynamism in pastoral ministry among the mendicant friars. This dynamism was especially marked in the Franciscan observants, known in Poland as the Bernardines after St. Bernardine of Siena.[17]

During even the most difficult years of the sixteenth century, the material bases of the Catholic Church were not fundamentally shaken. What is curious, even exceptional in the European context, is that the expropriation of Church goods never became a focal point for debates.[18] All during the period bishops held their positions in the Senate, a factor of great significance for the Polish political system given the importance of the Sejm. The loss of hundreds of parishes to the Protestants truly disorganized normal activities in many territories. Nonetheless, the loyalty to Catholicism of the peasant masses, petty nobility, and Polish middle class, confirmed almost everywhere, remains a striking phenomenon.[19] The reasons for this immeasurably important phenomenon and its significance are still debated today. However, one cannot rule out that it was in part the result of their relatively recent and successful conversion to Catholicism, as well as of the connections established between Catholicism and folk culture, connections frequently and sharply criticized by the demanding evangelism of the Protestants.

Among the religious orders, the weakened and yet active Bernardines and Dominicans distinguished themselves in these difficult

---

[17] Wiśniowski (1981), Kłoczowski (1968, 1983).
[18] On the economic factors relative to the goods of the Church, see Żytkowicz (1962). On the goods of the bishops, see Topolski (1955), Sobisiak (1960).
[19] See Urban (1959) on Małopolska, an area of special importance.

decades. The cathedral chapters seem to become especially important centers. From them–for example, Kraków–emanated on the one hand the sharpest internal criticisms of the existing situation and severe assessments of episcopal negligence, and, on the other, different initiatives and actions supporting order or promoting reform.[20]

The papal nunciature, established precisely in the mid-sixteenth century, played a substantial role in the Commonwealth, surely greater than in other countries. The nuncios, representing the pope, exerted influence on King Zygmunt August (1548-72), who at certain times came close to the idea of a national church. They at the same time mobilized the bishops to make joint pronouncements, and they supported the cathedral chapters in their reform activities.

From the 1550s onward, new forces clearly began to take shape. Stanisław Hozjusz was an important cardinal and a participant in the last phases of the Council of Trent. He was, as well, an articulate writer and theologian who gathered like-thinking persons around him. He also represented the new type of saintly bishop, i.e., a pastor with a deep sense of responsibility for the diocese entrusted to him. Transferred from Chelmno to Warmia, Hozjusz brought the new Jesuit order to Poland in Braniewo in 1564. This date, important also for the king's official acceptance of the decrees of the Council of Trent, can be seen as a turning point. The scale begins to tip in favor of the Catholics.[21]

The Society of Jesus would prove to be very important. Poles began to enter the Society in Vienna, where the Jesuit college had been in operation since 1552. In 1564, Stanisław and Paweł Kostka, sons of the Zakrocim castellan, were students there. Stanisław entered the order in 1567 in Rome, where he died the following year. He was beatified in 1670 and canonized in 1726.

With its establishment in Braniewo in 1564, the order began its expansion in the Polish-Lithuanian Commonwealth. When a Polish province was created ten years later, colleges already existed in Pułtusk, Wilno, Poznań, and Jarosław, as well as in Braniewo. Material aid was assured by the generous help of the bishops and also by King Stefan Batory (1576-86), who funded three great colleges on the northeastern

---

[20] Wollek (1972). We need many more such studies.
[21] Thorough studies: Wojtyska (1967, 1977). On the correspondence of the nuncios, see Wojtyska (1973), as well as Boratyński (1915) and Kuntze and Nanke (1923-50). The editing of the writings of Hozjusz is still in progress (1879-). We lack a good history of the Polish Jesuits, although recently sources have been gathered and published, e.g., Natoński (1969), Majkowski (1972).

borders in Połock, Ryga, and Dorpat with the plan of re-Catholicizing the Inflant lands (present-day Estonia and Latvia), which had only recently been converted to Protestantism. In its first generation the Society already attracted to itself in Poland many persons of distinction, both Poles and foreigners including some former Protestants. Jesuit secondary schools were tuition-free, accessible to all and equipped with a modern humanistic program highly esteemed in all Europe. They enjoyed tremendous popularity among both Catholics and Protestants. For a long time in Poland these schools encountered competition only from Protestant and German-language *gymnazia* in Gdańsk, Elblag, and Toruń, as well as a few schools established by groups disaffected towards the Jesuits. Kraków University, fearful of Jesuit competition, was nevertheless incapable of developing any program that could really threaten the clear dominance of the Society.[22]

Up to the end of the sixteenth century at the very least, tens of thousands passed through the schools of the Society, and this fact strongly marked both the clerical and secular intellectual elite of the country. In Poland and Lithuania at the beginning of the seventeenth century, twenty-five large colleges already existed in all the more important cities. Even today these buildings testify to the scope and dimension of this enterprise.

The ministry of the Society of Jesus extended, however, far beyond the schools. It included popular missions, beginning with sermons preached in all the major centers from the royal court on down. Jesuits engaged in sharp polemics with the Protestants; they produced an abundant theological and religious literature. In several regions, such as in the Grand Duchy of Lithuania where one could easily still find traces of paganism alongside active Protestant, Catholic, or Orthodox parishes, the Jesuits concentrated special effort. Here they created their own university in Wilno (1579). It was difficult for the local Protestants, despite the protection of the powerful Radziwiłłs, to counter the Jesuits' international elite. The revitalization of Catholicism there was also to a large extent the Jesuits' doing, as it was in a great many other parts of the Commonwealth.[23]

---

[22]On Kraków University: Barycz (1935), Lepszy (1964).
[23]Poplatek (1936), Rabikauskas (1979), Piechnik (1984).

III

One of the most obvious manifestations of Catholic victory first appeared in the 1560s, and then grew in subsequent years: the return of the Protestant nobility to their former Church. On the Ruthenian lands of the Grand Duchy of Lithuania, a large number of Ruthenian bojars, moreover, accepted Catholicism. These nobles had earlier cast off Orthodoxy for Protestantism only to find themselves ultimately in the Catholic Church. In due course the nobility there became almost completely Polonized.

At the end of the century, when the success of the Catholic Church was becoming ever more apparent, the Catholic Reform, in the more restricted sense of the term, gained further momentum. The new generation of bishops promoted it on a wide scale. They fundamentally reorganized their dioceses, strengthened the entire system of control and visitation, strove to raise the level of education and discipline of the clergy, and articulated in synods a general program of reform.[24]

The Council of Trent had recommended that a seminary be founded in each diocese. In practice this turned out to be a difficult task, realized only slowly over the course of the next hundred or even two hundred years. To a large extent, however, the Jesuit colleges immediately aided in preparing better candidates for the priesthood.

The zealous and responsible pastor had to have knowledge of each one of his parishioners.[25] To this end, the obligation of recording with precision baptisms, marriages, and burials was implemented. Parochial registers appeared, an invaluable source for the history of the people and families of each parish.

At the same time the activity of the religious orders intensified.[26] New candidates by the hundreds applied for admission, and new houses were established. This phenomenon took on an outright mass character during the first half of the seventeenth century. Everywhere requests

---

[24]For a general view of the changes in the dioceses, see Müller (1970). For analyses based on a single diocese: for Płock, see Müller (1975) and Góralski (1983); for Kraków, see Machay (1936), Wyczawski (1964). On the influence of Borromeo's example, see the forthcoming work by Wojtyska (1986). For studies on the basic sources: synods, Sawicki (1948-); visitation accounts, Litak (1962), Librowski (1964), Wiśniewski (1981); episcopal reports sent to Rome, Długosz (1937), Rabikauskas (1971-), Müller (1978). On the different situation in Silesia, see Sabisch (1975).

[25]Litak (1970). See also Patyga (1966), Olczak (1978).

[26]For a comprehensive treatment of the expansion of the religious orders, see Kłoczowski (1970); on the Dominicans, Kłoczowski (1975); on the rise of the monastery at Jasna Góra (Częstochowa) as a pilgrimage site, Witkowska (1984).

poured in for the orders' preachers, missionaries, confessors, chaplains for the increasing number of pilgrimage shrines, and organizers for confraternities.

These religious confraternities, with the Brethren of the Rosary at their head, became immeasurably popular and grew to formerly unheard-of dimensions. The social base for the entire movement was very broad, and its geographical range gradually encompassed the Commonwealth along with its Lithuanian and Ruthenian lands.

To a large extent, the patronage of the magnates and the great nobility assured the development of religious institutions and, in general, promoted Church construction. Many nobles removed Protestant ministers from their courts and replaced them with priests from the religious orders. Both diocesan and religious clergy were principally of plebeian background, especially middle-class, although there were a number of nobles, generally petty nobles, among them.[27] Within the relatively strong framework of religious or diocesan structures, the plebeian clergy was better protected than Protestant groups from the arbitrary actions of their secular patrons. Every priest had the support of a strong and, to a great degree, independent institution.

Judged in comparison with the rest of Europe, the expansion of Catholicism proceeded in a strikingly peaceful manner. Violence did occur, however, especially from the 1570s onwards in large cities with a preponderantly Catholic population, beginning with the capital city of Kraków.[28] The crowds, often students of the Jesuit schools, destroyed Protestant shrines, or, for instance, attacked funeral processions. Authorities did not always respond to these disturbances promptly or effectively. In a number of cities, moreover, Protestant churches were completely destroyed in the first half of the seventeenth century.

The promotion of Catholicism by the kings, especially after Zygmunt Waza III (1587-1632), had a major impact through the exercise of certain forms of political pressure, e.g., avoiding the nomination of Protestants for senatorial positions. This practice led to the Senate becoming almost completely Catholic. The Royal Tribunal, established in 1578 as the highest noble court, showed less and less tolerance over time for Protestants, particularly for the Polish Brethren, who were held suspect even by other antitrinitarians. In 1638, by sentence of the Sejm Court, the academy, church, and publishing house

---

[27] Gapski (1986), in preparation.
[28] Tazbir (1971).

of the Arians were closed in Raków, their best known and chief center. Without dismissing these various forms of pressure and oppression, one must nonetheless view them against the general practice of all victorious churches of the period regardless of their denomination. We should not in any case attribute the definitive emergence of Catholicism exclusively or even basically to pressures of this type.

IV

The reasons for Catholic success continue, in fact, to be debated by scholars. Studies of the mentality and religious culture of successive generations of Poles in the sixteenth century will surely produce important results. An important moment for the generation of the 1570s and 1580s, the generation that returned *en masse* to Catholicism, was brilliantly presented by Jan Błoński in his study (1967) of Mikołaj Sęp Szarzyński, perhaps the greatest Polish poet in the generation following Jan Kochanowski.[29]

Italian ties and a whole sense of tradition, so important in the consciousness of the Polish nobility and in its understanding of Humanism, basically brought the nobility to Catholicism. For a long time it was believed that, at least through a Council, the unification of Christians could be effected. Yet gradually this conciliatory position was destroyed, along with the hope of finding a common solution. The Wars of Religion in Europe and religious persecutions in Poland surely bear much responsibility for this change in perception. They helped engender pessimism and a sense of the immensity of sin and the tragedy of human existence. Serene objectivity and a humanistic optimism were replaced by the need for an inner truth, a mystical need for the personal bond of man to God which was in fact a characteristic of Protestant Christianity. What proved especially important for Catholicism was the emergence of the reform movements in Spain, particularly Spanish mysticism and asceticism, which were already apparent at the end of the fifteenth century and somewhat related to the *Devotio moderna,* with which Luther and Calvin also had some contact.

The Spiritual Exercises of Loyola and the writings of the Dominican, Luis de Granada, proved to be exceptionally important in this regard

[29]Błoński (1967).

in Poland during the 1570s.[30] At the very time the Jesuits arrived there, the first Polish translations of Luis appeared in print, and they quickly became popular. Luis's *Guide of Sinners* (first Polish edition, 1567) and his *Mirror of a Christian man* (first Polish edition, 1577) are somewhat similar to the *Exercises* in that they propose a practical pursuit of Christian virtues and daily exercise in them.

Catholic mysticism and asceticism, influenced to some extent by Christian Humanism, aimed at the formation of strong individuals ready to fulfill the tasks of life in all spheres. This led, for instance, in Sęp Szarzyński to his presentation of life as a task to be fulfilled; life in some way or other entailed a mission entrusted by God. Within this framework, the individual found a place for himself in the world, in the Church, in his country. Religion thus understood gave the individual a clear sense of life and personal involvement. Such a program, which skillfully linked the mystical and ascetical traditions with Humanism and with the exaltation of outright heroism in the human vocation, fitted well with the deeper psychological needs of new generations of Poles in the last decades of the sixteenth century. It perhaps finally decided the success of Catholicism.

This spirituality helped bring numerous men and women into the religious orders, but it also found application to people in all walks of life. The Jesuits, with Piotr Skarga traditionally seen as their leader, were especially successful here. The Commonwealth's actual needs at that time promoted, in part, the ideal of the Christian knight waging a holy war with the pagans. Sęp had already fully identified the knight's duty as religious, and he saw in the king the most vivid embodiment of the soldier who is a bulwark of Christianity.[31]

Published in Wilno in 1583, the memoir of Kasper Wilkowski, *The Reasons for Returning to the Common Faith,* includes a striking description of the long journey of this Arian who decided to accept the Catholic faith against the wishes of his family and against his friends, who pulled him in different directions. Compromise was not possible for Kasper because, as he wrote: "It concerns the soul, so everything that was a hindrance had to be set aside." After the years of inner unrest and indecision, this conversion began to bring him

---

[30]Górski (1962, 1980) has introscored the special significance of the last decades of the sixteenth century and the first decades of the seventeenth century for the history of spirituality and mysticism in Poland. See also Ciesielska-Borkowska (1939).

[31]Błoński (1967), and the still indispensable Kurdybacha (1938).

peace: "every day greater and greater confirmation, joy and enlightenment, by God's mercy."[32] Many examples exist of people who at the end of the sixteenth and particularly in the first decades of the seventeenth century realized in life the model of heroic holiness that the Catholic Reform proposed. Women from the Polish elite entered convents and monasteries. The Benedictine Congregation energetically directed by Magdalena Mortęska (1556-1633) attained to about twenty houses scattered throughout the Commonwealth.[33] We also have evidence of exceptionally devout wives and mothers who, usually after the death of their husbands, were able to fulfill even public tasks in the spirit of Christian and civic duty. There were many accomplished and responsible bishops, for instance, the heroic Hetman Stanisław Żółkiewski.[34] This phenomenon included persons, therefore, from all stations of life. True, the worsening situation of the peasants made it impossible for them, with rarer and rarer exception, to enter the world of any social elite. But from this peasant milieu, for example, came Stanisław Papczyński (1631-1701), founder of the Marian Fathers, the only order of male religious to be established in prepartition Poland. The cause for his beatification is under way.[35]

V

The Eastern Byzantine-Slavic Church, which included great Ruthenian territories in the Commonwealth and a sizable portion of their population, was decidedly affected by the general reform movements by the end of the sixteenth century. There is no doubt that this Church was in deep crisis, which is striking in comparison with what was happening in other churches in the very same country.[36] The weak education of its lower and higher clergy, its organizational confusion, its extensive dependence on secular powers, and its legal and social handicaps created the image of a clearly second- or third-rate Church in relationship to other institutions. The magnates and the Ruthenian nobility, as well as part of the middle class, were gradually

---

[32]Hernas (1973).
[33]Górski (1971, 1980).
[34]There is no contemporary biography of Żółkiewski; see, however, Prochaska (1927).
[35]Oskierka and Gustaw (1972).
[36]A basic work, Bieńkowski (1970); see also Śliwa (1974). For the viewpoint of Ukrainian historians, *Ukraine* (1971).

leaving it for Catholicism or, in the sixteenth century, often for Calvinism or antitrinitarianism. The expansion of Latin culture and Western Christianity, with the Jesuit schools in the lead, created the especially great danger of direct and threatening confrontation for the Eastern Church in the last decades of the century.

On the Polish side, interest in the Orthodox Church and its union with the Catholic Church, so clearly expressed by Stanislaw Orzechowski, later surfaced in a steady flow of reflective and polemical writings.[37] The Jesuits took up this issue in the 1570s, at that time proposing a unification of the Church with Rome. The bishops also began to move slowly towards this joint solution, reckoning that it would give them full equality with the Catholic Church in Senate seats, in the selection of bishops by chapters, in the independence of the lower clergy from secular patrons, and in the organization of schools for the clergy, as well as in other matters. At the same time they understood that they would preserve their autonomy in their organization and rituals, although they would break off relations with the patriarch in Constantinople. In this manner a whole movement of episcopal or, even more broadly, spiritual reform came about.

But the Eastern Church was opposed within its very framework by another movement represented by lay people gathered in religious confraternities, particularly in the two most important centers for the eastern lands of the Commonwealth–Lwów and Wilno. The confraternities wanted reforms under the patronage of the patriarch, the development of schools and full equality of the Ruthenian Orthodox with the Poles. In particular, the greatest Ruthenian magnate, Prince Konstantyn Wasyl Ostrogski (1527-1608), had his own plan for reform. In 1580 he even brought about the creation of the Ostrogska Academy, which was open to the study of Greek and Latin as well as Church Slavonic. Ostrogski also considered the possibility of union with the Catholics.[38]

In the end, the chief promoters of the union proved to be the bishops of the Eastern Church in the Commonwealth. Their delegations formally signed the Act of Union in the Vatican Palace on December 23, 1595, according to principles similar to those of the Union of Florence in the previous century. Opposition crystallized at home, however, with Prince Ostrogski and the confraternities at its head. When the Act of Union was announced at the synod in Brezno

[37]Redakcja (1979).
[38]Halecki (1958), Isaievicz (1960), Chynczewska-Hennel (1979).

in the autumn of 1586, it resulted in prolonged conflict. Ultimately, most of the bishops and diocesan clergy declared themselves for the union, but two bishops–from Przemyś and Lwów–as well as most of the monasteries remained in the Orthodox Church. Prince Ostrogski, a powerful man within the Commonwealth, became the chief protector of these so-called "Disuniates."

The government recognized the Uniates and their hierarchy as the only representatives of Eastern Christianity. Nonetheless, the Uniate bishops never obtained all they had expected. In particular, they were not allowed into the Senate. While the Uniates could count on the good will of Rome or the papal nuncios, they found the Latin bishops generally aloof.

The tension between the Uniates and the Disuniates, and also, frequently enough, between the Uniates and the Latin Catholics, seriously complicated the already established order of denominational relationships in the Commonwealth. (Many Latin Catholic priests and religious favored conversion from the Orthodox to the Latin Catholic Church rather than to the Uniate Church!) The murder in 1623 of the Uniate archbishop of Połock, Jozef Kuncewicz, by Orthodox crowds he had infuriated had an especially strong resonance in the whole country. The archbishop was recognized as a martyr and declared blessed in 1643, canonized in 1867.[39]

The Orthodox, practicing their faith in all the dioceses, aimed chiefly at creating their own hierarchy. They succeeded in this unofficially in 1620, and officially shortly after Władysław IV took power in the years 1632-35. Thus both Eastern Churches finally achieved recognition and stability in the Commonwealth.

For the Uniate Church the reign of the accomplished metropolitan, Welamin Rutski (1614-37) had special importance. He was active in a fundamental reform of the monasteries and in the creation of the order of St. Bazyl (the Basilians) on the model of the Latin orders, especially the Jesuits who were working closely with reform. The whole organization of the Uniate Church came to depend ever more on the Basilians, linked with the metropolitan. The Uniates began, for instance, to recruit bishops from the order.[40]

On the other hand, the Orthodox Church was organized by the metropolitan, Piotr Mohyla (1632-44). He was of a Moldavian hospodar family related by marriage to Polish magnates, a man deeply

---

[39]Rechowicz and Gustaw (1971).
[40]Welykyj (1956-).

influenced by Western culture as is clear in his theological writings. In Kiev, the main center of his activities, he created a college, later named the Mohyla Academy, which realized a program of studies influenced by Western culture adapted to the urgent needs of the Orthodox. Soon after Kiev fell definitively away from Poland and Peter I began to europeanize the Russian Church, Polish-Latin culture would influence Russia through the Academy. A great many bishops promoted this influence.[41]

VI

The Polish situation is made unique, therefore, by the coexistence not only of the classic faiths of the European Reforms–Catholic, Lutheran and Calvinist, and antitrinitarian–but also by the reforms of the Eastern Churches. Moreover, there are traces of intellectual and religious ferment among the non-Christian communities of the Commonwealth. One work can serve as an indication of that ferment, *The Confirmation of the Faith (Chizzuk emuna)* by Isaac, son of Abraham, a Karaite of the distant and superficially "provincial" Troks. This work includes an apology for the Mosaic Law and a polemic with Christians.[42]

Polish studies of the last thirty years have had a biased focus (harmful for a comprehensive view) on a group important in and of themselves, the Polish Brethren or Arians.[43] Today it is important to expand such studies to survey the whole religious phenomenon, without excluding anyone or omitting any religious or theological tradition. Existing works already allow us, indeed, to speak of the high quality of the activities and the intellectual and religious efforts of the Catholics. Their achievements, generally speaking, compare favorably with the level of intellectual culture of the epoch. As early as the mid-sixteenth century, a Polish theological "school" existed, centered to a large degree around Stanisław Hozjusz and tied to the Erasmian-humanistic tradition.[44]

The general development of Western theological thought at this time moved in the direction of so-called Positive Theology and relied

---

[41]Bendza (1982). On the academy, see Sydorenko (1977), sysyn (1984), Pritsak and Procyk (1984).

[42]Troki (1971).

[43]For an attempt to grasp the wider significance of Polish Socinianism, see Wrzecionko (1977).

[44]Rechowicz (1975).

directly on the Bible, along with certain Tridentine and post-Tridentine texts. The goal here was not so much elaborating a reasoning process along the traditional lines of the Scholastics, but the strengthening of the faith and love of God through the Bible, the Fathers of the Church, and the history of Christianity. The development of biblical studies, patristics, and Church history was the result of this orientation. Out of a practical and "devout" moral theology was slowly born a theology of the inner life. "Controversial" theology arose, as well, from religious polemics.

The Poles made substantial contribution in all these areas. Hozjusz was one of the most renowned writers of his day in all of Catholic Europe. The originality of Polish works on the Church rested in part on their concern for matters touching the Eastern Church. Among such authors special mention must be made of Stanisław Sokołowski (d. 1637) and Benedykt Herbest (d. 1593).[45]

The Polish Jesuits were in direct continuity with the first generation of the "Polish theological school." It is estimated that over fifty Jesuits in their first generation passed through a humanistic school and Kraków University before entering the order.[46] Along with polemical theology, which from the end of the sixteenth century concentrated more and more on the Polish Brethren, the Jesuits' most serious intellectual opponents, the early Jesuits continued and expanded works on Positive and ascetic-mystical theology in diverse ways.

It was of immense importance that, beginning with the Bible, texts fundamental to the whole Christian tradition and culture be translated into good Polish. The Bible had already been translated at the end of the Middle Ages. In 1561 the first complete printed text in Polish appeared, edited by Jan Nicz Leopolita (1523-72). Two years later appeared the full Protestant text of the so-called Radziwiłł Bible.[47] The Jesuits took advantage of these efforts and, thanks to Jakub Wujek, published clearly the best translation to exist in Poland for centuries. (The complete edition appeared in 1599.)

The Lives of the Saints from the Old and New Testaments, written for each day of the year by Piotr Skarga and, like his other works, translated

[45]Grabka (1945), Zdrodowski (1947), Zaorski (1957), Bochenek (1960). See also notes 14 and 21 above.

[46]Natoński (1975); on foreign Jesuits, Darowski (1978); on the teaching of philosophy, Darowski (1980).

[47]Kossowska (1968-69), Smereka (1975).

into excellent Polish, was to enjoy immense popularity.[48] From the entire company of important Jesuits, we must mention three in the field of ascetic-mystical theology: Mikołaj Leczycki (1574-1653), Kasper Druzbicki (1590-1662) and Daniel Pawłowski (1626-73). Both Leczycki and Pawłowski came from heretical families, not an unusual phenomenon for these first and, from a religious and intellectual perspective, most interesting generations of Polish Jesuits.[49]

Although all of the Reforms were sensitive to the ministerial care of their flocks, from the end of the sixteenth century only the Catholic Reform developed a truly immense pastoral campaign of a range and intensity hitherto unrealized in Poland. The elite, the Jesuits, and the bishops working closely with them strove to create an intellectual base for this campaign, adapted to Polish needs and circumstances. The comprehensive Pastoral Letter of the bishop of Kraków, Bernard Maciejowski, 1601, took on the character of a generally accepted ministerial guide. This letter referred to an earlier letter of a bishop who later became Cardinal Jerzy Radziwiłł and who, as the bishop working most closely with the Jesuits, published it again in Wilno in 1582. Once Radziwiłł became bishop of Kraków, he attached this same letter to the synod statutes of that diocese in 1593.[50]

VII

Catholic Reform, despite its momentum and dynamism, was unable to impose on Polish Catholicism as a whole the severe demands of a "heroic calling" for every Christian. The specific quality of Polish life and attitudes, including religious attitudes, was evident to all devout Catholic and other discerning observers arriving in Poland from Catholic Italy, Spain, or France. Even the notes and observations of the papal nuncios are interesting in this regard.[51] In spite of the piety of many of them, the nobles and magnates were far from ridding themselves of their traditional anticlericalism. In the fear that "Poland should turn into a kingdom of priests," for example, the Sejm of 1635

---

[48]There is no fully satisfactory monograph on Skarga; see, however, Berga (1916). See also Tazbir (1978), Williams (1981).

[49]Drużbicki (1963), Drzymala (1970).

[50]Brzozowski (1975); Bajda (1975) tries to draw general conclusions from existing studies, which are far from adequate.

[51]A still invaluable collection of accounts, partially in Polish translation, is Rykaczewski (1864).

forbade the transfer of real estate to the churches.[52] In practice, however, some of this land, which was the foundation for the wealth and significance of the nobility, later found its way by more or less legal means into church institutions. Certain legal checks and a lively opposition did preserve a distinction: church land became goods of mortmain and escaped the payments and partitions so characteristic of Poland where estates were always divided among all the children of a family.

In many important matters the Sejms did not yield to the demands of the Church. There was no talk of Church courts overturning the decisions of state courts or of the suspension of the Warsaw Confederation, which guaranteed religious tolerance. In the Sejm, in courts of law, and in normal social intercourse, the nobility of different faiths met without difficulty. Endless examples of this widespread phenomenon exist. To mention only one, Damiano Fonseca, a Spanish Dominican conducting a thorough visitation of the convents of his order in the Commonwealth in 1617-19, spent Christmas in 1617 at the court of Prince Jerzy Czartoryski on the occasion of the christening of the Prince's son. How puzzled he was to find Catholic, Orthodox, and Arian nobles there in the greatest harmony! What is more, in the course of these festivities the Prince demanded that the Dominican avoid a dispute with an Arian guest about the divinity of Christ.[53]

Only in such an atmosphere, doubtlessly slowly worsening but far removed from the intolerance dominating Europe, could one seriously attempt discussions among the faiths. A great advocate of such discussions was Władysław IV Waza (1632-48) along with a group of his close advisers, like Chancellor Jerzy Ossoliński and the wise and experienced Capuchin, Walerian Magni, a foreigner granted the Polish king's full confidence and openly sympathetic toward other faiths.[54] Although no direct results came of the thorough negotiations carried out with the Orthodox led by Piotr Mohyla, a man close to the king, and with the Protestants in the famous colloquium in Toruń in 1645, these negotiations testify to the special situation and atmosphere in Poland and to the Commonwealth's understanding of its basic interests in an era when religious wars were shaking the continent.

---

[52] Mazurkiewicz (1933).
[53] Kłoczowski (1973).
[54] Czapliński has attempted to examine all of Władysław IV's reign (1972). We are sorely lacking a good mongraph on Magni.

Only in such an atmosphere could there take place, as well, the aformentioned integration of Polish, Lithuanian, and Ruthenian nobles along with the ever more clear-cut and deeply rooted process of Polonization. These processes accompanied the voluntary conversion of the Ruthenian nobility to Catholicism, with the oldest and best families leading the way. At the same time the Commonwealth found place for Lutheran Gdańsk, for the Calvinist branch of the Radziwiłłs in Lithuania, and for the Orthodox. How strongly were Ruthenian nobles bound to the Commonwealth, like Konstantyn Ostrogski to Zygmunt III and Adam Kisiel, the Kievan governor close to Władysław IV![55] Yet we must not forget that from the contemporary perspective of the national consciousness of the Lithuanians and Ukrainians, the Polonization of their nobility is seen as their greatest loss during the period of coexistence within the Commonwealth.[56]

One must point out, on the other hand, the clearly weak aspects of a victorious Polish Catholicism, which are probably found to some extent in any denomination of "reforming" Christianity in the era. On a deeper level, one can examine just how well received were those heroic models proposed by the first generation of Jesuits, for example, the model of the Christian knight. In practice another model was becoming ensconced in the sixteenth century, that of the farmer in a "quiet and happy countryside" who unwillingly leaves his home and friends and neighbors for public service.[57] Any sort of rigorous, severe, or sharp demands clearly did not suit the Poles, whether these demands came from Calvin or from Charles Borromeo. Without a doubt the authentic and even ardent religiosity of the Poles was easily dissipated in the sea of Polish social life, in the hospitality the Poles valued so highly, and also in their easy loquacity, in the rhetoric of the meetings of the Sejm, and in incessant discussions.

This problem is clearly evident in the religious orders, and therefore also in the creation of the religious elite. One could say that the orders, including the Society of Jesus, shaped people in Poland to the same degree that they were shaped by the Poles and Polish society.[58]

---

[55]On Kisiel, see Wojcik (1966-67). For a history of Lutheran Gdańsk and its environs from a German perspective, Neumeyer (1971-77).

[56]For the viewpoint of contemporary Lithuanian historiography, see, e.g., Suziedlis (1970-78). For a history of the Ukraine, Chirovsky (1981-84); for a discussion of Polish and Ukrainian historians, see, e.g., Potichnyj (1980).

[57]Kurdybacha (1938).

[58]Kłoczowski (1970, 1973).

In Damiano Fonseca's description (1617-19) of the faults of the Polish Dominican community, which was at that time in full vigor, creating a hundred new houses in the Commonwealth in the seventeenth century, the weak aspects of Polish society are seen as concentrated in an omnipotent and dominant nobility that set an example for others. These faults were a lack of discipline and respect for authority, factional struggles, obstinacy in litigation, and alcoholism. In the end, the wise Fonseca found a compromise for the Dominicans that was accepted by all parties and assured the peace of this rent community. However, the thoroughly Polish character of that community offers us a sample of the difficulties facing anyone who tried consistently to effect any given reform in Poland. By the first half of the seventeenth century, we observe also among the Jesuits clear traces of a breakdown in its former momentum and quality of accomplishments, especially in their educational system. However, the heroic ideal, a model for every state of life, was rooted in the memory, recalled on different occasions, and sometimes even realized.

The approximately hundred-year period of these various and great reform movements had a colossal significance for the history of Polish society and the cultural and religious life of the Commonwealth. From an extended historical perspective, the victory of Catholicism in this atmosphere of religious tolerance should be underscored both in Polish history and general histories of Christianity. Moreover, today we understand better than previous scholars not only the similarities between all Christian reform movements in the sixteenth century, but also their similar failures. Thus, the limited success of Polish Catholicism in many areas was also in some sense its partial failure.

VIII

An important need in contemporary research is to view all the changes wrought by the Catholic Reform in the Polish-Lithuanian state in a wider comparative context, especially taking into account neighboring countries in the Catholic tradition like Bohemia and Hungary. Until now such research has been only weakly pursued. The importance of such a comparative view is apparent because of the close ties that bound this group of countries together in the Middle Ages and linked them to Western Civilization, as well as the substantive similarities in the changes effected in many areas.[59] Still, there are clear dissimilarities in the general sixteenth-century situation in each of these three countries. Hungary had undergone a division into three territories–one tied to and dependent upon Turkey, the autonomous Siedmiogrod, and finally the part in the hands of the Hapsburgs. The Czechs, on the other hand, were consistently under the rule of the Hapsburgs for centuries. The problem of the Protestant or Catholic Reform in the countries ruled by the Hapsburgs presents quite different problems for the scholar–the general national context here was, in any case, different from the one that so heavily weighed on the Commonwealth. In Czech territory and in Moravia, where since the fifteenth century the dissimilarity of the religious situation is so clear, elements of the classic Counter Reformation, in the sense that coercion was used to strengthen Catholicism, became particularly apparent after 1620, although it would be a mistake to attribute all religious changes there to that cause.[60]

The autonomy of the Hungarians in the Hapsburg nations was greater than in Czech lands; undoubtedly, coercion was less operative. The dynamism of the Catholic Reform in its confrontation with a strong Protestantism was especially apparent here in the begining of the seventeenth century. The symbol of the movement was the Primate, Pázmany. Aside from the extraordinary importance of the Jesuits, the part played by the Capuchins is here more clearly manifest than in Poland, where they arrived only at the end of the seventeenth century.[61]

It is also important to view the religious reforms in all these countries from a long-term perspective, *"la longue durée."* After all, the Catholic Reform included elements of a long standing program that continued not only through the seventeenth century but, under different circumstances, into the nineteenth and early twentieth. Given such an understanding of this historical process, it should be clear that though reforms suffered setbacks and periods of regression and

[59]Recently I undertook such a project for the fourteenth and fifteenth centuries in the wider framework of Slavic Europe (1984); Kloczowski (1987); *Bibliographie* (1965).

[60]For a characteristic book by a Czech scholar on the religious changes in Czech lands between 1460 and 1620, see Kalista (1974).

[61]Egyed (1973) gives a general survey of the history of the Catholic Church in Hungary up to 1914; Bucsay (1977) provides one for Protestantism. For recent works concerning Pázmány, see Miklós (1970, 1973), István (1979). On the Jesuits, László (1969-81), János (1963); on the Capuchins, Frey (1949). For his help in defining and assessing the Hungarians' position, I thank Professor József Török in Budapest.

though reforms suffered setbacks and periods of regression and stagnation, they also involved a certain continuity and clear undercurrents of new invigoration.

Without a doubt, a history of the socio-religious changes in the last few centuries has a fundamental significance for understanding the religious situation in these countries today. Although this thesis needs further verification, the degree of religious coercion exercised had an especially great significance over the long run. In the Polish-Lithuanian-Ruthenian lands there was significantly less coercion and a lack of church-state absolutism–factors that facilitated the creation through slow and voluntary processes of a specific culture linking constant elements of traditional folk religion with the impulses and requirements of reformed Christianity.[62] Later, under the difficult circumstances of foreign domination in the nineteenth and twentieth centuries, this culture would demonstrate great strength for survival, and the de-Christianizing processes would proceed more weakly here than elsewhere.

In Czech lands, however, where the national awakening in the nineteenth century took place largely in reaction to a whole set of attitudes forcibly imposed on the people by the Catholic Hapsburgs, the degree of their de-Christianization, exceptional for all of Central-Eastern Europe, became a striking phenomenon in the twentieth century. One can expect that further studies along this line–they are surely inadequate at present–will allow us to comprehend better and more deeply the complex set of questions only touched upon in this essay.

Bibliography

Ammann, A., *Abriss der ostslawischen Kirchengeschichte* (Vienna, 1950).

Backvis, Clause, *Individu et société dans la Pologne de la Renaissance* (Brussels and Paris, 1967).

Bajda, Jerzy, "Teologia moralna (kazuistyczna) w. 17-18," *Dzieje teologii katolickiej w Polsce,* ed. M. Rechowicz (Lublin, 1975), 2/1: 267-305.

---

[62]To a certain extent one could apply to this situation the judgment of Backis (1967), the accomplished Belgian expert on Polish culture in the sixteenth and seventeenth centuries: "Car nous touchons ici au paradoxe–paradoxe de pure apparence, puisq'on a affaire à une réalité historique indubitable et durable–que de ce mouvement d'individualisme humaniste, de cette ambiance de discussions incessantes, de cet affrontement perpétuel d'opinions et d'options vont sortir tout à la fois . . . un Etat extrement faible mais aussi une société prodigieusement solide, une sociétie cimentée par un vigoureux ésprit de corps."

Bardach, Juliusz, et al., *Historia państwa i prawa polskiego* (Warsaw, 1976).

Baron, Salo Wittmayer, *A Social and Religious History of the Jews*, XVI (New York and London, 1976).

Bartel, O., "Reformacja w Polsce 1518-1556," *Rocznik Teologiczny*, 8 (1966): 13-45.

Barycz, H., *Historia Uniwersytetu Jagiellonskiego w epoce humanizmu* (Kraków, 1935).

Bendza, M., *Prawosławna diecezja przemyska w latach 1596-1681, studium historyczne-kanoniczne* (Warsaw, 1982).

Berga, August, *Pierre Skarga* (Paris, 1916).

Bibliographie de la Réforme 1450-1648, 5 (Leiden, 1965).

Bieńkowski, Ludomir, "Organizacia Kościoła Wschondniego w Polsce," *Kościoł w Polsce*, ed., J. Kłoczowski, II (Kraków, 1970).

_____, Jerzy Flaga, and Zygmunt Sulowski, *Cartographie historique de la Pologne*, I (Leiden, 1971).

Błoński, Jan, *Mikolaj Sęp Szarzyński a początki polskiego baroku* (Kraków, 1967).

Bochenek, Jan, *Świetych obcowanie w nauce Stanisłasw Hozjusza* (Lublin, 1960).

Bogdanowicz, Leon, "The Muslims in Poland. Their Origin, History and Cultural Life," *Journal of the Royal Asiatic Society (October, 1942): 163-80.*

Boratyński, L., and J. A. Caligari, ed., *Nuntii Apostolici in Polonia: Epistolae et acta 1578-1581* (Kraków, 1915).

Brzozowski, M., "Teoria kaznodziejstwa (wiek 16-18)," *Dzieje teologii katolickie w Polsce*, ed. M. Rechowicz (Lublin, 1975), 2/1: 361-482.

Bucsay, M., *Der Protestantismus in Ungarn 1521-1978*, I (Vienna, 1977).

Chirovsky, N., *An Introduction to Ukrainian History*, 2 vols. (New York, 1981-84).

Chrzanowski, Tadeusz, *Działalność artystyczna Tomasza Tretera* (Warsaw, 1984).

Chynczewska-Hennel, Teresa, "Ostrogski, Konstanty," *Polski Słownik Biograficzny, XXIV* (Wrocław, 1979): 489-95.

Ciesielska-Borkowska, Stefania, "Mistycyzm hiszpanski na gruncie polskim," *Rozprawy Wydziału Filologicznego Polskiej Akademii Umiejętności, LXVI/1* (Kraków, 1939).

Czapliński, Władysław, "Blaski i cienie Kościoła katolickiego w Polsce w okresie potrydenckim," *Odrodzenie i Reformacja w Polsce* 14 (1969): 5-26.

_____, *Władysław IV i jego czasy* (Warsaw, 1972).

Czarnowski, Stefan, "La réaction catholique en Pologne à la fin du XVI et au debut du XVII s.," *La Pologne au XVIIIᵉ Congrès International des Sciences Historiques* (Warsaw, 1933), 2: 287-310.

Czartoryski, Pawel, "Średniowiecze," *Historia nauki polskiej*, ed. B. Suchodolski, I (Wrocław, 1970): 1-194.

Cytowska, M., ed., *Koresponden cja Erazma z Rotterdamu* (Warsaw, 1965).

Darowski, Roman, "Piotr Viana s.j. (1549-1609) i jego działalność filozoficzna w Polsce," *Odrodzenie i Reformacja w Polsce* 23 (1978): 37-53.

———, "Przepisy dotyczace nauczania filozofii w uczelniach jesuickich w Polsce w XVI wieku," *Studia z historii filozofii. Księga pamiątkowa z okazji 50-lecia pracy naukowej ks. Pawła Siwka s.j.* (Kraków, 1980): 47-85.

Davies, Norman, *Poland, Past and Present. A Select Bibliography of Works in English* (Newtonville, 1977).

———, *Heart of Europe. A Short History of Poland* (Oxford, 1984).

Długosz, Teofil, ed., *Relacje arcybiskupow lwowskich 1595-1794 (Lwów, 1937)*.

Drużbicki, O., *Kasper Drużbicki, teolog i mistyk polski 1592-1662*. Praca zbiorowa, Ateneum Kapłańskie, vol. 66 (Włocławek, 1963).

Drzymała, K., "Ks. Kasper Drużbicki," *Nasza Przezłość* 33 (1970): 143-65.

Dvornik, Francis, *Les Slaves* (Paris, 1970), a revised edition of the English version, *The Slavs in European History and Civilisation* (New Brunswick, 1958).

Dworzaczkowa, J., "Reformacja w Wielkopolsce," *Dzieje Wielkopolski,* ed. J. Topolski, I (Posnań, 1969): 542-73.

Egyed, Hermann, *A katolikus Egyház története Magyarországon 1914 ig* (Munich, 1973; rev. ed., 1982).

Fedorowicz, J. K., ed., *A Republic of Nobles: Studies in Polish History to 1864* (Cambridge, 1982).

Frey, Hyazinth, O. F. M., *Die Beziehungen der Kapuziner zu Ungarn bis zum Grundung des ersten Klosters (1595-1674)* (Budapest, 1949).

Gapski, Henryk, *Rekrutacja do zakonów męskich w Polsce w koncu XVI i w pierwszej połowie XVIII w.* (Lublin, 1986, in preparation).

Góralski, Wojciech, *Reformistyczne synody płockie na przełomie XVI i XVII wieku* (Płock, 1983).

Górski, Karol, *Od religijności domistyki* (Lublin, 1962).

———, *Matka Mortęska* (Kraków, 1971).

———, *Studia i materialy z dziejów duchowosci* (Warsaw, 1980).

Grabka, G., *Cardinalis Hosii doctrina de Corpore Christi mystico in luce saeculi XVI* (Washington D.C., 1945).

Halecki, Oskar, *Zgoda sandomierska 1570 r.* (Warsaw, 1915).

———, *Borderlands of Western Civilization* (New York, 1952).

———, *From Florence to Brest (1439-1596),* 2d ed. (Hamden, Conn., 1968).

Hernas, Czeslaw, *Barok. Historia literatury polskiej* (Warsaw, 1973).

Hozjusz, Stanisław, *Stanislai Hosii cardinalis et episcopi Varmiensis Epistolae et quae ad eum scriptae sunt tum etiam eius orationes legationes 1525-1579,* various editors (Kraków and Olsztyn, 1869-).

Hundert, Gershon David, and Gershon C. Bacon, *The Jews in Poland and Russia. Bibliographical Essays* (Bloomington, 1984).

Isaievicz, J., *Bratstvata ich rel' v rozvietku ukrainskoj kultury XVI-XVIII st.* (Kyiv, 1966).

István, Bitskey, *Humanista erudició és barokk világkép: Die Predigten von Péter Pázmány* (Budapest, 1979).

Ivinskis, Z., "Die Entwicklung der Reformation in Litauen bis zum Erscheinen der Jesuiten (1569)," *Forschung zur Osteuropean Geschichte* 12 (1967): 7-45.

János, Péteri, *As alsö jezsuiták Magyaroroszágon 1561-1567* (Rome, 1963).

Jobert, A., *De Luther à Mohila. La Pologne dans la crise de la chrétienté 1517-1648* (Paris, 1974).

Jörgensen, K. E. J., *Oekumenische Bestrebungen unter den polnischen Protestanten bis zum Jahre 1645* (Kopenhagen, 1942).

Kalista, Zdenek, "Die katholische Reform von Hilarius bis zum Weissen Berg," *Bohemia Sacra,* ed. F. Seibt (Schwamm, 1974).

Kamiński, Andrzej, *Lithuania and the Polish-Lithuanian Commonwealth, 1000-1795* (Seattle and London, in preparation).

Karzel, Othmar, *Die Reformation in Oberschlesien. Ausbreitung und Verlauf* (Würzburg, 1979).

Kłoczowski, Jerzy, ed., *Kościół w Polsce,* 2 vols., (Kraków, 1968-70).

_____, "Zakony na ziemiach polskich w wiekach średnich," *Kościół w Polsce,* ed. J. Kłoczowski, I (Kraków, 1986): 375-582.

_____, "Zakony męskie w Polsce w XVI-XVIII w.," *Kościół w Polsce,* ed. J. Kłoczowski II (1970).

_____, "Wielki zakon XVII wiecznej Rzeczypospolitej u progu swego rozwoju–Dominikanie polscy w świetle wizytacji generalnej z lat 1617-1619," *Nasza Przeszłość* 39 (1973): 103-80.

_____, ed., *Studia nad historią dominikanów w Polsce,* 2 vols. (Warsaw, 1975).

_____, ed., *Chrześcijaństwo w Polsce* (Lublin, 1980); expanded Italian version, *Storia del Cristianesimo in Polonia* (Bologna, 1980).

_____, ed., *Franciszkanie w Polsce średniowiecznej,* I (Kraków, 1983).

_____, *Europa słowiańska w XIV-XV w.* (Warsaw, 1984).

_____, *Dzieje chrześcijaństwa w polskiego,* 2 vols. (Paris, 1987).

_____, ed., *Histoire religieuse de la Pologne* (Paris, 1987).

_____, *Les Réformes en Europe centrale-orientale (la Bohême, la Hongrie, la Pologne avec la Lithuanie et la Ruthenie-l'Ukraine),* Histoire du christianisme, 8, ed. M. Venard (Paris, Desclée, 1987).

Kosman, Marceli, *Reformacja i Kontrreformacja w Wielkim Księstwie Litewskim w swietle propagandy wyznaniowej* (Wrocław, 1973).

Kossowska, Maria, *Biblia w języku polskim,* 2 vols. (Poznań, 1968-69).

Kot, Stanislaw, "La Reforme dans le Grand Duché de Lithuanie," *Annuaire de l'Institut de Philologie et d'Histoire Orientales et Slaves* 12 (1953): 201-61.

_____, *Socinianism in Poland. The Social and Political Ideas of the Polish Antitrinitarians* (Boston, 1957).

Kowalska, Halina, *Działalność reformatorska Jana Łaskiego* (Wrocław, 1969).

Krasiński, Walerian, *Historical Sketch of the Rise, Progress and Decline of the Influence which the Scriptural Doctrines have Exercised on that Country in Literary, Moral and Political Respects,* (London, 1838-40).

Kumor, Bolesław and Żdzisław Obertyński, ed., *Historia Kościoła w Polsce,* I/2 (Poznań, 1974).

Kuntze, E., Cz. Nanke, ed., *Nuntii Apostolici in Polonia. Epistolae et acta 1581-1585*, 2 vols. (Kraków, 1923-50).

Kurdybacha, Łukasz, *Staropolski ideal wychowawczy* (Lwów, 1938).

László, Lukács, *Monumenta Antiqua Hungariae* (Monumenta Historica Societatis Jesu), I (1550-79), II (1580-86), III (1587-92), (Rome, 1969-81).

Lecler, Joseph, *Histoire de la tolérance au siècle de la Réforme*, 2 vols. (Paris, 1955).

Lehman, J., *Konfesja Sandomierska na tle innych konfesji w Polsce XVI w.* (Warsaw, 1937).

Lepszy, Kazimierz, ed., *Dzieje Uniwersytetu Jagiellonskiego* (Kraków, 1964).

Librowski, Stanisław, "Wizytacje diecezji włocławskiej," *Archiwa, Biblioteki i Muzea Kościelne* 8 (Lublin, 1964): 5-180.

Liedke, Antoni, and Romuald Gustaw, "Hozjusz, Stanisław," *Hagiografia Polska. Słownik bio-biograficzny* (Poznań, 1971) 1:375-401.

Litak, Stanisław, "Akta wizytacji parafii z XVI-XVII w jako źródło historyczne," *Zeszyty Naukowe KUL* 5 (1962): 41-58.

_____, "Struktura i funkcje parafii w Polsce," *Kościół w Polsce*, ed. J. Kłowzowski (Kraków, 1970), 2:261-484.

_____, *Le temps des réformes et des lettres religieuses*, ed. J. Kłoczowski (Paris, 1987): 173-220.

Ljubović, Nikolaj, *Naćalo katolićskoj reakcii i upadok reformacii v Pol'še. Po neizdannym istoćnikam* (Warsaw, 1890).

Machay, Ferdynand, *Działalność duszpasterska kardynala Radziwiłła diskupa krakowskiego (1591-1600)* (Kraków, 1936).

Mączak, Antoni, "Od połowy XV wieku do rozbiorów," *Społeczeństwo polskie od X do XX wieku* (Warsaw, 1979): 227-453.

Majkowski, Józef, *Saint Stansilaus Kostka. A Pyschological Hagiography* (Rome, 1972).

Mazurkiewicz, Josef, *Ustawy, amortyzacyjne w dawnej Pwlsce* (Lwów, 1933).

Miklós, Öry, *Pázmány Péter tanulmányi évei* (Eisenstadt, 1970).

_____, "Kardinal Pázmány und die kirchliche Erneuerung in Ungarn," *Ungarn-Jahrbuch* 5 (1973): 76-96.

Müller, Wiesław, "Diecezja płocka od drugiej połowy XVI wieku do rozbiorów," *Studia Płockie* 3 (1975): 153-220.

_____, "Diecezje w okresie potrydenckim," *Kościół w Polsce*, ed. J. Kłoczowski (Kraków, 1970), 2:27-258.

_____, ed., *Relacje o stanie diecezji krakowskiej 1615-1756* (Lublin, 1978).

Natoński, Bronislaw, "Humanizm jezuicki i teologia pozytywno-kontrowersyjna w XVII-XVIII w. Nauczanie i piśmiennictwo," *Dzieje teologii katolickiej w Polsce*, ed. M. Rechowicz (Lublin, 1975), 2/1: 87-219.

_____, "Poczętki i rozwój Towarzystwa Jezusowego w Polsce 1564-1580," James Brodrick, *Powstanie i rozwój Towarzystwa Jesusowego*, I (Kraków, 1969): 414-76.

Neumeyer, Heinz, *Kirchengeschichte von Danzig und Westpreussen in evangelischer Sicht*, 2 vols. (Raustenberg, 1971-77).

Olczak, Stanisław, *Szkolnictwo parafialne w Wielkopolsce w XVII-XVIII wieku (w świetle wizytacji kościelnych)* (Lublin, 1978).

Oskierka, Bronisław Waldemar, and Romauld Gustaw, "Papczyński Jan Stanisław," *Hagiografia Polska. Słownik bio-biograficzny* (Poznań, 1972), 2:192-208.

Pałyga, J., "Duchowieństwo parafialne dekanatu kazimierskiego w XVII i XVIII wieku," *Roczniki Humanistyczne* 14/2 (Lublin, 1966): 16-42.

Petrowicz, G., *La Chiesa Armena in Polonia,* I (Rome, 1971).

Piechnik, Ludwik, *Początki Akademii Wileńskiej 1570-1599* (Rome, 1984).

Piwko, S., *Frycza Modrzewskiego program reformy państwa i Kościoła (Warsaw, 1979).*

———, "Andrzej Frycz Modrzewski–koncepcje reformy Kościoła," *Archiwum Historii Filosofii i Myśli Społecznej* 15 (1969): 59-90.

Poplatek, Jan, "Wykaz alumnów Seminarium Papieskiego w Wilnie 1582-1773," *Ateneum Wilenskie* 11 (1936): 1-66.

Potichnyj, Peter J., ed., *Poland and Ukraine. Past and Present* (Toronto, 1980).

Pritsak, Omeljan, and Oksana Procyk, "A Select Bibliography of Soviet Publications Related to the Kiev Academy and Its Founder, 1970-1983," *Harvard Ukrainian Studies* VII, 1/2 (1984): 229-50.

Prochaska, Antoni, *Hetman Stanisław Żółkiewski* (Warsaw, 1927).

Rabikauskas, Paulus, *Relationes status dioecesium in Magno Ducatu Lituaniae* (Rome, 1971-).

———, *The Foundation of the University of Vilnius, 1579* (Rome, 1979).

Rechowicz, Marian, and Romauld Gustaw, "Jozafat Jan Kuncewicz (Kunczyc)," *Hagiografia Polska. Słownik bio-biograficzny* (Poznań, 1971), 1:632-54.

———, "Po założeniu Wydziału Teologicznego w Krakowie (Wiek XV)," *Dzieje teologii katolickiej w Polsce* (Lublin, 1974), 1:93-148.

———, ed., *Dzieje teologii katolickiej w Polsce* (Lublin, 1974), 2/1-2.

Redakcja, (Polskiego Słownika Biograficznego), "Orzechowski Stanisław herbu Oksza (1513-1566)," *Polski Słownik Biograficzny* 24 (Wrocław, 1979): 287-92.

Rescius, Stanislaus, *Stanislai Hosii Vita* (Pelplini, 1938).

Rykaczewski, Erasm, ed., *Relacye nuncyuszow apostolskich i innych osób o Polsce do roku 1548-1690,* 2 vols. (Berlin, 1864).

Sabisch, Alfred, *Die Bischöfe von Breslau und die Reformation in Schlesien (Münster, 1975).*

Sawicki, Jakub, *Concilia Poloniae. Źródła i studia krytyczne,* vols. 2-10 (Warsaw, 1948-).

Schmydtowa, Zofia, *O Erazmie i Reju* (Warsaw, 1972).

Schramm, Gottfried, *Der polnische Adel und die Reformation 1548-1607* (Wiesbaden, 1965).

Śliwa, Tadeusz, "Kościół wschodni w monarchii Jagiellonów w latach 1506-1596," "Kościól unicki w Polsce w latach 1596-1696," "Kościół prawosławny w Rzeczypospolitej w latach 1596-1696," *Historia Kościoła w polsce,* ed. B. Kumor and Z. Obertyński, I/2 (Posnań, 1974).

Smereka, Władysław, "Biblistyka polska (wieki XVI-XVIII)," *Dzieje teologii katolickiej w Polsce,* ed. M. Rechowicz (Lublin, 1975), 1/1:221-60.

Sobisiak, W., *Rozwój latifundium biskupstwa poznańskiego w XVI do XVIII w.* (Poznań, 1960).

Stasiewski, B., *Reformation und Gegenreformation in Polen. Neue Erforschungsergebnisse* (Münster, 1960).

Suziedlis, Simas, et al., *Encyclopedia Lituanica,* 6 vols. (Boston, 1970-78).

Sydorenko, Alexander, *The Kievan Academy in the Seventeenth Century* (Ottawa, 1977).

Sysyn, Frank E., "Peter Mohyla and the Kiev Academy in Recent Western Works: Divergent Views on Seventeenth-Century Ukrainian Culture," *Harvard Ukrainian Studies* 8, 1/2 (1984): 155-87.

Szyszman, Szymon, *Le Karaïsme* (Lausanne, 1980).

Tazbir, Janusz, (the chapters on the sixteenth and seventeenth centuries) *History of Poland,* ed. Stefan Kieniewicz, (Warsaw, 1968).

_____, *Arianie i katolicy* (Warsaw, 1971).

_____, *A State without Stakes. Polish Religious Tolerance in the Sixteenth and Seventeenth Centuries* (Warsaw, 1973).

_____, *Piotr Skarga* (Warsaw, 1978).

Treterus, Thomas, *Theatrum Virtutum D. Stanislai Hosii* (Pelplini, 1938).

Topolski, Jerzy, *Rozwój latyfundium arcybiskupstwa gnieźnieńskiego od XVI do XVIII w.* (Poznań, 1955).

Troki, Isaac, *Faith Strengthened* (New York, 1971).

Ukraine. A Concise Encyclopedia. See "The Ukrainian Church," II (Toronto, 1971): 120-231.

Urban, Waclaw, *Chłopi wobec reformacji w Małopolsce w drugiej połowie XVI w.* (Kraków, 1959).

Weintraub, Wiktor, "Tolerance and Intolerance in Old Poland," *Canadian Slavonic Papers* 13 (1971).

Welykyj, A. G., ed., *Epistolae metropolitarum Kiioviensium catholicorum* (Rome, 1956-).

Williams, George Huntston, "Erasmianism in Poland: An Account and Interpretation of a Major though Ever Diminishing Current in Sixteenth-Century Polish Humanism and Religion, 1518-1605," *The Polish Review* 22 (1977): 3-50.

_____, "Protestants in the Ukraine during the Period of the Polish-Lithuanian Commonwealth," *Harvard Ukrainian Studies* 2 (1978): 41-72.

_____, *The Polish Brethren,* 2 vols. (Cambridge, Mass., 1980).

_____, "Stanislaus Hosius 1504-1579," *Shapers of Religious Traditions in Germany, Switzerland, and Poland, 1560-1600,* ed., Jill Raitt (New Haven, 1981), 157-74.

————, "Peter Skarga," *Shapers of Religious Traditions in Germany, Switzerland, and Poland, 1560-1600,* ed., Jill Raitt (New Haven, 1981), 175-94.

Wiśniewski, Jan, "Warmińskie wizytacje kromerowskie," *Archiwa, Biblioteki i Muzea Kościelne, 43 (1981): 181-202.*

Wiśniowski, Eugeniusz, "Parish Clergy in Medieval Poland," *The Christian Community in Medieval Poland,* ed. J. Kłoczowski (Wrocław, 1981): 119-48.

Witkowska, Aleksandra, "Kult jasnogórski w formach pątniczych do połowy XVII wieku," *Studia Claromontana* 5 (1984): 184-223.

Wojcik, Zbigniew, "Kisiel Adam Świetołdycz z Brusiłwa," *Polski Słownik Biograficzny,* XII (Wrocław, 1966-67): 487-91.

Wojtyska, Damian, *Cardinal Hosius, Legate to the Council of Trent* (Rome, 1967).

————, "Stan przygotowania do druku korespondencji nuncjuszów w Polsce do roku 1572," *Studia Źródłoznawcze* 18 (1973): 199-206.

————, *Papiestwo–Polska 1548-1563* (Lublin, 1977).

————, "Reformacja–Reforma Katolicka–Kontrreformacja," *Roczniki Teologiczno-Kanoniczne* 24/4 (1977): 223-49.

————, Św. Karol Boromeusz a Polska (U źródeł potrydenckiej odnowy pastoralnej Kościoła polskiego), in preparation.

Wollek, Ch., *Das Domkapitel von Płock 1524-1564. Gegenreformatorische Haltung und innerkirchliche Reformbestrebungen* (Cologne and Vienna, 1972).

Wrzecionko, P., ed., *Reformation und Frühaufklärung in Polen. Studien über den Sozinianismus und seinen Einfluss auf das westeuropäische Denken im 17. Jahrhundert* (Göttingen, 1977).

Wyczawski, Hieronim Eugeniusz, "Studia nad wewnątrznymi dziejami kościelnymi w Małopolsce na schyłku XVI w." *Prawo Kanoniczne* 7 (1964): 21-116.

Zaorski, Franciscus, *Doctrina card. Stanislai Hosii de coelibatu ecclesiastico adversus haereses saec. XVI* (Rome, 1957).

Zdrodowski, F., *The Concept of Heresy according to Cardinal Hosius* (Washington, D.C., 1947).

Zytkowicz, L., *Studia nad gospodarstwem wiejskim w dobrach kościelnych XVI w.* (Warsaw, 1962).

Popular Piety

Peter Burke

IF THE PHRASE, "the Copernican Revolution in History" had not already been applied to the work of Leopold von Ranke, it would be tempting to employ it to describe the rise of history "from below" in the last generation or so, for it is hard to think of a more profound shift in historical points of view. In the case of the Church, we see a movement away from official, institutional "ecclesiastical history" to a broader history of "religion" or "piety"; away from theology in the precise, technical sense, towards the study of attitudes, values and sentiments; away from the concerns of the clergy, and towards those of the lay majority. The connection between changes in the contemporary Church and this new perspective on the past will be obvious; it has not spread merely by contagion from secular history.

In this movement towards an unofficial history of the Counter Reformation, the French contribution has been of the first importance. It goes back at least as far as Lucien Febvre, co-founder of the journal *Annales*, whose famous "Question mal posée" was a manifesto for religious (as opposed to ecclesiastical) history. Febvre was most concerned with the French reformation, but his brief study of the inventories of Amiens charted, among other things, the rise of new forms of lay piety in the early seventeenth century, and reminds us that one of his masters was Henri Bremond, author of the great "literary history" of religious "sentiments" in the period.[1]

Febvre's approach to religious history in terms of sentiments and "mentalities" has not been lost on his successors. If it did not interest his most direct successor, Fernand Braudel, it did make an impression on Febvre's other heir, Robert Mandrou, who discussed popular Catholicism in his essay on French "psychology," 1500-1650, in his study of chap-books in the seventeenth and eighteenth centuries, and in his doctoral thesis on the witchcraft debate in seventeenth-century France.[2] This approach was of relevance to Gabriel Le Bras, a sociologist of religion who used quantitative methods but was also aware of the historical dimension in investigating the decline of popular piety in France. It also interested a few historians on the periphery of the *Annales*

---

[1]Febvre (1929, 1941).
[2]Mandrou (1960, 1964, 1968).

movement, while the main body was primarily concerned with economic and social history (Pierre Goubert, for example, ended by leaving religion out of his otherwise exemplary study of the Beauvaisis in the seventeenth century). Alphonse Dupront has devoted himself to the history of Christianity, Febvre-style, including popular religion; his own published works are probably outweighed, despite their distinction, by his influence on his students.[3] Jean Delumeau, who began as an economic historian, has made a massive contribution to the study of early modern Christianity, more especially Catholicism, in which popular piety has been increasingly emphasized.[4] In the next generation, four figures stand out. In the north, Robert Muchembled, whose approach combines Febvre and Delumeau with a dash of Marxism, has been particularly concerned with Artois and the Cambrésis, while his colleague Alain Lottin, a pupil of the institutional historian, Roland Mousnier, has worked on Lille.[5] In the South, Michel Vovelle, a Marxist historian of mentalities who is fascinated by statistics, has specialised on eighteenth-century Provence, and gathered a group of gifted pupils around him, some of whom are concerned with popular religion.[6] In the West, Alain Croix, who is equally attracted by Marxism, quantitative methods, and the history of sentiments, has produced a large and important book on the religion of the people in Brittany and its social and material environment.

The second country in which an important contribution has been made to our subject is Italy. Italy's Febvre was Ernesto De Martino, another man who burst through the frontiers between disciplines and is equally difficult to classify as an anthropologist, a sociologist, or a historian. His main concern was with the culture of contemporary southern Italy, including its religious culture, but he was always aware of its roots in the past. If his direct contribution to the history of the early modern period was relatively small, he inspired important work in others, notably Gabriele De Rosa (1971), who has himself created something of a school. It is in this context–or half in this context–that we should place the Italian historian with the greatest international reputation, Carlo Ginzburg. A pupil of Delio Cantimori, the historian of Italian heretics, Ginzburg has learned something from De Martino, and of course from De Martino's master, the unorthodox Sardinian

---

[3]Dupront (1966, 1978); Froeschlé-Chopard (1980).
[4]Notably in Delumeau (1976, 1978, 1983).
[5]Muchembled (1978, 1979, 1984); Lottin (1968, 1979, 1981, 1984).
[6]Vovelle (1973); Cousin (1983).

Marxist Antonio Gramsci.[7] In Italy as in France the history of popular piety, on the border between studies of popular culture and studies of the Counter Reformation, is characterised like the wider culture by a blend of (or a struggle between) Catholicism and Marxism.

More recently, some important work on popular Catholicism has appeared in England and the United States, to some extent inspired by the French example and in any case following similar lines to the retrospective sociology (more recently, retrospective anthropology) practised in France and Italy, which owes a great deal, directly and indirectly, to the approaches of Marx, Durkheim, and Weber. Particularly influential has been the work of Natalie Davis on sixteenth-century Lyons, comparing and contrasting the attitudes and practices of Catholic and Protestant groups in the city. John Bossy is more inclined to keep a certain distance from the theories of Durkheim and other sociologists, while remaining interested in their approaches.[8]

This new emphasis on the history of popular piety has brought problems in its wake. In the first place, there is the problem of what counts as "popular." Are we talking about the religion of the laity, even the learned,[9] or about that of "odinary people," the "subordinate classes," the peasants, or the illiterate? These groups overlap but they do not coincide. And should we not find room for the parish clergy, at least the country clergy, so close–at least in the sixteenth century–to the attitudes and values of their flocks?[10] Or are we talking about unofficial practices, whoever was involved in them? But in that case, what counts as "unofficial"? The sacraments are official by definition, but they may mean something different to different individuals or groups. And what about sacramentals? Are they unofficial or semiofficial? It is no wonder that historians, like anthropologists and sociologists, have been experimenting with alternatives like "practical religion," "local religion," and "the religion of the popular classes" in the plural. The center-periphery model implied by the term "local religion" has its attractions, here as in other fields, but the terms "central" and "local" are not as clear as they may look. Where, for example, should one place what is usually called the "popular piety" of seventeenth-century Rome?[11]

[7]Ginzburg (1966, 1972, 1975).
[8]Bossy (1970, 1973, 1975, 1984).
[9]Barbero (1981).
[10]Allegra (1978, 1981); O'Neil (1984).
[11]Ginzburg (1979); Christian (1981).

After disputes over definitions and problems of method, how can we know what the "inarticulate" thought or felt about their religion? If we use popular religious literature, for example, we run the risk of ignoring the illiterate and also of confusing what was produced for the people with what was produced by them. Even if we can be sure that a group of peasants or craftsmen or women read or listened to a particular devotional work, we do not know how they understood it. We do get this kind of information in the case of suspected heretics, since the Inquisition transcribed their answers (including gestures) with such care that their records have been compared to tape recordings or even videotapes; but we have to be on our guard for leading questions, and also take account of the problem of typicality. The Inquisition only interrogated a minority. We can follow the example of Le Bras and study the statistics for Easter confessions and communions, as collected by increasing numbers of bishops from Trent onwards; but the meaning of the fluctuations remains uncertain.[12] We can turn to material culture and study religious images and even the interior arrangements of village churches, adding to our other problems that of translating the language of objects into words.[13] All these approaches have their advantages; all have been practised by some of the historians discussed in this essay; all have their limitations; and combining their testimony, which seems the obvious solution, creates problems of its own. However, it is the best we can do in the presumptuous attempt to recover the unspoken assumptions, rather than the conscious beliefs, of the Catholic population of early modern Europe.

A third problem concerns concepts and values: theirs and ours, and of course the relation between the two. This large, pervasive, elusive problem crystallizes around a few recurrent value-laden terms. One, most common in France, is *déchristianisation;* it describes the decline of Christianity assumed to have taken place in France and elsewhere in Catholic Europe since the French Revolution. It raises the question of when France really was Christian, and that raises the meta-question, What is Christianity? If ordinary people in sixteenth-century France (say) regarded themselves as Christians, it is rather patronizing–and confusing–of modern historians to describe them, as Delumeau has sometimes done, as "pagans."[14] The English term "secularization" provokes even wider questions, for the boundary between the religious

[12]Le Bras (1955-6); Pérouas (1964).
[13] Froeschlé-Chopard (1980).
[14]Le Bras (1955-6), Delumeau (1971).

and the secular, like that between Christianity and "paganism," is not fixed for all time but subject to change. It has become commonplace to speak of the medieval "confusion" between the sacred and the profane; it would be better, because less anachronistic, to say that people in the Middle Ages drew a less sharp distinction between sacred and profane than was established during the Counter Reformation, or that they drew the distinction in a different place. Similar problems are raised by the term "superstition" which simply encourages ethnocentrism and anachronism. "We" are religious; "they" are superstitious. To make matters more confused, there are two distinctions between "Us" and "Them" superimposed here, that of the learned clergy of the Counter Reformation, and that of modern scholars, each with a tendency to see popular beliefs as the inverse of their own, and to treat the "little tradition" in a somewhat patronizing way.[15] The Bollandists were already writing of "little traditions of the people" *(populares traditiunculae)* in 1757. "Magic" is another awkward term. It is doubtless possible to give a fairly neutral and cross-cultural definition of magic, but in the western tradition the word has long been an emotive one, usually perjorative, whether contrasted with orthodox religion or with reason.

It is hard to decide whether confusion has been cleared up, or worse confounded, by the recent introduction into the discussion of the anthropologist's term "acculturation" to refer to changes in popular religion resulting from the pressure of elites, thus suggesting an analogy between these changes and the transformation of indigenous religions in Asia, Africa, and America in the colonial age. There is indeed an analogy, which was not lost on the Jesuits and others who called southern Italy and southern Spain the "Indies" of Europe.[16] However, this analogy is no more than partial. Learned culture and popular culture in Europe were not two cultures in the sense that western culture and (say) Peruvian culture were; they had been interacting for centuries, so the cultural distance between them was much less; so much so that the distinction is sometimes virtually impossible to draw at all.[17] These conceptual problems are inescapable and need to be borne in mind when considering recent research into different manifestations of popular piety, to which we now turn.

[15]Thiers (1679).
[16]Prosperi (1982).
[17] Dupront (1966); Muchembled (1978) Burke (1982).

Research has concentrated so far on the impact of the Counter Reformation on the people, the process of change sometimes described as "christianisation" or "acculturation," but here as "the reform of popular culture."[18] Most of the serious research is concentrated on France and Italy, and it tends, because of the way in which the records are organised, to take the form of monographs on particular dioceses such as Turin, Bologna, La Rochelle, Tarbes, Gap, and so on.[19] Within this framework, studies tend to deal in turn with the negative and the positive aspects of the reform. The negative side, more obvious, involves the suppression of whatever the bishops were coming to perceive as "superstitious," "pagan," immoral, or simply indecorous. Plays, festivals, images, customs, all came under scrutiny in order to be censored if not totally destroyed or abolished. Joking, dancing, and feasting in holy places such as churches or at holy times was particularly frowned on; a sharper distinction between the sacred and the profane than had been customary was gradually enforced. The Inquisition in Spain, Italy, and elsewhere was concerned on occasion with the same issues, although it put more effort into the detection of unorthodoxy. "Blasphemous" rituals which parodied the litany, for example, or "superstitious" remedies for illness were grist to its mill.[20]

On the positive side, there was the attempt to educate the people in their faith by means of schools, catechisms, and so on. In Italy, the so-called "schools of christian doctrine," which operated on Sundays and holidays, were established after–and in a few places even before–the Council of Trent, spreading from the pioneering dioceses of Milan (under Castellino da Castello and Carlo Borromeo) and Bologna (under Gabriele Paleotti) to cover much of northern Italy by 1600. In France, the movement to teach ordinary people, especially children, the rudiments of their faith was seventeenth- and eighteenth- rather than sixteenth-century and owed a good deal to organizations such as the Compagnie du Saint Sacrament and the followers of Jean-Baptiste de la Salle.[21] In school and out, an important means of popular instruction was the catechism, a short and simple instruction booklet usually in question-and-answer form. The catechisms of the Jesuits, Peter Canisius (1555) and Robert Bellarmine (1597), were often reprinted and translated. In this way the new medium of print became a weapon

---

[18]Burke (1978), ch. 8. For an earlier overview, Bossy (1970).
[19]Pérouas (1964); Prodi (1967); Soulet (1974); Tackett (1977).
[20]Ginzburg (1966); Bennassar (1979); Contreras (1982); O'Neil (1984).
[21]Bossy (1970); Erba (1979); Poutet (1971, 1976).

in the fight against "ignorance," "superstition," and of course "heresy."

" In France, cheap popular religious literature included the *Pensez-y-bien,* a meditation on the four last things; in Germany, the Capuchin Martin von Cochem's *Das Grosse Leben Christi* (1677), which went through at least twenty-two editions before the end of the century; and almost everywhere, the lives of certain saints.[22] Traditional media were not forgotten, as contemporary accounts of missions show. In Milan in the late sixteenth century, Carlo Borromeo made considerable use of processions to put his ideas across. The Jesuits did something similar in Naples in the 1650s. In Brittany later in the seventeenth century, the missionaries, Jesuits again, such as Michel Le Nobletz and Julien Maunoir, presented dialogues (between the living and the damned, for example) and made effective use of visual aids.[23] Hellfire sermons were part of the missionary's arsenal. "Teaching through fear," it has been called. Perhaps this was the only way for the missionary to leave an impression behind him when, after a few days in a given locality, he had to move on; but the media have a way of infecting the messages they broadcast, and it has been suggested that a consequence was an overemphasis on guilt in the Catholic as in the Protestant West.[24]

In describing the clergy's attempts to change the beliefs and values of the people, it is easy to overestimate the cultural distance between them, and also to see the role of the laity as a purely passive one. Some recent work corrects this false impression by pointing out that both partners in this "marriage" were prepared to adapt. The Jesuits and others built on popular religious traditions as well as trying to purify or even destroy some of them; and for their part, the laity soon made some of the new devotions their own.[25] To go beyond the rather bald statement that the people were not entirely passive, however, it is necessary to look at specific topics, problems, and institutions in a little more detail.

One institution central to lay piety which has attracted a good deal of research from Le Bras onwards is the confraternity.[26] One reason for this attention is the general interest of social historians in voluntary

[22]Signer (1963); Mandrou (1964).
[23]Buratti (1982); Dallaj (1982); Croix (1981); Soulet (1974).
[24]Delumeau (1978, 1983).
[25] Lottin (1979).
[26]Le Bras (1955-6); Agulhon (1966); Pullan (1971); Gerbet (1971); Soulet (1974); Grendi (1975); Galpern (1976); Tackett (1977); Froeschlé-Chopard (1980); Barbero (1981); Weissman (1982); Black (1985); etc.

associations, but another is precisely the desire to understand the laity's view of their religion. Confraternities became numerous in the late Middle Ages, but they continued to multiply in the early modern period. What kinds of people joined them? What did their members expect from them? To what extent were they independent of the clergy? How far did their organization and functions change after the Council of Trent? All these problems have preoccupied recent writers on the subject, and although a synthesis is still lacking, the outline of a general picture is emerging. The first point to make about them is their appeal; many people joined these voluntary associations in the towns and in the countryside. In the large village (or small town) of Altopascio in Tuscany in the late seventeenth century, nearly 25 percent of the total population of about six hundred people were inscribed in one confraternity alone, and there were others. In Santena in Piedmont at much the same time, 84 percent of testators left something to one or more of the confraternities of the parish, asking for the prayers of members or for their presence at the funeral. Not the least of their uses was to act as a kind of village burial society. In the towns at least, the confraternities tended to specialize in particular charitable functions–giving alms to the poor, visiting prisons, accompanying the condemned to execution, and so on. They also appealed to rather different clientèles, at least in France. In the later sixteenth century, the Penitents appealed to the elite, the Rosary to the poor. In the later eighteenth century, on the other hand, at least in the diocese of Gap, the Penitents were mainly for men and the Rosary for women, while in Vence and Grasse, the elite was moving from the Penitents to the Rosary and the Blessed Sacrament. In Venice, by contrast, rich and poor, nobles, citizens and commoners, men and women might join the same confraternity, but in the case of the six most prestigious (the *Scuole Grandi*), rich and poor were segregated within it. The politics of confraternities is not well documented and it is only just beginning to be studied, but it appears that they were mobilized against Protestants in late sixteenth-century France and in defence of the Catholic League, while in Italy there are signs that membership of a given confraternity might be associated with membership of a political faction.[27]

The confraternity was a kind of parish within the parish (as Le Bras once put it), and it is not surprising to find that the Council of Trent expressed unease about this independence. The bishops were

[27]Hardin (1980); Levi (1985).

ordered to visit them and check their accounts. There was a move to centralize them and place them more firmly under clerical control by grouping them into "archconfraternities," like the one of Santa Maria sopra Minerva, founded in Rome in 1539 and a model for others, or at least inspecting their statutes and accounts, as bishops were increasingly inclined to do. The higher clergy also tried to encourage the devotion to the Blessed Sacrament at the expense of the traditional cults of saints, and perhaps also to deflect them from flagellation to charity (as Borromeo did in the case of San Giovanni Decollato at Milan). Processions of flagellants remained common enough in Italy at least to attract the attention of a number of seventeenth-century visitors, but this particular form of the imitation of Christ's suffering during his passion seems to have gone out of favor in the following century. It used to be said that the confraternities went into decline after Trent. Recent research on seventeenth-century Italy, however, suggests that they were continuing to grow, perhaps in reaction to the spread of plague and famine. In the late eighteenth century in the south of France, a distinction between two kinds of confraternity is visible. The traditional brotherhoods of penitents, discouraged by the bishop, were gradually abandoned by the local elites, while the new brotherhoods of the Blessed Sacrament, the Rosary, and St Joseph were increasing in importance.[28] The fraternities did not fade away; they were abolished by governments (in France, in 1776 and 1792; in Florence, in 1785, and so on).

One of the attractions of confraternities was the part their members played in rituals. On Maundy Thursday, for example, the officers of some fraternities washed the feet of the ordinary members in imitation of Christ washing the feet of his disciples, a ritual that reaffirmed the sense of community that had brought the members together.[29] So did the annual feasts, which came under clerical attack after Trent, because they involved eating and drinking in a holy place. And so did the processions, by day or by night, in which the members wore their robes of black, white, or blue and carried their candles or whips. If we want to study the piety of ordinary lay people in this period, we must take a closer look at processions–religious rituals, many of which took place in the street rather than the church and allowed the laity (or some of them) to act rather than simply watch. Their importance for the participants is suggested by the amount of space devoted to them in

[28]Froeschlé-Chopard (1980).
[29]Weissman (1982).

three of the few surviving journals written by Catholic craftsmen in early modern Europe: those of Gianbattista Casali, a carpenter of Milan in the late sixteenth century; Bastiano Arditi, a tailor of Florence in the same period; and Pierre Ignace Chavatte, a serge-maker in Lille in the late seventeenth century.[30] Grand processions took place not only on the great days of the liturgical year, such as Corpus Christi, or on the festival of the local saint, but also to ask extraordinary favors. Whatever the educated clergy thought of the custom, processions to pray for rain (or for the rain to stop) remained commonplace after the Council of Trent. In the case of Brescia, for example, a local chronicle records processions of this kind in 1601, 1621, 1622, and 1623. "Agrarian devotions," as they have been called, remained strong in the villages. In the diocese of Paris in the seventeenth century, for example, the blessed sacrament might be carried to the vines to protect them from insects, although some of the higher clergy thought this irreverent and suggested the exorcism of the insects instead.[31]

Devotion to the saints remained traditional in many ways. There is evidence in some regions at least of popular cults of some new saints, the saints of the Counter Reformation itself, for example, such as Ignatius Loyola and Carlo Borromeo. The very name of the craftsman of Lille just mentioned, Pierre Ignace Chavatte, suggests that his parents were devoted to Ignatius (it should be added that in the early 1630s, when Chavatte was born, the town's allegiance was still Spanish, not French). In Milan in the early seventeenth century inventories testify to a widespread devotion to Carlo Borromeo, the local hero, since portraits of him were far from rare even in the houses of the relatively poor. His image also turns up in inventories in Amiens in the same period.[32] The 144 Italian communes who chose 238 new patrons between 1630 and 1699 gave 68 of their "votes" to Counter Reformation saints (9 for Filippo Neri, 7 for Francis Xavier, 6 for Ignatius Loyola).[33] St Isidore the ploughman, a twelfth-century Spanish peasant who was canonized in 1622, seems to have become popular fairly quickly not only around Madrid but as far away as Bavaria, the Tyrol, and Poland, where confraternities of peasants were named after him.[34] On the other hand, the new saints of the Counter Reformation

[30]Arditi (1970); Lottin (1968). Casali's journal has not been published, but is to be found in the Biblioteca Ambrosiana in Milan.
[31]Ferté (1962).
[32]Febvre (1941).
[33]Sallmann (1982).
[34]Tazbir (1969).

seem to have made little impact on the people of Brittany.[35] And if we turn to what ordinary people are recorded to have wanted or expected from the saints in this period, it seems to have changed little if at all from the Middle Ages. The saints were still predominantly supernatural healers, who specialized in particular ailments (St Roch in the plague, St Blaise in sore throats, and so on). The use of "Ignatius water" in Catholic Germany in the seventeenth and eighteenth centuries suggests that new saints could be incorporated into the system without too much difficulty. They may have been proposed to the people by the elites for specific purposes–St. Isidore as a symbol of obedience, and so on–but this was not necessarily how they were received. The "marriage" between Counter Reformation and popular culture was one that allowed for a measure of "negotiation." This model also has its uses in accounting for the choice of new saints when canonizations began again in 1588, after a hiatus of sixty-five years. The fifty-five saints canonized between 1588 and 1767 should be seen as the outcome of a process of negotiation, at times rather lengthy, between clergy and laity, center and periphery, learned culture and popular culture, in which many cults developed at the grass-roots but only a few were officially accepted.[36] Even the idea of sanctity differed between learned culture (where it was legally defined) and popular culture, where it was essentially unofficial. "Saint Masaniello, pray for us" was a cry heard in Naples in 1647, soon after the murder of the young fisherman who had led the revolt against Spain.[37]

The crucial question from our point of view is how ordinary people perceived the saints, and to answer it the best evidence is that of art–not the great masterpieces but the "repository art" of the early modern period. To investigate the religious assumptions of the mass of the Catholic population, a majority of whom were illiterate throughout the period, paintings and sculptures are sources of prime importance, even if they are hard to handle. The pioneering study of changes in religious art as an indicator of changing attitudes after the Council of Trent is of course that of Emile Mâle (1932), who drew attention to the importance of themes such as ecstasy and death and noted the reaffirmation in art of precisely the doctrines that the Protestants had challenged. He concentrated on major works of art commissioned by the clergy (the religious orders in particular). As these works were

[35]Croix (1981).
[36]Burke (1984).
[37]Sallman (1979); Burke (1983).

generally displayed in churches where everyone could see them and intended to encourage the devotion of the laity (or to channel it in particular directions), we cannot dismiss them as irrelevant to popular piety; but for our purposes the religious art of villages rather than towns, the work of local artists for the most part, is of greater value as evidence because its testimony is more direct. Ordinary people paid for most of it, which makes it likely that the images expressed a vision of the supernatural that was at the very least compatible with theirs. It is for this reason that the last few years have seen some historians of religion turn to iconography, to the altarpieces of village churches in Provence, for example, or Brittany; to the sculptures of churches in churchyards, again in Brittany; and to ex-votos, in Provence and elsewhere, which often record the name of the individual or family who commissioned the painting.[38] Others have studied devotional woodcuts, which were of course mass-produced by urban printers who were intent on making a profit, but were for that very reason in touch with popular demand.[39] One of their most important conclusions is exactly the reverse of Mâle's; what they emphasize is the persistence into the eighteenth century of an iconography that is essentially medieval, characterized, for example, by a frontal view of a saint, which suggests that the function of the image was to serve as a emanation of power rather than (as the clergy would have it) a form of instruction.[40] It is of course necessary to distinguish different kinds of popular religious image (the thaumaturgic image, the devotional image in the strict sense, and so on) and to register the gradual spread of a new iconography, but the overall impression of the cultural lag of the periphery behind the centre, the laity behind the clergy, the countryside behind the towns, is virtually overwhelming and an important corrective to traditional narratives of the Catholic Reformation which tended to exaggerate the pace of change.

After the rituals in which ordinary people participated, the images they looked at, the booklets they read or listened to, the occasional journals they kept, there remains one important approach to the religion of ordinary people: the history of everyday life, and the assumptions about religion it reveals. The rituals and prayers by which ordinary people tried to cope with the hazards of poor harvests, plague, and death have already been discussed, leaving us with the family, sex, and

---

[38]Vovelle and Vovelle (1970); Tapié (1972); Debidour (1953); Croix (1981); Cousin (1983).
[39]Adhémar (1968); Vecchi (1968).
[40]Froeschlé-Chopard (1980).

marriage. This historical field was first cultivated by the demographers in the 1950s and 1960s when they found they could not explain the behavior of Catholic populations without recourse to moral theology and canon law; it is now beginning to attract the interest of historians who want to know the extent to which the laity followed or resisted the instructions and advice of their priests and bishops, or whether changes in family structure had consequences for religion. John Bossy (1973, 1984), for example, points to the importance of kinship to the baptism and marriage rituals of the late Middle Ages, and to the decline of godparenthood in the early modern period, the result, he suggests, of the shift from the extended to the "concentrated" (if not quite "nuclear") family. Raul Merzario has studied dispensations for consanguinity and affinity in the diocese of Como to discover the Church's increasing control of marriage in this remote mountain region after the Council of Trent. In this confined area it was difficult for people not to marry within the prohibited degrees, but there was a marked decline in the degrees of consanguinity and affinity, as defined by the Church, and a shift towards asking for permission in advance instead of the traditional application for a dispensation simply to legitimize a *fait accompli*. An increase in the Church's control of behavior (or the internalization of the Church's rules) is suggested by the decline in parts of Catholic Europe of popular rituals of engagement (like the *créantailles* of Troyes), which were understood as authorizing sexual intercourse before marriage.[41] However, popular conformity in this area should not be exaggerated. In many parts of eighteenth-century France, the rate of births within eight months of marriage was as high as 10 or 15 or even in some regions 40 percent. In the Sologne in the eighteenth century the population seems to have been scrupulous in avoiding marriages during Advent and Lent, as the Church told them to, but in other ways they were sexually permissive.[42] If we turn to Spain, a part of Catholic Europe where the beliefs as well as the behavior of the laity were investigated with care, we find not infrequent examples of unorthodox views of sex and marriage. The Inquisition records tell of people who claimed that the married state was superior to that of celibacy or that fornication was not a mortal sin, at least not if one paid for it, or if one's spouse was asleep at the time (sleep being analogous to death).[43] One wonders how often similar views have gone unrecorded in areas that had no Inquisition.

[41]Flandrin (1978).
[42]Bouchard (1972).
[43]Dedieu (1979); Contreras (1982).

No account of "popular piety" in this period would be complete without some consideration, however brief, of popular impiety, and for this the Inquisition records are of course indispensable. They have received a good deal of attention from this point of view in the last decade or so, in both Italy and Spain. The main conclusion that has emerged is that (ethnic minorities apart), the majorty of cases were cases of blasphemy ("*Dio becco,*" "*Cristo bellaco y cornudo,*" and so on). Before Trent, the inquisitors were not inclined to take phrases like this too seriously. They were doubtless correct in treating them as momentary explosions of aggression, not as evidence of unorthodoxy. In the course of the sixteenth century, however, cases of this kind came to be punished more severely, probably in reaction to the spread of Protestantism; if heresy is seen as a form of blasphemy, blasphemy comes to look more and more like heresy. This change in the attitudes of the courts does not of course imply any change in the attitudes of the blasphemers themselves.

More interesting to historians of religion, and much more difficult to interpret, are the cases of laity who were hauled before the Inquisition because they had said that the host was nothing but a piece of bread; or that heaven and hell were "an invention of priests and friars, to make a profit," or that indulgences were just a trick (*las bullas son burlas*), or even that "everything is deceit" *todo es engaño*). Carlo Ginzburg's Menocchio is an extreme and voluble case of a wider phenomenon, though one which it is difficult to get into perspective. It is almost as difficult to decide what the unorthodoxy recorded in the trials meant to the individuals concerned–whether it was completely or only half-serious, whether it was felt to be compatible or incompatible with everyday religious practice–as it is to assess the importance or the typicality of the group. We have to avoid the opposite dangers of dismissing Menocchio as a maverick and treating him, as Ginzburg almost does, as a spokesman for traditional popular culture.[44]

So much for the present state of studies of popular piety. What of the future? In the immediate future there is room for a fair number of studies of ritual and imagery, in particular the kind just described. The social and cultural variation within Europe being what it is (or was), it is extremely unlikely that they will all turn up the same conclusions. In the cases of France and Italy studies of confraternities and of episcopal visitations are now so numerous that conclusions will soon be subject

[44]Ginzburg (1975); Contreras (1982).

to the law of diminishing returns (if that has not happened already); but in other parts of Europe systematic investigation of popular piety in this period has scarcely begun. In the case of Spain there have been important studies of Inquisition records, but little else. In that of Portugal, where these records are also abundant, even this research has scarcely begun, although a collective project assisted by the Gulbenkian Foundation is now under way.[45] Central Europe remains a largely neglected field, despite the turn of the younger generation of German historians to the history of popular culture and everyday life. The initiative was taken by the folklorists, and it is only very slowly that historians are beginning to follow their example.[46] In Poland, too, despite the tradition of interest in the history of popular culture–and in Catholicism–the harvest has so far been relatively poor.[47] In the Spanish Netherlands, now Belgium, there has been some useful work, though not as much as one might have expected given the richness of the sources.[48]

Historians who choose to work in one of these more or less undiscovered regions will have the advantage of late-comers in learning from the mistakes as well as the successes of the French and Italian pioneers. They will be well-advised not to attempt, for example, to isolate the "people" as an object of study, but to focus on the interaction between clergy and laity, rulers and ruled, the highly-educated and the more or less "uneducated" and on popular interpretations and transformations of the ideas spread by missionaries and reformers.

Once a broader geographical range of monographs is available, the top priority will be a systematically comparative study that attempts to identify what was common to the popular religion of Catholic Christendom and what was subject to local variations, and to discuss the success in this sector of the drive towards centralization and uniformity that followed the Council of Trent–if that is the true turning-point–for one object of a comparative study should be precisely to test that hypothesis. Some recent research has emphasized the continuity of the Counter Reformation reform of popular culture with that of the late Middle Ages, while other scholars have pointed out that developments in the eighteenth century are part of the same

[45]The present state of knowledge is surveyed in Bethencourt (1984).
[46]Brückner (1968); Hoerger (1984).
[47]Tazbir (1969) is an interesting exception.
[48]Cloeck (1971). N. Galpern promises a study of this subject. C. F. Lattin (1984).

movement.[49] In the field of popular culture–and perhaps not only there–
the generations after Trent must be placed in a religious *"histoire de
longue durée."*
     In this field of research, which necessarily privileges the unofficial
and the informal, it is particularly difficult to identify specific
instruments of scholarship. The decrees of councils and synods and the
records of episcopal visitations are better evidence for the contemporary
clerical view of the religion of the people than for that religion itself.
There can be no royal (or papal) road to the study of popular piety. As
for the centers of research, it is not surprising to find them difficult to
name in a field that is impossible to define with precision, and which
comes, historiographically speaking, at the point of intersection
between two very different traditions: the mainly institutional history
of the Church and the mainly secular study of popular culture.
Historians who like neatly circumscribed territories had better look
elsewhere for a subject. To other scholars, the fluidity and elusiveness
of this potentially enormous subject is a part of its charm and its
challenge.

Bibliography

Adhémar, Jean, *L'Imagerie populaire française* (Milan, 1968).
Agulhon, Maurice, *La sociabilité méridionale* (Aix, 1966).
Allegra, Luciano, *Ricerche sulla cultura del clero in Piemonte* (Turin, 1978).
_____, "Il parroco: un mediatore fra alta e bassa cultura," *Storia d'Italia, Annali,*
     4 (1981): 897-947.
Arditi, Bastiano, *Diario,* ed. R. Cantagallo (Florence, 1970).
Bennassar, Bartholomé et al., *L'inquisition espagnole* (Paris, 1979).
Bethencourt, Francisco, "Campo religioso e inquisicão em Portugal no século
     xvi, *Estudos Contemporaneos* 6 (1984): 43-60.
Black, Christopher, *Philanthropy and Salvation: Confraternities in
     Sixteenth-Century Italy* (forthcoming, 1985).
Bossy, John, "The Counter-Reformation and the People of Catholic Europe,"
     Past and Present 47 (1970): 51-70.
_____, "Blood and Baptism," *Studies in Church History* 10 (1973): 129-43.
_____, "The Social History of Confession," *Transactions of the Royal Historical
     Society* 25 (1975): 21-38.
_____, "Godparenthood: the Fortunes of a Social Institution in Early Modern
     Christianity," *Religion and Society in Early Modern Europe,* ed. Kaspar von
     Greyerz (London, 1984): 194-201.
Bouchard, Gérard, *Le village immobile: Sennely-en Sologne* (Paris, 1972).

---

[49]Sauzet (1983); Allegra (1978).

Brückner, Wolfgang, "Popular Piety in Central Europe," *Journal of the Folklore Institute* 5 (1968): 158-74.

Buratti, A., et al., *La città rituale: la città e lo stato di Milano nell'età di Borromeo* (Milan, 1982).

Burke, Peter, *Popular Culture in Early Modern Europe* (London, 1978).

———, "A Question of Acculturation?" *Scienze, Credenze Occulte, Livelli di Cultura,* ed. P. Zambelli (Florence, 1982): 197-204.

———, "The Virgin of the Carmine and the Revolt of Masaniello," *Past and Present* 99 (1983): 3-21.

———, "How to be a Counter-Reformation Saint" *Religion and Society in Early Modern Europe,* ed. K. von Greyerz (London, 1984): 45-55.

Christian, William, *Local Religion in Sixteenth-Century Spain* (Princeton, 1981).

Cloeck, M, "Religious Life in a Rural Deanery in Flanders," *Acta Historiae Neerlandicae* (1971).

Contreras, Jaime, *El santo oficio de la inquisición en Galicia, 1560-1700* (Madrid, 1982).

Cousin, Bernard, *Le miracle et le quotidien: les ex-voto provençaux images d'une société,* (Aix, 1983).

Croix, Alain, *Le Bretagne aux 16ᵉ et 17ᵉ siècles,* 2 vols. (Paris, 1981).

Dallaj, Arnaldo, "Le processioni a Milano nella Controriforma," *Studi Storici* (1982).

Davis, Natalie Z., "The Sacred and the Body Social in Sixteenth-Century Lyons," *Past and Present* 90 (1981): 40-70.

Debidour, Victor-Henry, *La sculpture bretonne* (Rennes, 1953).

Dedieu, Jean-Pierre, "Christianisation en nouvelle Castille," *Mélanges de la Casa de Velazquez, 15 (1979): 261-94.*

Delooz, Pierre, *Sociologie et canonisations* (Liège and The Hague, 1969).

Delumeau, Jean, "De l'aujourd'hui à l'hier de l'occident chrétien," *La religion populaire,* ed. B. Plongeron (Paris, 1976): 99-107.

———, *La peur en occident* (Paris, 1978).

———, *La péché et la peur* (Paris, 1983).

De Rosa, Gabriele, *Vescovi, popolo e magia nel Sud* (Naples, 1971).

Dupront, Alfonse, "La religion populaire dans l'histoire de l'Europe occidentale," *Revue de l'histoire de l'Église de France* 64 (1978): 185-202,

Febvre, Lucien, "Une question mal posée," trans. K. Folca as "The Origins of the French Reformation," *A New Kind of History,* ed. P. Burke (London, 1973), ch. 4.

Ferté, Jeanne, *La vie religieuse dans les campagnes parisiennes, 1622-95* (Paris, 1962).

Flandrin, Jean-Louis, *Le sexe et l'occident* (Paris, 1981).

Frijhoff, Willem, "The Late Middle Ages and Early Modern Times," *Official and Popular Religion,* ed. P. H. Vrijhof and J. Waardenburg (The Hague, 1979): 71-100.

Froeschlé-Chopard, Marie-Hélène, *La religion populaire en Provence orientale au XVIIIᵉ siècle* (Paris, 1980).

Galpern, Neil, *The Religions of the People in Sixteenth-Century Champagne* (Cambridge, Mass., 1976).

Ginzburg, Carlo, *I benandanti* (Turin, 1966), trans. A. and J. Tedeschi as *The Night Battles* (Baltimore, 1983).

———, "Folklore, magia, religione," *Storia d'Italia* 1 (Turin, 1972): 603-76.

———, *Il formaggio e i vermi* (Turin, 1975), trans. A. and J. Tedeschi as *The Cheese and the Worms* (Baltimore, 1981).

Grendi, Edoardo, "Le confraternite a Genova fra i secoli xvi e xvii," *Atti della Società Ligure di Storia Patria* 5 (1975): 241-305.

Harding, Robert, "The Mobilisation of Confraternities against the Reformation in France," *Sixteenth Century Journal* 11 (1980): 85-104.

Hoerger, Hermann, "Organisational Forms of Popular Piety in Bavaria," *Religion and Society in Early Modern Europe*, ed. K. von Greyerz (London, 1984): 212-22.

Hoffman, Philip T., *Church and Community in the Diocese of Lyon* (Princeton, 1984).

Julia, Dominique, "La réforme post-tridentine en France," *La società religiosa* (Naples, 1973): 311-97.

Le Bras, Gabriel, *Etudes de sociologie religieuse*, 2 vols. (Paris, 1955-56).

Levi, Giovanni, *L'eredità immateriale: carriera di un esorcista nel Piemonte del '600* (Turin, 1985).

Lottin, Alain, "La catechèse en milieu populaire," *Les intermédiaires culturels*, ed. M. Vovelle (Paris, 1981).

———, *Vie et mentalité d'une Lillois sous Louis XIV* (Lille, 1968).

———, "Contre-réforme et religion populaire: un mariage difficile mais réussi aux 16ᵉ et 17ᵉ siècles en Flandre et en Hainau," *La religion populaire*, ed. G. Dubuscq (Paris, 1979): 53-63.

———, *Lille cittadelle de la Contre-réforme?* (Lille, 1984).

Mâle, Emile, *L'art religieux après le concile de Trente* (Paris, 1932).

Mandrou, Robert, *Introduction à la France moderne* (Paris, 1961).

———, *De la religion populaire aux 17ᵉ et 18ᵉ siècles* (Paris, 1964).

Merzario, Raul, *Il paese stretto: strategie matrimoniali nella diocesi di Como, secoli xvi-xviii* (Turin, 1981).

Muchembled, Robert, *Culture populaire, culture des élites* (Paris, 1978). English trans. Baton Rouge 1985.

———, "The Witches of the Cambrésis," *Religion and the People*, ed. J. Obelkevich (Chapel Hill, 1979).

———, "Lay Judges and the Acculturation of the Masses," *Religion and Society in Early Modern Europe*, ed. K. von Greyerz (London, 1984): 66-78.

O'Neil, Mary, "Sacerdote ovvero strione: Ecclesiastical and Superstitious Remedies in Sixteenth-Century Italy," *Understanding Popular Culture*, ed. S. Kaplan (Berlin, 1984), ch. 4.

Pérouas, Louis, *Le diocèse de La Rochelle de 1648 à 1724* (Paris, 1964).

Poutet, Yves, "L'education de la piété du peuple d'après l'oeuvre de L. B. de La Salle," *La piété populaire de 1610 à nos jours*, ed. J. M. Debard (Paris, 1976): 71-95.

Prodi, Paolo, *Il cardinale Gabriele Paleotti,* 2 vols. (Rome, 1959-67).

Prosperi, Adriano, "Otras Indias," in *Scienze, Credenze Occulte, Livelli di Cultura,* ed. P. Zambelli (Florence, 1982): 205-34.

Sallmann, Jean-Michel, "Il santo e le rappresentazioni de santità," *Quaderni Storici* 41 (1979): 584-602.

_____ "Image et fonction du saint dans la région de Naples," *Mélanges de l'Ecole Française de Rome* 91 (1979): 827-73.

_____, "Il santo patrono cittadino nel '600," *Per la storia sociale e religiosa del Mezzogiorno,* ed. G. Galasso and C. Russo, (Naples, 1980-2), 2: 187-208.

Sauzet, Robert, "La religion populaire bas-Languedocienne au 17ᵉ siècle," *La religion populaire* (Paris, 1979): 103-8.

_____, "Aux origines du refus des jeux et divertissements dans la pastorale catholique moderne," *Les jeux à la Renaissance,* ed. P. Ariès and J.-C. Margolin (Paris, 1983): 649-58.

Signer, Leutfrid, *Martin von Cochem: eine grosse Gestalt des rheinischen Barock* (Wiesbaden, 1963).

Soulet, Jean-François, *Traditions et réformes religieuses dans les Pyrenées centrales au 17ᵉ siècle* (Pau, 1974).

Tackett, Timothy, *Priest and Parish in Eighteenth-Century France: A Social and Political Study of the curés in a diocese of Dauphiné, 1750-1791* (Princeton, 1977).

Tapié, Victor-Louis, *Retables baroques de Bretagne* (Paris, 1972).

Tazbir, Janusz, "Die gesellschaftlichen Funktion des Kultus des heiligen Isidor des Pflügen in Polen," *Acta Poloniae Historiae* 20 (1969): 120-37.

Thiers, Jean-Baptiste, *Traité de la superstition* (Paris, 1679).

Vecchi, Alberto, *Il culto delle immagini nelle stampe popolari* (Florence, 1968).

Vovelle, Gaby, and Michel Vovelle, *La vision de la mort et de l'audelà en Provence d'après les autels des âmes de Purgatoire* (Paris, 1970).

Vovelle, Michel, *Piété baroque et déchristianisation en Provence au dix-huitème siècle* (Paris, 1973).

Weissman, Ronald, *Ritual Brotherhood in Renaissance Florence* (New York, 1982).

The Counter Reformation and Women: Religious and Lay

Kathryn Norberg

IN THE PAST TEN YEARS renewed interest in the history of women has focused considerable attention upon Protestant women, and a number of historians have asked why women joined the Reform and what they gained once they did. The distaff side of the Reformation is, in consequence, fairly well known.[1] But if Protestant women have enjoyed the attentions of scholars, their Catholic sisters have been less fortunate. Despite the presence of such important figures as Teresa of Avila, Angela Merici, and Louise de Marillac, the women of Counter Reformation Europe have not been the subject of a sustained analysis. Few historians have asked how the Church affected women, or whether it undermined their autonomy or improved their status. Fewer still have produced answers to these questions.

Historians of Protestant women have posed them, and it is they who have produced the interpretation that still dominates the field. According to traditional wisdom, Protestantism enhanced the position of women by sanctifying the family, instituting divorce, and admitting women to the priesthood of all believers. In contrast, Catholicism in the sixteenth and seventeenth centuries meant "business as usual." Catholic women were still excluded from the priesthood and their roles as mothers and wives were depreciated by a Church that still preferred celibacy to the family. On the whole, these scholars argue that the Reformation improved the position of women. Despite dissent from such notable scholars as Natalie Davis, this view continues to prevail and was recently reiterated in an important synthesis. The argument is all the more compelling given the undeniable fact that many women actually did join the ranks of the Reformed.[2]

Although this view has long dominated thinking about women and the post-Tridentine Church, it fails to satisfy for one simple reason: the sixteenth and seventeenth centuries did not mean "business as usual" as far as Catholicism was concerned. As recent research has demonstrated, to assume that medieval conditions persisted into the

---

[1]See Irwin (1982).
[2]Davis (1975): 65-97; Irwin (1982); Ozment (1984).

seventeenth century is to make a serious error. Trent and the host of reformers who followed in the Council's wake changed Catholicism and with it the position of women both within and outside the Church. This essay will discuss those changes and also summarize recent research. Because inquiry into the status of women in Catholic Europe has only just begun, I will have as many suggestions as conclusions to offer. But after considering the impact of the Counter Reformation upon women, both religious and lay, we should be able to arrive at an informed, if only tentative, picture of the position of Catholic women.

Female Religious

Any discussion of women in Catholic Europe must begin with the religious, with the convents and congregations that sheltered a significant number of European women. Immediately one encounters problems, for aside from reference manuals like the *Dizionario degli istituti di perfezione,* studies are most rare. No general survey comparable to Eckenstein's work on medieval religious exists. There are a number of old monographs, usually written by amateur historians, which concern the histories of individual houses. These studies can be extremely useful, but they are often hidden in local journals or regional libraries. I have included a partial listing of such works and have undoubtedly slighted Spain and Italy, which are not my regions of specialty. A considerable body of work on individual nuns, in particular the founders of orders, also exists. The literature on Teresa of Avila, for instance, is vast, and only a few fundamental works are listed here.

All studies of women religious, be they individual biographies or histories of orders, must deal, sooner or later, with the great innovation of the Council of Trent–compulsory claustration. The Council sought to remedy the abuses that had sprung up in convents by sealing them off from the outside world.[3] Ever since, obligatory claustration has been assailed by scholars and churchmen, and there is little doubt that it represented an overly simple solution to a complex problem. If nothing else, it was often inappropriate. Scholars have probably been too quick to assume that problems of a sexual nature afflicted late medieval and renaissance convents. In sixteenth-century Aix-en-Provence, as Claire

---

[3]On the decrees of Trent and subsequent Popes, see Creytens (1965).

Dolan's work has shown, the nuns suffered more from poverty than lechery.[4] In Avila, the sisters of Teresa's first convent left their cloister, not because they were debauched, but because the convent could not afford to feed them. They had to return home to the bed and board of their parents or risk starvation. The imposition of claustration probably did nothing to improve the nuns' fortunes. In Seville, at least, as Mary Elizabeth Perry has observed, nuns were thus deprived of alms for which they might otherwise have begged.

Trent's adoption of strict claustration for women's orders would appear at first glance to support those who believe that the Counter Reformation limited women's options. That the ruling worked against women cannot be denied, but it was not necessarily the product of the Church alone. Secular society also demanded that the nuns be "dead to the world." In Lyon, for instance, the archbishop insisted that the Visitandines adopt strict claustration because, he contended, no wealthy family would send its daughter to a house that was not cloistered. Families would fear, he claimed, that the daughter might one day lay claim to her brothers' inheritance.[5] On the question of claustration, then, the Church was responding in part to the needs of secular society and to the demands of elite families eager to maintain their patrimony.

Whether or not the Church bore responsibility for the cloistering of women religious, we are still left wondering if claustration actually did work a hardship on sixteenth-century and seventeenth-century nuns. Here recent research has indicated that, as far as some religious orders were concerned, the Tridentine edicts concerning claustration had little or no effect. Carla Russo's work on the nuns of Naples leaves one with the impression that a great many religious houses escaped claustration. In Naples, the religious resisted all attempts on the part of the ecclesiastical hierarchy to lock their gates and diminish their independence.[6] Other houses, especially aristocratic houses, may also have avoided reform, that is, claustration.

Also exempted were many of the religious orders created after Trent. Here, the legacy of the Counter Reformation is ambiguous: on the one hand, the churchmen of the sixteenth and seventeenth centuries sought to lock up nuns; on the other, they set them free. Angela Merici and Francis de Sales did not intend the Ursulines and the Visitation to be cloistered. Where they failed, Vincent de Paul succeeded, and the

---

[4]Dolan (1981): 42-82.
[5]Devos, (1973): 23-30.
[6]Russo (1970).

Daughters of Charity never knew claustration. Nor did scores of other semi-religious organizations or "congregations" created in localities throughout Europe. Several older works deal with these new, "active" orders whose members lived out in the world, nursing and teaching.[7] Recently, an unpublished Ph.D. dissertation by Judith Combes Taylor has dealt with the emergence of teaching "congregations" in the Parisian area, and more work of this kind is needed. Until the women of the congregations and the Third Orders are included in our picture of post-Tridentine society, we will not be able to assess the impact of Trent upon female religious.

But then there are many questions about nuns and convents, in the strict sense of the word, that still need to be answered. How many nuns were there in early modern Europe, and how did their numbers vary over time? In an important study of the Visitation of Annecy, Roger Devos has found that the number of sisters in that convent declined in the last part of the seventeenth century and continued to do so for at least a century. Was the same true in other houses? As yet, we have little statistical evidence concerning the population of feminine religious houses.

We must also learn why women entered the convent. Literary evidence suggests that convents functioned as warehouses for the unmarriageable. Richard Trexler has demonstrated just how vital the convent was to the Florentine family faced with astronomical dowries and too many daughters. Trexler's article reminds us that the history of religious women must also take into account the history of the family, but it is hazardous to apply the Florentine case to the rest of Europe. Moreover, the Church itself struggled to prevent "forced vocations." According to the decrees of Trent, solemn vows could only be taken at the age of eighteen and only after examination by the Bishop. On this issue, the Church showed greater concern for the independence of women than did secular society. But did the Church succeed in thwarting the wishes of families? Not really, for as Roger Devos's study shows, many young girls were still placed in the convent at a tender age, before sixteen.[8] To be sure, they did not take their final vows until eighteen as canon law required, but at that time they were highly unlikely to rebel against their parents' wishes by asking to leave an institution that was all they had ever known. Secular society appears to have triumphed on this point, but only further research will reveal just how complete was the victory.

---

[7]Chalenard (1950); Dainville (1949); Vaillaret (1947).
[8]Devos (1973): 264-67.

If we do not know why women joined the convent, we are equally ignorant of who joined, or of what social groups produced female religious. Roger Devos's study of the Visitation provides invaluable information on the social background of one group of nuns. Basing his study upon exhaustive work in both convent archives and notarial sources, Devos demonstrates that nuns of the choir came primarily from the nobility, both of robe and sword. Of more modest origins were the other sisters of the order, who sprang from the lower echelons of the legal professions and whose stay in the convent was neither permanent nor comfortable. Consequently, a kind of social stratification existed within each convent and between orders as well. The nursing orders have yet to receive the attention of a social historian, but it is likely that they appealed to less prosperous social groups.[9] Although the founder of the Daughters of Charity was Louise de Marillac, a daughter of the nobility of the robe, the first member of the order was Marguerite Naseau, a simple shepherdess when Vincent de Paul met her. Was she typical of the sort of women who joined nursing and teaching orders? Of course, almost every house required a dowry as well as additional fees for clothing, room, and board. Did all this represent a substantial sum? At the Visitation of Annecy it did, but the Annecy chapter was fairly aristocratic. Were other convents just as demanding, and did religious vows thus constitute an option for only a small percentage of the female population? The current state of research does not allow us to answer these questions.

Nor do we know as much as we might about the financial situation of early modern convents. Presumably documentation abounds in the local archives, but as yet there are few studies which try to determine just how rich–or poor–the convents were.[10] Most houses in sixteenth-cenutry Spain existed in constant financial crisis.[11] In Aix-en-Provence, the feminine religious houses were destitute by comparison to male orders.[12] Were early modern convents, like contemporary women's colleges, constantly beset with financial problems? My guess is that most were and that their impoverishment had serious consequences for life inside the convent. Novices may have

---

[9]Colins Jones's forthcoming book on the Daughters of Charity in France should provide much-needed information on an extremely important order.

[10]Documents concerning the financial affairs of convents are abundant in the French archives with which I am most familiar. Also, Carla Russo's work suggests that the same is true of Italian records.

[11]Perry (1978); Ortiz (1970).

[12]Dolan (1981): 42-82.

been admitted more for their dowries than their vocations. Roger Devos cites the stubborness, if not desperation, of the ladies of the Visitation, who did not mind dickering with the families of prospective nuns when a dowry was in question. Angelique Arnauld may have refused, as she claimed, to "bargain over girls," but many other mother superiors probably could not afford such scruples.

The origins of this impoverishment lay deep in Catholic doctrine: women were excluded from the priesthood, and consequently they could not receive the bequests for redemptive Masses which accounted for a substantial portion of the monasteries' income. In the seventeenth century Catholic laymen and women bequeathed money for Masses in their wills, and male orders profited, especially the friars who had made of the liturgy of the dead their speciality. The nuns, of course, could not tap this source of wealth. Some female religious tried to find an alternative to the stipend-bearing Masses. The sisters of Bon Pasteur of Lyon offered the benefits of their devotions to lay women. One could purchase a "bouquet" consisting of a sister's saying the rosary, wearing an iron girdle, holding her arms in the position of the cross, abstaining from wine, applying the whip, and so forth. The "menu" changed with the religious holidays and annually.[13] But how different were these prayers and mortifications from those of any lay person? Because they could not administer the sacraments, the nuns were hardly distinguishable in this regard from the devout laity when it came to one of the central mysteries of the Church.

As a result, female religious suffered a distinct handicap, and Trent aggravated the situation. The problem was more than just material or economic; it was also spiritual. As a piety centered upon the sacraments emerged in the years after the Council, some nuns, in particular those in old medieval orders, must have wondered just what their role was in the Christian community. They must have asked how their vocation contributed to the salvation of other souls and the dissemination of a renewed Catholicism. In this light the appearance of so many "active" orders makes sense. If nuns could not save souls by celebrating the Mass, they could save them by nursing and teaching. An active role in the world allowed the nuns to overcome or at least mitigate the difficulties posed by their gender. If they could not enjoy a special relationship with the sacraments, they could do God's work in other ways.

---

[13]Archives departementales du Rhone, 14 H 7. I am grateful to Ann Elwood, who is preparing a dissertation on French nuns in the seventeenth and eighteenth centuries, for this reference.

Of course, there was another way for women to establish a special relationship with God, one of which they had often availed themselves in the past: mysticism. Mysticism has always been a peculiarly feminine business, and few eras have produced as many female mystics as the sixteenth and seventeenth centuries. Teresa of Avila is the most celebrated, but she has hundreds, if not thousands, of counterparts. In Spain alone, there were thousands of *beatae* or devout women who lived in a community but who had taken only simple vows, and this figure does not include female hermits or lay visionaries.[14] Despite a large body of work, particularly concerning Teresa herself, I am inclined to agree with William Christian that the relationship between women and mysticism has yet to be fully explored. Recently, Michel De Certeau has offered a fresh perspective on this issue. In an extremely stimulating study, he has argued that mysticism, as cultivated by Teresa and exported to France, was inherently, indeed structurally feminine. Certainly, the Church authorities thought that women were given to mystical visions, in particular false visions. Female mystics, including Teresa herself, received no encouragement from the post-Tridentine Church. On the contrary, almost all were harassed. Mysticism may have provided yet another alternative to women, but it was an alternative that the official Church found appropriate for only a few.

The mystic is perhaps the most glamorous of all female religious; her more pedestrian sisters should not be forgotten. Only a few historians have as yet tried to determine just what went on in the average early modern convent. Using judicial records, Judith Brown has revealed one side of convent life through the experiences of the extraordinary Benedetta Carlini. Literature written by the nuns themselves has provided M-C. Guesdre with information on the spiritually cultivated in the convents. Convent literature, specifically chronicles, has also supplied Judith Combes Taylor with invaluable information on attitudes and practices. Apparently, as M-C. Guesdre believes, a lot of writing went on in convents. The chronicles of Visitandines, Ursulines, and Benedictines, to name only sources in French archives, await a historian.[15]

So too does the crucial issue of contracts between the convent and laywomen. In principle, the convents were sealed, but in fact they were, it appears, permeable. Certain orders, the Visitandines for example,

---

[14]Christian, Local Religion , 171.
[15]See bibliography in Guesdre (1964) for further information.

actually welcomed laywomen.[16] Francis de Sales made special provision for laywomen's retreats, and the houses of Annecy and Grenoble frequently hosted devout ladies. Did other houses follow suit? Financial exigencies would have encouraged them to create special ties with wealthy women who were potential benefactresses. Francis de Sales certainly believed that ties between laywomen and nuns were quite ordinary in Italy. The subject requies further investigation, for if laywomen found spiritual nourishment inside the convent, then post-Tridentine Catholicism provided believers with a feminine alternative to the male-dominated religious life of the parish.

Laywomen

Most Catholic women, of course, lived outside the convent. Our knowledge of lay women's religiosity in the early modern period, previously virtually nonexistent, has been greatly expanded by the multiplication of studies on popular religion. Historians (like churchmen before them) have tended to place early modern women under one of two rubrics. Either a woman was heterodox, or she was orthodox. As in the past, the heterodox have received more attention than the conventional. Erik Midelfort's comprehensive bibliography on the subject exempts me from treating the vast and growing literature on witchcraft. Much less voluminous is the body of work on women's religious practice that was not classed as black magic but was not considered orthodox either. William Christian has dealt with the Spanish women who had celestial visions;[17] Jean-Pierre Schmitt has described the women of southeastern France who remained loyal to the cult of a greyhound, Saint Guinefort. Women are certainly not absent from the literature on popular religion: they appear frequently but usually as members of the community, parishioners, heretics, adherents of peculiar sects–rarely as women. We need a sustained analysis of heterodox devotions that were peculiarly feminine in form or purpose. For instance, Saint Guinefort appealed to women because he [it] cured children and infants. Other saints and, of course, the Virgin probably attracted women because they offered help in other peculiarly feminine predicaments. Christian mentions in passing the devotions

---

[16] Rollet (1975): 201-02.
[17] Christian, *Apparitions* (1981).

invoked at the time of childbirth and the relics devised to help a woman through a difficult confinement. Delumeau cites the case of a saint used (and physically abused) by Breton women who wanted to call their sailor husbands back from the sea. A catalog of such practices and a description of how they changed over time might enrich considerably our understanding of feminine piety. So too would some notion of the Church's success (or more likely failure) in stamping out such feminine devotions. At the same time, we might benefit from a more precise knowledge of women's rituals surrounding rites of passage, such as marriage. Surely women had their own practices, their own customs. If we are unaware of them, it is probably not because they failed to exist, but because historians of popular religion have not yet fully heeded Gabriel Le Bras's admonition that the history of religious practice must take into account gender.

Of course the Church opposed women's heterodox practices when it encountered them. Did it seek to replace them with its own devotions designed specifically for women and practiced mainly by women? Did it substitute a new form of women's religion for the old? It is hard to say, for women's orthodox religious practices are even less well known than their heterodox devotions. Years ago Bremond made a cursory examination of the rather large body of devotional literature intended for women. A close scrutiny of the catechisms, "hours," and spiritual treatises designed for women might indicate just what virtues the Church sought to instill in women. At the same time, the experience through which many upper-class women passed–the convent school–deserves closer examination. We need to know what sort of experience women had in these institutions and if they promoted a type of devotion different from that of men.

Convent schools and books on contemplation appealed to the wealthy. Yet studies of women's spirituality need not be limited to the elite. How are we to approach the religious practices of common women? One avenue might be the confraternity or sodality. Historians long believed these to be purely male organizations, but some recent studies have shown that female and mixed confraternities existed or were established throughout Europe in the seventeenth century.[18] Rosary confraternities had first spread in the late Middle Ages, but women's groups appear to have multiplied in large numbers only with the Counter Reformation. Such associations, however loose, provided

[18]Hoffman (1984); Norberg (1979).

an arena for feminine spirituality and extended to women a type of religious life previously the privelege of men. Upper-class women, too, benefitted from the creation of sodalities. Usually these were charitable confraternities, of which Saint Vincent de Paul's Daughters of Charity is the most famous. These groups tended to bring together elite women for mutual spiritual advantage and for good works, be it the sheltering of orphans, the nursing of the sick, or even the rehabilitation of prostitutes. Such groups gave elite women opportunities outside the home even if they did tend to cultivate the notion of women as nurturer.[19] The companionship gained in the charitable confraternity provided a remedy to the growing isolation of women, especially elite women, in the family. On the whole, the confraternities constituted one of the few acceptable outlets for feminine energies in a secular world that limited women to the home.

Through confraternities the church reformers sought to win women over to Catholicism. In France at least there is indication that they succeeded over the long term. Michel Vovelle in his innovative study of Provençal wills found that eighteenth-century women remained true to the Church while their husbands abandoned it. Studies of wills in Grenoble, Lyon, and Paris have confirmed Vovelle's findings and established that a distinct conversion of women occurred in the seventeenth century, a conversion that withstood the skepticism of the Enlightenment.[20] As more work is completed, we may have to revise this picture somewhat, but for the moment, it appears that the reformers won women to their cause. Why? I have already suggested a number of answers: the Church created confraternities and devotions specifically for women. Historians of popular religion have additional hypotheses. Philip Hoffman has recently argued that the Catholic reformers condemned and undermined male sexual violence, an achievement which worked to the advantage of women. Marc Venard believes that the rise of the priest interposed a third party between a woman and her husband and thereby increased her autonomy. Whatever the causes, one thing is clear: post-Tridentine Catholicism, like its Protestant rival, attracted women and retained their loyalties long after their husbands had gone over to disbelief. The strongest case for Protestant superiority when it comes to women–the support of women for the Reformation–no longer seems so convincing.

[19]Norberg (1979).
[20]Hoffman (1984); Norberg (1985); Chaunu (1978).

We have come back the the problem posed at the outset of this essay: which offered more autonomy to women, the Protestant or the Catholic Reformation? In view of what we have just learned, Natalie Davis's response to this question seems most accurate.[21] Both confessions, she argues, promoted the status of women but in different ways. The Protestant Church assimilated women to men's roles, that is, offered them access to positions previously monopolized by men. The Tridentine Church retained the separation of men's and women's roles, but multiplied the latter so that women had greater choice. Neither confession provided genuine liberation; how could they in a period virtually unparalleled in its misogyny? Undoubtedly our appreciation of the position of women will change as research continues. With the emergence of a genuine history of Catholic women, we may revise our interpretation. In fact historians may amend their notions about post-Tridentine Catholicism as a whole.

Bibliography

Aubert, J-L, *La Femme: antiféminisme et christianisme* (Paris, 1975).

Bayonne, G. S., *Caterina de Ricci, la santa di Prato* (Prato, 1960).

Bremond, Henri, *A Literary History of Religious Thought in France,* 2 vols. (New York, 1928).

Brown, Judith, *Immodest Acts: The Life of a Lesbian Nun in Renaissance Italy* (New York, 1986).

Caraman, Philip G., *St. Angela. The Life of Angela Merici, Foundress of the Ursulines, 1474-1540* (New York, 1964).

Casadei, Alfredo, "La donna della riforma italiana." *Religio* 12 (1937): 133-41.

Chalendard, M., *La promotion de la femme à l'apostolat* (Paris, 1950).

Chaunu, Pierre, *La mort à Paris aux XVIᵉ, XVIIᵉ, et XVIIIᵉ siècles* (Paris, 1978).

Chaussy, Dom Yves, *Les Benedictines et la réforme catholique en France au XVIIᵉ siècle* (Paris, 1975).

Christian, William, *Apparitions in Late Medieval and Renaissance Spain* (Princeton, 1981).

———, *Local Religion in Sixteenth-Century Spain* (Princeton, 1981).

Cognet, L., *La mère Angélique et son temps,* 2 vols. (Paris, 1922-24).

Creytens, Raimondo, "La riforma dei monasteri femminili dopo i Decreti Tridentini," *Il Concilio di Trento e la riforma tridentina, atti del convegno storico internazionale* (Rome, 1965): 45-84.

D'Addario, Arnaldo, *Aspetti della controriforma a Firenze* (Rome, 1972).

Dainville, François de, "Accès à la vie active des religieuses," *Vie spirituel* 81 (1949): 36-61.

[21]Davis (1975): 65-97.

Davis, Natalie, *Society and Culture in Early Modern France* (Stanford, 1975).

———, and Jill Conway, *Society and the Sexes: A Bibliography of Women's History in Early Modern Europe, Colonial America and the United States* (New York, 1981).

De Certeau, Michel, *La Fable mystique XVIᵉ-XVIIᵉ siècle* (Paris, 1982).

Deleito y Pinuela, José, *La vida religiosa española bajo el cuarto Felipe; santos y pecadores* (Madrid, 1952).

Delumeau, Jean, *Le Catholicisme entre Luther et Voltaire* (Paris, 1971).

Devos, Roger, *Vie religieuse féminine et société: L'Origine sociale des Visitandines d'Annecy aux XVIIᵉ et XVIIIᵉ siècles* (Annecy, 1973).

Dolan, Claire, *Entre tours et clochers. Les gens d'église a Aix-en-Provence au XVIᵉ siècle* (Sherbrooke, 1981).

Domínguez, Ortiz, Antonio, *La sociedad española en el siglo XVII* (Madrid, 1970).

Duran, Marie Angeles, "Notas para el estudio de la estructura social de España en el siglo XVIII," in *Mujer y sociedad en España, 1700-1975,* Ministerio de Cultura Estudios Sobre Mujer (Madrid, 1982).

Eckenstein, Lina, *Women under Monasticism* (New York, 1963).

Efrén de la Madre de Dios, and Otger Steggink, *Tiempo y vida de Santa Teresa* (Madrid, 1977).

Egido, Teófanes, "El ambiante histórico de Santa Teresa," *Introducción a la lectura de Santa Teresa* (Madrid, 1978): 43-103.

Frey, Linda, Marsha Frey, and Joanne Scheider, *Women in Western European History: A Select Chronological, Geographical and Topical Bibliography from Antiquity to the French Revolution* (Brighton, 1982).

Guesdre, M-C, "La femme et la vie spirituelle," *XVIIᵉ siècle* 62-63 (1964): 47-77.

Guilhem, Claire, "Devaluation des discours féminins," *Histoire de l'Inquisition,* ed. Bernard Bennassar (Paris, 1979): 197-240.

Herve-Bazin, F., *Les grands ordres et congrégations des femmes* (Paris, 1889).

Hoffman, Paul, *Theories de la femininité aux XVIIᵉ et XVIIIᵉ siècles: de Descartes à Cabanis* (Paris, 1975).

Hoffman, Philip T., *Church and Community in the Diocese of Lyon, 1500-1789* (New Haven, 1984).

Hufton, Olwen, "Women in History: Early Modern Europe," *Past and Present* 101 (1983): 125-41.

Irwin, Joyce, "Society and the Sexes," *Reformation Europe: A Guide to Research,* ed. Steven Ozment (St. Louis, 1982): 343-61.

Jegou, Marie-André, *Les Ursulines du faubourg Saint Jacques à Paris, 1607-1662: Origine d'un monastère apostolique* (Paris, 1981).

Kendrick, T. D., *Mary of Agreda: The Life and Legend of a Spanish Nun* (London, 1967).

Le Bras, Gabriel, *Etudes de sociologie religieuse* (Paris, 1956).

Le Brun, François, ed., *Histoire des catholiques en France* (Toulouse, 1980).

Liebowitz, Ruth, "Virgins in the Service of Christ: The Dispute over an Active Apostolate for Women during the Counter Reformation," *Women of Spirit: Female Leadership in the Jewish and Christian Traditions,* eds. Rosemary Ruether and Eleanor McLaughlin (New York, 1979).

Llamas Martínez, Enrique, *Santa Teresa y la Inquisición española* (Madrid, 1972).

Longhurst, John, "La Beata Isabel de la Cruz ante la Inquisición, 1524-1529," *Cuadernos de historia de España* 15-16 (1957): 297-303.

Loysel, *Des aumônes dotales ou dots moniales avant 1789* (Paris, 1908).

Martin, Mère Marie de Saint Jean, OSU, *Ursuline Methods of Education* (Rahway, N.J., 1946).

Midelfort, Erik, "Witchcraft, Magic and the Occult," *Reformation Europe: A Guide to Research*, ed. Steven Ozment (St. Louis, 1981): 183-211.

Molinari, F., "Visite pastorali nei monasteri femminili di Piacenza nel secolo XVI," *Il Concilio de Trento e la riforma tridentina* (Rome, 1965): 679-733.

Monica, Sister, *Angela Merici and Her Teaching Idea, 1747-1540* (New York, 1927).

Newton, W. Ritchey, "Port Royal and Jansenism: Social Experience, Group Formation and Religious Attitudes in Seventeenth Century France," Unpublished Ph.D. dissertation, University of Michigan, 1974.

Norberg, Kathryn, "Women, the Family and the Counter Reformation: Women's Confraternities in the Seventeenth Century," *Proceedings of the Western Society for French History* 6 (1979): 55-63.

_____, *Rich and Poor: Grenoble 1600-1814* (Berkeley, 1985).

Oliver, Sister Mary, *Mary Ward, 1585-1645* (New York, 1959).

Orcibal, J., *La rencontre du Carmel thérèsien avec les mystiques du nord* (Paris, 1959).

Ozment, Steven, *The Reformation and the Family* (New Haven, 1984).

Paschini, Pio, "I monasteri femminili in Italia nel 500," *Problemi di vita religiosa in Italia nel Cinquecento* (Padua, 1960): 31-61.

Perry, Mary Elizabeth, "'Lost Women' in Early Modern Seville: The Poetics of Prostitution," *Feminist Studies* 4 (1978): 195-214.

Platelle, H., *Les chrétiens devant la miracle* (Paris, 1968).

Renault, Emmanuel, *Sainte Thérèse d'Avila et l'experience mystique* (Paris, 1970).

Rollet, Henri, *La condition de la femme dans l'Eglise* (Paris, 1975).

Rosa, G. de, *Vescovi, popolo e magia nel sud: ricerche di storia socio-religiosa dal XVII al XIV secolo* (Naples, 1971).

Russo, Carla, *I monasteri femminili di clausura a Napoli nel secolo XVII* (Naples, 1970).

Schueller, Th., *La Femme et le saint, La Femme et ses problèmes d'après François de Sales* (Paris, 1970).

Schmitt, Jean-Claude, *Le saint levrier. Guinefort, guérisseur d'enfants depuis le XIII siècle* (Paris, 1979).

Taylor, Judith Combes, "From Proselytizing to Social Reform: Three Generations of Female Teaching Congregations, 1600-1720," Unpublished Ph.D. dissertation, Arizona State University, 1980.

Tomás (Alvárez) de la Cruz, "Santa Teresa y la polémica de la oración mental: Sentido polémico del 'Camino de la perfección'," *Santa Teresa en el IV Centenario de la Reforma Carmelitana* (Barcelona, 1963): 41-61.

Trexler, Richard, "Le célibat à la fin du moyen age: Les Religieuses de Florence," *Annales, Economies, Sociétés, Civilisations* 27 (1972): 1334-50.

Venard, Marc, *L'église d'Avignon au XVI siècle,* 4 vols. (Lille, 1980).

Villaret, Michel, *Les congrégations mariales* (Paris, 1947).

Vovelle, Michel, *Piété baroque et déchristianisation en Provence au XVII͑ siècle* (Paris, 1973).

Weaver, Ellen, "Cloister and Salon in 17th Century Paris," *Beyond Androcentrism: New Essays on Women and Religion,* ed. Rita M. Gross (Missoula, 1977): 159-80.

_____, "Women and Religion in Early Modern France: A Bibliographic Essay on the State of the Question," *Catholic Historical Review* 67 (1981): 50-59.

Weiner, Dora B., "A Guide to Research in Archives of Active French Women's Orders," *French Historical Studies* 9 (1975): 362-64.

Wright, Wendy M., *Bond of Perfection: Jeanne de Chantal and François de Sales* (New York, 1985).

Zanette, E., *Suor Arcangela, monaca del Seicento veneziano* (Venice-Rome, 1961).

Zarri, Gabriella, "Le sante vive, Per una tipologia della santità femminile nel primo Cinquecento," *Annali delli Instituto storico italo-germanico in Trento* 6 (1980): 371-446.

Religious Orders of Men, Especially the Society of Jesus

John Patrick Donnelly, S.J. *

General Information

MEMBERS OF MALE RELIGIOUS ORDERS wrote most of the Catholic theology and spirituality produced during the period 1550-1700. They also supplied most of the personnel for the foreign missions, staffed the Inquisition, and engaged extensively in the ministry of the Word. These important activities are discussed elsewhere in this volume.

During the late Middle Ages the reputation of the orders declined so far that the zealous churchmen who wrote the *Consilium de Emendanda Ecclesia* of 1537 urged that no new religious orders be allowed and that the existing ones be consolidated into a few basic types. Instead, new forms of the religious life sprang up, and several old orders experienced a marked revival. Religious orders and congregations have been keenly conscious of their historical roots and have generally held up their early history as a source of inspiration for their members. Moreover, since most of the orders produced large numbers of writers and scholars, their history has been cultivated and an enormous number of primary sources and secondary studies are available. The quality of this material is uneven. Biography, much of it hagiographic, and local studies are dominant genres. On the other hand many orders have historical institutes, often connected with their Roman headquarters, which publish journals and critically edit collections of documents.[1]

No scholars of the stature of Fernand Braudel or Hubert Jedin dominate the historiography of the orders, and the most insightful historians of the religious life, David Knowles and Jean Leclercq, are medievalists. For the early modern period progress has come not by breakthroughs but by steady increment.

*The author wishes to thank the editor, William Bangert, Robert Bireley, and Michael Zeps for suggestions that greatly improved this essay.

[1]The first section of the bibliography lists the more important journals and the addresses of the historical institutes of the religious orders.

The fundamental tool for the study of religious orders is the DIP–*Dizionario degli istituti di perfezione;* seven of a projected nine volumes have appeared since 1974. This encyclopedia is less well known than it deserves to be, perhaps because many scholars do not read Italian well and because its title is opaque–"institutes of perfection" is canonical jargon for all the orders, congregations, and groups that take the three religious vows. DIP stresses Catholic orders but includes articles on Protestant, Orthodox, and non-Christian monasticism. There is an entry for each religious order. DIP's bibliographies can be updated by those in *Revue d'histoire ecclésiastique,* mostly under the subtitle *corporations religieuses.* RHE also lists some 500 journals that it surveys, including almost all the historical journals of the orders. The annual *Literaturbericht* of the *Archiv für Reformationsgeschichte* gives fewer but more detailed notices.

A useful survey of the entire subject is Dom Robert Lemoine's *Le monde des religieux;* covering the period 1563-1789. More stimulating but controversial is Raymond Hostie, *Vie et mort des ordres religieux.* Published in a series devoted to psycho-religious studies, it attempts a comparative examination of different orders from the Egyptian desert to Vatican Council II and argues that most orders have a built-in life-cycle. Hostie considers the Benedictines an exception to this pattern because each monastery is largely autonomous. His biological analogy may be questioned, but his daring and his comparative method deserve admiration. Hostie points out, as have other scholars, that the foundation of religious orders comes in waves and usually corresponds to crises in church history. One wave was the early thirteenth century; another was the second quarter of the sixteenth century. New foundations were fewer in the seventeenth century and were largely confined to France (Vincentians, Christian Brothers, Sulpicians, Eudists, Missions étrangères de Paris), where the Wars of Religion had delayed the Catholic Reformation. Hostie provides thirty pages of maps and statistical tables that make clear the numerical growth of the main religious orders during the period 1540-1700. The Dominicans doubled from 15,000 to 30,000. The Franciscans grew from 50,000 to 110,000 if one combines Conventuals, Observants, and Capuchins. Contrary to a widespread assumption, the older forms of religious life, particularly the mendicants, remained the most popular throughout the Counter Reformation. Continuity and reform within the older orders, therefore, deserve more study than they usually receive.

The Society of Jesus

This essay stresses the Jesuits, nonetheless, because their impact on the age was greater and because their historiography is richer. This was their golden age, comparable to that of the mendicants in the thirteenth century. A deeper investigation of the Jesuits suggests problems and resources for research more effectively than would an even-handed survey of all the orders.

The most important research center is the Institutum Historicum Societatis Iesu (IHSI). The IHSI houses a specialized library and some twenty scholars immediately adjacent to the headquarters and central archives of the Society in Rome. The IHSI publishes four major series. The *Archivum Historicum Societatis Iesu,* a semi-annual journal, has been appearing since 1932. It welcomes scholarly articles in any major western language, publishes reviews, and provides a very detailed annual bibliography. The largest project of the IHSI is the *Monumenta Historicum Societatis Iesu* (MHSI), which now includes more than 125 substantial volumes of documents on early Jesuit history. Eighteen volumes of the MHSI contain the writings of St. Ignatius of Loyola, plus four more of sources for his life. Other volumes reprint the papers of his early companions. Souces for previous founders of religious orders are often scanty or mixed with myth, but evidence for a scientific life of Loyola is massively available. More than forty volumes of the MHSI deal with Jesuit missionary work in the Orient and the Americas. These are often invaluable sources for the history of the countries involved. A few volumes of the missions cross into the seventeenth century; all the rest relate to the sixteenth century. The IHSI has also published more than forty monographs in its *Bibliotheca* (BIHSI) series. Examples are Manuel Ruiz Jurado's study of early Jesuit novitiates, and five monographs dealing with Jesuit architecture. A final series published by the IHSI is the *Subsidia,* which largely contains membership lists and bibliographies. The great bibliographic work on the Jesuits is László Polgár's *Bibliographie sur l'histoire de la Compagnie de Jésus 1901-1980.* The first volume covers the Society as a whole (6,215 entries); the second volume treats the countries of Europe (6,751 entries). Another volume is projected for non-European countries, as are three additional volumes on individual Jesuits. IHSI will shortly publish the *Encyclopedia of Jesuit History* in both English and Spanish editions.

Edmond Lamalle has described the central archive of the Jesuits in Rome (Borgo S. Spirito 5), whose holdings are especially rich for the years 1550-1600. During the next century most letters sent to Rome were no longer preserved. The archive contains important material on rural missions. There are also Jesuit provincial archives; particularly good are those in London (114 Mount Street) and at Chantilly outside Paris. At some point the Jesuits were suppressed or exiled by every European government; their papers were taken over and not always returned. The papers of the Lower German Province are at the province archives (5 Köln, Stolzestrasse 1a), but the Jesuiten Abteilung of the Hauptstaatarchiv zu München houses 3,000 manuscript numbers relating to the Upper German Province. It is worth noting here that several state libraries in Rome once belonged to religious orders and still contain materials for their history, for example, the Biblioteca Angelica for the Augustinians and the Biblioteca Casanatense for the Dominicans.

Research on St. Ignatius of Loyola produces about eighty published items a year, most of which deal with his spirituality, especially *The Spiritual Exercises,* yet there is still no fully adequate biography. Too much research, moreover, has concentrated on his pre-Jesuit career. Only after his arrival in Rome and the foundation of the Jesuits does he become an important historical figure. André Ravier's *Ignace de Loyola fonde la Compagnie de Jésus* gives a good account of the Roman years and of the Order's foundation. The new study of St. Ignatius from his correspondence as general by Dominique Bertrand is among the most serious and comprehensive that we possess.

Loyola in his earlier years is best interpreted as a pilgrim, the image he himself used. His last ten years should be viewed in comparison with other founders of religious orders. This is the perspective of David Knowles's short *From Pachomius to Ignatius: A Study in the Constitutional History of the Religious Orders.* Unfortunately, Loyola and the Jesuits continue to be pictured in military stereotypes. In fact Loyola was never a soldier, but a minor courtier who doubled as a gentleman volunteer for a few months. Good scholars now realize that Jesuit obedience is not military obedience, but the misunderstanding persists in much of the literature.

Loyola's relations to Erasmus and humanism were more positive than his early biographers admitted. By doing away with compulsory austerities, special garb, and the choral recitation of the office, by stressing education and *bonae litterae,* and by seeking unity with God in and through apostolic activies the Jesuits partly answered Erasmian criticism and reshaped the religious life to the needs and mentality of a new age. Jesuit colleges were a major force in institutionalizing humanist educational ideas.[2]

William Bangert's *A History of the Jesuits* presents a reliable overview of the Society as a whole. A generation ago the most common introduction came through James Brodrick's sympathetic biographies of the early Jesuits. Still older were the multi-volume histories of the order under the Old Regime in the various major Catholic countries; although outdated, all these works contain a wealth of detail. Space does not permit a discussion of them, but they are listed by Polgár. Better and more recent are Mario Scaduto's volumes on the Italian Jesuits during the generalate of Diego Laínez and Horacio de la Costa's *The Jesuits in the Philippines, 1581-1768.*

The church-related schools founded by the Jesuits as a form of ministry were a striking innovation not found in earlier centuries, and education turned out to be the most important single ministry of the new Order. By 1626 there were 444 Jesuit colleges and 56 seminaries. Most colleges covered the equivalent of American junior high school through junior college, but a few were full-fledged universities. L. Lukács has edited the documents on educational theory and practice that led up to the *Ratio Studiorum* of 1599, which became normative for all Jesuit schools. The rise of Jesuit education in France has been described by François de Dainville; a later phase is central to a massive study by Marc Fumaroli, which successfully related the Jesuits to larger cultural currents. Useful for the educational work of the German Jesuits is Karl Hengst's *Jesuiten an Universitäten und Jesuitenuniversitäten.* Gian Paolo Brizzi has studied the colleges of nobles operated by the Jesuits in Italy. The most important of all Jesuit schools in the sixteenth century was the Collegio Romano; a recent study by William Wallace shows how the Jesuit professors there contributed to the development of Galileo's thought. How the Jesuits adapted on the fringes of the Catholic world emerges from the works of Vello Helk on the college at Dorpat in Estonia and Luis Martín on the college of San Pablo in Peru. Jesuit schools threatened older schools, but these seldom put up effective opposition except when the Jesuits tried to establish themselves in university towns. They met bitter opposition in Paris, Louvain, Prague, Cracow, and Padua. These struggles have left rich records that have been studied in isolation. A general study of local opposition to the new Jesuit schools is needed.

[2]Olin (1969); Fumaroli (1980).

Theater was an important adjunct to Jesuit colleges, which were attended by such famous dramatists as Lope de Vega, Calderón, Molière, and Voltaire. There is an introduction in English to Jesuit drama by William McCabe. The recent multi-volume works on Jesuit theater in German speaking lands by Jean-Marie Valentin and Elida Maria Szarota would seem to exhaust that area, but more work is needed for other countries. Jesuit theater stressed spectacle and a baroque blending of the arts in the service of piety. Several Jesuits, especially lay brothers, achieved note as architects (G. Tristano) or painters (A. Pozzo) or both (G. Valeriano), and the Jesuits influenced major artists such as Ammannati, Rubens, and Bernini. There is considerable literature on the Jesuits and the fine arts, but the area still needs research. Good starting points are the essays edited by Rudolph Wittkower and Irma Jaffe on the Jesuits and baroque art. Among Jesuit poets St. Robert Southwell has attracted the most attention. Recently Anthony Raspa has traced Jesuit influence on six Elizabethan and Jacobean poets. The same sort of research on Continental writers should prove even more interesting.[3]

The political involvement of the Jesuits has been denounced down through the centuries. The Jesuits themselves were keenly aware of how political involvement hurt their reputation, and the Fifth General Congregation in 1593 forbade Jesuits to meddle in affairs of state. But some involvement with rulers was inevitable, for even foundation and endowment of colleges entailed dealing with political leaders. Oskar Garstein has made an exhaustive study of the unsuccessful Jesuit efforts to convert Sweden with the help of John III and Sigismund III. Lynn Martin has shown that in France Emond Auger shaped the piety and backed the policies of Henry III, while other Jesuits supported the League. Much of Jesuit Gallicanism in the seventeenth century awaits its historian. The best book on a Jesuit confessor's influence on policy (the rigorous stance of Ferdinand II in the Thirty Years' War) is Robert Bireley's study of William Lamormaini.

The Jesuits and the other religious orders often provided chaplains for Catholic armies and navies during the early modern period. Among the prominent Jesuits who wrote manuals of devotion for soldiers were Peter Canisius, Antonio Possevino, and Thomas Sailly. These books, which have not been studied, might shed light on Jesuit anti-Protestantism and add historical dimension to current debates on Christian attitudes toward war and peace.

---

[3]Raspa (1983); Fumaroli (1980).

Protestant opposition to the Jesuits largely followed earlier Protestant critiques of the religious life itself. Pascal's attack on Jesuit moral theology is well known. More interesting, however, are the attacks of conservative Catholics such as Melchor Cano and Étienne Pasquier, since they alert us to how radical some Jesuit innovations seemed.[4] It is worth noting that other religious groups with a monastic tradition such as Eastern Orthodoxy and Buddhism never developed anything comparable to the Jesuits.

There have been a number of studies of Jesuit economic activity in the seventeenth century, especially of agricultural enterprises in Latin America, but an overview of Jesuit finances would be useful.[5] Financial stringency, probably reflecting the general economic and demographic slowdown of the seventeenth century, forced the Jesuits to turn away prospective novices and perhaps helped dry up initiative. More work is required on the social background of novices and their reasons for entering the Society. It seems that from Claudio Aquaviva's generalate (1581-1615) onward most novices came from the Jesuit colleges and received a standardized priestly training. Earlier, the age and background of novices was much more mixed and the training more individualized. There is room for a study of how this changing background affected Jesuit attitudes.

Compared to either the lower classes or members of strict monastic orders the Jesuits ate regularly and well. How did this affect life expectancy? Statistical evidence is abundant. Likewise statistical studies of perserverance rates in the various orders would seem feasible. Cliometricians have not yet exploited the many printed necrologies of the religious orders.

This volume contains a separate chapter on missionary work in the Orient, where the Jesuits took the lead. In Latin America the friars did the main work, but the Jesuits also played a major role. On the Mexican Jesuits there is Zambrano's bibliography in fifteen volumes, and the semi-independent republic that the Jesuits established for the Indians of Paraguay has attracted many writers; a recent survey is Philip Caraman's *The Lost Paradise.*

[4]Pasquier's attack has been edited recently (1982) with a long introduction.
[5]Cushner (1982); Konrad (1980).

The Other New Orders

The Theatines (1524), Barnabites (1430), and Somaschi (1534) all antedate the Jesuits as clerks regular but did not go so far in adapting the religious life to the needs of an active ministry. They remained quite small and spread more slowly outside Italy. The Theatines were the largest and most important, not least because they proved a seedbed of reforming bishops. The Roman journal *Regnum Dei* specializes in Theatine history. A. Gentili has written an introduction to Barnabite history and spirituality. Those interested in the Somaschi should start with DIP. Although not strictly a religious order, the Oratory of St. Philip Neri shared some characteristics of an order. For a model local study, see Jacques Maillard's *L'Oratoire à Angers aux XVIIeme et XVIIIeme siècle*. Another small order was the Piarists of Scolope, who ran elementary schools in Italy and Central Europe and were recognized as a religious order in 1621. The correspondence of their founder, St. José da Calasanz (1557-1648), and his associates has been published by Georgius Sántha and Claudius Vilá Palá.

The Capuchins, more numerous than the Jesuits and founded before them, can be classified both as a new order and as a reformed branch of the Franciscans. Still useful are Cuthbert of Brighton's two volumes on the Capuchins and the Counter Reformation. More recent is Melchor de Pobladura's three-volume history of the order. Callisto Urbanelli's two-volume study on the Capuchins in the Marches is not just another local study, as the order began there. The 450th anniversary of the order was the occasion of a conference at Camerino on its origins; the published acts contain many valuable papers, including one on Capuchin historiography. The Capuchins at the end of the seventeenth century can be seen in great detail (more than 2,000 pages) in the account of Filippo Bernardi, the secretary who accompanied the general in a tour of the European house from 1691 to 1698. Raoul Mauzaize has written a detailed study of the Capuchin Parisian province in the early seventeenth century, and Metódio da Nembio has studied Capuchin missionary work in Brazil. The Capuchin Historical Institute has been publishing a *Monumenta* series since 1937 and *Collectanea Franciscana*, a journal devoted to Capuchin history. Volume 50 (1980) of the *Collectanea* contains a review of the Institute's work. About every six years the same Institute publishes *Bibliographia Franciscana;* the volume completed in 1980 covers the years 1964 to 1973 and contains 8,844 entries dealing with all branches of the Franciscans.

The leadership in founding new orders and reforming old ones that Italy and Spain enjoyed during the sixteenth century shifted to France in the seventeenth century. The indefatigable G. Rigault has devoted nine volumes to the Christian Brothers of St. Jean Baptiste de la Salle. For the Vincentians (also called the Congregation of the Mission or Lazarists) founded by St. Vincent de Paul, there is a history by J. Herrera. The papers at a conference commemorating the four-hundredth anniversary of Vincent de Paul's birth in 1581 have recently been published.[6]

The Older Orders

If *ecclesia semper reformanda est,* the same can be said for religious orders. Even before 1517 there were reform movements, for instance those in Spain under Ferdinand and Isabella described by José García Oro. In many ways reforming old orders was more difficult than founding new ones, as the inertia of the past had to be overcome. New orders did not face schisms, which often resulted from reform, or the constant threat of legal action by recalcitrant members. In France, for example, successful reform movements not only required a strong nucleus of supporters within local houses but also agreement from the crown, the Parlement, the pope with his curia, and, in the case of the mendicants, the order's Roman headquarters. Hubert Jedin's biography of Girolamo Seripando, general of the Augustinians, illustrates vividly the problems and frustrations facing reformers. Perhaps religious who resisted reform deserve more sympathy than they usually get: after all they had made their vows and commitment to a concrete way of life, which was suddenly being upset in the name of ancient texts. Moreover, reform sometimes, as under the stern Abbot de Rancé, consisted mainly in greater fasting and corporal austerity.

The starting point for research on the Benedictines is Oliver Kapsner's three-volume bibliography. The standard survey of Benedictine history is by Philibert Schmitz in seven volumes. For seventeenth-century France there are good mongraphs on the Benedictines by Dom Yves Chaussy and Maarten Ultee and on the Cistercians of the Strict Observance by Louis Lekai and Polykarp Zakar. A. J. Krailsheimer's biography of de Rancé traces the origins of the Trappists. Easily the most important Carthusian community was that

---

[6]*Vincent de Paul* (1982).

at Cologne, which became a publishing center and resisted efforts to Protestantize the archbishopric. Gerald Chaix tells its story in three volumes. The Benedictines continued to attract vocations from England and sent missionaries to England during the seventeenth century; this survival, or rather resurrection, of English monasticism is ably studied by David Lunn.

Although the sixteenth and seventeenth centuries represent at least a respectable silver age for the Dominicans and Franciscans, the historiography is somewhat disappointing. Much of it concentrates on mission work or on great individuals like Bartolomé de Las Casas. A. W. Walz, however, has examined the work of the Dominicans at the Council of Trent. The 1981 issue of *Archivum Fratrum Praedicatorum* contains an index for the previous fifty years which guides scholars to a mass of specialized research. Gustavo Parisciani has traced reform among the Franciscan Conventuals, while Benignus Millett's *The Irish Franciscans, 1657-1665* describes the destruction of a flourishing mission by Oliver Cromwell. The literature on the smaller mendicant orders is richer. For the Minims there is P. J. S. Whitmore's *The Orders of the Minims in Seventeenth Century France*. For the Augustinians there is a survey by David Gutiérrez covering the years 1518-1648. Much more detailed are the studies of the individual German Augustinian provinces by Adalberto Kunzelmann. The second and third volumes of Joachim Smet's *The Carmelites* deal with the period 1550-1750, and P. W. Janssen has traced the reform of the French Carmelites in the seventeenth century. The chapter on spirituality in this volume deals with the great Spanish Carmelite mystics.

Past Tendencies and New Directions

The most important distinction among historians of religious orders is between "insiders" (members of the order under study) and "outsiders." In quantity the insiders easily outnumber the outsiders. Insiders are understandably sympathetic to religious life in general and to their own order in particular, so that sophisticated historians generally allow for this factor, just as they do for other sorts of institutional, religious, or national sympathies. Inside historians likewise tend to stress continuity in the order's traditions, while being less aware of how epoch and nation profoundly affect the way religious life is lived and how even an order's spirituality is bent to new needs. A more serious defect of inside history flows from its narrow focus on a single religious order. Even though the historical institutes of many orders are in Rome, the scholars from these institutes seem to have little contact with one another, so that comparative history of the orders remains a field for future research.

Much inside research has dealt with individual leaders, especially saints, with constitutional and institutional questions and event-history, but recently the sorts of questions raised especially by the *Annales* school have begun to interest inside historians so that graphs, tables, and cliometrics appear increasingly in their writings. The strength of the inside historians at the Roman research institutes parallels that of local historians a generation ago: careful archival work and a mastery of the printed sources. They also have a lived experience of their tradition and the ways in which constitutions and customs translate into practice. The dominant role of inside historians during the last century, however, is passing.

Outsiders are more likely to have professional training as historians and often bring new questions and new quantitative techniques to old texts. Many have a better grasp of the larger history of an era or a country and are more inclined to comparative studies. On the other hand, some outside history can be superficial or journalistic, and it sometimes ignores the specifically religious motivation of the orders, often subjecting it to political or psychological reductionism.

There was a time when outside historians seeking documents in the archives of the religious orders were often regarded with suspicion, whereas today the outsider can expect less red tape and more help than in many state archives. The archives of some religious orders are well catalogued, so that they can be investigated systematically. The historical journals of most orders publish in any major western language and welcome contributions from outsiders.

The lack of comparative history of the religious orders noted earlier has left largely unanswered how the old and new orders influenced one another and how both adapted to changing mentalities and institutions in the culture around them. For example, the centralized model of the Jesuits and the more active papacy and papal curia of the Counter Reformation surely worked to give the generals of the friars and their Roman headquarters a more prominent role, but growing nationalism and the new monarchies, especially in Spain and France, were equally strong forces. These opposing tendencies, both characteristic of the modern era, should be prominent in any comparative study of the orders. No less important was the interaction of spiritualities. Loyola left the Jesuits his *Spiritual Exercises* and the ideal of "the contemplative in action," but the Jesuits and the other new orders did not develop comprehensive treatises on their spirituality and understanding of the religious life until the early seventeenth century. Meanwhile, several popes tried to make the Jesuits return to older practices that were widely considered as integral to the religious life. More subtle was the influence of mendicant spirituality, especially in Spain. It was the newer spirituality–often mystical–rather than the medieval heritage, that attracted Spanish Jesuits, notably St. Francis Borgia, and led many to compromise Loyola's stress on active ministry. The influence was not all one way. The newer orders deeply influenced the old, especially the friars.

Older studies tend to stress continuity, presenting an order's history as the unfolding and growth of the seed planted by the founder, whose charism each new generation should replicate. There is a temptation to see change as deviation. In fact all the orders, both old and new, were constantly challenged to adapt to new conditions. Future studies should try to show not only how the orders contributed to larger cultural currents but how these affected the orders, their life and thought, what they lost and what they gained. Such studies would contribute greatly to a still larger question: to what degree was the Church after Trent and society in Catholic lands still medieval or distinctly new and modern? Was the Counter Reformation really one road to modernization? Specialized studies, the bricks for building a new synthesis, are abundant, but the architects will need interdisciplinary training, daring, and a new vision.

Bibliography

SELECTED JOURNALS AND HISTORICAL INSTITUTES:
Analecta Augustiniana, Institutum Historicum Ordinis S. Augustinii, Via del Sant' Offizio, 25 00193 Rome
Analecta Cicterciensia, Piazza del Tiempio de Diana, 14 00153 Rome
Analecta Mercedaria, Institutum Historicum Ordinis de Mercede, Via di Torre Gaia, 120 00133 Rome
Archivum Fratrum Praedicatorum, Istituto storico Domenicano, Largo Angelicum, 1 00184 Rome
Archivum Historicum Societatis Iesu, Institutum Historicum Societatis Iesu, Via dei Penitenzieri, 20 00193 Rome
Archivum Scholarum Piarum, Piazza de' Massimi, 4 00186 Rome
Augustiniana, Louvain, Belgium

Carmelus, Institutum Carmelitanum, Via Sforza Pallavicini, 10 00193 Rome
Cistercian Studies, Beerhem, Belgium
Collectanea Franciscana, Istituto storico Cappuccini, Circonv. occidentale, 6850
00163 Rome
Miscellanea Franciscana, Via del Serafico, 1 00142 Rome
Regnum Dei: Collectanea Theatina, Piazza Vidoni, 6 00195 Rome
Revue Bénédictine, Maredsous, Belgium
Studi Francescani, Biblioteca di Studi Francescani, Via A. Giacomini, 3 50132
Florence
Studia Monastica, Montserrat, Spain

GENERAL WORKS:

Boaga, Emanuele, O.C., "Aspetti e problemi degli Ordini e Congregazioni
religiose nei secoli XVII e XVIII," *Problemi di Storia della Chiesa* (Naples,
1982): 91-135.

Lemoine, Robert, O.S.B., *Le monde des religieux* (Paris, 1976).

THE SOCIETY OF JESUS:

Bangert, William, S.J., *A History of the Society of Jesus* (St. Louis, 1972).

_____, *A Bibliographical Essay on the History of the Society of Jesus: Books in English*
(St. Louis, 1976).

Bertrand, Dominique, *La politique de S. Ignace de Loyola* (Paris, 1985).

Bireley, Robert, S.J., *Religion and Politics in the Age of the Counterreformation*
(Chapel Hill, 1981).

Brizzi, Gian Paolo, *La formazione della classe dirigente nel seisettecento* (Bologna,
1976).

Caraman, Philip, S.J., *The Lost Paradise* (New York, 1976).

Codina Mir, Gabriel, S.J., *Aux sources de la pédagogie des jésuites: Le "modus
parisiensis"* (Rome, 1968).

Costa, Horacio de la, S.J., *The Jesuits in the Philippines, 1581-1768* (Cambridge,
Mass., 1961).

Cushner, Nicholas, *Farms and Factory: The Jesuits and the Development of Agarian
Capitalism in Colonial Quito, 1600-1767* (Albany, 1982).

Dainville, François de, S.J., *Les Jésuites et l'education de la société française. La
naissance de l'humanisme moderne* (Paris, 1940).

Fumaroli, Marc, *L'âge de l'eloquence: Rhétorique et "res literaria" de la Renaissance
au seuil de l'époque classique* (Geneva, 1980).

Garstein, Oskar, *Rome and the Counter-Reformation in Scandinavia,* 4 vols. (Olso,
1963-). Vols. 3 and 4 in progress.

Helk, Vello, *Die Jesuiten in Dorpat, 1583-1625. Ein Vorpostern der
Gegenreformation in Nordösteuropa* (Copenhagen, 1977).

Hengst, Karl, *Jesuiten an Universitäten und Jesuitenuniversitäten* (Munich, 1981).

Konrad, Herman, *A Jesuit Hacienda in Colonial Mexico: Santa Lucia 1576-1767*
(Stanford, 1980).

160   *Catholicism in Early Modern History*

Lamalle, Edmond, S.J., "L'archivo di un grande Ordine religioso. L'Archivo Generale della Compagnia di Gesù," *Archiva Ecclesiae 24-25 (1981-82): 89-120.*

Lukács, L., S.J., *Monumenta Paedagogica Societatis Iesu,* 3 vols. (Rome, 1965-74).

McCabe, William, S.J., *An Introduction to Jesuit Theater* (St. Louis, 1984).

Martin, A. Lynn, *Henry III and the Jesuit Politicians* (Geneva, 1973).

Martín, Luis, *The Intellectual Conquest of Peru. The Jesuit College of San Pablo, 1568-1768* (New York, 1968).

Olin, John, "Erasmus and St. Ignatius Loyola," *Luther, Erasmus and the Reformation,* ed. John Olin et al. (New York, 1969).

Pasquier, Etienne, *Le Catéchisme des Jésuites,* ed. Claude Sutto (Sherbrooke, Canada, 1982).

Polgar, László, S.J., *Bibliography of the History of the Society of Jesus* (Rome, 1967).

Raspa, Anthony, *The Emotive Image. Jesuit Poetics in the English Renaissance* (Fort Worth, 1983).

Ravier, André, S.J., *Ignace de Loyola fonde la Compagnie de Jésus* (Paris, 1974).

Ruiz Jurado, Manuel, S.J., *Origenes del noviciado en la Compañía de Jesús (Rome, 1980).*

Scaduto, Mario, S.J., *Storia della Compagnia di Gesù in Italia. L'epoca di Giacomo Lainez 1556-1565,* 2 vols. (Rome, 1964-74).

Szarota, Elida Maria, *Das Jesuitendrama im deutschen Sprachgebiet, 2 vols. (Munich, 1979).*

Valentin, Jean-Marie, *Le théâtre des Jésuites dans les pays de langue allemande (1554-1680),* 3 vols. (Bern, 1978).

Wallace, William, *Galileo and his Sources. The Heritage of the Collegio Romano in Galileo's Science* (Princeton, 1984).

Wittkower, Rudolf, and Irma Jaffe, eds., *Baroque Art: The Jesuit Contribution* (New York, 1972).

Zambrano, Francisco, S.J., *Diccionario bio-bibliografico de la Compañía de Jesus en Mexico,* 15 vols. (Mexico City, 1961-77).

OTHER NEW ORDERS:

Bernardi, Filippo, O.F.M. Cap. (Phillipus de Firenze), *Itinera ministri generalis Bernardini de Arezzo (1691-1698).* I: *Per Hispania.* II: *Per Galliam.* III: *Per Flandriam et Germaniam.* IV: *Per Italiam.* ed. Marianus D'Alatri (Rome, 1968-73).

Berthelot de Chesnay, C., *Les missions de saint Jean Eudes* (Paris, 1968).

Cuthbert of Brighton, O.F.M. Cap., *The Capuchins: A Contribution to the History of the Counter-Reformation,* 2 vols. (London, 1929; reprinted Port Washington, 1971).

Gentili, A., *I Barnabiti: Manuale di storia e spiritualità* (Rome, 1967).

Herrera, J., *Historia de la congregación de la Misión* (Madrid, 1949).

Maillard, Jacques, *L'Oratoire à Angers aux XVIIeme et XVIIIeme siècles* (Paris, n.d.)

Mauzaize, Raoul, O.F.M. Cap., *Histoire des Frères Mineur Capuchins de la province de Paris (1601-1660)* (Blois, 1967).

Melchor de Pobladura, O.F.M. Cap., *Historia generalis Ordinis Fratrum Minorum Capuchinorum,* 3 vols. (Rome, 1947-51).

Metódio da Nembio, O.F.M. Cap., *Storia dell' attività missionaria dei minori Cappuccini nel Brazile (Rome, 1958).*

Picard, Émile, "Les Théatins de Sainte-Ann-La-Royale (1644-1790)," *Regnum Dei* 36 (1980): 99-374.

Rigault, G., F.E.C., *Histoire générale de l'Institute des Frères des Écoles Chrétiennes,* 9 vols. (Paris, 1937-53).

Sántha, Georgius, and Claudius Vilá Palá, Sch. P., eds., *Epistolarium Coaetaneorum S. Josephi Calasanctii 1600-1648.* 6 vols. (Rome, 1977-81).

Urbanelli, Callisto, O.F.M. Cap., *Storia dei cappuccini delle Marche.* Vol. I: *Origini della Riforma cappuccina 1525-1536.* Vol. II: *Vicende del primo Cinquantennio 1535-1585* (Ancona, 1978).

Vincent de Paul. *Actes du Colloque international d'études vincentiennes–Paris, 25-26 Septembre 1981* (Rome, 1982).

450° *dell'Ordine cappuccino. Le origini della riforma cappuccina. Atti del Convegno di studi storici. Camerino 18-21 Settembre 1978* (Ancona, 1979).

THE OLD ORDERS:

Chaix, Gérald, *Réforme et Contre-Réforme catholiques. Recherches sur la chartreuse de Cologne au XVI° siècle,* 3 vols. (Salzburg, 1981).

Chaussy, Yves, O.S.B., *Les Bénédictines et la réforme catholique en France au XVII° siècle* (Toulouse, 1975).

García Oro, José, *La Reforma de los religiosos españoles en tiempo de los reyes católicos* (Valladolid, 1969).

Gutiérrez, David, *Die Augustiner von Beginn der Reformation bis zur katholischen Restauration 1518-1646* (Rome, 1975).

Janssen, P. W., O. Carm., *Les origines de la Réforme des Carmes en France au XVII° siècle* (The Hague, 1963).

Jedin, Hubert, *Papal Legate at the Council of Trent: Cardinal Seripando* (St. Louis, 1947).

Kapsner, Oliver, O.S.B., *A Benedictine Bibliography,* 3 vols. (Collegeville, Minn., 1962-82).

Krailsheimer, A. J., *Armand-Jean de Rancé. His Influence in the Cloister and the World* (Oxford, 1974).

Kunzelmann, Adalberto, O.S.A., *Geschichte der deutschen Augustiner-Eremiten,* 7 vols. (Würzburg, 1976).

Lekai, Louis J., *The Rise of the Cistercians of the Strict Observance in Seventeenth Century France* (Washington, D.C., 1968).

Lunn, David, *The English Benedictines, 1540-1688, from Reformation to Revolution* (London, 1980).

Miele, M., O.P., *La Riforma domenicana a Napoli nel periodo post-tridentino (1583-1725)* (Rome, 1963).

Millett, Benignus, *The Irish Franciscans, 1651-1665.* (Rome, 1964).

Parisciani, Gustavo, O.F.M.-Conv., "La Riforma Tridentina e i Frati Minori Conventuali," *Miscellanea Francescana* 83 (1983): 499-1021.

Schmitz, Philibert, O.S.B., *Histoire de l'ordre de Saint-Benoît,* 7 vols. (Maredesous, 1948-56).

Starling, A., O. Carm., *Der Karmelitengeneral Nikolaus Audet und die Katholische Reform des XVI Jahrhunderts* (Rome, 1959).

Smet, Joachim, O. Carm., *The Carmelites: A History of the Brothers of our Lady of Mount Carmel,* 4 vols. (Darien, IL, 1975-82).

Ultee, Maarten, *The Abbey of St. Germain des Prés in the Seventeenth Century* (New Haven, 1981).

Walz, A., O.P., *I Domenicani al Concilio di Trento* (Rome, 1961).

Whitmore, P. J. S., *The Order of Minims in Seventeenth Century France* (The Hague, 1967).

Zakar, Polykarp, *Histoire de la stricte observance de l'ordre cistercien depuis ses débuts jusqu'au généralat du cardinal de Richelieu* (Rome, 1966).

Spirituality in the Sixteenth and Seventeenth Centuries

Massimo Marcocchi

Renovation in the Spanish Church

SPAIN DOMINATED THE SIXTEENTH CENTURY with its political power as well as its artistic and literary achievements. Even in the area of religion, it was a world of great vigor. Within the Spanish Church lively reform movements developed, and among these the "observantist" movements in convents and monasteries held a special importance.

With the Dominicans the reform began with Alvaro de Zamora (d. 1430), who founded the strict observance Convent of Escalaceli at Cordova. From there sprang the renewal of the communities of San Esteban at Salamanca and of San Gregorio at Valladolid, where Luis de Granada and Bartolomé Carranza were trained. In the first two decades of the sixteenth century, the movement begun by Juan Hurtado de Mendoza, who was under the spell of Savonarola and hence spread Savonarola's ideas, gained strength. If it is perhaps excessive to speak, as does Beltrán de Heredia (1943), of a Savonarolian invasion, the influence of the Dominican both as a spiritual writer and reformer was nonetheless strong.

Among the Franciscans the observantist movement found expression in three great writers in the first half of the sixteenth century: Alonso de Madrid with the *Arte para servir a Dios* (1521), Francisco de Osuna with the *Tercer abecedario espiritual* (1527), and Bernardino de Laredo with the *Subida del monte Sion* (first edition, 1535; second edition, 1538). Osuna and Laredo taught that the soul must detach itself from itself and from all creation, must make itself "deaf," "dumb," and "blind" to the senses and to the higher faculties of the soul (*no pensar nada*), and must effect internal silence and recollection (recogimiento) in order to permit the penetration of divine action.[1]

Among the Benedictines the Congregation of Valladolid was formed, to which the monastery of Montserrat in Catalonia adhered.

---

[1] De Ros (1936, 1948, 1963); Andrés Martín (1975).

Its abbot, García Jiménez de Cisneros, introduced daily mental prayer alongside traditional liturgical piety, and for this purpose composed his *Ejercitatorio de la vida espiritual* (1500), influenced by the ideals of the *Devotio moderna.*[2] Through the *Ejercitatorio* a vast movement fostering methodological mental prayer developed, a movement represented by the Franciscan, Pedro de Alcántara, the Dominican, Luis de Granada, and above all by Ignatius Loyola with his *Spiritual Exercises,* to name just a few. Cisnero's book enjoyed an extraordinary success, and its sources, meaning and progressive elaboration have all been studied.[3] From this context emerged the secular priest, Juan de Avila (1500-69), one of the most impressive figures of sixteenth-century Spain. His writings are collected in a critical edition in six volumes begun by Sala Balust (d. 1965) and completed by Francisco Martín Hernández.[4]

Another noteworthy phenomenon in Spain in the first half of the century was the numerous editions and translations of classics of spirituality, like the works of John Climacus, Augustine, Gregory the Great, Bonaventure, Catherine of Siena, Angela da Foligno, Ludolf the Carthusian, and Savonarola. Also important were the writings of the Rhenish and Flemish mystics (Tauler, Suso, Herp, and Ruysbroeck), whose influence has been studied by Groult, Orcibal (1966), and Alventosa Sanchis. The phenomenon still needs, however, further research.

The Alumbrados of Castile

From about 1510 onwards mystical tendencies began to take hold in certain Franciscan convents. As recent historiography has demonstrated, this phenomenon arose at different times in different places, and did not always have the same characteristics.[5] Isabel de la Cruz, a Franciscan terciary, and Pedro de Alcaraz, a layman won over by Isabel, meditated on the medieval mystics as well as on the Bible, which they explained to their disciples. They considered vocal prayer harmful; they extolled mental prayer and opposed fasting, ascetic practices, the veneration of the saints; they abhorred sensible devotion and belittled external works, which they described as *ataduras,* traps,

---

[2]Leturia (1957).
[3]Leturia (1957); Cusson (1968); Bernard (1969).
[4]*Obras completas* (1970-71).
[5]Bataillon (1937); Selke (1952-1956); Domingo de S. Teresa (1957); Márquez (1972); Andrés Martín (1975); Nieto (1978).

and sought perfection through internal illumination (*alumbramiento*) and the direct union of the soul with God. Alcaraz was well aware that man is inclined toward evil and that, if God does not help him, he is lost. It is therefore necessary to abandon oneself (*dejar, dejamiento, dejado*) to the action of God.

Alcaraz was not concerned about Church reform, but Franciscans like Fray Melchor and Francisco de Ocaña longed for a spiritual Church and predicted the advent of an angelic pope. In the Franciscan, Juan de Cazalla, and his sister, Maria, the mother of many children, the spirituality of the *alumbrados* was much influenced by Erasmus. Emphasis was thus placed on the reading of the Bible and on the necessity of an internalized and evangelical piety.

The phenomenon of the *alumbrados* poses a series of delicate and complex problems. First of all, it is necessary to discriminate between *recogidos* and *dejados,* a distinction already clear in the sixteenth century: "*Aliud es dejamento, aliud es recogimiento,*" says Juan de Avila. For the *recogidos,* reaching the summit of the mountain of perfection presupposed the acquisition of the moral and theological virtues. The *dejados,* on the other hand, concerned themselves only with living at the summit of *dejamiento* and not with the ascent from the foot of the mountain. For the *dejados* oral prayer is harmful; for the *recogidos* oral prayer is good, meditation on the Passion of Christ is better, the prayer of *recogimiento* is best.[6] One must also distinguish the *alumbrados* of Toledo from those later found at Llerena in Estremadura, whose illuminism was less spiritual and considered.[7]

Marcel Bataillon compared Erasmian thought with illuminism and at times almost equated them. In reality, the *alumbrado* movement did not spring from Erasmus but was born earlier. Nevertheless, some affinities can be established between the two, for example, the necessity of an internalized Christianity. Erasmus's *Enchiridion militis christiani* was in fact read by the *alumbrados.* It must also be pointed out, however, that the *alumbrados* were animated by an acute sense of sin and by a mystic tendency that one seeks in vain in Erasmus. For E. Asensio the *alumbrados* of Toledo are not sons of Erasmus, even less of Luther, but rather have their roots in the *Devotio moderna* and in the tradition represented by Bernard, Bonaventure, Angela da Foligno, and Catherine of Siena.

[6]Andrés Martín (1975).
[7]Heredia (1947); Sala Balust (1963).

In this context, characterized by a variety of positions and open to European currents of thought through the court of Charles V, the books of Erasmus, translated into Castilian, were circulated; thus were spread the Erasmian ideals, a phenomenon that reached its moment of greatest splendor between 1525 and 1535. Bataillon's *Erasme et l'Espagne*, published in 1937 and translated into Spanish with revisions in 1950 and 1966, remains fundamental. This classic of contemporary historiography tends, however, to overestimate the influence of Erasmus. Asensio and Andrés Martín have reevaluated Erasmus's importance, as indicated above. For Asensio, the Franciscan element "*es mucho más potente y caudalosa que la erasmista.*"[8] With the failure of its dream of universal peace and especially because of its intrinsic inadequacies, Erasmian thought soon wore itself out. "It did not have within itself the strength," Eugenio Garin wrote in 1939, reviewing Bataillon's work, "to make martyrs or overturn the world." Erasmus was a moderate man who fled excesses; he supported an irenic system in which freedom and grace collaborate. His ideal of morality and interiority, admirable in itself, was incapable of producing new impulses and energies. The folly of Christ was felt by him in too prudent a fashion.[9]

St. Teresa of Avila

Teresa of Jesus and John of the Cross, the most representative figures of mystical Spain, sank roots in this soil, from which they derived lifeblood and their very temperment. For a long time Teresa stood almost isolated by an inaccessible and meta-historical greatness that refused to measure itself against the social, economic, cultural, and religious conditions of sixteenth-century Spain. According to hagiographic legend, Teresa owed everything to her own experiences, or rather, to divine inspiration. Teresa's internal experience, of extraordinary intensity, remains without doubt the fundamental reference point for understanding her writings, but it is undeniable that this experience was also nourished by the works she read and by the influences of her surroundings.

Thanks to the studies by G. Etchegoyen, R. Hoornaert, F. de Ros (1936, 1948), and L. Oechslin, we are able to clarify the nature of some of the influences on her, even if their relative impact has not yet been

[8]Asensio.
[9]Garin (1939): 741.

determined with complete certainty. The question of sources is, in fact, complex, because, with the exception of the Bible, Teresa never indicated the authors for her sources through a delicate process of comparisons. Teresa had, moreover, an amazing capacity for assimilation and invention.

Some facts are, however, now certain. Teresa was familiar with Scripture and with works of spiritual literature like the *Imitation of Christ*, the *Life of Christ* by Ludolf the Carthusian, and the *Flos sanctorum*.[10] Among the writings of the Fathers, she knew the *Moralia in Job* of Gregory the Great and the *Confessions* of Augustine in the Spanish version of 1554. Also among the authors known by Teresa are certainly Francisco de Osuna and Bernardino de Laredo, who exercised a profound influence on her, as F. de Ros has made evident. Yet another influence, more direct than books, was exerted by the Carmelite tradition in which Teresa was deeply rooted, and by her confessors, who belonged to various schools of spirituality (Jesuit, Dominican, Carmelite, Franciscan), as well as by personalities like the austere Franciscan, Pedro de Alcántara, even though he was never her confessor.[11]

Her surroundings were also a strong influence. Teresa breathes air saturated with the chivalrous ideals and military undertakings of the Spain of her time, and she mixes memories of the struggles of the *reconquista* with the adventures of the soul. Images, comparisons and metaphors deriving from military vocabulary abound in her writings: Jesus is "the great captain;" God is "His Majesty"; the Christian is the soldier of Christ; the soul is compared to a castle surrounded by seven walls.[12]

A recently ascertained fact, Teresa's Jewish-convert ancestry, has attracted attention in the latest historiography.[13] The discovery in 1946 of a manuscript in the Real Cancillería of Valladolid revealed that Teresa's maternal grandfather, a merchant of Jewish descent, converted to Christianity in 1485. To what degree does this fact throw light upon Teresa's outlook? One must proceed here with balance, neither overemphasizing the fact nor ignoring it.

We know, for instance, that honor (*honra*) was linked with belonging to the Old Christians, those without the Jewish stain in their

[10]Herraíz (1979).
[11]Oechslin, (1946); Lépée (1947); Efrén de la Madre de Dios-Stegginck (1968).
[12]Ricard-Pélisson (1968).
[13]Egido (1982).

blood. The *conversos* were impure and did not have *honra*. Teresa reinterprets the principle of *honra* because the value of a person does not stem from noble titles, the pureness of one's blood, or wealth, but rather from the intensity with which one lives the relationship with God. At the convent of St. Joseph, Teresa initiated a regime of equality among the nuns, refusing to admit titles and claims of ancestry, and she established manual labor as normative for all.

Her Jewish ancestry might help explain some of her characteristic traits. Teresa wrote sublime mystical pages, but she also concerned herself with economic matters and juridical processes; she sparkled with initiative, business and diplomatic abilities, common sense. It is not possible, however, to go much beyond this; we do not think it is legitimate to indicate a causal relationship between Teresa's mysticism and her belonging to a family of converts.

There has long been an abundant literature on Teresa's spirituality, but to a large degree it has been apologetic and devotional. Studies from a more detached viewpoint began to appear in the 1940s,[14] but only in the last thirty years have they acquired critical depth, the achievement especially of Carmelite scholars. Typical of this more recent literature is the tendency to read Teresa in the light of the theological and spiritual issues of our own times.

The Carmelite, Tomás de la Cruz, in an essay in 1962 that marked a turning point in the evaluation of Teresa, outlined the content of Teresa's mystical experience (the Trinity, Christ, the Church, sin, grace). In the wake of this essay, further studies of the themes and aspects of Teresian doctrine have been undertaken. Thus, F. Domínguez Reboiras reconstructed the doctrine of grace in Teresa; A. García Evangelista analyzed Teresa's idea of "inhabitation"; M. Herráiz (1980, 1981) studied the sense of God in Teresian doctrine and experience and focused on the characteristics of Teresian prayer; Tomás de la Cruz (1966) studied the theme of the Church.

The Christological dimension that Tomás de la Cruz in 1962 considered the essential point of Teresa's spirituality remained in the shadows. In the 1970s, in connection with a renewed interest in Christological questions by contemporary Christian theologians, some efforts were made in this direction, but only with the work of the Carmelite, S. Castro (1978, 1981), has the Christology of Teresa been reconstructed with both rigor and breadth. Castro sees Jesus Christ as

---

[14]Lépée (1947, 1951); Oechslin (1946).

the originating principle of Teresa's mystical experience, the foundation on which the structure of Teresa's doctrine and spirituality is based. Even when one reaches the summit of the spiritual journey in which it would seem that one must do without every sensible reality, Teresa does not stray from the humanity of the Lord, for the mystical marriage binds only with the Word made flesh. The experience of Christ permeates all of Christian life. Morality consists in the following of Christ; prayer is the orbit in which one grasps the mystery of Christ who lives in man. According to Castro, the nucleus of Teresa's experience is no longer, therefore, prayer, as has sometimes been maintained, because prayer is the gate to mystery, not the mystery itself.

Teresa's thoughts on "the world" have also been studied, thanks to the interest in that question in contemporary spirituality and theology. This theme was absent in the essay by Tomás de la Cruz cited above. The researches of U. Dobhan and S. Castro (1981) have pointed out that the term appears frequently in Teresa and often assumes a negative meaning because it stands for all that is inimical to the spiritual life. In Teresa, however, the word also has a positive meaning, because it can be used to indicate "creation," which bears in itself traces of God.

Teresa described the spiritual journey through a system of symbols, often enigmatic and difficult to decipher. With extraordinary intuition she observed that in the symbolic process one finds the only valid method that permits expression of the mystical experience. Symbolic language is allusive, capable of joining one evocatively to the experience that one wishes to communicate, and it is inexhaustible, that is, rich and polyvalent. When the mystical life finds stability in the castle (the fifth "mansion"), for instance, Teresa introduces the symbol of the silkworm that becomes a butterfly. As the worm, now mature, enters the cocoon, dies, and leaves transformed into a butterfly, so the soul dies and finds itself permeated by God. To describe the union with God, Teresa uses the symbol of the stream that flows into the sea from which it can no longer be separated. But other images that even better express the permanence of the two personalities in union also occur, for example, the nuptial metaphor. Study of Teresian symbolism found a pioneer in the person of G. Etchegoyen. Recently J. Castellano Cervera has offered, in a concrete application of the silkworm symbol, some further keys to reading symbolism in Teresa. A general study of the problem, however, is still lacking.

St. John of the Cross

John of the Cross, likè Teresa, has long been considered an isolated writer, debtor in all things to divine inspiration. Today scholars are convinced that John is deeply related to the spiritual tradition of sixteenth-century Spain. As with Teresa, the question of sources is complex because, apart from the Bible and an occasional patristic *topos,* John does not cite the authors from whom he draws. Furthermore, John was well educated and was familiar with a much wider range of writings than Teresa. Some points, however, seem rather clear, even if they cannot claim to be absolutely definitive or exhaustive.

The Scriptures are for John the source *par excellence.* Vilnet's study has shown that John seeks in them the explanation and confirmation of his mystical experiences.[15] For John, the language of the Bible sets the norm for mystical language; indeed, it is the first source of mystical language. His reading of Scripture is not, therefore, scientific, and it cannot be reduced to the limits set by professional exegetes. John was also profoundly influenced by Dionysius the Areopagite from whom he understood above all the negation of the things of the senses as the path to the ineffable God.[16]

At Salamanca (1564-68) John received a philosophical and theological formation that left a strong mark on him. Predominant is the influence of Thomistic doctrine, which through the efforts of the Dominicans permeated the university community.[17] John may have absorbed other currents of thought as well. Morel (I, 1960) has shown the existence of both anti-Thomastic and anti-Aristotelian trends at Salamanca, and has recalled that the Carmelite order had its own tradition, represented in particular by Baconthorp and Michele da Bologna. John's reading of the poets Garcilaso and Boscán[18] and the meeting with Luis de León probably also date back to the Salamanca years.[19] This period has attracted the attention of all who have studied John's doctrine–from Baruzi to Morel, following on Bruno de Jésus-Marie and Crisógono de Jesús–for the purpose of grasping the influence of John's intellectual formation on his internal experience.

[15]Vilnet (1949); Nieto (1979).
[16]Chevallier (1959): 41-45.
[17]Bruno de Jésus-Marie (1929).
[18]Milner (1951).
[19]Baruzi (1926): 130-33.

John in fact attempted to explain his experience by making use of philosophical and theological categories.

The influence exerted by the Rhenish and Flemish mystics appears today above all ever more evident and important, thanks to the study by J. Orcibal (1966), who in an accurate analysis confirmed and enhanced the intuitions of Bruno de Jésus-Marie and Crisógono de Jesús. The influence of Moslem mysticism on John has been studied by Asin Palacios (1932) and L. Baralt López. These authors present suggestive insights into a problem of great relevance, still in need of investigation: the diffusion and depth of Islamic mysticism in Spain. John was, in any case, an impassioned reader, who however assimilated and transformed what he read and integrated it into his personal synthesis. In addition to literary sources, John was strongly influenced by the Carmelite tradition, which he consistently encountered in his office as confessor and in his relationship with Teresa of Jesus.[20]

Along with this research, which admittedly does not penetrate directly to the meaning of John's message but rather helps understand his historical origins, studies aimed at reconstructing in whole or in part the spiritual doctrine of John of the Cross are also in great evidence. The twentieth century has indeed reaffirmed John's great authority in the field of mysticism (in 1926 he was proclaimed a Doctor of the Church), and all suspicions that the quarrel over Quietism placed on his works have faded away.

John's writings have been abundantly probed from a variety of viewpoints–philosophical, theological, psychological, literary, sociological, linguistic–that have produced a range of interpretations that often place John's works in a cultural framework quite different from the one in which they were produced; they impose conceptual schemes extraneous to them at the risk of misunderstanding their meaning. It is obviously impossible here to give a complete account of the problems research has raised and the results it has attained. We shall merely underline a few aspects that seem particularly pertinent.

Some studies have reflected, for instance, upon the literary genre of John's works. Others raise questions of content. Does John confine himself, for example, to imparting rules for spiritual direction, or does he confront the ontological reality of the divine, situating himself therefore on a more objective plane? Because John's works were read primarily in conventual circles, some scholars formed the opinion that

[20]Crisógono de Jesús (1946).

John was merely a great teacher of prayer, intent on leading souls to union with God. J. Maritain attempted to establish this opinion on a scholarly basis in an article in 1931, in which he defined John as a "*praticien de la contemplation,*" and denied him any doctrinal worth. John, according to Maritain, points to the road leading to transforming union but says little or nothing about the nature of divine reality. He is, in short, a spiritual director who brings a pedagogical, rather than an ontological, approach to his affirmations.

In opposition to this interpretation, several scholars have vindicated the doctrinal value of John's writings, finding in the saint a great spiritual guide, of course, but above all a teacher of doctrine.[21] Thence arises the necessity of elaborating a synthesis that integrates the mystic and the theologian in a complementary vision including both doctrine and experience. It must nonetheless be insisted that John of the Cross is not so much interested in defining the nature of God, the person of Christ and grace as realities in themselves as he is in teaching in a perspective of spiritual dynamism how these are present to man and lead to his deification.

Authors agree, in any case, that union with God is at the center of John's works at the levels of both doctrine and experience. Yet John's mysticism, centered around intimate union with God, is marked by a trait that seems to negate it: the transcendence of God and its corollary, the negation of the tangible/sensible, in that no created element can be an effective means of arriving at divine union; no such element can have in itself any "proportion" with God.

The theological virtues are, however, a suitable and "proportioned" means by which to bring about union with God, infinitely far from His creatures by reason of His transcendence. Studies have revealed the centrality and the originality of the theme of theological life in John, both as synthesis of the communion between God and man and as a basis for the mystico-theological structure of his writings.[22] For John, each theological virtue has profound meaning. Concerning faith, for example, G. Moioli (1982) has provided some subtle observations on the relationship between "*credere*" and "*intelligere*" in John, demonstrating that his reflections develop not out of *intelligo ut credam* but rather *credo ut intelligam*. The union of man with God by means of the theological virtues is realized in Jesus Christ, so that John's mysticism assumes a markedly Christocentric character. For John, all

---

[21]Morel (1960-61); Ruiz (1968).
[22]Ruiz (1959, 1968, 1980).

that we can understand of God is contained in the revelation that Christ made of the Father; faith in a transcendent God is the faith in a God revealed in Christ.[23]

In John of the Cross as in Teresa, the spiritual journey is described through symbols.[24] Where conceptual language cannot but fail, John trusts that, while symbolic language will not totally reveal the mystery, it can suggest what his ineffable experience has shown him about God. John of the Cross does not in principle underestimate the conceptual-discursive language of scholastic theology, but he has a sharp sense of its limits as a "wisdom" about the mystery of God.

Among John's favorite symbols is "night." This crucial expression and experience of the mystical process, to which John provides an absolutely original contribution, has been penetratingly analyzed.[25] "Night" is the darkness in which the soul finds itself during the process of purification from sensible/worldly and spiritual appetites; night is faith for the intellect, the road along which the soul journeys towards union with God; night is the incapacity of reason to understand anything of God's being; it is experience, as in Dionysius, of the divine transcendence that renders fleeting all concepts.

Since man participates in the union with his whole being, since he is the active and passive subject of the relationship, John of the Cross is driven to analyze man in both his stable structure and his dynamism. In recent years, thanks to the lively interest in such questions in contemporary culture, the anthropological theme in John has attracted attention. Scholars have analyzed central notions like "the powers of the soul" (intellect, memory, will), *sentido-espiritu-sustancia* of the soul and the "depth" of the soul, and they have noted the essentially Aristotelian and Thomistic roots, with elements derived from Augustine, of John's anthropological conception.[26]

The link that John finds between the theological virtues and the powers of the soul have also been studied. Faith empties the intellect, making natural knowledge obscure. Hope, understood as the exclusive search for God, is united with memory, since the soul, desiring God's possession, renounces all else and therefore purifies memory of all

[23]Giovanna della Croce (1964); Lucien-Marie de Saint-Joseph (1968).
[24]Baruzi (1926); Morel (III, 1961).
[25]Ruiz (1972, 1980, 1985); Stein (1957).
[26]Pacho (1961); Ruiz (1981).

remembrances that could cause the return of desire for earthly things.[27] Charity frees the will from all affection and pleasure that is not God. Interesting perspectives on John of the Cross have been opened by linguistical studies. This leads us to M. Huot de Longchamp's work, *Lectures de Jean de la Croix: Essai d'anthropologie mystique.* Emphasizing the inadequacy of existing works on this subject, in particular the *Concordancias* of Luis de San José (Burgos, 1948), Huot proposes to decipher John's *corpus* by the network of signs through which he expresses himself, to note the key words and clarify their meaning, grasping what is, one might say, right before our eyes by the very nature of the words–in short, to follow the movements of the experience as they are expressed in the modulation of the language and the texture of the words. At the root of Huot's work lie both the desire to read the text in itself, free from extraneous schemes, and the rejection of "systematic" readings that attempt to impose on John of the Cross their own conceptual systems. (Among the examples adduced by Huot are the works by Baruzi and Morel.) This is a difficult book, almost esoteric in its technicality, yet important. The exclusively philological viewpoint raises, nonetheless, some reservations, as if John's discourse could not in any way imply more general and profound issues. We feel that while the linguistic approach can furnish useful tools for interpretation, it does not get to the mystical experience itself.

Renovation in France and the Abstract School

With the decline of the *siglo de oro* in Spain, France took the lead spiritually and intellectually. The French Church came out of the religious wars exhausted, but from the time of the Edict of Nantes (1598) showed signs of recovery that would grow into a full spiritual rebirth. Within the old religious orders reform movement intent on restoring the observance of the rules arose; new orders, like the Jesuits, the Capuchins and Minorites were introduced into France; and–the greatest innovation–associations of secular priests practicing "the common life" (*apostolica vivendi forma*) were formed and exercised their ministries throughout the world (the Oratory of Bérulle, the Congregation of the Mission of Vincent de Paul, the Company of St. Sulpice of J.-J. Olier, the Company of Jesus and Mary of John Eudes).

[27]Bord (1971).

Between 1550 and 1610 spiritual literature in France lived on borrowings. The most significant phenomenon in this sector, as the research of Dagens, Huijben (1930-31), and Van Schoote demonstrates, was the edition and translation of the Rhenish-Flemish mystics, which after a weak reception in the first half of the century gained great vigor in the second. Intertwined with the diffusion of these northern authors was that of the Spaniards, especially St. Teresa and St. John of the Cross. The Italian spiritual tradition radiated to France through the works of Caterina da Genova,[28] the *Combattimento spirituale* by the Theatine, Lorenzo Scupoli, the *Pratica dell'orazione mentale* by the Capuchin, Bellinntani da Salò, and the *Breve compendio di perfezione cristiana* by the Jesuit, Achille Gagliardi. In 1608 Feuillant François Goulu prepared a translation of Dionysius the Areopagite. This diffusion of foreign works saturated the French environment with rich traditions that were at the root of the spiritual growth of the *grand siècle*.

This renewal influenced the lay world as well; within the nobility and the middle class, groups of devout men formed who gathered to cultivate the life of prayer and to promote ministerial initiatives. A significant place in this framework belongs to the circle surrounding Madame Acarie, who was at the center of the movement for spiritual renewal that characterized French Catholicism in the first decades of the seventeenth century.

The most noteworthy personality of this circle was Benoît de Canfield (1562-1610), a convert from Anglicanism to Catholicism, who in 1586 entered the Capuchins of Fauberg Saint-Honoré. In a book published in 1609 (*La règle de perfection*), but already circulating in manuscript in 1593, Canfield outlined a spirituality whose summit was the absorption of the human will into the divine; this summit was achieved directly, passing over all intermediaries, including the humanity of Christ. Christ is therefore the road to divine being, but not the last boundary of the spiritual journey.

An heir to the Rhenish-Flemish tradition, Benoît de Canfield has never ceased to impose himself ever more clearly as an author of primary importance for French spirituality of the seventeenth century, as is clear from the researches of Bremond, Cognet, and above all Optat de Veghel, who analyzed the sources of the *Règle* (Bonaventure, Herp, Caterina da Genova, *Theologia germanica*). Research on the English

---

[28]Goré (1968).

Capuchin has been crowned by a critical edition of the *Règle* by J. Orcibal (1982). (This undertaking is even more remarkable considering the complicated story that lies behind the editing and publication of the book.) Because of its abstract and speculative nature, Canfield's mysticism was inaccessible to the ordinary Christian, but had a strong influence in monastic society and in the "devout circles" of seventeenth-century France.

Supportive of Canfield's approach were the Capuchin, Laurent de Paris; the Carmelite, Jean de Saint Samson; the Berullians, Condren and Olier; the Jesuits, Surin and Lallemant; the laymen, Bernières and Renty; and, at the end of the century, Madame Guyon. Despite this approval, the *Règle* soon provoked suspicion and opposition, and was to remain at the center of the controversy over forms of mysticism. Orcibal (1959) illustrates one phase of this controversy by studying the conflict that exploded at the beginning of the seventeenth century between the representatives of the Carmelite Reform, Girolamo Gracián and Tommaso di Gesù, both linked to the Christocentric spirituality of Teresa of Avila, and the Capuchins of the Spanish Netherlands influenced by the metaphysical mysticism of the Rhenish-Flemish tradition imported into France by the Abstract School related to Canfield.

Francis de Sales

At Madame Acarie's circle could be found, although in different modes, the two greatest spiritual figures of the seventeenth century: Francis de Sales and Pierre de Bérulle. During a sojourn in Paris in 1602, the Savoyard, Francis de Sales (1567-1622), formed a friendship with Madame Acarie and frequented her circle. Thus he had the opportunity to acquaint himself with "abstract" mysticism. He was not, however, attracted to it because he found it obscure and complicated, lacking in warmth and affect. In the *Introduction to the Devout Life* (1609), de Sales proposed a spirituality more in touch with concrete reality, rich in psychological wisdom, balanced, attainable in fulfilling the duties of one's state of life, not a privilege of exceptional spirits: an idea of spirituality quite different from the "abstract" school. By the time it was published, nevertheless, St. Francis had to some extent already outgrown the *Introduction*. Indeed, certain perspectives had opened up for him that he had not revealed to Filotea. In fact, he had withheld them from her.

In order to understand this evolution, Cognet (1958, 1966) places great emphasis on Francis's meeting in 1604 with Madame Jane Frances de Chantal, who, already advanced in the practice of contemplation, revealed new spiritual horizons to him. Contrary to Bremond, who dates the beginning of Francis's mystical journey in 1602, Cognet maintains, correctly in my opinion, that in 1602 Francis, even though having already had some contemplative experiences, still moved in a substantially ascetic world. His meditations on the writings of St. Teresa begun in 1604 and then his encounter with the first Visitandines provoked his further evolution.

The Carmelite, Pierre Sérouet, has indicated the influence of Teresa on de Sales, though he considers marginal that of John of the Cross. Sérouet places great stress on the Paris sojourn of 1602 (*"année cruciale"*), because at Madame Acarie's circle Francis met Jean de Brétigny, who in 1601 had published the French translation of Teresa's works and who was involved with Bérulle in introducing the Carmelites into France. All this inclines us to believe that Francis, who did not know Spanish, had the opportunity to approach Teresa's works through this translation. While the *Introduction to the Devout Life* bears few traces of Teresa's spirit, her mark is strong in the *Treatise on the Love of God,* particularly in books VI, VII, VIII and IX, which constitute the core of the work.

From his reading and from his association with persons of high spiritual understanding was born the *Treatise* (1616), which expands on the intent of the *Introduction.* In a thorough analysis, the Jesuit, A. Liuima, has shown the sources utilized by de Sales: classical authors, the Fathers of the Church, spiritual writers, theologians, and above all Scripture. His inventory of the sources of the *Treatise* is compiled with such care that one sometimes has the impression that Liuima clings so closely to these texts and to their original meaning that he does not pay sufficient attention to the living thought of de Sales itself with its remarkable powers of assimilation and transformation. In reality, however, Liuima's work is not only a study of sources, but also an attempt to grasp the evolution of de Sales's thought. Liuima concludes that de Sales's personality was marked in a decisive manner by the spirituality of St. Ignatius. While it is legitimate to admit this influence, it is less so, in our opinion, to make it exclusive. We must keep in mind that a number of factors contributed to the genesis of St. Francis's ideas and realize, therefore, that it is unwise to emphasize only one of them.

In addition to de Sales's sources, research has also concentrated on the content of the *Treatise*. Scholars have studied the doctrine of pure love that forms the heart of Francis's spiritual message,[29] the anthropology that recognizes in man, however fallen, a predisposition for a relationship with God,[30] and a Christocentrism understood not as a "devout" Christocentrism, which considers Christ as a model, but as a "mystic" Christocentrism, which sees in Christ the principle that transforms man.[31]

Berullian Christocentrism

Scholars have shown great interest in Pierre de Bérulle (1575-1629). The credit belongs to Henri Bremond, who, in the third volume of his *Histoire littéraire du sentiment religieux en France* (1921), removed the curtain of silence that cloaked the French Oratorian and restored him and his work to us. Especially after the Second World War, Berullian studies have increased in quantity and have corrected any imprecisions found in Bremond. They have also brought to light some new features in his spirituality.

Two works by J. Dagens are of fundamental importance: the edition of Bérulle's *Correspondance* (1937-39) and the study published in 1952, *Bérulle et les origines de la restauration catholique (1575-1611)*. This excellent work is not a biography of Bérulle but an essay on his philosophical and theological formation until 1611, the eve of the foundation of the Oratory. Dagens' fine research makes evident that Bérulle, an extremely well educated man and an untiring reader, was a matrix in which many elements were fused: the tradition of Augustine and the Greek Fathers (especially Cyril of Alexandria and Gregory of Nyssa), the heritage of Dionysius the Areopagite and of Bonaventure, the contributions of Rhenish-Flemish mysticism and of Caterina da Genova, the tradition of the Italian humanists.

While evaluating the *Correspondance* of Dagens' work, J. Orcibal (1965) confronted the problem of Bérulle's spiritual evolution. For Orcibal this evolution becomes clear only in the measure in which one established the chronology of the *Oeuvres de piéte*, published and

[29]D'Angers (1970).
[30]Cognet (1966).
[31]Lajeunie (1966).

unpublished.[32] Orcibal concentrates his attention above all on Bérulle's youthful formation, marked by the influence of Rhenish-Flemish mysticism. A testimony to this influence was Bérulle's adaptation into French of Achille Gagliardi's *Breve compendio di perfezione cristiana* (1597). In this short treatise Bérulle described the progress of the soul, which by means of successive "abnegations" arrives at total passivity. Christ is not mentioned, whereas Gagliardi had insisted on the relationship between the humiliation at Gethsemane and the trials of the spiritual life.

Of particular importance because of reference to the Savior, although not easily interpreted, are the notes made by Bérulle in 1602 during his retreat with the Jesuits of Verdun. Orcibal denies Dagens' theory that pinpoints this experience as Bérulle's passage to Christocentrism, since the mention of Christ would have been determined by the prescriptions of the *Spiritual Exercises;* Orcibal instead dates the passage at the years 1605-6, even though the decisive document is a letter to the Duchess of Montpensier of October, 1608.

The sources of Berullian Christocentrism are to be sought, according to Orcibal, in his encounter with the piety of the Carmelites (whom he introduced into France) in the *Nombres de Cristo* of Luis de León and in his long activity as a controversialist. The *Trois discours de controverse* (1609), replete with patristic texts for polemics with the Calvinists, reveals the new orientation by the prominence given to the Incarnation, the Eucharist, and the Mystical Body. Orcibal then analyzes the great themes of Bérulle's maturity, such as the doctrines of "states," "annihilation," and "relation" (the dependence on God of His creatures). In Bérulle's last work, the *Vie de Jésus* (1629), Platonic and Dionysian themes are again in evidence, inspired by the Rhenish-Flemish tradition of apophatic or negative theology. Orcibal outlines, therefore, the evolution of a spirituality marked by diverse influences but that revolves about several constants. His research, exemplary in its wealth of documentation and rigorous analyses, marked a fundamental step in studies on Bérulle.

Later research has taken Orcibal's work into account when analyzing specific aspects of Berullian doctrine. For example, M. Dupuy studied Bérulle's concept of the priesthood; G. Moioli (1964) analyzed some key works of Berullian language; and F. G. Preckler examined the concept of "states," that is, of the mysteries of the life of Christ,

---

[32]Orcibal (1962).

which, although historically grounded, remain everlasting in their power.

We must welcome this enthusiam for studies on Bérulle, but at the same time regret that a complete edition of his works to accompany the *Correspondance* has not yet appeared. We must in fact read Bérulle's works in the old editions of Bourgoing (1644) and Migne (1856). Many writings, including the "*Collationes*" of 1611-15, are as yet unpublished.

Bérulle strongly influenced not only the members of his Oratory (Bourgoing, Gibieuf, Seguenot, Condren, Quesnel, Duguet) but also Saint-Cyran, Olier, Eudes, Vincent de Paul, Marie de l'Incarnation, Mectilde del SS. Sacramento, the French Carmelites and the layman, Bernières. Nonetheless, it must be pointed out on the basis of recent historiography that these *spirituels,* while dependent upon Bérulle, still maintained their own physiognomy. In short, no "orthodox" Berullians, servilely faithful to the model, exist.

Typical is Charles de Condren (1588-1641), Bérulle's successor as head of the Oratory. Sensitive to the ideas of the "abstract" school, he bends Berullianism towards a docrine of annihilation. The originality of Condren's spirituality consists in the notion of "sacrifice," linked in turn to the notion of "destruction." According to Condren, the creature pays homage to the Creator not by adoration, but by sacrifice, that is, the destruction of oneself after the pattern of immolated victims.[33]

The ideas of Bérulle and Condren influenced by way of Olier the Congregation of Saint-Sulpice, and through Bernières, the Ursuline nun, Marie de l'Incarnation. Recent years have seen a heightened interest in Marie, thanks to the Benedictine, G. Oury of the Abbey of Solesmes, who published an edition of her correspondence. Before the Second World War, Dom Jamet had begun the publication of these letters, but by 1939 only two volumes (up to 1652) had appeared. Oury decided not to continue Jamet's work but to begin anew. He published all 278 letters of Marie in one volume (1971), with copious historical and doctrinal notes. On the basis of his research for the *Correspondance,* Oury constructed the first critical biography of Marie de l'Incarnation. To Oury's foundational studies must now be added the works by A. Thiry, R. Michel, and G. Boucher. Despite these researches, a full-scale study of the Ursuline sister's spiritual doctrine still does not exist.

Some would say that the Christocentrism of Bérulle touched also Duvergier de Hauranne, abbot of Saint-Cyran. To Orcibal (1962) goes

[33]Galy (1951).

the credit for having recovered for us the dense spiritual physiognomy of Saint-Cyran and its relationship to the Berullian tradition. (He thereby destroyed the idea that Jansenism was a uniform and undifferentiated monolith.) Nourished by an anti-humanistic bias, Saint-Cyran's spirituality is characterized by a tragic sense of human fragility and of acute need for salvation through grace. Saint-Cyran derives from Augustine not so much a doctrine of grace and predestination as a conception of Christian life. Like the Augustinianism of Bérulle, that of Saint-Cyran looks to lived Christian experience and does not attempt to form theories. An incomparable spiritual director, Saint-Cyran influenced individuals and communities: Antoine Arnauld, Angélique Arnauld, the nuns of Port-Royal, and the "recluses" of Port-Royal, who beginning in 1637 abandoned political and social life in order to dedicate themselves to prayer, penance, the study of the Bible and the Fathers, and–following the example of the Cistercians and Carthusians–manual labor.

The works of Orcibal, Cognet, and Taveneaux have revealed that Jansenism was not only a theological dispute, not only a controversy with the Holy See, not only a tangle of scathing and often captious polemics, but also a life of prayer, of love of the Bible, of Eucharistic devotion, penitential discipline, and service to the poor–all elements rooted in a profound spirituality.[34]

Vincent de Paul and Service to the Poor

Vincent de Paul, scarcely inclined to adapt himself to an overly subtle and intellectual message, was also influenced by Bérulle's Christocentrism, but he filtered it through his own sensitivities. In fact, Vincent replaced the speculative dimensions of Berullian spirituality with an active and practical charity, and he effected the "adhesion" to Christ (we deliberately use the term dear to Bérulle) by means of "adhesion" to the poor. The influence of Francis de Sales and Ignatius Loyola, however, can also be traced in Vincent–in his predilection for a spirituality based on solid virtues, diffident of mystical languors, fleeing from the exceptional. Vincent also gave welcome to the voluntarism of Benoît de Canfield, understood as full conformity to the will of God, even though he consistently distrusts Canfield's unrealistic perspective. Vincent de Paul is an eclectic who assumes

[34]Taveneaux (1973).

various stances–unified however by one characteristic: service to the poor.

To Defrennes, Dodin, and Ibañez goes the credit for bringing to light the specific notes of Vincentian spirituality and underlining his eminent position in seventeenth-century France. They do this in contrast with Bremond and Cognet, who relegated Vincent to a secondary role in Bérulle's shadow. Within this spirituality, as L. Mezzadri has eminently demonstrated, is included Vincent's opposition to Jansenism, whose peremptory and radical message, elitist and aristocratic, was incomprehensible to the people of the French countryside as they suffered from famine and wars and were defenseless against the powerful.

Recent studies have tried to reconstruct the cultural context in which Vincent de Paul worked in the conviction that, in order to understand Vincent, one must understand seventeenth-century France–marked as it was by political hegemony, by the splendor of the Court, by a cultural and artistic renaissance, but also by famines, wars, and peasant uprisings. Praiseworthy products of this critical direction are the study by Ibañez, the biography by J. M. Roman, and the Acts of the international colloquium of 1981.[35] To evaluate the freshness of this orientation, we must remember that Coste's classic biography in 1932 was pivotal for understanding Vincent's personality, but left in shadow the social, political, and economic milieu in which he lived.

The Spirituality of the Jesuits

If the spirituality of Saint-Cyran and his friends is marked by a sharp anti-humanism, the ascetical-voluntaristic orientation in spirituality is predominant among French Jesuits, in conformity with a general tendency of the Society. The path to holiness is characterized not by a repudiation of nature but by transferring to a supernatural plane the movement of the will; the journey takes a direct course in which any singularity is foreign. The fundamental intuition is clear: nature in its deepest substance is, despite sin, oriented towards God; the work of grace builds on this predisposition of nature, strengthens it, perfects it.[36]

While the ascetical-voluntaristic direction is predominant among the French Jesuits, it is not exclusive. The results of an inquiry, *De*

[35]Ibañez (1977); Roman (1981); Vincent de Paul (1983).
[36]De Guibert (1953).

detrimentis Societatis, promoted in 1606 by the General of the Society, Claudio Aquaviva, are revealing. This document has been carefully studied by M. de Certeau (1965). Several Jesuits in their replies denounce the *immoderatae occupationes externae* that deny them the necessary time for prayer as the root of the evils that afflict the Society. They do not repudiate the labors of ministry but rather, against the dangers that accompany them, they invoke a return to a prayer that is more contemplative than discursive. The uneasiness that the inquiry reveals gave birth in the years 1625-40 to a trend that, though substantially faithful to the Ignatian tradition, turned it in a mystical direction. This was done particularly under the influence of Herp and Benoît de Canfield. The most representative exponents of this trend are L. Surin (1600-65) and L. Lallemant (1588-1635), whose spirituality has been well studied by M. de Certeau (1966) and by F. Courel.

Madame Guyon and Fénelon

Madame Guyon (1648-1717) finds her place in the mystical trends of the century; in fact, she represents their most extreme outcome. Through her confessor, Bertot, she entered into relationship with the circle of Caen and became imbued with the ideals of "abstract" mysticism. She also was influenced by Francis de Sales, the *Life* of Jane Frances de Chantal by Henri de Maupas, and Spanish mysticism, particularly John of the Cross. L. Cognet (1967) has studied her spiritual journey, which was characterized by a progressive process of annihilation in the tradition of Canfield, understood by her as the effort of the soul to empty itself of all that is possessed and to desire only what God desired.

In her description of passive purification, Guyon was indebted particularly to John of the Cross. Her anti-intellectualism is radical. God, who is unattainable by the intellect, must be sought in the deepest depths of the soul. Guyon teaches, therefore, "prayer of the heart" in contrast to "prayer of the mind," that is, methodical and discursive prayer. Much of her writing remains unpublished, preserved in Paris (Bibliothèque Nationale and the Seminary of Saint-Sulpice), Oxford, and Lausanne. The publication of these unpublished works and the preparation of a modern edition of those already in print is much to be desired.

In Paris in 1688 the young abbot Fénelon met Madame Guyon and initiated a friendship that marked *"le début de son calvaire et l'éclosion de son génie théologique et mystique."*[37] Fénelon, who at the time was overwhelmed by a spiritual aridity (*sècheress*) brought on by an overly intellectual piety, discovered in Guyon the possibility of warm religious experience that resulted from abandonment to the will of God, forgetfulness of self, indifference to all created things, spiritual infancy.

Meanwhile, Fénelon, who before meeting Madame Guyon had little familiarity with mystical literature, began to meditate upon the writings of Francis de Sales, Teresa of Avila, John of the Cross, Caterina da Genova, the Rhenish-Flemish authors and Benoît de Canfield. Thus he arrived at the elaboration of a spiritual perspective that the researches of Bremond, and later of Joppin, Varillon (1954, 1957), and J.-L. Goré (1956, 1957), have amply described, while placing it within the context of the cultural and religious life of the seventeenth century.

These studies show that Fénelon's interior experience, although deeply influenced by Guyon, resulted in a personalized vision of the spiritual life in which humanism (*l'esprit classique*) and devotion harmoniously met. The critical edition of his *Correspondance* by J. Orcibal is of fundamental importance for understanding him, as well as for other spiritualities at the turn of the century. The first volume serves as an introduction, two contain the letters, and two contain notes and commentary. These last are perhaps unsurpassed in their field for the wealth of their philological and historical commentary.

The Debate over Quietism

Beginning in 1691, the ideas of Madame Guyon began to raise suspicions that spilled over onto Fénelon. These were the first skirmishes in the controversy that will keep the two most prestigious personalities of the French Court–Fénelon and Bossuet–occupied for several years on opposite sides of the debate. Thanks to studies by Cognet (1958), Zovatto, Orcibal (1968), and especially Le Brun, we are now able to understand the nature of the controversy, which is not only the meeting ground of two eminent personalities but which also articulates, in essence, the contrast between two different conceptions of Christian perfection. In this quarrel personal rivalries, pressures from Louis XIV, royal jealousies, relations with the Holy See, and intrigues

---

[37]Varillon (1957): 51.

with Roman agents on both sides play important roles. Le Brun also emphasizes the distrust of the French national "genius" towards the mystical current from Spain.[38]

With Fénelon the grand era of seventeenth-century French spirituality ends (the *"invasion mystique"* of which Bremond wrote). The condemnation by Innocent XII of twenty three propositions extracted from Fénelon's *Maximes des Saints* (1699) and the earlier condemnation of the Spaniard, Miguel de Molinos (1687), helped place these mystical movements into crisis. But the "twilight of the mystics," as Cognet (1958) indicates, resulted not only from the condemnation of Quietism, but from anti-mystical tendencies that began to arise in France in the first half of the seventeenth century and the affirmation, beginning in 1660, of psychological interests that, with their concern with analysis and introspection, opposed a spirituality that aimed at transcending conceptual and discursive forms. The study of moral problems displaced the spirituality of the mystics.

Nicole, Bourdaloue, Bossuet, and Tronson mark the advent of an intellectualized religion which for Paul Hazard was one of the components of the "European crisis of conscience." Also contributing to the decline of mysticism in France was the diffusion of a rationalistic mentality arising from the study of philosophy and science and ever more reluctant to lend credence to extraordinary experiences. The more awkwardly intense expressions of mysticism, especially in communities of women religious, and the sometimes morbid taste for unusual phenomena added fuel to the anti-mystical trend. The most important factor, however, was the emergence of a spiritual perspective immersed in the realities of the day and wary of experiences that implied withdrawal into oneself, escape into a private world, and a spiritual narcissism. In this context, the lives of Vincent de Paul and of Marie de l'Incarnation, who left France for a mission in Canada, are emblematic.

Achille Gagliardi, Lorenzo Scupoli and Filippo Neri

The splendor of the Spanish and French schools must not allow us to forget authors from other geographical areas like the States of Italy. The Italian Jesuit, Achille Gagliardi (1537-1607), for instance,

---

[38]Le Brun (1972): 642.

wrote one of the most significant works of sixteenth-century spirituality, the *Breve compendio di perfezione cristiana*. Adapted by Bérulle and recommended by Surin, it was placed on the Index of Prohibited Books in 1703 and remained in the shadows until about 1930, when a renewal of interest in its influence on French spirituality developed. In the eleventh volume of his *Histoire littéraire du sentiment religieux*, Bremond emphasized its *"prodigieuse importance."*

Following on the work by French scholars and basing himself on unpublished documents, the Jesuit, Pietro Pirri, published between 1945 and 1960 three important essays on the *Compendio*. These essays link the book to the *"zelatori"* in the Society who were intent on its spiritual reform through an emphasis on contemplation. Although serious and critical studies on Gagliardi have been published, some problems remain unresolved. A critical edition of the *Compendio* would be welcome. Manuscripts discovered by Pirri reveal in fact that the printed versions are defective. Also lacking is a profile of Gagliardi's spirituality based not only on the *Compendio* but on his *De interiori doctrina*, preserved unpublished in the Roman Archives of the Society of Jesus. We need a biography of Gagliardi, one of the most representative figures of second-generation Jesuits in Italy. Such a biography might well throw light on the religious ferment within the Society, on the role played in politics by Jesuits between the sixteenth and seventeenth centuries, and on their relationship with Charles Borromeo.

Several problems remain unsolved even regarding the *Combattimento spirituale* (1589) of the Theatine, Lorenzo Scupoli. Together with Gagliardi's *Compendio*, it comprises one of the most significant works of Italian spirituality between the two centuries. We need an edition of the *Combattimento* that would provide a reliable text. We also need a comprehensive study of it that would elaborate, for example, on the anti-humanistic character of Scupoli's spirituality and define the influences on him of Ignatian, Franciscan (Alonso de Madrid) and Dominican (Battista da Crema) spiritualities. While these influences are often mentioned, they have not been studied in any depth.[39]

Recent studies on Philip Neri, a figure of immense importance and prestige who inspired Bérulle's foundation of the Oratory, often fail to meet rigorous standards of scholarship. New light could be shed on

[39]De Ros (1954); *Regnum Dei* (1958).

him from the huge *corpus* of the Acts of his canonization published some years ago.[40] A positive note does come from the labors of the Oratorian, Antonio Cistellini, who initiated the publication of the *Memorie oratoriane* in 1974 and has planned a series of *Testi e studi oratoriani*. The series opened with the re-edition of the dialogue of Cardinal Agostino Valier (Valerio), *Philippus sive de christiana letitia,* and of other ancient documents of the Oratory.[41]

We would like to complete this *excursus* into Italian spirituality of the second half of the sixteenth century with two great women: the Carmelite, Maddalena de' Pazzi, whose teaching has been reconstructed by B. Secondin, and the Dominican, Caterina de'Ricci, about whom important information can be gleaned from the volumes of the *Collana ricciana* edited by Guglielmo di Agresti. Secondin identifies Augustine, Bernard, Catherine of Siena, Ludolf of Saxony and Alonso de Madrid as the writers who most influenced Maddalena de'Pazzi. This evidence confirms one of the special characteristics of sixteenth-century Italian spirituality: its continuity with the traditions of previous centuries. Thus the doctrine of pure love, vigorously espoused by Caterina da Genova, continues in Gagliardi; the Capuchin, Bellintani da Salò, finds his roots in the tradition of Bonaventure; and Caterina de'Ricci belongs to the tradition of Savonarola and his followers.

Bibliography

Alventosa Sanchis, Joaquín, "Los escritores nordicos y los espirituales españoles," in *Corrientes espirituales en la España del siglo XVI* (Barcelona, 1963): 527-42.

Andrés Martín, M., *Los recogidos: Nueva vision de la mística española (1500-1700)* (Madrid, 1975).

Asensio, Eugenio, "El erasmismo y las corrientes espirituales afines," *Revista de filología española* 36 (1952): 31-99.

Bataillon, Marcel, *Erasme et l'Espagne* (Paris, 1937); *Erasmo y España* (Mexico-Buenos Aires, 1950; rev. ed., 1966).

Baralt López, Luce "Simbología mística musulmana en San Juan de la Cruz y en Santa Teresa de Jesús," *Nueva revista de filología hispánica* 30 (1981): 21-91.

Baruzi, Jean, *Saint Jean de la Croix et le problème de l'expérience mystique* (Paris, 1926; 2d ed., 1931).

---

[40] *Il primo processo* (1957-63).
[41] *Collectanea vetustorum* (1982).

Beltrán de Heredia, V., *Las corrientes de espiritualidad entre los Dominicanos de Castilla durante la primera mitad del siglo XVI* (Salamanca, 1943).

———, "Un grupo de visionarios y pseudoprofetas que actuá durante los ultimos años de Filipe II," *Revista española de teología* 7 (1947): 373-97, 483-534.

Bernard, Charles, "Signification des Exercises de Saint Ignace," *Revue d'ascétique et de mystique* 45 (1969): 241-61.

Bord, André, *Mémoire et espérance chez Jean de la Croix* (Paris, 1971).

Boucher, Ghislaine, *Du Centre à la Croix, Marie de l'Incarnation (1599-1672): Symbolique spirituelle* (Sillery and Montreal, 1976).

Bruno de Jésus-Marie, *Saint Jean de la Croix* (Paris, 1929; 2d rev. ed., 1962).

Castellano Cervera, Jesús, "Lectura de un símbolo teresiano," *Revista de espiritualidad* 41 (1982): 531-66.

Castro, Secondino, *Cristología teresiana* (Madrid, 1978).

———, *Ser cristiano según Santa Teresa (Madrid, 1981)*.

———, "Teología teresiana del mundo," *Revista de espiritualidad* 40 (1981): 381-405.

Chevallier, Ph. *Saint Jean de la Croix, docteur des âmes* (Paris, 1959).

Cognet, Louis, *Crépuscule des mystiques* (Tournai, 1958).

———, *De la dévotion moderne à la spiritualité française* (Paris, 1958).

———, *La spiritualité moderne.* I: *L'essor, 1500-1650* (Paris, 1966).

———, "Guyon," in *Dictionnaire de spiritualité* 6:1306-36.

Collana ricciana, ed. Guglielmo di Agresti (Florence, 1962 ff.).

Collectanea vestustorum ac fundamentalium documentorum congregationis Oratorii sancti Philippi Nerii, ed. Antonio Cistellini (Brescia, 1982).

Courel, F., ed., "Introduction" to *La Vie et la doctrine spirituelle du père Louis Lallemant* (Paris, 1959).

Crisógono de Jesús, *Vida de San Juan de la Cruz* (Madrid, 1946; 2d ed., 1983).

Cusson, Gilles, *Pédagogie de l'experience spirituelle personelle: Bible et Exercices spirituels* (Bruges-Paris, 1968).

Dagens, Jean, *Bérulle et les origines de la restauration catholique (1575-1611)* (Bruges, 1952).

D'Angers, Julien Eymard, *L'humanisme chrétienne au XVIIᵉ siècle: S. François de Sales et Yves de Paris* (La Haye, 1970).

De Canfield, Benoît, *La règle de perfection,* ed. J. Orcibal (Paris, 1982).

De Certeau, Michel, "Surin et la 'nouvelle spiritualité'" in J.-J. Surin, *Correspondance* (Paris, 1966).

———, "Crise sociale et reformisme spirituel au début du 17 siècle: Une 'nouvelle spiritualité' chez les Jésuites français," *Revue d'ascétique et mystique* 41 (1965): 339-86.

Defrennes, Pierre, "La vocation de Saint Vincent de Paul: Étude de psychologie surnaturelle," *Revue d'ascétique et mystique* 13 (1932): 60-86, 164-83, 294-321, 398-411.

De Guibert, Joseph, *La spiritualité de la Compagnie de Jésus* (Rome, 1953); trans., *The Jesuits: Their Spiritual Doctrine and Practice* (Chicago, 1964).

1963): 283-96.

————, *Un maître de sainte Thérèse, Le père François de Osuna: Sa vie, son oeuvre, sa doctrine spirituelle* (Paris, 1936).

————, *Un inspirateur de sainte Thérèse: Le frère Bernardin de Laredo* (Paris, 1948).

————, "Aux sources du Combat spirituel: Alonso de Madrid et Laurent Scupoli," *Revue d'ascétique et mystique* 39 (1954): 117-39.

Dictionnaire de spiritualité.

Dizionario degli istituti di perfezione.

Dobhan, U., *Gott, Mensch, Welt in der Sicht Teresas von Avila* (Frankfurt a/M., 1978).

Dodin, André, *Saint Vincent de Paul et la charité* (Paris, 1960).

Domingo de S. Teresa, *Juan de Valdés: Su pensamiento religioso y la corrientes espirituales de su tiempo* (Rome, 1957).

Dupuy, Michel, *Bérulle et le sacerdoce* (Paris, 1969).

Efrén de la Madre de Dios, and Otger Steggink, *Tiempo y vida de Santa Teresa* (Madrid, 1968).

Egido, Teófanes, "Santa Teresa y su circunstancia histórica," *Revista de espiritualidad* 41 (1982): 9-27.

Etchegoyen, Gaston, *L'amour divin: Essai sur les sources de sainte Thérèse* (Bordeaux-Paris, 1923).

Evangelista García, A., "La experiencia mística de la inhabitación," *Archivo teológico granadino* 16 (1953): 62-326.

Fénelon, F., *Correspondance*, ed. J. Orcibal, 5 vols. (Paris, 1972-76).

Gagliardi, A., *Breve compendio di perfezione cristiana*, a cura di M. Bendiscioli (Florence, 1951).

Galy, J., *Le sacrifice dans l'Ecole française de spiritualité* (Paris, 1951).

Garin, Eugenio, "Erasmo e la Spagna," *Rinascita* 2 (1939): 741.

Giovanna della Croce, "Christus in der Mystik des hl. Johannes von Kreuz," *Jahrbuch für mystische Theologie* 10 (1964): 9-123.

Goré, J. Lydie, *La notion d'indifférence chez Fénelon et ses sources* (Paris, 1956).

————, *L'itinéraire de Fénelon: humanisme et spiritualité* (Paris, 1957).

————, "La fortune de sainte Catherine de Gênes au XVIIe siècle," in Supplement to no. 35 of *Studi francesi* (May-August, 1968): 63-77.

Groult, P., *Les mystiques des Pays-Bas et la littérature espagnole du siezième siècle* (Louvain, 1927).

Herraíz García, Maximiliano, "La palabra de Dios en la vida y pensamiento teresiano," *Teología espiritual* 23 (1979): 17-53.

————, *Solo Dios basta* (Madrid, 1980).

————, *La oración: historia de amistad* (Madrid, 1981).

Hoornaert, R., *Sainte Thérèse écrivain: son milieu, ses facultés, son oeuvre* (Paris, 1922).

Huijben, J., "Aux sources de la spiritualité française du XVIIe siècle," *La vie spirituelle*, Supplement 25 (1930): 113-39; 26 (1931): 17-46, 75-111; 27 (1931): 20-42, 94-122.

Huijben, J., "Aux sources de la spiritualité française du XVIIᵉ siècle," *La vie spirituelle,* Supplement 25 (1930): 113-39; 26 (1931): 17-46, 75-111; 27 (1931): 20-42, 94-122.

Huot de Longchamp, M., *Lectures de Jean de la Croix: Essais d'anthropologie mystique* (Paris, 1981).

Ibañez, José Maria, *Vicente de Paul y los pobres de su tiempo* (Salamanca, 1977).

Joppin, G., *Fénelon et la mystique du pur amour* (Paris, 1938).

Juan de Avila, *Obras completas,* ed. Luis Sala Balust and Francisco Martín Hernández, 6 vols. (Madrid, 1970-71).

Lajeunie, Etienne-Marie, *Saint François de Sales* (Paris, 1966).

Le Brun, Jacques, *La spiritualité de Bossuet* (Paris, 1972).

Lépée, Marcel, *Bañez et sainte Thérèse* (Paris, 1947).

_____, *Sainte Thérèse d'Avila: La réalisme chrétien* (Paris, 1947).

_____, *Sainte Thérèse mystique* (Paris, 1951).

Leturia, Pedro de, "Génesis de los Ejercicios de san Ignacio y su influjo en la fundación de la Compañía de Jesús," *Estudios Ignacianos* II (Rome, 1957): 3-55.

_____, "La 'Devotio moderna' en el Montserrat de S. Ignacio," *Estudios Ignacianos* II (Rome, 1957): 73-88.

Liuima, Antanas, *Aux sources du Traité de l'Amour de Dieu de Saint François de Sales,* 2 vols. (Rome, 1959-60).

Lucien-Marie de Saint-Joseph, *L'expérience de Dieu: actualité du message de saint Jean de la Croix* (Paris, 1968).

Marcocchi, M., *La spiritualità del Seicento francese tra giansenismo, e quietismo* (Rome, 1983).

Marie de l'Incarnation, *Correspondance,* ed. G. Oury (Solesmes, 1971).

Maritain, Jacques, "Saint Jean de la Croix, practicien de la contemplation," *Etudes carmélitaines* 16 (1931): 62-109.

Márquez, A., *Los alumbrados. Origines y filosofía* (Madrid, 1972).

Mezzadri, Luigi, *Fra giansenisti e antigiansenisti: Vincent de Paul e la congregazione della missione (1624-1737)* (Florence, 1977).

Michel, Robert, *Vivre dans L'Esprit: Marie de l'Incarnation* (Montreal, 1975).

Milner, Max, *Poésie et vie mystique chez saint Jean de la Croix* (Paris, 1951).

Moioli, Giovanni, "Contributo allo studio del vocabolario della devozione berulliana al Verbo incarnato," *Miscellanea Carlo Figini* (Varese, 1964): 305-25.

_____, "Sul tema 'Fede e linguaggi della fede' in Giovanni della Croce," *Teologia* 7 (1982): 171-204.

Morel, Georges, *Le sens de l'existence selon saint Jean de la Croix,* 3 vols. (Paris, 1960-61).

Nieto, C. José, "The heretical *alumbrados dexados:* Isabel de la Cruz and Pedro Ruiz de Alcaraz," *Revue de littérature comparée* 52 (1978): 293-313.

_____, *Mystic, Rebel, Saint: A Study of St. John of the Cross* (Geneva, 1979).

Oechslin, Louis, *L'intuition mystique de sainte Thérèse* (Paris, 1946).

Orcibal, Jean, *La rencontre du Carmel thérésien avec les mystiques du Nord* (Paris, 1959).

———, *La spiritualité de Saint-Cyran avec ses écrits de pieté inédits* (Paris, 1962).

———, "Les 'Oeuvres de pieté' du cardinal de Bérulle: Essai de classement des inédits et conjectures chronologiques," *Revue d'histoire ecclésiastique* 57 (1962): 813-62.

———, *Le cardinal de Bérulle: Evolution d'une spiritualité* (Paris, 1965).

———, *Saint Jean de la Croix et les mystiques rhéno-flamands* (Paris, 1966).

———, "Documents pour une histoire doctrinale de la querelle du quiétisme: Le procès de Maximes des Saints devant le Saint-Office (1697-1699)," *Archivio italiano per la storia della pietà* 5 (1968): 389-507.

Oury, Guy, *Marie de l'Incarnation, 2 vols.* (Quebec, 1978).

Pacho, Eulogio, "La antropología sanjuanista," *Monte Carmelo* 69 *(1961): 47-90.*

Palacios, Asin, "Un précurseur hispano-musulman de saint Jean de la Croix," *Etudes carmélitaines* 17 (1932): 113-67.

———, *Storia della spiritualità moderna* (Rome, 1984).

Pirri, Pietro, "Il p. Gagliardi, la dama milanese, la riforma dello spirito e il movimento degli zelatori," *Archivum Historicum Societatis Jesu* 14 (1945): 1-72.

———, "Il 'Breve compendio' di Achille Gagliardi al vaglio di teologi gesuiti," *Archivum Historicum Societatis Jesu* 20 (1951): 231-53.

———, "Gagliardiana," *Archivum Historicum Societatis Jesu* 29 (1960): 29-129.

Preckler, Fernando Guillén, *"Etat" chez le cardinal de Bérulle* (Rome, 1974).

Il primo processo per s. Filippo Neri, ed., G. I. della Rocchetta, et al., 4 vols. (Vatican City, 1957-63).

Reboiras, F. Domínguez, "'El amor vivo de Dios': Apuntes para una teología de la gracia desde los escritos de Santa Teresa de Jesús," *Compostellanum* 15 (1970): 5-59.

Regnum Dei 14 (1958), NOS. 54-56.

Ricard, Robert, and Nicole Pélisson, *Etudes sur sainte Thérèse* (Paris, 1968).

Roman, J. M., *San Vicente de Paul: Biografía* (Madrid, 1981).

Ruiz, Salvador Federico, *Introdución a San Juan de la Cruz* (Madrid, 1968).

———, "Estructuras de la vida teologal," *Monte Carmelo* 88 (1980): 367-87.

———, "Metodo e strutture di antropologia sanjuanista," in *Temi di antropologia teologica* (Rome, 1981): 403-37.

———, "El simblo de la noche oscura," *Revista de espiritualidad* 44 (1985): 79-110.

Sala Balust, Luis, "En torno al grupo de alumbrados de Llerena," *Corrientes espirituales en la España del siglo XVI* (Barcelona, 1963): 509-23.

Secondin, Bruno, *Santa Marie Maddalena de' Pazzi: Esperienza e dottrina* (Rome, 1974).

Selke, Angela, "Algunos datos nuevos sobre los primeros alumbrados," *Bulletin hispanique* 54 (1952): 125-52; 58 (1956): 395-420.

Selke, Angela, "Algunos datos nuevos sobre los primeros alumbrados," *Bulletin hispanique* 54 (1952): 125-52; 58 (1956): 395-420.

Sérouet, Pierre, *De la vie dévote à la vie mystique: Sainte Thérèse d'Avila, Saint François de Sales* (Paris, 1958).

Stein, Edith, *La science de la Croix: Passion d'amour de saint Jean de la Croix* (Louvain-Paris, 1957).

Taveneaux, R., *La vie quotidienne des Jansénistes* (Paris, 1973).

Thiry, André, *Marie de l'Incarnation: Itinéraire spirituel* (Paris, 1973).

Tomás de la Cruz, "Santa Teresa de Jesús contemplativa," *Ephemerides carmeliticae* 13 (1962): 9-62.

_____, "Santa Teresa de Avila, hija de la Iglesia," *Ephemerides carmeliticae* 17 (1966): 305-67.

Valier, Agostino, *Il dialogo della gioia cristiana*, ed. Antonio Cistellini (Brescia, 1975).

Van Schoote, Jean-Pierre, "Les traducteurs français des mystiques rhéno-flamands et leur contribution à l'élaboration de la langue dévote à l'aube du XVIIᵉ siècle," *Revue d'ascétique et de mystique* 39 (1963): 319-37.

Varillon, F., "Introduction" to Fénelon's *Oeuvres spirituelles* (Paris, 1954).

_____, *Fénelon et le pur amour* (Paris, 1957).

Vilnet, Jean, *Bible et mystique chez saint Jean de la Croix* (Paris, 1969).

Vincent de Paul: Actes du colloque international d'études vincentiennes, Paris, 25-26 septembre 1981 (Rome, 1983).

Wright, Wendy M., *Bond of Perfection: Jeanne de Chantal and François de Sales* (New York, 1985).

Zovatto, Pietro, *La polemica Bossuet-Fénelon: Introduzione critico-bibliografica* (Padua, 1968).

From India to Japan
European Missionary Expansion, 1500-1650

John W. Witek, S.J.

THROUGH ITS DECREE on the missions, *Ad Gentes,* the Second Vatican Council that ended in 1965 gave added impulse to scholarly interest and research on mission history. Only some of the principal works of anthropologists, liturgists, and historians that have been shaping this field of inquiry during the past two decades can be covered in this essay. The focus is on the first century of the Christian missionary enterprise in Asia, that is, until about the middle of the seventeenth century. Inclusion of developments into the late eighteenth century would require a separate, and much longer, study.

Discussion of recent literature about these missions written in native languages such as Japanese, Chinese, or others is excluded, as many historians for whom this volume is intended may not possess such language capability. It should be noted that it is widely, and wisely, taken for granted today that younger historians of the missions must know not just the languages of the area but above all its history and civilization in order to place the role of the mission in a wider context. This contextualization has enhanced a number of the studies under discussion herein. But this is not to deprecate the enormous labor of those scholars who continue to collect and publish the letters of the missionaries or who have traced the developments of European expansion from strictly European sources. Anyone embarking on this field soon realizes that vast amounts of data still need to be gathered before a comprehensive study and, even more so, a comparative study of these missions can be achieved.

The order of presentation follows the path of European expansion into Asia. The Portuguese reached India, from which they pushed to Southeast Asia, that is, to the Moluccas and also into Malacca, which they seized in 1511. Macao was transformed into a commercial town under Portuguese control forty-six years later. From these two ports missionary expansion developed even as the Spaniards crossed the Pacific and entered the Philippines.[1] In a series of articles still under

---

[1]Boxer (1974), Noonan (1973-74); see also Boxer (1978).

way, all the papal documents on Portuguese expansion in the sixteenth century are being assembled and analyzed.[2]

South Asia

A significant advance in our understanding of the development of Christianity in India in the sixteenth and seventeenth centuries has resulted from the publication of two survey histories, one by J. Thekkedath, the other by S. Neill. The second of a projected multi-volume series, Thekkedath's study covers the years 1542 to 1700, i.e., from the arrival of St. Francis Xavier until the diverse missionary efforts occasioned by the coming of missionaries "from other traditions." One of its chief strengths is the comparative regional analysis of the growth of Christianity in various areas of India, such as Tamil Nadu, North India, and Kerala. Neill's work differs in that, after a rapid overview of the presence of Christianity before the arrival of Xavier, it proceeds to intertwine the story of the Thomas Christians, Roman Catholics, and Protestants. Perhaps more than Thekkedath, Neill underlines the differences among these three groups. Both writers are aware, however, of the conflicts that existed at that time within the administrative structures of the Catholic Church and its religious orders. Although apparently ending with studies in 1980, Neill's bibliography is especially helpful, for it is divided according to the book's chapters, critically analyzes each entry and indicates divergent scholarly views on some issues discussed in the text. Both of these surveys are highly welcome, since the very few histories of Christianity in India that exist have focused separately on the Roman Catholic missions, the Protestant missions, or on other topics. Such narrower confines have been swept away by emphasizing an integral historical approach toward all Christians in India.

Major trends in research on the missions in India have ranged from attempts to arrive at a deeper understanding of the Thomas Christians to studies of administrative systems and personnel or the search for and discovery of important manuscripts that the missionaries sent to Europe. These are part of an emerging pattern of scholarship that continues to evolve from disparate elements.

The presence of the Portuguese in India led to the discovery of the Thomas Christians, also known as Syro-Malabar Christians. A. M.

---

[2]Witte (1984-85).

Mundadan has indicated a frequently encountered problem in earlier Indian historiography, whether political, economic or religious–the lack of substantial evidence from Indian records. To comprehend the relationships of the Portuguese and the Thomas Christians, he used the fragmentary native evidence and the more extensive Portuguese materials. Contacts between the two groups helped the Thomas Christians become more aware of doctrinal matters, but they very strongly opposed *padroado* jurisdiction and the possibility of enforced latinization. The Jesuits began a ministry among these Christians in 1575. But the problems of mixing the two groups led to an irreparable split under the Jesuit bishop of Cranganore whose "rigid character," in the words of Thekedathu, did not make governing these Christians any easier.[3]

Such research highlights two issues whose study is only beginning to set a trend: administrative structures and personnel. Until the Congregation for the Propagation of the Faith was established in 1622, Rome appointed bishops through Portugal and the *padroado* and to some extent through Spain and the *patronato*. As Propaganda entered the Indian scene by creating a role for vicars apostolic and by bringing in other religious orders especially from France and Italy, the lines of administration of the mission became complex. This problem has not yet been the focus of any monograph, but some lines of inquiry are found in Josef Wicki's study on the *padroado*'s early years in India.[4]

Studies about personnel focus both on individuals and on several religious orders. Georg Schurhammer's multi-volume biography of Xavier is based on extensive research pursued for many decades. Its wealth of data on the missionary himself and on the vast territory he traveled from India to Japan offers an incomparable glimpse into comparative sixteenth-century Asian history. The *Documenta Indica* collection of Jesuit letters, which is now up to 1594, sheds light on the problems of personnel working under vastly different conditions from those in Europe.[5] The researches of Achilles Meersman led to the publication of his authoritative work on the Franciscan provinces up to 1835. He admitted he could not achieve his hope of writing a thorough history because of the lack of documentation. In fact, the *Conquista Espiritual do Oriente,* written in 1635 but published only two decades ago, provides much vital information about Franciscan

[3]Thekedathu (1972): 164.
[4]Wicki (1972).
[5]Wicki (1948-84).

missionary activity.[6] On the Augustinians, T. A. López and A. Hartmann have written lengthy articles that could well be developed into monographs. The fourth and fifth archbishops of Goa, both Dominicans, proved to be capable reformers in the spirit of the Council of Trent.[7] This is an intriguing topic in Indian history that needs to be pursued further.

The missionaries' understanding of the native civilization is an intricate but significant aspect of mission history. Studies of several recently found manuscripts of the Jesuits, Heinrich Roth and Roberto de Nobili, have led to a reassessment of their leadership in Indology. Roth's writings on Sanskrit philology and Vedanta thought were known in Europe a decade after his death in 1668, but his Sanskrit grammar and related documents, discovered only in 1967 in Rome, indicate that he was the first European pioneer in Sanskrit language studies.[8] The earlier Jesuits had concentrated on Persian and the study of Islam with the idea of affecting change in the Mughal Empire. For Roth, however, the key to possible conversion of the great majority of the people, who were Hindus, not Muslims, was through knowledge of Sanskrit. Similarly, the discovery of several Tamil and Latin works on adaptation of Catholicism to India and its customs has created a clearer appreciation of this missionary.[9]

Xavier Rajamanickam has also shown that Nobili wrote at least one Sanskrit work, though others have also been ascribed to him. On these documents research is still in progress. Nobili's works include catechisms and sermons he delivered, and these too need further scrutiny to ascertain in depth his missionary methods. Nonetheless, Richard de Smet has already shown that Nobili gained insights into the thought of Sankara (788-820), the foremost leader of the Vedanta school, which since the ninth century had been the prevailing philosophy of India. Nobili sought interconnections of Christian ideas with this Hindu system that was so pervasive among the intellectual elite of India.

---

[6]Trindade (1962-67).
[7]Wicki (1968, 1978).
[8]Camps (1969); see also Correia-Afonso (1981).
[9]Rajamanickam (1971, 1972a, 1972b).

Southeast Asia

Recent historiography on the missions in the vast and diverse area of Southeast Asia has focused on two regions, the Moluccas and the Philippines. This strategic zone for the commercial interests of several European countries was also the crossroads where the *padroado* and the *patronato* with their differing ecclesiastical jurisdictions intersected. Of all the Jesuit missions in Asia, only the Moluccas have now been thoroughly documented, by Hubert Jacobs. The mission, begun in the days of Xavier and dependent on the *padroado* administration in India, was forced to break those ties as the Spanish military from the Philippines seized Ternate in 1606. Spanish Jesuits replaced their Portuguese confreres and continued the mission until 1682. A more significant struggle, however, was that between the Christians and the Muslims, for it was in this area that the furthest extent of the Muslim world in Asia was being attained. As Jacobs has suggested, research in Muslim sources is needed if in order to arrive at a full and balanced view of the conflict.

Recent studies on the Philippines have caused us to realize that two interlocking realities characterized that area: it was a mission open to several religious orders, and it was at the same time a station from which to reach other parts of Asia. In sixteenth-century Spain, the mendicant orders and the Jesuits had a common desire to evangelize China. Mexico was considered the first stop and the Philippines as the second on the way to the Middle Kingdom.[10] By 1567 Spanish religious authorities knew that travel from Seville to Japan or China was possible by this route in about six months, compared to two years by way of Portugal, Goa, and Macao. The Philippines thus became a target for missionary activity in order to establish a base for further missionary expansion. The increasing presence of Chinese on the islands was utilized by the Augustinians to learn several southern Chinese dialects and thereby gain entry into China. The Spanish massacre of the Chinese in 1603, however, dispelled for a time any possibility of such an entry.[11] Several decades later a few Jesuits from the Philippines eventually reached China, which had been their ultimate mission goal.[12] Studies of these phenomena underline the need to abandon the view that missionaries were those who left Europe, reached a designated post and

[10]Beckmann (1963-64).
[11]Chan (1978).
[12]Sebes (1978).

stayed there until death.

The Philippines was, however, a mission in its own right. Recent research has examined the roles played in the endeavor by the religious orders as well as by the episcopate. The Augustinians who accompanied the first conquerors of the Philippines made great strides in conversions.[13] This did not mean they agreed with every move of the government, since Fray Martín de Rada eloquently defended the rights and customs of the Filipinos against the Manila authorities.[14] His latest biography emphasizes that Rada's quixotic life was not always fathomable to his peers, and that the conquest cannot be viewed as a total destruction of all Filipino mores. Recently found documents have revealed additional aspects of the evangelization methods of the Franciscans.[15] This data can be evaluated quite positively with a newer approach, a comparative study of published catechisms, grammars, and a sixteenth-century Tagalog manuscript of the Decalogue.[16] This methodology reveals the social and religious customs of the Filipinos and the extent to which the missionaries tried to transform their non-Christian way of life.

Publication of the annals of the early Philippine church and the acts of the first synod in Manila helped lay the groundwork for further research.[17] Horacio de la Costa (1969) has presented a useful survey of episcopal jurisdiction. Lucio Gutiérrez has analyzed in depth the career of the first bishop, Domingo de Salazar, O.P., who struggled for justice and humanization in the conquest of the islands.

Beyond the island of Luzon, Samar and Leyte were also the focus of missionary endeavor. In a series of articles as part of an ongoing project, a Dominican and a Franciscan have been editing a manuscript of the Jesuit, Ignacio Alzina, who labored on both of those islands.[18] In the seven installments published thus far, descriptions of towns, piratical raids, native uprisings, and missionary methods are included. Several of these topics de la Costa had already discussed in his history of the Jesuits in the Philippines (1967). The availability of the complete Alzina manuscripts augurs well for a realistic understanding of the development of the mission as it interacted with the local populace.

---

[13]San Agustín (1975).
[14]Galende (1980).
[15]Fuertes (1982, 1983).
[16]Rosales (1984).
[17]"Anales" (1967-69), "Actas" (1969).
[18]Fernández and Kobak (1979-83).

East Asia

The principal foci of research on the missions of China and Japan have been the search for documentation, studies on the founders of these missions, and the beginnings of the Chinese Rites controversy. There is a vast array of subtopics within each of these themes, but space limitations prevent their presentation.

For an understanding of the Japan mission, which was at first granted to the Jesuits alone, the works of Josef Schütte are indispensable. His introductory volume lays out his worldwide search for archival materials to prepare the publication of the letters from the mission.[19] In the first volume of the *Monumenta Historiae Japóniae,* he published the catalogues of the personnel from 1553 to 1654. He continued searching for more manuscripts at the Royal Academy of History and the National Archives in Madrid.[20] The publication of the volumes of letters was interrupted by his death in 1981, but the work is under way once more.

The apostolate of Xavier and his immediate successors in Japan has been analyzed from several perspectives. The last volume of Schurhammer's biography depicts in great detail Xavier's extraordinary role as a missionary. Despite Schurhammer's clear admiration for Xavier, this is a critical biography that highlights the mistakes Xavier made in the initial stages of his work in Japan and also casts light on the evolution of his project of accommodating the Church to the Japanese. In fact, this development of accommodation in Japan contrasts with a different policy he had followed in India. The immediate successors of Xavier in Japan did not thoroughly implement this newer policy, but upon the arrival of Alessandro Valignano as Visitor thirty years later, a plan of evangelization much less western-oriented was adopted. An English translation of Schütte's two volumes describing Valignano's missionary principles is now available.[21] One of the more glaring needs in this field is a full-length biography of Valignano to help us better comprehend his progressive leadership concerning the missions in India, China, and Japan.

"Catechumenizing" and the liturgy as the steps the missionaries followed to explain the faith to the Japanese are the focus of some

---

[19]Schütte (1968).
[20]Schütte (1975, 1976, 1978-79).
[21]Schütte (1980-85), Willeke (1975).

significant research by López Gay.[22] Conceptualizing basic beliefs and using different language styles to explain them to the upper and lower classes were only the first phase of the missionary enterprise. Another was the adaptation of the liturgical reforms of the Council of Trent, especially regarding sacred music, services for the dead, and the dispensing of the sacraments to the Christians. Sociological analysis of such religious and cultural contact explains some of the difficulties the Japanese experienced in their attempts to understand their new faith.

The acceptance of Christian doctrine by the Japanese, who believed their emperor and their land were divine, is the theme of one of the more important recent works. In *Deus Destroyed*, George Elison has argued that, although there was a Christian attempt at an ethical synthesis and an evolution of a policy of accommodation, the missionaries' "cultural contribution to Japan was nil," a statement that he qualifies later.[23] By translating the tracts of the leading apostates, including Fabian Fucan, Elison underscores the rift between some of the Japanese intelligentsia and the Church. Yet the very strong adherence to their faith among the majority of the Japanese Christians, elite and peasant alike, has become even clearer from the recently discovered letter of a leading Christian daimyo, Takayama Ukon, and by a study of the Shimabara Rebellion.[24] The causes for the Rebellion no longer can be ascribed only to the cruelty of the local daimyo, but are seen to be due as well to the economic hardships faced by the "persecuted Christians."[25]

Two histories of Japan written by the missionaries themselves disclose their extensive knowledge of the country. João Rodrigues's overview of the sixteenth-century Church in Japan is now available in an English translation. Michael Cooper's biography of Rodrigues explores much further the impact of this young Portuguese boy who came to Japan, became a Jesuit, and then later an influential interpreter for the missionaries and merchants with the highest officials.[26] Although some parts of Luis Frois's history have been available in German for some time, the entire multi-volume work has only recently begun to appear. It helps in understanding Japanese society and culture as the European missionaries experienced them. One of the more

[22]López Gay (1966, 1970, 1971-72).
[23]Elison (1973): 248.
[24]"A Samurai," (1981).
[25]Sebes (1979).
[26]Cooper (1973, 1974).

significant insights it offers is that the great military unifier, Toyotomi Hideyoshi, had more definite attitudes towards Japanese religion and Christianity than historians of Japan have contended during the last several decades.[27]

The cultural interchange of the European missionaries and the Japanese are the focus of several recent works. Michael Cooper (1965) has published an important anthology of reports on Japan by Europeans that touch on language, housing, clothing, and similar topics. A complementary, scholarly study (1971) offers six essays on the missionary presence. Its more than a hundred illustrations are very helpful for attaining some impression of the impact of the missionaries, especially in Namban (Southern Barbarian) art.

All of these studies on the missions in Japan have been widely received within certain circles, but they cannot compare to the audience in the United States and abroad that saw the 1980 television series *Shogun* based on the novel of the same name. In reviewing a collection of essays on methods of learning from the novel, G. Cameron Hurst remarked on the absence of any comment on the missionaries in the volume and added that it was "hard to imagine a more defamatory view of any religious group than Clavell's depiction of the Jesuits."[28] An analysis of this issue in the novel and in the television series, which altered some parts of the novel, remains an unfinished task.

Several lines of inquiry about the China mission have been particularly effectively pursued in recent years–studies about leading missionaries, collections of documents, and theoretical questions of missiology. These publications mark distinct advances in mission history. As several of the authors are primarily sinologists, they saw the need to address mission issues as part of Chinese history.

Biographical data on the Jesuits in China and an outline of the mission up to 1800 appeared in the indispensable *Répertoire des Jésuites de Chine.*[29] Updating the earlier work of A. Pfister (1932-34), this biographical registry offers more details and includes secondary literature for each entry. Although many of the annual Jesuit letters from the mission were published within a few years after their receipt, only recently has a list of these letters sent from China and widely read in Europe been completed.[30] There is no published collection of the

[27]Wicki (1984).
[28]Hurst (1981).
[29]Dehergne (1973).
[30]Dehergne (1980).

many letters the Jesuits sent to Rome, although preparation of the first volume of them is under way. In fact, the only continuous publication of missionary letters from sixteenth- and seventeenth-century China is the *Sinica Franciscana* collection, which now covers up to 1692.[31]

On the occasion of the fourth centenary of the entry of Matteo Ricci into China in 1583, several symposia were held and their proceedings have appeared. Before the centenary two noteworthy studies about Ricci were completed. G. Harris focused on Ricci's mission from an anthropological perspective as "an effort at guided culture change" in China. This lengthy article moved the focus from the person of Ricci to his accommodation policy and its effects in China. Citing both Chinese and western sources, the outstanding sinologist, W. Franke, sketched, however, a remarkable biography of Ricci. At the international meeting in Macerata (Ricci's birthplace) and in Rome, some of Europe's foremost sinologists and historians of the missions presented the results of new research on several aspects of Ricci's life and work. These include the impact of Ricci's publications on the diffusion of European culture in Japan and on Goethe's understanding of Chinese thought.[32] Forty papers were presented at the international symposium in Taipei, and they include study of the foundations of intercultural exchange that Ricci created and that permeated the mission in later years.[33]

An important factor in Ricci's reception in China was his prodigious memory based on his memory place system, which Jonathan Spence has described in an impressionistic sketch of Ricci. As an apostle in China, Ricci was a "prophet of action and a precursor" who had no elaborate theory of evangelization, according to Yves Raguin, but presented a "global message" that was religious, human, and scientific.[34] Scholars in the People's Republic of China have evinced a generally positive appreciation of Ricci.[35] They are not very dissimilar from their sixteenth-century counterparts in their evaluation of Ricci's principal work on the Christian principles, which has recently appeared in an English translation.[36]

Assessments of the possible compatibility of Christianity and Confucianism presented by Ricci and his successors are one of the more

[31]Van den Wyngaert (1929-75).
[32]Cigliano (1984).
[33]Lo (1983).
[34]Raguin (1985): 20.
[35]Nalet (1984).
[36]Sebes (1984), Ricci (1985).

significant advances in recent studies of the China mission. Utilizing Chinese Buddhist–not necessarily Confucian–writings against Ricci, Jacques Gernet has argued that bridging the gap was nearly impossible. Linguistic and morphological structures oriented Chinese and Western thought in different directions, since religious and intellectual traditions on each side resulted from basically diverse philosophical and socio-political systems. D. Lancashire had earlier discussed such Buddhist reactions to Christianity (1968-69), but Gernet was unaware of these essays. In a further analysis of the first encounter of Christianity in China, John Young contends that "Confucianism and Christianity could not have been reconciled without a fatal compromise on both sides." Ricci's policy of accommodation was not necessarily self-defeating, however, though its failure was inevitable in China, as those who tolerated Christianity "understood it from a Confucian perspective."[37]

Gernet and Young were unaware of each other's work, and neither reflect any acquaintance with German scholarship. Monika Übelhör's study on Hsü Kuang-ch'i, the agronomist-scholar who later became a convert, highlights his place in early Chinese Christianity.[38] Moreover, her analysis of the intellectual currents in late Ming China as they intersected with the work of the Jesuits is seminal.[39] Prospects in China for the reception of Western ideas at the opening of the seventeenth century were bright, but the Jesuits could not overcome the intolerant trends that developed toward the end of the Ming period. Lancashire (1969) also has discussed the anti-Christian polemics of the era. David Mungello has surveyed the impact that Jesuit accommodation had on seventeenth-century European assimilation of information about China.

At first in the mission itself and later in Europe, the Chinese Rites controversy became a formidable problem not settled until the definitive papal decree of 1742, *Ex quo singulari*. Research on this topic has been gradually emerging so that scholars outside mission history can now have recourse to several significant studies. The encyclopedia article by Francis A. Rouleau remains a fundamental guideline. The origins of the controversy, especially as it came to the attention of the Propaganda by 1643, has been studied by utilizing several important archives in Rome.[40] Trying to show that the Franciscan friars were "not

---

[37]Young (1983): 127-28.
[38]Übelhör (1968-69).
[39]Übelhör (1972).
[40]Margiotti (1979a).

rigid stereotypes" or "reactionaries" in China, J. S. Cummins has surveyed the differences of their missionary methods from those of the Jesuits. Yet the leading Franciscan expert on China, Fortunato Margiotti, in the same collection of essays with Cummins (1979b), notes that Franciscan attitudes in the Rites controversy moved from intransigent rigorism to a gradual agreement with the Jesuit views until the Holy See decided otherwise, and then to the acceptance of Rome's decrees.

It was Martino Martini who presented the Jesuit views in the controversy to the Holy See. Joseph Sebes (1983a) has studied his role by reconstructing the argumentation found in Martini's manuscripts. Further dimensions of Martini as a geographer and historian who mediated to Europe accurate data about China are the subject of other essays in this set of proceedings from a conference at Trent.[41] To date, however, no overall history of the Chinese Rites controversy based on the abundant manuscripts and printed literature of the seventeenth and eighteenth centuries has appeared. A brief review of the issue occurs in the opening chapters of G. Minamiki's recent work, which is principally concerned with events in Manchukuo and Japan in the 1930s.

After such broad strokes on a wide geographic canvas, a reader may wonder if there have been any attempts at surveying all of these missions in Asia in a universal historical perspective. Joseph Sebes (1983b) has outlined in a perceptive essay some of the essential elements necessary to develop a comparison of the religious missions among the civilizations of India, China, and Japan. In the first volumes of a much longer projected work, Donald Lach has portrayed the impact of Asia on Europe from the beginning of the missionary enterprise. There is no doubt that European readers of missionary reports were truly beginning to understand world history during the late sixteenth century. Moreover, by a wide-ranging analysis of the seventeenth-century Jesuit method of accommodation in various parts of the world, Wolfgang Reinhard has pointed out its lack of success in Asia compared to its partial success in America. Emphasizing that the pioneers in Asia of such cultural contact were Italians and Germans, not Spaniards, Portuguese, or French, he thereby shows some of the pitfalls of such a comparative view, for the French did not develop a missionary presence in China and elsewhere in Asia until the following century.

[41]Melis (1983).

These three studies in any case suggest frameworks for analyzing missionary history in a wide perspective.

From the short survey presented above, it is clear that traditional history, not the *Annales* school, is thus far characteristic of research in this field. Such a result has occurred, not because the latter may be inapplicable, but because there are many questions that need answers before such newer history can be undertaken. Perhaps the first need is more research tools, like the publication of documents somewhat akin to the *Documenta Indica* and the *Sinica Franciscana*. Documentary collections on the Jesuit missions in China and Japan are forthcoming, but whether other religious orders will follow suit is not known. Then too, the publication of a calendar of manuscripts about Asian missions in the archives of Propaganda Fide and the Vatican would be invaluable. Admittedly, these may only be a small beginning when one considers the vast manuscript holdings of other depositories in Europe and Asia.

With such tools, future research can focus on biographies of individual missionaries besides those already discussed. Full-length studies about Valignano, Niccolò Longobardo, Antonio Caballero de Santa Maria, and many others will disclose the many currents of opinion within a religious order and also among the orders. Such studies will offer insights into how missions were conducted, not just in the principal cities but especially among the towns and villages. The prior training of the missionaries, the preparation and use of catechists, visiting outlying stations dependent on a principal residence, and the development of a catechesis intelligible in the local area are but a few of the topics that will lead to a better understanding of the dynamics of a mission region. Only then can one determine whether and how the missionary presence changed the local area and its customs. Moreover, none of these missions in this period has been subjected to an economic historical analysis. That Jesuits were involved in trading in Japan, which was eventually prohibited by superiors, is known. But the economic life of the ordinary missionary, the religious houses, and the provinces of an order, their linkage with the European trading companies, and their dependence on charitable funds donated in Europe are some themes that need to be scrutinized in conjunction with the few economic studies about these countries and their subregions now under way.

By the middle of the seventeenth century, the Chinese Rites controversy began to create divisions among several religious orders, among the hierarchy on the missions and among various papal

Congregations in Rome. This was not merely a jurisdictional dispute, but it involved individuals in Rome whose attitudes and theological training affected the issue. It was the Asian missionaries who, serving peoples whose thought and civilized lifestyles were so different from their European counterparts, first began to question those in the Church who assumed that unification had been achieved after the Council of Trent. Their questions became part of the Church's dialogue with the world beyond Europe.

These are, in sum, only some suggestive lines of inquiry for the future of a field that has shown vitality in the past two decades. In "crossing the multiple threshold of history," Fernand Braudel has observed, "all doors seem good. Unfortunately none of us can know them all."[42] The history of the missions in Asia to 1650 (and even later) has a great number of doors, only a few of which this essay has entered.

Bibliography

"Actas de Primer Sinodo de Manila, 1582-1586," *Philippiniana Sacra* 4 (1969): 425-537.

"Anales eclesiásticos de Filipinas," *Philippiniana Sacra* 2 (1967): 177-202; 457-86; 695-714; 3 (1968): 147-72; 451-75; 597-627; 4 (1969): 273-95.

Beckmann, Johannes, "China im Blickfeld der mexikanischen Bettelordern des 16. Jahrhunderts," *Neue Zeitschrift für Missionswissenschaft* 19 (1963): 81-92, 195-214; 20 (1964): 27-41, 89-108.

Boxer, Charles R., "Macao as a Religious and Commercial Entrepot in the 16th and 17th Centuries," *Acta Asiatica* 26 (1974): 64-90.

_____, *The Church Militant and Iberian Expansion, 1440-1770* (Baltimore, 1978).

Braudel, Fernand, *On History* (Chicago, 1980).

Camps, A., "Fr. Heinrich Roth, S.J. (1620-1668) and the History of his Sanskrit Manuscripts," *Zeitschrift für Missionswissenschaft und Religionswissenschaft* 55 (1969): 185-95.

Castro, Manuel de, "Fr. Marcelo de Ribadeneira, O.F.M. Vida y escritos," *España en Extremo Oriente. Filipinas, China, Japón, Presencia Franciscana, 1578-1978*, ed. V. Sánchez and C. S. Fuertes (Madrid, 1979): 181-246.

Chan, Albert, "Chinese-Philippine Relations in the Late Sixteenth Century and to 1603," *Philippine Studies* 26 (1978): 51-82.

Cigliano, Maria, ed., *Atti del Convegno Internazionale di Studi Ricciani. Macerata-Rome, 22-25 Ottobre 1982* (Macerata, 1984).

Cooper, Michael, *They Came to Japan. An Anthology of European Reports on Japan, 1543-1640* (Berkeley, 1965; paperback ed., 1981).

[42]Braudel (1980): 131.

_____. ed., *The Southern Barbarians. The First Europeans in Japan* (Tokyo, 1971).

_____. *This Island of Japón. João Rodrigues' Account of 16th-Century Japan* (Tokyo, 1973).

_____. *Rodrigues the Interpreter. An Early Jesuit in Japan and China* (New York, 1974).

Correia-Afonso, John, ed., *Letters from the Mughal Court. The First Jesuit Mission to Akbar, 1580-1583* (St. Louis, 1981).

Costa, Horacio de la. *The Jesuits in the Philippines, 1581-1768* (Cambridge, 1967).

_____. "The Episcopal Jurisdiction in the Philippines," *Studies in Philippine Church History*, ed. G. H. Anderson (Ithaca, 1969): 44-64.

Cummins, J. S. "Two Missionary Methods in China: Mendicants and Jesuits," *España en Extremo Oriente. Filipinas, China, Japón. Presencia Franciscana, 1578-1978*, ed., V. Sánchez and J. S. Fuertes (Madrid, 1979): 33-108.

Dehergne, Joseph, *Répertoire des Jésuites de Chine de 1552 à 1800* (Rome and Paris, 1973).

_____. "Les lettres annuelles des missions jésuites de Chine au temps des Ming, 1581-1644," *Archivum Historicum Societatis Jesu* 49 (1980): 379-92.

Elison, George. *Deus Destroyed. The Image of Christianity in Early Modern Japan* (Cambridge, 1973).

Fernández, Pablo, and Cantius J. Kobak, "Piratical Raids and Native Uprisings in 17th Century Samar and Leyte," *Philippiniana Sacra* 14 (1979): 351-414, 510-68.

_____, "XVIIth Century Jesuit Missions in Samar and Leyte," *Philippiniana Sacra* 15 (1980): 262-319, 478-632.

_____, "Report on the Administration of the Sacraments (Unction of the Sick and Marriage) and the Works of Mercy in XVIIth century Samar and Leyte," *Philippiniana Sacra* 16 (1981): 438-500.

_____, "Descriptions of the Towns of Sulat and Tubig, Bobon and Catarman and of the Palapag Uprising in 1649," *Philippiniana Sacra* 17 (Jan-Apr., 1982): 122-85.

_____, "Aftermath of Sumodoy's Rebellion in Palapag." *Philippiniana Sacra* 17 (May-August, 1982): 106-77.

_____, "Description of the Towns of Basay, Balangigan and Guiuan in 1668," *Philippiniana Sacra* 17 (Sept.-Dec. 1982): 136-89.

_____, "The Bisayan Uprising of 1649-1650. A Mid-17th Century Account," *Philippiniana Sacra* 18 (1983): 89-157.

Franke, Wolfgang, "Ricci, Matteo," *Dictionary of Ming Biography*, ed. L. C. Goodrich and Fang Chao-ying, 2 vols. (New York, 1976), 2:1137-44.

Frois, Luis, *Historia de Japam*, ed. J. Wicki. 4 vols. to date (Lisbon, 1976-).

Fuertes, C. S. "El radicalismo evangelico de Fr. Juan Pobre de Zamora," *Archivo Ibero-Americano* 42 (1982): 751-807.

_____, "Los Franciscanos y la evangelización de Filipinas, 1578-1600," *Archivo Ibero-Americano* 43 (1983): 311-63.

Galende, Pedro G., *Apologia pro Filipinos. The Quixotic Life and Chivalric Adventures of Fray Martin de Rada, O.S.A. in the Defense of the Early Philippinos.* (Manila, 1980).

Gernet, Jacques. *China and the Christian Impact. A Conflict of Cultures.* (Cambridge, 1985).

Gutiérrez, Lucio, "Domingo de Salazar's Struggle for Justice and Humanization in the Conquest of the Philippines, 1579-1594," *Philippiniana Sacra* 14 (1979): 219-82.

Harris, George L. "The Mission of Matteo Ricci, S.J. A Case Study of an Effort at Guided Culture Change in China in the Sixteenth Century," *Monumenta Serica* 25 (1966): 1-168.

Hartmann, A. "The Augustinian Mission in Bengal, 1579-1834," *Analecta Augustiniana* 41 (1978): 159-213.

Hurst, G. Cameron, review of *Learning from Shogun,* ed. Henry Smith (Santa Barbara, 1980) in *Journal of Asian Studies* 41 (1981): 158-59.

Jacobs, Hubert, ed., *Documenta Malucensia,* 3 vols. (Rome, 1974-84).

Lach, Donald F., *Asia in the Making of Europe,* 2 vols. to date, (Chicago, 1965).

Lancashire, Douglas, "Buddhist Reaction to Christianity in Late Ming China," *Journal of the Oriental Society of Australia* 6 (1968-69): 82-103.

_____, "Anti-Christian Polemics in Seventeenth-Century China," *Church History* 38 (June, 1969): 218-41.

Lo, Kuang, ed., *International Symposium on Chinese-Western Cultural Interchange in Commemoration of the 400th Anniversary of the Arrival of Matteo Ricci, S.J., in China* (Taipei, 1983).

López, T. A., "La Orden de San Agustín en la India, 1572-1622," *Studia* (July, 1974): 563-707, (December, 1974): 145-236.

López Gay, J., *El Catecumenado en la misión del Japón del S. XVI* (Rome, 1966).

_____, *La Liturgia en la misión del Japón del siglo XVI* (Rome, 1970).

_____, "Las corrientes espirituales de la misión del Japón en la segunda mitad del siglo XVI," *Missionalia Hispanica* 28 (1971): 323-58, 29 (1972): 61-101.

Margiotti, Fortunato, "I Riti cinesi davanti alla S. C. de Propaganda Fide prima del 1643," *Neue Zeitschrift für Missionswissenschaft* 35 (1979): 132-53, 192-211.(a)

_____, "L'Atteggiamento dei Francescani Spagnoli nella questione dei Riti Cinesi," *España en Extremo Oriente. Filipinas, China, Japón. Presencia Franciscana, 1578-1978,* ed. V. Sánchez and C. S. Fuertes, (Madrid, 1979): 125-80.(b)

Meersman, Achilles, *The Ancient Franciscan Provinces in India, 1500-1835* (Bangalore, 1971).

Melis, G., ed., *Martino Martini, geografo, cartografo, storico, teologo. Trento 1614-Hangzhou 1661* (Trent, 1983).

Minamiki, George, *The Chinese Rites Controversy from Its Beginnings to Modern Times* (Chicago, 1985).

Mundadan, A. M., *The Arrival of the Portuguese in India and the Thomas Christians under Mar Jacob, 1498-1522* (Bangalore, 1967).

Mungello, David E., *Curious Land. Jesuit Accommodation and the Origins of Sinology* (Stuttgart, 1985).

Nalet, Yves, "Ricci et son oeuvre vus par la Republique populaire en Chine," *Recherches de Science Religieuse* 72 (1984): 71-80.

Neill, Stephen, *A History of Christianity in India. The Beginnings to A.D. 1707* (Cambridge, 1984).

Noonan, L. A., "The First Jesuit Mission to Malacca. A Study of the Use of the Portuguese Trading Centre as a Base for Christian Missionary Expansion during the years 1545 to 1552," *Studia* 36 (1973): 391-457; 37 (1974): 317-85.

Pfister, L., *Notices biographiques et bibliographiques sur les Jésuites de l'ancienne mission de Chine, 1552-1773*, 2 vols. (Shanghai, 1932-34; reprint ed., Nendeln, 1971).

Raguin, Yves, "Matteo Ricci. An Example of Inculturation," *Lumen Vitae* 40 (1985): 19-35.

Rajamanickam, Xavier. *Roberto de Nobili on Adaptation* (Palayamkottai, 1971).

_____, *The First Oriental Scholar* (Tirunelveli, 1972).(a)

_____, *Roberto de Nobili on Indian Customs* (Palayamkottai, 1972).(b)

Reinhard, Wolfgang, "Gelenkter Kulturwandel im 17. Jahrhundert. Akkulturation in den Jesuitenmission als universalhistorisches Problem," *Historische Zeitschrift* 223 (1976): 529-90.

Ricci, Matteo, S.J., *The True Meaning of the Lord of Heaven (T'ien-chu Shih-i)*, ed. E. J. Malatesta (St. Louis, 1985).

Rosales, Antonio M., *A Study of a 16th-Century Tagalog Manuscript on the Ten Commandments. Its Significance and Implications* (Honolulu, 1984).

Rouleau, Francis A., "Chinese Rites Controversy," *New Catholic Encyclopedia*, 3:611-17.

"A Samurai and Christianity: An Important Letter of Takayama Ukon Discovered," *The East* 17 (1981): 53-56.

San Agustín, Gaspar de, *Conquistas de las islas Filipinas, 1565-1615*, ed. Manuel Merino, O.S.A. (Madrid, 1975).

Sánchez, Victor, and Cayetano S. Fuertes, eds., *España en Extremo Oriente. Filipinas, China, Japón. Presencia Franciscana, 1578-1978* (Madrid, 1979).

Schurhammer, Georg, *Francis Xavier. His Life, His Times*, trans. J. Costelloe, 4 vols. (Rome, 1973-82).

Schütte, Josef Franz, *Introductio ad Historiam Societatis Jesu in Japónia, 1549-1650. Ac Proemium ad Catalogos Japóniae Edendos ad Edenda Societatis Jesu Monumenta Historica Japóniae Propylaeum* (Rome, 1968).

_____, ed., *Monumenta Historica Japóniae, I (Rome, 1975)*.

_____, *Japón, China, Filipinas en la colección 'Jesuitas. Tomos' de la Real Academia de la Historia* (Madrid, 1976).

———, "Documentos del 'Archivo del Japón' en el Archivo Histórico Nacional de Madrid," *Missionalia Hispanica* 35/36 (1978-79): 137-283.

———, *Valignano's Mission Principles for Japan*, trans. J. J. Coyne, 2 vols. (St. Louis, 1980-85).

Sebes, Joseph, "Philippine Jesuits in the Middle Kingdom in the 17th Century," *Philippine Studies* 26 (1978): 192-208.

———, "Christian Influences on the Shimabara Rebellion, 1637-1638," *Archivum Historicum Societatis Jesu* 48 (1979): 136-48.

———, "Martino Martini's Role in the Controversy of Chinese Rites," *Martino Martini, geografo, cartografo, storico, teologo. Trento 1614-Hangzhou 1661*, ed. G. Melis (Trent, 1983): 472-92.(a)

———, "A Comparative Study of Religious Missions in Three Civilizations: India, China, and Japan," *Colloque internationale de sinologie, III, Appréciation par l'Europe de la tradition chinoise à partir du XVII' siècle* (Paris, 1983): 271-290.(b)

———, "The Summary Review of Matteo Ricci's *T'ien-chu shih-yi in the Ssu-k'u ch'uan-shu tsung-mu t'i-yao*," *Archivum Historicum Societatis Jesu* 53 (1984): 371-93.

Smet, Richard de, "Robert de Nobili and Vedanta," *Vidyajyoti* 40 (1976): 363-71.

Spence, Jonathan, *The Memory Palace of Matteo Ricci* (New York, 1984).

Thekedathu, Joseph, *The Troubled Days of Francis Garcia, S.J., Archbishop of Cranganore, 1641-1659* (Rome, 1972).

Thekkedath, J., *History of Christianity in India*, II: *From the Middle of the XVIth Century of the End of the XVIIth Century, 1542-1700* (Bangalore, 1982).

Trindade, Paulus de, *Conquista espiritual do Oriente*, ed., F. F. Lopes, 3 vols. (Lisbon, 1962-67).

Übelhör, Monika, "Hsü Kuang-ch'i und seine Einstellung zum Christentum. Ein Beitrag zur Geistesgeschichte der späten Ming-Zeit," *Oriens Extremus* 15 (1968): 191-257; 16 (1969): 41-74.

———, "Geistesströmungen der späten Ming-Zeit die das Wirken der Jesuiten in China begünstigten," *Saeculum* 23 (1972): 172-85.

Van den Wyngaert, A., G. Mensaert, and F. Margiotti, ed., *Sinica Franciscana*, 8 vols. to date (Quaracchi-Florence, 1929-75).

Wicki, Joseph, *Documenta Indica*, 16 vols. to date (Rome, 1948-84).

———, "D. Henrique de Tavora, O.P. Bischof von Cochin, 1567-78, Erzbischof von Goa, 1578-81," *Neue Zeitschrift für Missionswissenschaft 24 (1968): 111-21.

———, "Das portugiesische Padroado in Indien, 1500-1580," *Neue Zeitschrift für Missionswissenschaft* 28 (1972): 275-87.

———, "Fr. Vincente de Fonseca, O.P. 5. Erzbischof von Goa, 1583-1587," *Neue Zeitschrift für Missionswissenschaft* 34 (1978): 122-29.

———, "Toyotomi Hideyoshi in der 'Historia de Japam,' des P. Luis Frois, Erster Beitrag, 1583-1587," *Neue Zeitschrift für Missionswissenschaft* 40

The Council of Trent

Giuseppe Alberigo

1. The New Image of the Council

THE RENEWED INTEREST IN THE RELIGIOUS HISTORY of the Cinquecento characteristic of our century found one of its principal objects in the Council of Trent. Many German Catholics, especially, felt the need to understand their religious past. Bit by bit the ecumenical movement began to persuade them that the divisions among Christians were not irreversible but were the result of historical forces that needed analysis and an approach that was neither resigned nor fatalistic.[1]

Since the beginning of the twentieth century, therefore, German Catholics have dedicated a great deal of energy to the gathering, ordering, and publishing of the sources of the Council. The most imposing result of these initiatives is the seventeen volumes of *Concilium Tridentinum*. The volumes include not only the official minutes, but also diaries, letters, treatises, and memoranda written during the Council. These thousands and thousands of pages, practically inaccessible for the previous three and a half centuries, have allowed us to reconstruct and appreciate in a new way the troubled history of the Council and its significance.

This accomplishment is due above all, as is well known, to the work of the eminent historian and convinced Catholic, Hubert Jedin.[2] His history of the Council, a monumental enterprise published in five volumes between 1948 and 1975, has opened to our eyes the inner workings of the Council as well as its ecclesiastical and political context. Upon this base we have finally overcome the sterile alternatives of the completely negative assessment of the Council by the Servite, Paolo Sarpi, and the altogether positive one by the Jesuit, Sforza Pallavicino.[3] The Council, no longer an object of religious controversy, has found its place within history and not outside it, either as demon or *deus ex machina*.[4] Our appreciation of Trent has in the process been profoundly affected.

[1]Zierlein (1979-80).

[2]Alberigo (1980). For a complete bibliography of Jedin's publications, see Samulski and Butterini (1980).

[3]For examples of the older historiography, see the pertinent volumes of Ludwig Pastor's *History of the Popes,* as well as Michel (1938), Richard (1930-31), Cristiani (1948). The new orientation is already evident in Schreiber (1951).

[4]Jedin (1963), Alberigo (1965-67).

211

Above all, we now clearly realize that by the time the Council convened on 13 December 1545, it was already too late to achieve the peace between the warring factions for which the Council had been called. The long, complicated, and often contradictory mishaps through which the idea to resolve the religious problem by means of a council had to pass wrought havoc in the crucial decades between 1520 and 1545. Thus, when Paul III finally convoked the Council, the confessional division was already a reality, the generation that had lived through the original events was passing from the scene, and Christians had become accustomed to living in discord and conflict with one another. The self-interest of various groups had crystallized.

Culpability for the dramatically long delay in calling the Council weighs heavily upon almost all the leaders of Europe, but it weighs most of all upon the papacy and the Roman Curia, victims trapped in their own political designs. The papacy feared from the Council an attack on its prerogatives, and the Curia feared that a real reform "in head and members" would reduce the powers that had accrued to Rome in recent centuries.

The image of a council guided by a clear program for the restoration and vindication of the Church has been completely dissipated by the research of the past forty years. Indeed, the bishops gathered at Trent were few and often bewildered, overwhelmed by a rupture in the religious unity of the West that they did not really understand, uncertain whether the pope really wanted a Council or whether, in truth, he would not think they were spurred by an excessive and inappropriate zeal by the very fact that they even appeared at Trent.[5] Practically none of these bishops had any first-hand knowledge of the preaching and writing of the Reformers; they had to depend for this almost exclusively on the theologians present at the Council.

Their understanding of the pastoral and disciplinary problems of the Church, however, was on quite a different level, for many of them had immediate experience of the lamentable situation of the Church in this regard. We have long known that the Emperor, Charles V, wanted the Council to deal only with such reform, whereas Pope Paul III insisted that only doctrinal issues be discussed so that Protestant doctrines could be quickly condemned. These two perspectives originate, obviously, from two very different evaluations of the problem that exploded in Germany with Luther. According to the Emperor, the

---

[5]Alberigo (1956-57), Jedin (1956).

problem was essentially caused by ecclesiastical abuses and immorality, especially of the clergy. According to Rome, the only important issue was the doctrinal dissent of the Protestants, which it understood as simply a collection of ancient heresies refuted long ago.

The Council found a middle way between these two extremes by deciding to discuss alternatively a doctrinal and a disciplinary issue. This resulted in a slow and wearisome process, but one that corresponded to the reality in which the Church found itself. We must note, moreover, that the Council judiciously imposed upon itself the obligation to respond in every instance to the issues raised by the Protestants and did not yield to the temptation merely to construct independent of them a Catholic *Summa* dealing with the major issues under attack.

2. Problems of the First Period (1545-47)

The first period of the Council lasted from 13 December, 1545, to 11 March, 1547, and included eight Sessions of which the Fourth, Fifth, and Sixth were the most important from a dogmatic point of view. The Fourth Session approved two decrees concerning Scripture. The first of these fixed the canon and reaffirmed alongside the Bible the authority of apostolic–as distinct from ecclesiastical–traditions. It thus repudiated the Protestant principle of *sola Scriptura* while not entering into the question of the sufficiency of the Scripture, which some of the bishops defended upon the authority of Vincent of Lerins. The second decree declared the authority of the Vulgate, but it did not prohibit critical editions in the original languages or translations into the vernacular. The Fifth Session approved the decree on Original Sin, which condemned both a Pelagian optimism and what the Council understood as the Lutheran doctrine of the total corruption of human nature.

The decree on justification, approved in the Sixth Session, is the most masterful doctrinal statement of the entire Council. Although the result of protracted discussion, it still bears the imprint of the drafts prepared by Girolamo Seripando, General of the Augustinians, who was in this matter close to the positions of the so-called Evangelicals. He had even defended, unsuccessfully, the doctrine of "double justification" that Contarini had accepted at the Diet of Ratisbon (1541).

The decree on justification succeeded in both safeguarding the gratuity of grace and affirming the necessity of free cooperation with it on the part of man. Justification was presented as a true sanctification of the creature due to the inherence in him of grace. Through that grace, the justified person was made capable of performing meritorious works, but without this capability implying any prejudice to the sufficiency of the merits of Christ. Human merit was in fact nothing other than itself a gift from God, so that the Christian had to place all trust in God and none in himself.[6]

On disciplinary issues, by contrast, the results of the first period were disappointing. The Council was, in fact, far from having an easy course. The vagaries of imperial, French, and papal politics impinged upon Trent and repeatedly threatened its very existence. Thus, in March of 1547 Paul III's distrust of the Emperor led to the transfer of the Council to Bologna, an act that paralyzed it–the Spanish bishops flatly refused to leave Trent–and culminated in its formal suspension in 1549. If a council at Trent was a cause of perplexity and distrust for Protestants, its transfer to Bologna confirmed their worst suspicions of Rome's desire to destroy it.[7]

Only in 1551 did Pope Julius III reopen the deliberations at Trent, this time with the hope of Protestant participation. The reality of the rupture ultimately brought this hope to naught. Trent was to remain an exclusively "Roman Catholic" council. The religious and political realities of Europe continued to impose upon the Council ever more narrow perspectives, serious and urgent though these in fact were.

In many regions of Europe, Catholicism had been on the defensive for decades. It seemed incapable of overcoming its decadence and its disciplinary and doctrinal disarray, which the polemical denunciations of the Protestants aggravated and kept before the public eye without surcease. The new forces working for reform, like the Society of Jesus, tried to find ground upon which to stand and to overcome the distrust and skepticism about reform that increasingly characterized ecclesiastical circles.[8]

---

[6]Geiselmann (1962) reinterpreted the decree on tradition. On the vernacular, see Schmidt (1950). On the decree on justification, see Rückert (1972), and the fundamental study by Cavallera (1943-52). See also Maxcey (1979), Schäfer (1980), and Olazaran (1957). The observations by Küng (1957) are also pertinent.

[7]Jedin's attribution to M. Cervini of the responsibility for the transfer to Bologna is not altogether convincing. On Bologna, see Carcereri (1910), Jedin (1952, 1960a).

[8]Scaduto (1970-74).

3. The Failure of the Second Period (1551-52)

Cardinal Marcello Crescenzio presided during this phase of the Council assisted by two experts in German affairs, Cardinals Pighino and Lippomani. The problem of Germany was, in fact, expected to dominate the Council because of greater participation by the German episcopacy and because the advent of some delegations of Lutherans had been announced. The rivalry between France and the Emperor again made itself felt; whereas at Bologna some French prelates had put in an appearance, they were now completely absent from Trent due to an express prohibition by King Henry II.

The sacraments were at the center of the deliberations during this period. The Seventh Session reaffirmed their objective efficacy (*ex opere operato*). Taking account of work done at Bologna, the Council dealt with the Eucharist,[9] Penance,[10] and Extreme Unction. The disciplinary decrees were no more satisfactory than in the previous period.

Pressure from the Emperor did in fact bring to Trent between October of 1551 and March of 1552 some delegates of Lutheran princes and cities. Their presence proved unproductive, for they insisted on conditions that could not be met, e.g., a re-examination of all the decrees of Trent already approved. The Council, without having achieved any notable results, was again suspended at the end of March when the Elector, Maurice of Saxony, now allied with France, renewed the war of the Lutheran princes against Charles V.

In 1555 the election of Gian Pietro Carafa as Pope Paul IV took the Catholic Church a step further towards "Counter Reformation," in the more restricted sense of the term. He consigned to the Roman Inquisition, for instance, authority not only over heresy but also over the reform of morals. Juridical processes for heresy were instigated against Cardinals Pole and Morone, and the latter was imprisoned in Rome.[11] Paul IV promulgated in 1559 the first papally authorized *Index auctorum et librorum prohibitorum*, whose severity was so extreme that even St. Peter Canisius judged it inapplicable; it prohibited, among other things, all vernacular translations of the Bible. The Pope, moreover, had no intention of reconvening the Council.[12]

---

[9]Wohlmuth (1975).
[10]Arendt (1981).
[11]Firpo and Marcatto (1981-).
[12]Jedin (1934).

4. The Third Period (1561-63) and Conclusion

After the death of Paul IV, the Council was reopened in 1561 by Pius IV. France finally began to play a role,[13] and Calvinism was now a clear issue. The problem of episcopal residency was addressed almost immediately. Even in the first period, this problem had evoked lively discussions because of the request of many bishops, especially Spaniards, to declare the obligation to be of divine law (*jus divinum*). Such a declaration would have rendered papal dispensations from residency impossible. The same proposal was now made again by Archbishop Guerrero of Granada,[14] with the support of the papal legates–Cardinals Gonzaga and Seripando. Curialists at the Council, led by the third legate, Cardinal Simonetta, opposed it strenuously on the grounds that it compromised papal primacy. Pius IV after some hesitancy sided with the later group, and the legates decided to suspend discussion of the matter. The Council then proceeded to further decrees on the Eucharist and on the Sacrifice of the Mass.[15]

The problem of residency, still unresolved, returned in October, 1562, in conjunction with discussion of the sacrament of Holy Orders. The Spanish bishops were supported by some Italians and by the French under the leadership of Charles de Guise, Cardinal of Lorraine, who arrived at Trent in November.[16] These bishops maintained that not only the duty of residency but also episcopal authority was *jus divinum*. The resulting conflict with the Curialists (the so-called *zelanti*) provoked such a severe crisis that the Council came to a grinding halt for ten months. The deaths in March of both Gonzaga and Seripando were doubtless hastened by the fatigue and tensions occasioned by the situation.[17]

Cardinal Morone, their successor, achieved a compromise. The Twenty-Third Session affirmed that the episcopacy was of divine institution, but did not specify the origin of episcopal powers. It also affirmed that the duty of residence was of divine "precept" (*praeceptum divinum*), a term that still allowed the pope to dispense from the

---

[13]Fischer (1972).
[14]López Martín (1971), Martín Gonzalez (1974).
[15]Duval (1985).
[16]Evennett (1940).
[17]There is no critically satisfactory biography of Gonzaga. On Seripando, see Jedin (1947). On the legate S. Hosius, see Wojtyska (1967).

obligation.[18] This Session also provided for the creation of seminaries for the training of the clergy.[19]

Morone's skills most clearly came into play, however, in his formulation of a general program of reform that represented a compromise between the episcopacies of the various nations and the Roman Curia. Discussed in the summer and autumn of 1563, it was approved in the last two Sessions of the Council, which also defined the sacramental character of Matrimony,[20] and dealt with Purgatory, indulgences, and the cult of the saints.

Morone's reform decrees provided norms for the nomination of cardinals and bishops, prescribed diocesan synods each year and provincial synods every third year, and insisted that every bishop annually conduct a visitation of his whole diocese. These decrees are the center of Tridentine reform. They represent, however, much less than reformers had hoped for in the earlier decades of the century.[21] The authority of the bishops, moreover, lacked a solid doctrinal foundation, which exposed it to limitations imposed by the centralizing tendency of the Curia and by the exemptions enjoyed by the religious orders.[22] Nonetheless, in these decrees Trent rendered the great service of depicting the ideal of the bishop as pastor, as a man inspired by the supreme norm of *salus animarum*. The ideal would find an incarnation in St. Charles Borromeo.[23].

5. Achievements and Limitations of Trent

As is obvious, the monolithic image of the Council must yield to the reality of an assembly whose personnel changed over the course of a full generation, with quite diverse sensibilities, experiences, and cultural perspectives operative as the years passed. (This is an aspect of the Council that needs further study.) More important still, each period of the Council faced situations in Church and society that were different. Even inside the Council, lively and at times acrimonious debates took place. The Protestants were absent, but surely present were various national pressures and theological positions that begot tensions

---

[18]Jedin (1965), Alberigo (1965), Trisco (1975).
[19]O'Donohoe (1957), Telch (1971).
[20]Duibhdhiorma (1978).
[21]Prosperi (1969).
[22]Jedin (1960b), Alberigo (1985a), Trisco (1981).
[23]Jedin and Alberigo (1985).

difficult to resolve.[24] The more than two hundred bishops that participated in the last period of the Council reflected farily well the range of attitudes and theologies that coexisted in European Catholicism at the time. This polyhedral quality of Trent is one of the discoveries for which we are indebted to Jedin. The Council was, in other words, anything but monochromatic, single-minded, or docile and submissive to Rome, as the popes would probably have preferred. Two examples will illustrate what I mean. In the course of the debate over episcopal residency, Diego Laínez, the first successor of Ignatius Loyola as General of the Society of Jesus, sustained the scholastic opinion that episcopal authority consisted in a sacramental *potestas ordinis*, received with consecration to the episcopacy, and in a disciplinary *potestas jurisdictionis*, received from the pope. Despite the authority of the Jesuit theologian, many bishops disagreed with him and insisted that every bishop received in his consecration not only a *potestas ordinis* but as well a share in the responsiblity to guide the whole Church. This might seem to be a too subtle distinction, but the fact that at Trent Laínez's views did not receive formal sanction was decisive for the future. It allowed the affirmation of the doctrine of episcopal collegiality four centuries later at Vatican Council II.[25]

The second example concerns papal authority and ecclesiology. Although these were without doubt two burning issues in the debates with the Protestants, the Council in effect deemed them not ready for direct discussion. Indeed, in all the decrees of Trent one finds hardly a mention of the pope and his powers, just as one finds no decree on the Church in any way comparable to the *De ecclesia* of Vatican II.[26] Here, as elsewhere, the great diversity of viewpoint within the Council made unanimity or quasi-unanimity impossible, which was the condition required for approval of its decrees.

Nonetheless, the image of Trent that has monopolized historiography is that of a Council that "refounded" Catholicism on the eve of the modern era, giving it in its doctrinal and disciplinary decrees a new *Summa* that left untouched no aspect of the faith, of Catholic life, or of the Church. Both Trent's detractors and its apologists very soon created the myth of a Council that was all-encompassing in its scope and imbued with a single and organic unity of viewpoint.

[24]De Castro (1944-46), Gutiérrez (1951), Walz (1961), Rogger (1952), Alberigo (1959).
[25]Alberigo (1964).
[26]Alberigo (1964), Donghi (1980).

6. The Struggle over Interpretation

This interpretation dominated Catholic life for centuries, and even today shows an extraordinary power of survival despite the demythologizing of it in the past several decades. How did it come into being? Crucial is what occurred in the years immediately after the close of the Council.[27] In fact, between 1564 and 1580 a close and decisive battle was waged over the Council. Its center was not Trent but Rome.

The first phase of this battle consisted in the conflict between those who besought the Pope, Pius IV, to accept the decrees of Trent in their entirety and thus to publish them immediately, down to the very last syllable, and those who under the pretext of prudence urged him to wait awhile or, in any case, to proceed selectively by omitting or correcting some of the decrees, especially those dealing with reform. This phase came to a rapid conclusion. Pius IV decided to promulgate the decrees without any delay and in their integrity. His action put the papacy at the head of the movement for the implementation of the Council and over against the confused and conflicting appreciation of the Council entertained by various political entities and the deaf ears of many ecclesiastics.[28]

The Pope's wise, even prophetic, decision dispelled from Rome the distrust and hesitation felt there about the Council. At the same time, it opened a new phase of the battle over interpretation. It was now not a question of taking a position more or less favorable to the Council, but of how the Council was to be inserted into the living reality of Catholicism.[29] Again, two tendencies emerged.

The first appeared quickly, had its center in Rome, took flesh in a series of notable popes, and hinged upon the principle of centralized and uniform direction by Rome of the renewal of the Church. The second tendency, symbolically incarnated in Borromeo, archbishop of Milan, placed its emphasis on an appreciation of the local churches and their energies. This emphasis rested on the conviction that Trent would be transmitted into the life of the Church above all by a vast, dynamic, and differentiated movement of reception.

[27] Alberigo (1981, 1985b).
[28] Prodi (1972).
[29] Alberigo (1958).

These two orientations confronted each other in the years when the young Borromeo left Rome and his papal uncle, assumed with great zeal his episcopal ministry in Milan, and dedicated himself to a faithful and integral implementation of the Council. Borromeo's determination brought into his service a generation of generous men pledged to the revival of Catholicism. On the other hand, it aroused ever more bitter resistance and opposition from the clergy of Milan, from Spanish politicians in both Milan and Madrid, and from adversaries of reform in the churches of the province of Milan, of which Borromeo was the metropolitan.

7. Borromeo's Example

All this hostility, which almost always was directed not just against Borromeo but against the implementation of the reform decrees of Trent, acquired an unexpected gravity when it found echo and support in Rome. There the decisions of St. Charles, especially those found in the provincial synods over which he presided, were subjected to an obstructionism that was as tenacious as it is surprising. In Milan the enemies of the archbishop went so far as to attempt his assassination. They did not succeed, but in any case his early death (3 November 1584) seemed destined to ease the tensions and, indeed, to open the way for an implementation of the Council according to the Roman model.

St. Charles's reputation for sanctity, however, spread so rapidly in the seemingly moribund Catholicism of Europe as to constitute a cultural phenomenon of exceptional importance and interest–a phenomenon still insufficiently analyzed by scholars. We nonetheless clearly see that in his holiness Borromeo joined "private" and "public" virtue, that even his most severe ascetical practices were directly linked with his indefatigable dedication to ministry. Even for those who did not know him personally, Charles Borromeo stood for a bishop pledged without reserve or qualification to the implementation of Trent. Thus the Council and Borromeo were intimately associated with each other in the minds of many people. The great Council had found a great saint to mediate its reception by the Church.

Those who held the fate of the Roman Church in their hands regarded this development with distrust. The publication of the biography of Borromeo written by his faithful secretary, Carlo Bascapè, was doggedly obstructed. When the process of his canonization was concluded in September, 1610, Cardinal Roberto Bellarmino voted in favor of it before Pope Paul V, but he outlined a Roman image of Borromeo that was destined to become official, according to which he was always to be depicted. With determination Bellarmino maintained that Borromeo's sanctity consisted only in private virtues (love of God and neighbor, contempt of world and self). The great Jesuit theologian avoided precisely any reference to Borromeo's pastoral concerns and activity, which he evidently considered irrelevant. In line with this assessment, Rome decreed that St. Charles was henceforth to be pictured in his robes as cardinal, not as bishop.[30]

The long battle over how to interpret and implement the Council was finally concluded. The publication of the Tridentine Profession of Faith, of the Missal, of the Breviary,[31] and especially the Catechism provided appropriate instruments for affirming the ideal of a uniform implementation of the decrees of the Council. This ideal was strengthened by the nuncios and "apostolic visitors" sent from Rome. The local churches indeed assimilated the identification of Trent with Borromeo, but the elaboration of the official image of the Council was a work reserved to the papal theologians and Congregations of the Roman Curia. That task had long since been withdrawn from the spontaneous creativity of the bishops and their churches.

8. The Reception of the Council

We are far from having an adequate and comprehensive picture of how the Council was applied and received. Studies in the past decade, however, have emphasized a fundamental distinction between the Council and its decisions, on the one hand, and, on the other, the style (*tridentinism*) that dominated its implementation from the seventeenth to the nineteenth century. Once again, actual experience of great events has helped historians understand the past. In this instance, the Second Vatican Council and the early stages of its implementation have provoked a more attentive and dynamic reading of the relationship between Trent and its application.

[30]Headley (1987).
[31]On the Profession of Faith, see Jedin (1974), Alberigo (1978), esp. pp. 60-63. On the liturgical books, Jedin (1966).

What happened regarding Trent was that with the passage of time these two terms became identified, so that our understanding of the Council was filtered through the image of it circulated during the centuries of implementation. Only by uncovering the hidden but decisive battles described above has it been possible, now that we have a critically acceptable history of the Council, to realize that Trent has an historical identity not coextensive with the injunctions that guided its application through the centuries. Thus we have overcome a misinterpretation that was due to the long inaccessibility of the sources pertaining to the Council, but due as well to the need of post-tridentine Catholicism, and especially the papacy, to present itself as the unquestionably faithful projection of the great Council.

In fact Rome promoted, perhaps unwittingly, an interpretation of the Council that was alien to the spirit that animated it and to the understanding of it that those had who took part in it. In order to respond better to various pressures of the day, the Council had to be presented, it seems, as a systematic, complete and exhaustive response to every problem. In such a perspective Rome intransigeantly reserved to itself the interpretation of the conciliar decrees. It thereby blocked the reductionist tendencies of the circles within the Church hostile to reform, but it at the same time refused to recognize the necessity of local adaptation. Thus was born the uniformity and passivity of modern Catholicism. Only political power was able at times to obtain some mitigation–usually for only a short while and at the cost of bitter conflicts.[32] In the same way, polemics with the Protestants and the battle with Rationalism led to the desire for a theology complete and determined in all details. This was a theology of a kind that the bishops at Trent repeatedly refused to formulate, conscious as they were of their own limitations but also of the value of freedom in theological speculation and of the sovereignty of the Word of God over every theological system. [33]

Although the Roman Catechism had already pointed the way,[34] it fell to Roberto Bellarmino to provide systematic and closed formulation of the new Catholic theology, presenting it as almost a transcription of the Council. Under the aegis of the Council, Catholic theology in the post-tridentine era closed a great number of open questions, which at Trent were indeed recognized as such. The effect was to put a blight

[32] Jedin and Prodi (1979).
[33] López Rodríguez (1973).
[34] Rodríguez and Lanzetti (1982, 1985), Lanzetti (1984).

on theological pluralism and to promote a false identification of the certainties of faith with theological intransigeance. It consequently became customary to refer to Trent for warrant for theological opinions favored by Rome, while at the same time minimizing any confrontation of these opinions with the text of the Bible. This complex, long-lived phenomenon can appropriately be designated *tridentinismo* because of its jealously defended, but ambiguous, relationship to the Council of Trent.

Bibliography

1. SOURCES
Concilium Tridentinum. Diariorum, actorum, epistolarum, tractatuum nova collectio, ed. Societas Goerresiana, 13 vols. in 17 (Freiburg i/Br., 1901-67). The complete text of all the decrees published in *Conciliorum Oecumenicorum Decreta,* ed. G. Alberigo, et al., 3d ed. (Bologna, 1973): 657-799; this volume will soon appear in English (Sheed and Ward, London) under the editorship of Norman Tanner.
Calini, M., *Lettere conciliari 1561-63,* ed. A. Marani (Brescia, 1963).
Gutiérrez, C., ed., *Trento: un Concilio para la unión (1550-1552): Fuentes (1549-1551 + 1552-1553) (Cartas, despachos, nóminas, etc.) (Madrid, 1981).*
Jedin, Hubert, *Krisis und Wendepunkt des Trienter Konzils, 1562-1563* (Würzburg, 1941).
Susta, J., ed., *Die Römische Kurie und das Konzil von Trient unter Pius IV,* 4 vols. (Vienna, 1904-14), the correspondence of the legates during the last period.

2. CLASSIC HISTORIOGRAPHY
Sarpi, P., *Istoria del Concilio Tridentino* (London, 1619), now critically edited by G. Gambarin, 3 vols. (Bari, 1935).
Pallavicino, P. S., *Istoria del Concilio di Trento,* 3 vols. (Rome, 1656-57); see Hubert Jedin, *Der Quellenapparat der Konzilsgeschichte Pallavicinos* (Rome, 1940).

3. CRITICAL HISTORIOGRAPHY
Alberigo, Guiseppe, *I vescovi italiani al Concilio di Trento 1545-47* (Florence, 1959).
——, "L'ecclesiologia del Concilio di Trento," *Rivista di Storia della Chiesa in Italia* 18 (1964): 227-42.(a)
Bäumer, R., ed., *Concilium Tridentinum* (Darmstadt, 1979), a collection of studies by various authors, with rich bibliography, pp. 541-53.
Il Concilio di Trento e la riforma tridentina, 2 vols. (Rome and Freiburg i/Br., 1965), acts of the international convention at Trent, 1963.

Jedin, Hubert, *Das Konzil von Trient. Ein Überblick Über die Erforschung seiner Geschichte* (Rome, 1948).

_____, *Geschichte des Konzils von Trient*, 4 vols. in 5 (Freiburg i/Br., 1948-75).

Lecler, J., et al., *Latran V et Trente*, 2 vols. (Paris, 1975-81).

4. SECONDARY WORKS

Alberigo, Giuseppe, "Cataloghi dei partecipanti al Concilio di Trento editi durante il medesimo," *Rivista di Storia della Chiesa in Italia* 10 (1956): 345-73; 11 (1957): 49-94.

_____, "Studi e problemi relativi all'applicazione del Concilio di Trento in Italia," *Rivista storica italiana* 70 (1958): 239-98.

_____, *Lo sviluppo della dottrina sui poteri nella Chiesa universale. Momenti essenziali tra il XVI e il XIX secolo* (Rome, 1964): 11-101.(b)

_____, "Le potestà episcopali nei dibattiti tridentini," in *Il Concilio di Trento* (1965), 1:471-523.

_____, "Vues nouvelles sur le Concile de Trente à l'occasion du centenaire," *Concilium* 1 (1965-67): 65-79.

_____, "L'unité de l'Eglise dans le service de l'Eglise romaine et de la papauté (XIe-XXe siècle)," *Irénikon* 51 (1978): 46-72.

_____, "Hubert Jedin (1900-1980)," *Cristianesimo nella Storia* 1 (1980): 273-78.

_____, "Du Concile de Trente au tridentinisme," *Irénikon* 54 (1981): 192-210.

_____, "L'episcopato nel cattolicesimo post-tridentino," *Cristianesimo nella Storia* 6 (1985): 71-91. (a).

_____, "La reception du Concile de Trente par l'Eglise catholique romaine," *Irénikon* 58 (1985): 300-20. (b)

Arendt, H. P., *Bussakrament und Einzelbeichte. Die tridentinischen Lehraussagen Über das Sündenbekenntnis und ihre Verbindlichkeit für die Reform des Bussakramentes* (Freiburg i/Br., 1981).

Carcereri, L., *Il Concilio di Trento dalla traslazione a Bologna alla sospensione* (Bologna, 1948).

Cristiani, L. *L'Eglise à l'époque du concile de Trente* (Paris, 1948).

de Castro, J. *Portugal no Concilio de Trento*, 6 vols. (Lisbon, 1944-46).

Cavallera, F., "La session VIe du Concile de Trente sur la justification (13 janvier 1547)," *Bulletin de littérature ecclésiastique* 44 (1943): 229-38; 45 (1944): 91-112, 220-31; 46 (1945): 54-64; 47 (1946): 103-12; 49 (1948): 21-31, 231-40; 50 (1949): 65-76, 146-68; 53 (1952): 99-108.

Donghi, R., "Credo la Santa Chiesa Cattolica." *Dibattiti pretridentini e tridentini sulla Chiesa e formulazione dell'articolo nel Catechismo Romano* (Rome, 1980).

Duibhdhiorma, C. S. O., (C. S. McDermott), *The Tridentine Canon on the Sacramentality of Marriage (Canon 1, Session XXIV, 1563): Its Elaboration, Its Teaching and Its Scope* (Rome, 1978).

Duval, A., *Des Sacrements au Concile de Trente* (Paris, 1985).

Evennett, H. O., *The Cardinal of Lorraine and the Council of Trent* (Cambridge, 1940).

Firpo, M., and D. Marcatto, ed., *Il processo inquisitoriale del card. Giovanni Morone. Edizione critica* (Rome, 1981-).

Fischer, W. P., *Frankreich und die Wiedereröffnung des Konzils von Trient 1559-1562* (Münster, 1972).

Geiselmann, J. R., *Die Heilige Schrift und die Tradition* (Freiburg i/Br., 1962).

Gutiérrez, C., *Españoles en Trento* (Valladolid, 1951).

Headley, John M., ed., *San Carlo Borromeo: Catholic Reform and Ecclesiastical Politics in the Second Half of the Sixteenth Century* (Washington, D.C., 1988).

Jedin, Hubert, "Kirchenreform und Konzilsgedanke 1550-1559," *Historisches Jahrbuch* 54 (1934): 401-31.

———, *Papal Legate at the Council of Trent: Cardinal Seripando,* trans., F. C. Eckhoff (St. Louis, 1947).

———, "Der kaiserliche Protest gegen die Translation des Konzils von Trient nach Bologna," *Historisches Jahrbuch* 71 (1952): 184-96.

———, "Rede- und Stimmfreiheit auf dem Konzil von Trient," *Historisches Jahrbuch* 75 (1956): 73-93.

———, "Il significato del periodo bolognese per le decisioni dogmatiche e l'opera di riforma del Concilio di Trento," *Problemi di vita religiosa in Italia nel Cinquecento* (Padua, 1960): 1-16. (a)

———, "Delegatus Sedis Apostolicae und Bischöfliches Gewalt auf dem Konzil von Trient," *Festgabe Frings* (Cologne, 1960): 462-75. (b)

———, "Das Konzil von Trient in der Schau des 20. Jahrhunderts," *Jahres- und Tagungsbericht des Görres-Gesellschaft (1963): 14-24.*

———, "Der Kampf um die bischöfliche Residenzpflicht 1562/63," *Il Concilio di Trento* (1965), 1:1-25.

———, "Das Konzil von Trient und die Reform der liturgischen Bücher," *Kirche des Glaubens. Kirche der Geschichte,* 2 vols. (Freiburg i/Br., 1966), 2:499-525.

———, "Zur Entstehung der Professio fidei tridentina," *Annuarium Historiae Conciliorum 6 (1974): 369-75.*

———, and Paolo Prodi, ed., *Il Concilio di Trento come crocevia della politica europea* (Bologna, 1979).

———, and G. Alberigo, *La figura ideale del vescovo secondo la Riforma cattolica,* 2d ed. (Brescia, 1985).

Küng, Hans, *Rechtfertigung. Die Lehre K. Barths und eine katholische Besinnung* (Einsiedeln, 1957).

Lanzetti, R., "Francisco Foreiro, o la continuidad entre el Concilio de Trento y el Catecismo Romano," *Scripta theologica* 16 (1984): 451-58.

López, Martín, J., *La imagen del obispo en el pensamiento teológico-pastoral del don Pedro Guerrero en Trento* (Rome, 1971).

López, Rodríguez, T., "'Fides et mores' en Trento," *Scripta theologica* 5 (1973): 175-221.

Martín Gonzalez, A., *El cardenal Don Pedro Pacheco, obispo de Jaen, en el Concilio de Trento (Un prelado que personifacó la politica imperial de Carlos V),* 2 vols. (Jaen, 1974).

Maxcey, C. E., "Double Justice, Diego Laínez and the Council of Trent," *Church History* 48 (1979): 269-78.

Michel, A., *Le décrets du concile de Trente* (Paris, 1938).

O'Donohoe, J. A., *Tridentine Seminary Legislation: Its Sources and Its Formation* (Louvain, 1957).

Olazaran, J., ed., *Documentos inéditos Tridentinos sobre la justificación* (Madrid, 1957).

Prodi, Paolo, "Note sulla genesi del diritto nella chiesa post-tridentina," *Legge e Vangelo* (Brescia, 1972): 191-223.

Prosperi, Adriano, *Tra evangelismo e controriforma. G. M. Giberti (1495-1543)* (Rome, 1969).

Richard, P., *Histoire du Concile de Trente* (Paris, 1948).

Rodríguez, P., and R. Lanzetti, *El catecismo romano: fuentes e historia del texto y de la redación* (Pamplona, 1982).

————, *El manuscripto original del Catecismo Romano* (Pamplona, 1985).

Rückert, H., "Promereri. Eine Studie zum tridentinische Rechtfertigungsdekret," *Vorträge und Aufsätze zur historischen Theologie* (Tübingen, 1972): 264-94.

Samulski, R., and G. Butterini, "Bibliographie Hubert Jedin," *Annali dell'Istituto Storico italo-germanico in Trento* 6 (1980): 287-367.

Scaduto, Mario, *Storia della Compagnia di Gesù. L'epoca di G. Laínez*, 2 vols. (Rome, 1964-74).

Schäfer, Ph., "Hoffnungsgestalt und Gegenwart des Heiles. Zur Diskussion um die doppelte Gerechtigkeit auf dem Konzil von Trient," *Theologie und Philosophie* 55 (1980): 204-29.

Schmidt, H., *Liturgie et langue vulgaire. Le problème de la langue vulgaire chez les premiers Réformateurs et au Concile de Trente* (Rome, 1950).

Schreiber, G., *Das Weltkonzil von Trient*, 2 vols. (Freiburg i/Br., 1951).

Telch, P., "La teologia del presbiterato e la formazione dei preti al Concilio di Trento e nell'epoca post-tridentina," *Studia Patavina* 18 (1971): 343-89.

Trisco, Robert, "The Debate on the Election of the Bishops in the Council of Trent," *The Jurist* 34 (1975): 257-91.

————, "Reforming the Roman Curia: Emperor Ferdinand I and the Council of Trent," *Reform and Authority in the Medieval and Reformation Church*, ed. G. F. Lytle (Washington, 1981): 143-337.

Walz, A., *I domenicani al Concilio di Trento* (Rome, 1961).

Wohlmuth, J., *Realpräsenz und Transsubstantiation im Konzil von Trient. Eine historisch-kritische Analyse der Canones 1-4 der Sessio XIII*, 2 vols. (Bern, 1975).

Wojtyska, H. D., *Cardinal Hosius, Legate to the Council of Trent* (Rome, 1967).

Zierlein, F., "Sebastian Merkle und die Erforschung des Konzils von Trient," *Ellwanger Jahrbuch* 28 (1979-80): 9-104.

Doctrine and Theology

Jared Wicks, S.J.

CATHOLICS PRODUCED A HUGE QUANTITY of doctrinal and theological works in the sixteenth and seventeenth centuries. Controversy was recurrent concerning salvation, roles and authority in the Church, and a host of ethical issues. Defense of the tradition against Protestant claims called forth argumentative writing by talents great and small, while other individuals turned to the constructive exposition of the faith. New speculative approaches were flourishing by 1600, but rancorous debate had by then erupted inside the Church between Banezian Thomists and Molinists, and controversy continued through the seventeenth century, above all, between Jansenists and Jesuits.

Instruments of Research

The most ambitious exposition of early modern Catholic theology was to be volumes 18-19 of the Fliche-Martin *Histoire de l'Eglise.* Unfortunately, Willaert (1960) breaks off in the midst of the doctrinal problems of the period 1563-1648, and the proposed volume 18/2 has not appeared. Volume 19, Préclin and Jarry (1955) on 1648-1789, has been found seriously deficient on Jansenism, a movement around which numerous issues of the period coalesced. Therefore, the recommended works of first orientation are the concise chapters on theology in *Handbuch der Kirchengeschichte,* volumes 4 (1967) and 5 (1970), translated as volumes 5-6 of *History of the Church,* under the general direction of Hubert Jedin and John P. Dolan. Volume 5 (English edition) includes good surveys on the early controversialist theologians and the doctrinal colloquies by Erwin Iserloh and sure-handed presentations by Jedin on the Council of Trent, renewed scholasticism, and the emergence of positive theology. Volume 6 contains the precious final writings of Louis Cognet on Jansenism in the context of seventeenth-century French Catholicism.

An important regional survey is Andrés (1976-77), on Spanish theology from 1470 to 1570, a work one hopes will be complemented by a survey of developments after Melchor Cano's synthesis, say, down to the publications of Suárez's posthumous works in the 1620s. Many areas of doctrine in the early modern period are treated competently in the fascicles of the *Handbuch der Dogmengeschichte.* Köster (1982) on

228 Catholicism in Early Modern History

original sin and the human condition is an example. Theiner (1970) is valuable on the emergence of moral theology as a distinct discipline in this period.

For building and updating bibliographies, the *Archivo Teológico Granadino,* published in Granada, Spain, provides an annual descriptive bulletin on the history of theology between 1500 and 1800. The two Louvain publications, *Revue d'histoire ecclésiastique* and *Ephemerides theologicae Lovanienses,* provide massive bibliographies that list all relevant books and articles.

Controversial Theology

Recent work is modifying the conventional perjorative assessment of the pre-Tridentine Catholic controversialists. These early apologists suffer by comparison with Luther's verve and incisiveness, but whereas Joseph Lortz judged most Catholic works of the first quarter-century of Reformation argument to be barren and superficial, Pierre Fraenkel recently asserted their basic concern for Christian revelation and for a meaningful cosmic vision of universal order.[1] Bäumer (1980) reviews Hubert Jedin's extensive work, which was usually appreciative of the controversialists. Recent fascicles on the modern period in *Handbuch der Dogmengeschichte,* e.g. Schäfer (1984), give respectful attention to the positions and arguments of the controversialists. Pelikan (1984): 246-74, is a dense and accurate survey of the early Catholic responses to Luther. One can add the easily forgotten point that the early controversialists articulated a host of convictions to which Trent eventually gave concise official sanction and which authors like Stapleton and Bellarmine formulated comprehensively for modern Catholicism.

For work with the sixteenth-century controversialists, Klaiber (1978) provides a list of 355 authors and their works. Gilmont (1979) showed that Klaiber's work is not exhaustive or definitive, but it does present all the representative figures. Desgraves (1984), on controversy in seventeenth-century France, is bibliographical reporting of the highest quality. *Katholische Theologen der Reformation,* edited by Erwin Iserloh (1984-86), sketches concisely the life, thought, and major works of early opponents of the Reformation.[2]

---

[1]Lortz (1968). He rightly excepts Cajetan, Gropper, and Contarini from this negative view, to which Fraenkel (1978, 1983) implicitly responds.

[2]Wicks (1978) provides Cajetan's controversial works in annotated English translation or summary. Strand (1982) illustrates the work of Esmer, Dietenberger, and

At the center of this reassessment of the controversialists stand the critically edited texts of *Corpus Catholicorum*, which has recently had important additions. Three works allow us to trace the main lines of early responses to Reformation polemics against the sacrifice of the Mass: Emser (1959), Eck (1982), and Schatzgeyer (1984). Eck exemplified the methodological reorientation from speculation to amassing biblical and patristic warrants, thus initiating the positive theology that became a mainstay of Catholic teaching in the modern era. The valuable edition of Eck's 1525 *Enchiridion locorum communium*[3] shows ecclesiology and papal authority becoming the topics of first import, thereby setting Catholic thought on a trajectory leading through Pighi's *Hierarchiae ecclesiasticae assertio* (1538) to Bellarmine's *Controversies* (1586-93) and the dominance of institution, hierarchy, papacy, and obedience in classical modern Catholic ecclesiology.

At the Diet of Augsburg (1530) Johann Fabri, then of Constance but soon to be bishop of Vienna, directed a committee of theologians in producing the *Confutatio* of the Lutherans' Augsburg Confession.[4] This moderate rebuttal satisfied both Papal Legate Campeggio and the Erasmian advisers of Charles V and was a step toward the first reunion colloquy of the Reformation era. The agreements on doctrine and the impasse on practices (communion *sub una,* celibacy, the Mass) in late August 1530 still await further editions of the *acta* and full monographic analysis,[5] as do the recriminatory Catholic writings that followed Melanchthon's *Apologia* for the Augsburg Confession.[6]

Eck in spreading a vernacular Bible. Wicks, *Cajetan* (1983) traces Cajetan's career through 1521, highlighting his exchanges with Luther in 1518. Wicks, "Roman Reactions" (1983) reworks the last matter in English. Hallensleben (1985) is a broad-based, quite favorable, study of Cajetan on anthropology and soteriology.

[3]Eck, ed. Fraenkel (1979). Eck, trans. Battles (1979), gives in English the 1541 edition of the *Enchiridion*, the eighth and last revision during Eck's lifetime.

[4]*Confutatio* (1979), also in Corpus Catholicorum, with the contemporary German and Latin texts of 1530 on facing pages. Iserloh, *Confessio* (1980), contains convention papers with the ensuing debates on the full range of theological and political issues raised at Augsburg in 1530.

[5]Eugène Honée is preparing an edition of the documents assembled in 1532 by Hieronymus Vehus of Baden. Immenkötter (1973) provides a concise report on the colloquy of 1530, which Immenkötter and Gerhard Müller update in Müller (1980). Wicks (1980) documents the mixture of belligerence and moderation marking the Lutheran-Catholic dialogue of 1530.

[6]Pfnür (1970): 272-384, treats the doctrine of justification set forth by Catholics in the immediate aftermath of Augsburg. One text from this time, Arnoldi von Usingen (1978), recently discovered in manuscript, confirms Pfnür's thesis that the agreements on sin and justification in August 1530 were quickly forgotten as Catholics went back to attacking Luther's views of the early 1520s that had been significantly nuanced at

On the humanist wing of the anti-Lutheran alignment, Erasmus's critique of Luther recently received two divergent interpretations. Chantraine (1981) oscillates between stress on Erasmus's traditional views and an ecumenical fascination with Luther's dialectics. Boyle (1983) interprets *De libero arbitrio* from the fresh perspective of its rhetoric of persuasion, thus coming to a new formulation of the stark opposition between Erasmus's affable and sensitive pedagogy and Luther's penchant for prophetic denunciation and dogmatic assertions.

St. Thomas More's polemic against the Reformation is newly accessible in four volumes of the esteemed Yale *Complete Works*.[7] Two recent monographs aid considerably in grasping More's religious stance. Fox (1983) underscores More's insistence on human responsibility to obey God's laws and use the ecclesial aids Providence has given. Gogan (1982) traces More's ecclesial ideas. For More, past ecclesial traditions and the present faith of the worldwide Christian community are essential criteria of truth. Early on, More had advised Henry VIII to treat papal authority "more slenderly" in defending the seven sacraments, and to the very end More was reserved about papal claims. His attention to the Spirit's work of inspiring consensus made his ideas an alien body in the papal-centered institutionalism of Stapleton and Bellarmine. More's vision of the imperiled yet militant individual, however, anticipates well the spirituality of the Catholic elite of the confessional era.

In our ecumenical age scholarly interest gravitates naturally to the partial and short-lived doctrinal agreements formulated at the Diet of Regensburg (1541).[8] C. Augustijn has shown that personal contacts before and during the Diet enabled Protestant participants to perceive the Christian dedication and broad theological competence of Johann Gropper and Gasparo Contarini.[9] Contarini, however, insisted on explicit mention of transubstantiation in any formula of agreement on eucharistic doctrine. Gignola Fragnito observed tellingly that Contarini, Legate to the Diet, was less prepared to treat sacraments

---

Augsburg. Dietenberger (1985) is the Corpus Catholicorum edition of a work composed in the immediate aftermath of the breakdown of dialogue in 1530.

[7]More (1969, 1973, 1979, 1981). Six other writings from More's decade as a controversialist await publication.

[8]Fundamental, now, is the critical edition of the *Liber Ratisbonensis* in Pfeilschifter, 6 (1974): 21-88.

[9]Augustijn, in Müller (1980): 43-54, with a good review of recent literature on the Regensburg colloquy.

with the Lutherans than to pursue a dialogue with them on justification.[10] Contarini's dogmatic firmness combined with Wittenberg's refusals to revise the image of the Roman Antichrist to thus scuttle hopes for doctrinal reconciliation.

We can note three significant areas of recent scholarship on controversial thought in the post-Tridentine era during which the lines of division hardened. Thomas Stapleton of Douai and Louvain (d. 1598) has emerged as a significant exponent of the doctrinal points settled at Trent. O'Connell (1964) introduces Stapleton and his times quite well. Seybold (1967) explains amply but uncritically Stapleton's theology of justification, with its Tridentine stress on human collaboration with divine grace. Schützeichel (1966) is a model monograph on the ecclesial magisterium in Stapleton, showing how resolutely he subordinated Scripture and tradition to authoritative hierarchical teaching in the transmission of revelation. Facing aggressive Calvinists, Stapleton had no interest in sympathetic dialogue with appeals to *sola gratia* and *sola Scriptura*.[11]

Among the representative and influential figures of the Counter Reformation Church, Caesar Baronius exerts a magnetic effect on historians. Recently Cyriac Pullapilly provided an adequate biographical narrative and Martina Mazzariol a bibliography of Baroniana complete to 1981.[12] This, however, only sets the stage for a clash of interpretations concerning the apologetical aims of Baronius's *Annales ecclesiastici*. All agree that he marshalled massive documentation in favor of the historical legitimacy of papacy and hierarchy. A first critical question is whether such an apologia really met the contention of Protestant opponents that the centuries subsequent to the emergence of the papacy witnessed innovations in doctrine that obfuscated the apostolic legacy of truth. Baronius gave little attention to doctrine, subordinating everything to defense of the institutional Church. The further question arises whether Baronius's zeal was not exploited by

---

[10]Fragnito (1983): 186f. This compact portrayal is the best recent treatment of the many-sided Contarini.

[11]Recent work on Robert Bellarmine has not focused on his controversial theology but has ranged over his long career, beginning with his critique of Baius in Louvain in the 1570s and extending through his involvement as doctrinal factotum in the Roman Curia, i.e., concerning the Vulgate, the *de auxiliis* controversy, Paolo Sarpi and Venice, James I, and Galileo. Galeota (1981) touches the main issues.

[12]Pullapilly (1975); Mazzariol, in De Maio (1982): 815-952.

those concerned not with understanding the Church's past but with maintaining hierarchical authority.[13] Clearly the Counter Reformation ecclesiastical mind was loathe to acknowledge past or present change in Catholic doctrine and institutional forms. Plausibly, it was "the father of ecclesiastical history" who reinforced a prejudice against history itself, understood as creative adaptation and development.

Two older monographs, Polman (1932) and Snoeks (1951), have not been superseded as thematic studies of the argumentative use of history in a large number of Counter Reformation theologians. The most significant recent works of this scope are George Tavard's expositions (1969, 1978) on Scripture and tradition in seventeenth-century French and English Catholic apologists. Tavard discovered profound accounts of the Word of God in the Church and of its transmission through the close interaction of biblical text and traditional interpretation. Tradition, however, is at times referred to another word as well, the word that the Spirit writes in the hearts of believers. The English Catholic recusants of the early seventeenth century argued frequently that a "judge of controversies" was needed in biblical and religious matters that are otherwise obscure and confused. A later strain of recusant thought presented tradition as a universal cultural process and found in Christian doctrinal transmission an essential component in the genesis and maintenance of faith. Major recusant writers such as Christopher Davenport, Thomas White, Henry Holden, and John Sergeant deserve further monographic study.

The New Systematic Theology

Recent study has treated the expository compendia produced for Catholic pastors in the mid-sixteenth century. Among these manuals the *Tewtsche Theologey,* published in 1528 by Berthold Pürstinger, Bishop of Chiemsee, was a landmark first effort at fusing biblical and traditional teaching into an organic whole for a literate adult readership. Marx (1982) shows how Berthold went beyond arguments against a Lutheran *sola fide* to inculcate a submissive, trusting relation to God

---

[13]Jedin (1978) is mostly in praise of Baronius, while the contributors to De Maio (1982) are more critical, especially De Maio, Mastellone, and Norelli. Pullapilly's final assessment stresses Baronius's preference for textual quantity over quality and his tenacity regarding whatever was good for the papacy.

that readily clothes itself in good works and submits to sacramental remedies against sin.

Johann Gropper's *Enchiridion* of 1538 was widely appreciated in the quarter-century after its appearance.[14] Meier (1975) gives basic information on the origin, structure, and diffusion of the *Enchiridion*. Braunisch (1974) analyzes Gropper's critical dialogue on justification in comparison with Melanchthon's *Loci communes* of 1535, while Meier (1977) presents Gropper's teaching on the priesthood, for which he was both resolute defender and advocate of reform in the image of a biblical and patristic ideal of pastoral service. José Tellechea Idígoras's edition gives easy access to the famous catechism of Bartolomé Carranza (1972), published in 1558 to counteract the tide of Protestant literature then engulfing northern Europe. Carranza, soon to be the victim of inquisitorial mania, combined Thomistic clarity with an unctious portrayal of belief in the redemptive grace of Christ. Ongoing research should further clarify Carranza's dependence on Gropper and the influence Carranza had in spite of the subsequent prohibition of his book.[15]

Peter Canisius's book of adult instruction, the *Summa doctrinae christianae,* came out in 1555 and was revised in 1566 to conform more closely to Trent's doctrinal decrees. Canisius sought above all to give well-argued answers to the issues of Reformation controversy. In contrast, Julius Pflug's more Erasmian *Institutio christiani hominis* of 1562 was less apologetical and more concerned to foster a personal religiosity of trust in God, joy in his consolations, and active dedication to the works of mercy.[16] Canisius's success and the lack of Pflug reprints reflect well the religious priorities of the confessional age.

Significant recent scholarship has dealt with the *Catechismus Romanus* of 1566. Bellinger (1970) underscores its balanced

---

[14]Gropper (1977) is R. Braunisch's edition of Gropper's correspondence down to 1547, to be followed by a volume that will document Gropper's hardening against the Reformation. Pfeilschifter, 2 (1960): 192-305, is a critical edition of Gropper's reform statutes of 1536, the best sixteenth-century Catholic program for local church reform.

[15]Tellechea Idígoras (1973) demonstrated Carranza's dependence on Gropper for the exposition of a single creedal article. He also studied Carranza's transcriptions of Melanchhon's *Loci communes* in 1546 at Trent (1979). His edition of the *Comentarios* (1972) lists his fifty-four publications on Carranza down to 1971.

[16]Offele (1965) studies Pflug's adult catechism, giving a modern German translation on pp. 49-148.

presentation of doctrine, contrasting with the anti-Protestant emphases of Canisius. The Roman manual says little about purgatory and indulgences, and on justification it seems to soft-pedal the role of free, human collaboration with grace. For the *Catechismus Romanus*, the Protestants are still among the *fideles*, although offending against Church discipline. In a word, the compendium mandated by Trent was not narrowly Tridentine. Rodríguez and Lanzetti (1982) have studied the authors of the Roman Catechism, who drew on Carranza extensively and thereby on Gropper's *Enchiridion*. Their oft-noted Thomism in sacramental doctrine comes from Domingo de Soto's commentary on Book IV of Lombard, published at Salamanca in 1557-60.[17]

Mention of Soto and Salamanca introduces a subject of major importance, the Thomistic revival inspired by the lectures of Francisco de Vitoria in Salamanca, 1526-46. Recent scholarship on Spanish Thomist systematics concerns three main areas: theological method, ecclesiology, and justification and grace.

The premier methodological treatise of early modern Catholic theology is Melchor Cano's *De locis theologicis*, published posthumously in 1563. This codification of doctrinal sources resembled humanistic systematizations of the sources of rhetorical invention. Cano's ten *loci* are the documentary fields where one discovers evidence for the continuity of Catholic doctrine.[18] Three significant issues have been raised about Cano's achievement. López Martínez (1962) argues that Cano's manual in fact laid down the sources for censoring and prosecuting those suspect of heterodoxy, an activity that became a near obsession in the last years of Cano's life, 1555-60.[19] Muñoz Delgado (1978) maintains that the option for humanist method and Thomistic ethics brought with it the restoration of an analytically weak logic and an Aristotelian cosmology that had been surpassed by recent scientific proposals. Cano's *loci* organized the work of dogmatic theology, but

[17]Bellinger (1983) provides a bibliography of editions of the *Catechismus Romanus*, but should be used with the third chapter of Rodríguez and Lanzetti (1982), which gives a stemma of editions. The forthcoming critical edition of the *Catechismus* will use the original manuscript discovered in 1985–as reported in Rodríguez and Lanzetti (1985).

[18]Andrés (1976-77), 2: 386-424, treats Cano's *De locis* in its historical context. Belda Plans (1982): 175-385, gives an extensive early text on the doctrinal sources by Cano, probably from 1543.

[19]Andrés (1976-77) 2: 311-29, describes how Spanish culture was transformed in these years by official distrust and suspicion of the critical and experiential dimensions of religious thought.

Salamantine Thomism was alienated from early modern scientific thought, e.g., that of Vitoria's contemporary, Copernicus. Klinger (1978) underscores Cano's importance for classical modern Catholic ecclesiology, especially for orienting theological inquiry to past magisterial teaching. The integrating factor in theology for Cano is authority, since the overriding issue is certainty about the doctrinal *datum,* not understanding its meaning.

Antón (1986) narrates the history of ecclesiology in the second millenium down to Bellarmine, devoting four substantial chapters to sixteenth-century Catholics. Spanish Thomists loom large in Ulrich Horst's contributions (1978, 1982) to the history of Catholic ecclesiology. Horst's report extends from Thomas Aquinas to Vatican I, but the Salamantine commentators on Aquinas's *Summa* represent a critical turning point. Vitoria, formed in Paris, had recognized the great potential of councils for enacting reform. But by the late 1550s, the dominant ecclesiological concern had shifted from reform to the grounding of a single instance or tribunal of unassailable doctrinal validity. Perceiving the Reformation as a morass of subjectivism, Catholic confessional ecclesiology sought above all to lay the basis for absolute assurance of dogmatic truth. Sarmiento (1976) presents and analyzes a representative text, the ecclesiological lectures of Mancio de Corpus Christi, O.P., given in Salamanca in 1564. Mancio, student of Vitoria and Soto, was in turn the teacher of Luis de Léon, St. John of the Cross, Francisco Suárez, Domingo Bañez, and Gregory of Valencia. Bellarmine added erudition to this ecclesiology, but the main direction had been set even before his Louvain lectures of 1570-76. Here the Roman Pontiff was the living rule of faith, a norm affording the faithful the definitive judgments they could accept without reserve.

Luther had also sought certitude and found it in the Gospel word of forgiveness that faith alone apprehends. Trent set forth the Catholic alternative in its "Decree on Justification" in early 1547. Recent research has clarified both the antecedents and consequences of this doctrinal declaration.

Horn (1972) studies Andrés de Vega, a spokesman at Trent for Scotist views on faith, grace and *caritas,* and merit. Vega's *Opusculum de iustificatione* appeared in time to contribute to the Tridentine discussions. In 1548 he published a full-scale commentary on Trent's decree, especially valuable for the differentiations made regarding the intent and doctrinal weight of different assertions in the decree.[20] Vega

---

[20]Both of Vega's treatises are accessible in reprint: *De iustificatione doctrina universa,* 2 vols. (Ridgewood, N.J., 1964).

can put an orthodox construction on *sola fide*, and leaves room for an existential certitude of grace. Practically contemporary with Vega's commentary was the treatise, *De natura et gratia*, published in 1547 by Domingo de Soto, who had been Vitoria's colleague in the founding years of the new Salamantine tradition.[21] Under the same title, Augustine had vindicated the role of grace in healing nature's weakness and wounds. But Soto responded to the needs of his day with a purified scholastic exposition of justification, taking care to specify nature's powers and limits, whether on its own or under the influence of grace.

But new controversies soon erupted over nature and grace. In 1565 the theological faculties of Alcalá and Salamanca condemned propositions extracted from the works of Michael Baius of Louvain, and two years later most of the propositions reappeared in Pius V's bull, *Ex omnibus afflictionibus*, censuring Baius's views of human nature, the fall, and redemptive grace.[22] Grossi (1968) explains Baius's attempt to demonstrate from Augustine the deep wound afflicting fallen human nature. Baius would then overcome a Lutheran extrinsically imputed righteousness by reappropriating Augustine's transforming *gratia sanans* as a dire need for fallen humans. Catholic thought was not ready, however, to jettison convictions about human post-lapsarian natural integrity that had been systematized in high scholastic theories of created nature and supernatural grace. Robert Bellarmine's refutations of Baius, formulated in Louvain in the early 1570s, have been edited by Galeota (1966). The young Bellarmine shows how Catholic thought on the supernatural served paradoxically to guard the basic soundness, on its own level, of fallen nature.

Baius and his disciples continued to disseminate Augustinianism at Louvain. In 1586 they accused the Jesuit, Leonard Lessius, of a Pelagian view of salvation, since he had taught that God's election takes account of foreknown free choices.[23] A papal nuncio silenced both sides in July, 1588, but soon Lessius was heartened by the book of his confrere, Luis

---

[21]Soto's second edition (Paris, 1549) is also available in reprint (Ridgewood, N.J., 1965). Basic works on him are Beltrán de Heredia (1960), Becker (1966, 1967), and Martín de la Hoz (1984).

[22]There is a reprint, *Michaelis Baii opera* (Ridgewood, N.J., 1964), of the works originally published in Amsterdam in 1696 under Jansenist auspices. The critical edition of the Spanish censures and of the bull of Pius V against Baius is in van Eijl (1953).

[23]On an allied issue, Lessius (1974) gives texts on the divine-human collaboration in biblical authorship, where Lessius was attacked by Bañez, who, consistent with his views on grace, held verbal dictation by God. Artola (1983) recounts the controversy.

Molina, lately professor at Evora in Portugal. Molina set forth a complex but acute case for predestination being logically subsequent to God's foreknowledge of human free decisions for the good. Molina had been working out his ideas on grace and predestination since 1568 while commenting on Aquinas's *Summa,* quite independently of developments in Louvain. Bitter attacks on Molina, for exalting human freedom in a manner redolent of Pelagianism, followed hard upon the publication of his *Concordia* in 1588, especially from Spanish Dominicans led by Domingo Bañez of Salamanca. Molina came within an eyelash of papal censure, but Pope Paul V decided in 1607 to allow divergent accounts of salvation to coexist in Catholic theology.

Today we are in an improved situation for study of the controversy over just how God's *auxilia* of grace function in the realization of his purposes. Johann Rabaneck's stately edition of Molina's *Concordia* was published in 1953, based on the revised edition of 1595 prepared by Molina himself. Beltrán de Heredia (1968) provides a Dominican counterstatement, offering a number of anti-Molina documents, such as the lengthy *Apologia Fratrum Predicatorum* prepared by Bañez and his confreres in 1595. Stöhr (1980) is an edition of four briefer Dominican critiques from a hitherto neglected manuscript. Fresh over-all interpretations of the controversy are rare, although interesting partial studies have appeared.[24] A promising line of interpretation was advanced by Dino Pastone at the Baronius congress (1979), with emphasis on Molina's interest in the inner-wordly pedagogies by which a person is guided toward the best use of freedom in concert with God's interior gifts of grace. Baronius opposed Molina's ideas during the Roman hearings, albeit with rather conventional arguments against innovations in theology and oblivious to the theoretical support Molina gave to Jesuit apostolic activism throughout the world.[25]

Social Ethics

Contemporary concerns over peace, human rights, and the "theologies of liberation" give added relevance to the numerous recent publications on early modern social ethics, where primary material

---

[24] In addition to its bulletin, *Acrhivo Teolgico Granadino* publishes lengthy articles on the *de auxiliis* controversy, such as Peinado (1968), on Jesuit variations on Molina's theology.

[25] Pastone, in De Maio (1982): 232-51.

abounds.[26] Our report will be selective, touching on three areas: the Salamantine founders of the new ethics, theological themes in Bartolomé de las Casas, and recent work on the moral teaching of Francisco Suárez.

Recent publications of texts of Francisco de Vitoria and Domingo de Soto strengthen the basis for the study of the early modern Thomist doctrines of natural law, human rights, political authority, and the just war. Teófilo Urdánoz published in 1960 a handy and inexpensive Latin-Spanish edition of the thirteen *relectiones* of 1528-43 in which Vitoria applied his Thomist principles to specific ecclesiological and ethical problems.[27] The introductions to the recently published Vitorian texts are ample and informative, but tend to celebrate Vitoria's intellectual independence, acuity, and internationalist vision of human solidarity to the extent that they fail to note his moments of trepidation and confusion. For more balanced assessments one can consult Noreña (1975), Fernández-Santamaria (1977), and Ramón Hernández's essay in Ramos (1984).

Vitoria's colleague, Domingo de Soto, elaborated a comprehensive ethical teaching in his *De iustitia et iure,* first published in 1553-54, which appeared in 1967-68 in a Latin-Spanish edition with lengthy introductions by Venancio Carro. Numerous scholastic authors followed in Soto's wake with treatises bearing the same title. Suárez's *Tractatus de legibus* brought this genre to near perfection in 1612. Soto and those following him treat natural and positive law, justice, ownership and the obligation of restitution, respect for life, truth-telling, contracts and usury, special obligations of clergy and religious, and tithes and simony. Clearly, these treatises articulate a major component of modern Catholic moral doctrine.

A recurring "case" was the conquest of American lands and peoples by Spanish adventurers. Vitoria gave nuanced justification for Spanish tutelage over the Indians and for a limited use of force in dealing with obstacles to evangelization. But beginning with Juan de la Peña, who

---

[26]In Ramos (1984): 661-99, Luciano Pereña catalogued eighty-nine authors writing on social justice in sixteenth-century Spain. Hanke (1949) is the fundamental work on efforts to clarify the moral issues stemming from the discovery of America and the subsequent conquest and colonization. Hamilton (1963) remains the best introduction.

[27]More recent editions of individual *relectiones* on the conquest, Vitoria (1967, 1981), give a critical apparatus not found in the 1960 edition. These two recent works in the series of Latin-Spanish editions, *Corpus Hispanorum de Pace,* include numerous other texts otherwise not easily accessible.

lectured at Salamanca 1559-65, arguments were given against titles to dominion and for Spanish obligations to make restitution to the Indians for ill-gotten property and riches.[28]

Bartolomé de las Casas (1484-1566) continues to be studied by an international band of scholars. His advocacy as "Defender of the Indians" and his planning of mission projects is increasingly recognized as resting on a corpus of doctrinal convictions forged as his Thomist tradition intersected with "the signs of the times" in the New World. Las Casas's denunciations of plunder, exploitation, and illegitimate seizure of power show theology serving the public advocacy of justice and a forceful effort to form consciences. Historians of colonial society may question the actual effectiveness of his interventions, but there is no doubting his impact on the drafting–if not on the execution–of Spanish colonial law and on Popes Paul III and Pius V. Also, he provided obligatory reading for the Salamantine masters of the later sixteenth century.[29]

A major text, Las Casas's *Apologia* against the imperialist ideologue, Juan Ginés de Sepúlveda, was published in 1975 with a facsimile of the only known Latin manuscript and a Spanish translation by Angel Losada.[30] Stafford Poole's English translation of the *Apologia*, Las Casas (1974), goes with the introductory volume, Hanke (1974). Doctrinally, Las Casas asserts inalienable human equality, establishment and transfer of government authority only with the consent of the governed, respect before the consciences of those erring in good faith (even those practicing human sacrifice!), respect for the social fabric resulting from alien cultures, and, above all, evangelization intertwined with the promotion of peace and justice. In passing, we note the sharp rebuttal by Las Casas of the titles by which Vitoria had legitimated the conquest.[31] A recent monograph summarizes Las Casas's political and

---

[28]The two volumes of Peña (1982) contain added materials on colonization, war, and human rights, through excerpts from Carranza, Cano, Covarrubias, Soto, Castro, Sotomayer, Mancio, Luis de Léon, Bañez, Molina, Toledo, and Suárez.¹

[29]On Las Casas and Paul III's declaration of Indian rights in *Sublimis Deus* (1537), see Manuel Giménez Fernández's biographical sketch in Friede and Keen (1971): 88. Parish (1980): xxiii, indicates Las Casas's influence on Pius V's policy and on early Jesuit mission strategy. Vidal Abril, in Peña (1982), 2: 489-518, documents the increasing presence of Lascasian themes at Salamanca from 1560 to 1600.

[30]Sepúlveda (1975), beginning with the text of Las Casas's adversary, given in facsimile of the 1550 printing, and in Spanish on pp. 49-82. The Las Casas translation, pp. 101-93, has helpful notes and indices.

[31]Sepúlveda (1975), Appendix 2, fol. 237vf. In English, Las Casas (1974): 340.

social thought in thirty-one theses, and then happily terms him the "apostle of human freedom."[32]

For an initial approach to scholarship on Las Casas, Friede and Keen (1971) is a valuable mosaic of studies by a generation of specialists. The recent French introduction, Mahn-Lot (1982), is splendidly concise and informative. As a guide for study, Raymond Marcus provides a still useful selective bibliography of sources and studies, in Friede and Keen (1971), while Pérez Fernández (1981) gives an exhaustive inventory of 331 known writings of Las Casas. The latter's 1984 chronology gives detailed information on Las Casas's places of residence, travels, and activities. Of particular doctrinal interest in the new scholarship is Las Casas's understanding of the ministry of the bishop, where he shows affinities with the pre-Tridentine Italian reformers Contarini, Giustiniani, and Querini.[33] Another doctrinal area, studied especially in Cantù (1975), is the Lascasian elaboration of the obligation of restitution, imposed at times as a condition of absolution upon the colonizers.[34]

Domingo Bañez, O.P., (d. 1604) and Francisco Suárez, S.J., (d. 1617) loom large in the third generation of Spanish scholasticism. The bulky treatises of the latter are influential personal syntheses of metaphysics, speculation on revealed doctrine, and social thought. Recent work has included both text-editions and dissertations in the first two areas, but we concentrate here on Suárez's social thought.[35]

Pereña Vicente (1954) offered a critical edition of Suárez's texts on the just war, and beginning in 1971 he collaborated on the publication of an ambitious edition of the comprehensive *De legibus*. Both editions provide extensive appendices with relevant further texts from Suárez and his contemporaries.[36] A partial edition (1965) of the

---

[32]Queralto Moreno (1976): 360.

[33]Cantù (1973-74) surveys the topic well. Parish (1980) is an elegant edition of the document in which Las Casas stated his aims as a bishop.

[34]Las Casas's histories described another evil visited upon the New World peoples, a host of contagious diseases against which they had no immunities, beginning with smallpox on Hispanola in 1518. On this tragic story, see Crosby (1982): 35-63.

[35]Santos-Escudero (1980) gives a Suárez bibliography of 754 entries, covering the period 1948-1980. Castellote (1980) surveys recent editions offering texts notably improved over the nineteenth-century *Opera omnia*.

[36]All editions mentioned in this paragraph give the Latin original and a modern Spanish translation on facing pages. The eight volumes of *De legibus* published 1971-81 (in the *Corpus Hispanorum de Pace*) cover the first four of the ten books. Suárez (1967-68) gives a facsimile of the 1612 edition of *De legibus*, with Spanish translation.

Defensio fidei gives the important chapters on popular sovereignty from Suárez's refutation of the divine-right monarchism of James I of England. A further edition (1978-79), combining ample introductions with an edition of Book VI of the apologia against James I, shows Suárez delineating the limits of royal sovereignty. Pereña Vicente (1954) stressed the Spanish imperial context of Suárez's political thought, in which war is a limited instrument for serving justice and defending the faith. An ambiguity remains, however, because just-war theorizing begins with a reinforcing legitimation of war directed against Christian pacifists like Erasmus, which can overshadow both the restraints elaborated in treating legitimate reasons for war and the limits on how a state should wage war.[37] Wilenius (1963) has produced a competent survey that highlights Suárez's contributions to a theory of rightful resistance to tyranny, his accentuation of the common good over individual property rights, and his subordination of all individual rights to corporate values and the legal order. Elutério Elorduy, in the long introduction to the edition of Suárez (1965), clarifies the limited and residual character of Suarezian popular sovereignty. Soder (1973), the most comprehensive recent monograph on Suárez, sets forth his internationalist principles, correcting Pereña's assertion of Suárez's creativity on war and delineating the prevalence in Suárez of the objective order of nature and law over individual human rights.

Jansenists and Antijansenists

Four decades of fruitful study have produced broad agreement that seventeenth-century Jansenism was not a monolithic religious and social movement. Numerous works by Jean Orcibal point in this direction. Lucien Ceyssens's article of 1954 is an early statement of Jansenist pluriformity, and Louis Cognet's succinct account (1961) concludes that it is impossible to encompass the Jansenist movement

---

[37]In his works on the just war tradition, James T. Johnson (1975, 1981) presents the contributions of Vitoria and Suárez under the perceptive heading, "Secularized Just War Doctrine," because of their effort to lay down principles of universal applicability not dependent on Christian faith.

with a single intellectual position, such as that reflected in the five censured propositions of 1653. A good statement of this general view is the last chapter of Sedgwick (1977), where emphasis falls on the Jansenist assertion of individual responsibility in the face of the absolute claims of crown and Church hierarchy. The problems of definition are treated deftly by Pierre Hurtubise (1983), who, however, argues that beneath all the variety–in part due to the dialectic of fierce controversy– the Jansenists are identifiable as post-Tridentine reformed Catholics of a northern type, elitist and severe in the degree of their break with "the world." A tragic vision of the human condition marks off Jansenists from Catholics of a Mediterranean, humanistic bent, ready to insert themselves actively and confidently into the world. Progressive and adaptive forces in Catholic spirituality and theology occasioned the Jansenist archaizing and restorational ideal.

The problem of definition arises in part because of the twin paternity of the movement. Bishop Cornelius Jansenius wrote the massive *Augustinus* of 1640, but Abbé Saint-Cyran, was then already directing the early members of Port-Royal and numerous friends and supporters of the movement. Orcibal's volumes (1947-62) contain the correspondence of both Jansenius and Saint-Cyran, along with numerous short works of the latter published for the first time. At the center of Orcibal's *Les origines* is a large "life and times" of Saint-Cyran, complemented by an account of his spiritual teaching as Berullian and Salesian, as well as Jansenist. Orcibal is preparing a biography of Jansenius, the stern Louvain professor who was bishop of Ypres in the last three years of his life. The best brief account of Jansenius is Lucien Ceyssens's article (1968) in the Belgian, *Biographie Nationale.*[38]

Two other editions demonstrate the variety within second-generation French Jansenism. Goldmann (1956) exposes the extremism of Martin de Barcos (1600-78), promotor of retreat from all contact with a sick and sinful world. But Arnauld and Nicole (1965) provide a critical edition of the textbook of logic brought out under Port-Royal auspices in 1662 for schooling young people in clear thought and cogent argument–replete with examples of sophisms arising from *amour-propre* and syllogistic argument to the conclusion that pagans practice no real virtue.[39]

---

[38]Jansenius's *Augustinus* is available in facsimile reprint from Minerva Verlag (Frankfurt/M., 1964).

[39]James (1972) sets forth the thought of Nicole on grace, apologetics, mystical prayer, and ethics.

The study of Jansenism carries one beyond doctrine and theology into Church politics, spirituality, social history, and French literature. For example, the nine thick volumes of sources published by Lucien Ceyssens for the period 1640-82 of set purpose eschew doctrine and theology in order to document the litigation, alliances, and intrigues that accompanied Jansenism.[40] Ceyssens's interests are many, but he recurrently unmasks the chicanery and pressure politics employed by the antijansenists. Ceyssens (1980) shows the incompetence and manipulative tactics surrounding the preparation of *Cum occasione,* the condemnation of the five Jansenist propositions by Pope Innocent X in 1653.[41]

Among seventeenth-century "disciples of St. Augustine," none exercises broader appeal than Blaise Pascal. Mesnard (1969) gives a brief presentation of Pascal's theological endeavors in a book originally published in the Desclée series, *Les Ecrivains devant Dieu.* Miel (1969) investigates the corpus of doctrinal convictions underlying Pascal's work, with a valuable chapter on the heretofore neglected *Ecrits sur la grâce.* Sellier (1970) carefully documents the broad formative influence of St. Augustine on Pascal. Assiduous study of Augustine shaped Pascal's view of the sick heart of man, the sovereignty of grace, and the need lovingly to seek out God's truth hidden beneath figurative expressions. Sellier (1982) sets forth Pascal's Christology of Gethsemane and of the hidden Presence in the reserved Eucharist. Wetsel (1981) inserts Pascal's proposed case for the credibility of Christianity into the work of biblical interpretation at Port-Royal. Pascal followed important leads set forth by Isaac le Maistre de Sacy (1613-84), whose commentaries were a determined last-ditch defense of traditional, prophetic-typological reading of all Old Testament passages, which was soon to fall before a more rational and historical criticism.

These works dismantle the misleading image of Pascal as the genial amateur with exquisite expressive talents ranging far beyond any theological expertise. Other recent studies have led to an important

---

[40]Vázquez (1979) is a helpful guidebook to Ceyssens's work into 1978.

[41]Ceyssens, however, can give an innocuous and misleading view of the *Augustinus.* See, for example, Ceyssens (1980): 372, on the aim of Jansenius as simply to furnish the Pope with a *summa* of Augustine, to aid in solving the suspended *de auxiliis* deliberations. But Jansenius laced his work with over 300 references to Suárez, Vázquez, Molina, and Lessius, who are charged with departing from the Church's approved *doctor gratiae.* He clearly was out to secure the condemnation of Lessius, as noted by Orcibal (1948-62) 5: 82. Plausibly, the real beginning of Jansenius's struggle was the reprinting (1609) of Molina's *Concordia* in nearby Antwerp, with Lessius's *De gratia efficaci* following in 1610.

textual reconstruction of the *Pensées* and include both minute literary analyses and some striking efforts to make Pascal relevant for contemporary theology. But the five works noted above serve to secure Pascal's place as a major figure in early modern Catholic thought. The work of Lucien Ceyssens makes one acutely aware of the raw force of seventeenth-century antijansenist efforts. The theologians of this reaction could claim affinities with Renaissance convictions about human freedom and dignity and could offer their work as the theoretical complement to the missionary approach of the Church to sub-Christian Europeans and to non-European peoples. Some of these theologians are better known from recent work, such as Denis Petau, studied in Hofmann (1976), and Juan de Lugo, presented in Olivares (1984).

Conclusion

Our survey has moved clockwise from Germany to Rome and then on to Salamanca. From Spain theological issues brought us to Louvain and then to Paris in the French *grand siècle*. The movement itself indicates the relevant centers of research and study, to which we can add precision by mentioning Munich and Münster in Germany, the Centro de Estudios Postridentinos in Granada, Spain, and the outstanding library of the French Jesuits at Chantilly near Paris.

The main lacuna in our review concerns biblical interpretation. Among influential Tridentine Catholic theologians one has to go beyond controversialists, systematicians, and moralists to include Sixtus of Siena (d. 1569), Juan Maldonato (d. 1583), Alfonso Salmerón (d. 1585), Emmanuel Sa (d. 1596), and Cornelius à Lapide (d. 1637). Each of these, and many more, had a formative impact on many through their scripture commentaries.[42] Here is a large, uncharted field for research, where influential Catholic spokesmen argued with Valla and Erasmus, criticized the Reformers, and passed on to preachers and students a classical Catholic world-view. The significance of their teaching can be glimpsed by reflection upon the concern for "the truth of the Scripture" in 1633, when Urban VIII and his theologians

---

[42]Schmitt (1985) treats the life and times of Maldonato. Reinhardt (1981-83) begins assembling the roster of Spaniards who published biblical commentaries between 1500 and 1700.

fatefully took disciplinary action against Galileo's heliocentrism.[43] –But the commentators had more, much more, to say to Tridentine Catholics.

Bibliography

The author is grateful for having access, while preparing this survey, to the collections and services of The Newberry Library, Chicago.

Andrés Martín, Melquiades, *La teología española en el siglo XVI,* 2 vols. (Madrid, 1976-77).

Antón, Angel, *El misterio de la Iglesia. Evolucion histórica de la ideas eclesiologicas,* vol. 1 (Madrid-Toledo, 1986).

Arnauld, Antoine, and Pierre Nicole, *La logique: ou L'art de penser, contenant, outre les règles communes, plusieurs observations nouvelles, propres à former le jugement,* ed. Pierre Clair and François Girbal (Paris, 1965).

Arnoldi von Usingen, Bartholomeus, *Responsio contra Apologiam Philippi Melanchthonis,* ed. Primoz Simoniti (Würzburg, 1978).

Artola, Antonio M., *De la revelación a la inspiración. Les origines de la moderna teología católica sobre la inspiración bíblica* (Bilbao, 1983).

Bäumer, Remigius, "Hubert Jedin und die Erforschung der katholischen Kontroverstheologie des 16. Jahrhunderts," *Annali dell'Istituto storico italo-germanico in Trento* 6 (1980): 65-83.

Becker, Karl Josef, "Tradición manuscrita de las prelecciones de Domingo de Soto," *Archivo Teológico Granadino* 29 (1966): 125-80.

_____. *Die Rechtfertigungslehre nach Domingo de Soto. Das Denken eines Konzilsteilnehmer vor, in und nach Trient* (Rome, 1967).

Belda Plans, Juan, *Los lugares teológicos de Melchor Cano en los Comentarios a la Suma* (Pamplona, 1982).

Bellinger, Gerhard, *Der Catechismus Romanus und die Reformation. Die katechetische Antwort des Trienter Konzils auf die Haupt-Katechismen der Reformation* (Paderborn, 1970).

_____. *Bibliographie des Catechismus Romanus ex Decreto Concilii Tridentini ad Parochos, 1566-1978* (Baden-Baden, 1983).

Beltrán de Heredia, Vicente, *Domingo de Soto, Estudio biográfico documentado* (Salamanca, 1960).

_____. *Domingo Bañez y las controversias sobre la gracia* (Salamanca, 1968).

Boyle, Marjorie O., *Rhetoric and Reform, Erasmus' Civil Dispute with Luther* (Cambridge, Mass., 1983).

---

[43]D'Addio (1983-84) and Wallace (1984) are enlightening recent accounts of Galileo's encounters, both intellectual and canonical, in Rome.

Braunisch, Reinhard, *Die Theologie der Rechtfertigung im "Enchiridion" (1538) des Johannes Gropper. Sein kritischer Dialog mit Philipp Melanchthon* (Münster, 1974).

Cantù, Francesca, "Per un rinnovamento della coscienza pastorale del Cinquecento: il vescovo Bartolomé de las Casas ed il problema indiano," *Annuario dell'istituto storico italiano per l'età moderna e contemporanea* 25-26 (1973-74): 3-118.

———. "Evoluzione e significato della dottrina della restituzione in Bartolomé de las Casas," *Critica Storica*, n.s. 12 (1975): 231-319.

Carranza, Bartolomé, *Comentarios sobre el Catechismo christiano*, ed. José I. Tellechea Idígoras, 2 vols. (Madrid, 1972).

Castellote, Salvador, "Der Stand der heutigen Suárez-Forschung auf Grund der neu gefundenen Handschriften," *Philosophisches Jahrbuch* 87 (1980): 134-42.

Ceyssens, Lucien, "Le jansénisme. Considerations historiques preliminaries à sa notion," *Nuove recerche sul giansenismo* (Rome, 1954): 3-32. Reprinted in L. Ceyssens, *Jansenistica minora*, 3 (Malines, 1957), fascicle 24.

———. "Jansenius," *Biographie Nationale* 34 (Brussels, 1968): 459-86.

———, "L'authenticité des cinq propositions condamnées de Jansénius," *Antonianum* 55 (1980): 368-424.

Chantraine, Georges, *Erasme et Luther, libre et serf arbitre. Étude historique et théologique* (Paris, 1981).

Cognet, Louis, *Le Jansénisme* (Paris, 1961).

Die Confutatio der Confessio Augustana vom. 3. August 1530, ed. Herbert Immenkötter (Münster, 1979).

Crosby, Alfred W., *The Columbian Exchange* (Westport, Conn., 1972).

D'Addio, Mario, "Considerazioni sui processi a Galileo," *Rivista di storia della chiesa in Italia* 37 (1983): 1-52; 38 (1984): 47-114.

De Maio, Romeo, et al., eds., *Baronio storico e la controriforma. Atti del convengo internazionale di studi, Sora 6-10 ottobre 1979* (Sora, 1982).

Desgraves, Louis, *Répertoire des ouvrages de controverse entre Catholiques et Protestants en France (1598-1685)*, 2 vols. (Geneva, 1984).

Dietenberger, Johannes, *Phimostomos scripturariorum Köln 1532*, ed. Erwin Iserloh and Peter Fabisch (Münster, 1985).

Eck, John, *Enchiridion of Commonplaces Against Luther and Other Enemies of the Church*, trans. Ford L. Battles (Grand Rapids, 1979).

———. *Enchiridion locorum communium adversus Lutherum et alios hostes ecclesiae (1525-1543)*, ed. P. Fraenkel (Münster, 1979).

———. *De sacrificio missae libri tres (1526)*, eds. Erwin Iserloh, Vinzenz Pfnür, and Peter Fabisch (Münster, 1982).

van Eijl, Edouard, "Les censures des universités d'Alcala et de Salamanque et la censure du Pape Pie V contre Michel Baius (1565-1567)," *Revue d'histoire ecclésiastique* 48 (1953), 719-76.

Emser, Hieronymus, *Schriften zur Verteidigung der Messe*, ed. Theobald Freudenberger (Münster, 1959).

Fernández-Santamaria, José A., *The State, War, and Peace. Spanish Political Thought in the Renaissance 1516-1559* (Cambridge, 1977).

Fox, Alistair, *Thomas More. History and Providence* (New Haven, 1983).

Fraenkel, Pierre, "An der Grenze von Luthers Einfluss: Aversion gegen Umwertung," *Zeitschrift für Kirchengeschichte* 89 (1978): 21-30.

————. "Le schéma, l'image et la cible: Luther vu pars ses adversaires romains," *Luther et la Réforme allemande dans une perspective oecuménique* (Chambéry-Geneva, 1983): 339-63.

Fragnito, Gignola, "Contarini, Gasparo," *Dizionario biografico degli Italiani* 28 (Rome, 1983): 172-92.

Friede, Juan, and Benjamin Keen, eds., *Bartolomé de las Casas in History. Toward an Understanding of the Man and His Work* (DeKalb, Ill., 1971).

Galeota, Gustavo, *Bellarmino contro Baio a Lovanio. Studio e testo di un inedito bellarminiano* (Rome, 1966).

————. "Robert Bellarmin (1542-1621)," *Klassiker der Theologie,* ed. Heinrich Fries and Georg Kretschmar, 2 vols. (Munich, 1981-83), 1:346-62.

Gilmont, Jean-François, "La bibliographie de la controverse catholique au XVIᵉ siècle," *Revue d'histoire ecclésiastique* 74 (1979): 362-71.

Gogan, Brian, *The Common Corps of Christendom. Ecclesiological Themes in the Writings of Sir Thomas More* (Leiden, 1982).

Goldmann, Lucien, ed., *Correspondence de Martín de Barcos* (Paris, 1956).

Gropper, Johannes, *Briefwechsel,* vol. 1 (1529-1547), ed. Reinhard Braunisch (Münster, 1977).

Grossi, Vittorino, *Baio e Bellarmino interpreti di S. Agostino nelle questioni del soprannaturale* (Rome, 1968).

Hamilton, Bernice, *Political Thought in Sixteenth-Century Spain. A Study of the Political Ideas of Vitoria, De Soto, Suárez, and Molina* (Oxford, 1963).

Hanke, Lewis, *The Spanish Struggle for Justice in the Conquest of America* (Philadelphia, 1949).

————. *All Mankind is One. A Study of the Disputation Between Bartolomé de Las Casas and Juan Ginés de Sepúlveda in 1550 on the Intellectual and Religious Capacity of the American Indians* (DeKalb, Ill., 1974).

Hallensleben, Barbara, *Communicatio. Anthropologie und Gnadenlehre bei Thomas de Vio Cajetan (Münster, 1985).*

Hofmann, Michael, *Theologie, Dogma und Dogmenentwicklung im theologischen Werk Denis Pitau's* (Bern, 1976).

Horn, Stephan, *Glaube und Rechtfertigung nach dem Konzilstheologen Andrés de Vega* (Paderborn, 1972).

Horst, Ulrich, *Papst-Konzil-Unfehlbarkeit. Die Ekklesiologie der Summen-kommentare von Cajetan bis Billuart* (Mainz, 1978).

————. *Unfehlbarkeit und Geschichte. Studien zur Unfehlbarkeitsdiskussion von Melchior Cano bis zum I. Vatikanischen Konzil* (Mainz, 1982).

Hurtubise, Pierre, "Jansénisme ou jansénismes: visages d'un courant spirituel," *Modernité et non-conformisme en France à travers les âges,* ed. Myriam Yardeni (Leiden, 1983): 67-79.

Immenkötter, Herbert, *Um die Einheit im Glauben. Die Unionsverhandlungen des Augsburger Reichstages im August und September 1530* (Münster, 1973).

Iserloh, Erwin, ed., *Confessio Augustana und Confutatio. Der Augsburger Reichstag 1530 und die Einheit der Kirche* (Münster, 1980).

_____, ed., *Katholische Theologen der Reformationzeit*, 3 vols. (Münster, 1984-86).

James, Edward D., *Pierre Nicole, Jansenist and Humanist. A Study of His Thought* (The Hague, 1972).

Jedin, Hubert, *Kardinal Caesar Baronius. Der Anfang der katholischen Kirchengeschichtsschreibung im 16. Jahrhundert* (Münster, 1978).

Johnson, James T., *Ideology, Reason, and the Limitation of War. Religious and Secular Concepts, 1200-1740* (Princeton, 1975).

_____. *Just War Tradition and the Restraint of War. A Moral and Historical Inquiry* (Princeton, 1981).

Klaiber, Wilbirgis, *Katholische Kontroverstheologen und Reformer des 16. Jahrhunderts. Ein Werkverzeichnis* (Münster, 1978).

Klinger, Elmar, *Ekklesiologie der Neuzeit. Grundlegung bei Melchior Cano und Entwicklung bis zum Zweiten Vatikanischen Konzil* (Freiburg, 1978).

Köster, Heinrich, *Urstand, Fall und Erbsunde. Von der Reformation bis zur Gegenwart* (Freiburg/B., 1982).

Las Casas, Bartolomé de, *In Defense of the Indians,* trans. Stafford Poole (DeKalb, Ill., 1974).

Lessius, Leonard, *De sacra scriptura,* ed. Antonio M. Artola (Victoria, 1974).

López Martínez, Nicolas, "Tradición y Inquisición española (Segunda mitad del siglo XVI)," *Burgense* 3 (1962): 177-213.

Lortz, Joseph, "Wert und Grenzen der katholischen Kontroverstheologie in der ersten Hälfte des 16. Jahrhunderts," *Um Reform und Reformation,* ed. August Franzen (Münster, 1968): 9-32.

Mahn-Lot, Marianne, *Bartolomé de las Casas et le droit des Indiens* (Paris, 1982).

Martín de la Hoz, José, "Las relecciónes teológicas de Domingo de Soto: cronología y ediciones," *Scripta Theologica* 16 (1984): 433-42.

Marx, Gerhard, *Glaube, Werke und Sakramente im Dienste der Rechtfertigung in den Schriften von Berthold Pürstinger, Bischof vom Chiemsee* (Leipzig, 1982).

Meier, Johannes, "Das *Enchiridion christianae institutionis* (1538) von Johannes Gropper. Geschichte seiner Entstehung, Verbreitung und Nachwirkung," *Zeitschrift für Kirchengeschichte* 86 (1975): 289-328.

_____. *Der priesterliche Dienst nach Johannes Gropper (1503-1559)* (Münster, 1977).

Mesnard, Jean, *Pascal* (University, Ala., 1969).

Miel, Jan, *Pascal and Theology* (Baltimore, 1969).

Molina, Luis, *Liberi arbitrii cum gratiae donis, divina praescientia, providentia, praedestinatione et reprobatione concordia,* ed. Johannes Rabeneck (Oña and Madrid, 1953).

More, Thomas, *Responsio ad Lutherum,* trans. Sister Scholastica Mandeville, ed. John M. Headley, 2 vols. (New Haven, 1969).

———. *The Confutation of Tyndale's Answer*, ed. Louis A. Schuster, et al., 3 vols. (New Haven, 1973).

———. *The Apology*, ed. Joseph B. Trapp (New Haven, 1979).

———. *A Dialogue Concerning Heresies*, ed. Thomas Lawler et al., 2 vols. (New Haven, 1981).

Müller, Gerhard, ed., *Die Religionsgespräche der Reformationszeit* (Gütersloh, 1980).

Muñoz Delgado, Vicente, "Lógica, ciencia y humanismo en la renovación teológica de Vitoria y Cano," *Revista española de teología* 38 (1978): 205-71.

Noreña, Carlos G., "Vitoria, Salamanca, and the American Indians," in *Studies in Spanish Renaissance Thought* (The Hague, 1975): 36-149.

O'Connell, Marvin R., *Thomas Stapleton and the Counter Reformation* (New Haven, 1964).

Offele, Wolfgang, *Ein Katechismus im Dienst der Glaubenseinheit. Julius Pflugs "Institutio Christiani Hominis" als katechetischer Beitrag zur interkonfessionellen Begegnung* (Essen, 1965).

Olivares, E. "Juan de Lugo (1583-1660), datos biográficos, sus escritos, estudios sobre su doctrina y bibliografía," *Archivio Teológico Granadino* 47 (1984): 5-129.

Orcibal, Jean, *Les origines du Jansénisme*, 5 vols. (Louvain and Paris, 1947-62).

Parish, Helen Rand, *Las Casas as Bishop. A New Interpretation Based on His Holograph Petition* (Washington, D.C., 1980).

Peinado, Jesus, "Evolución de las formulas molinistas sobre la gracia eficaz durante las controversias *de auxiliis*," *Archivo Teológico Granadino* 31 (1968): 5-191.

Pelikan, Jaroslav, *The Christian Tradition*, vol. 4, *Reformation of Church and Dogma (1300-1700)* (Chicago, 1984).

Peña, Juan de la, *De bello contra insulanos. Intervención de España en America. Escuela Española de la Paz, Segunda generación 1560-1585*, eds. Luciano Pereña et al., 2 vols. (Madrid, 1982).

Pereña Vicente, Luciano, *Teoría de la guerra en Francisco Suárez*, 2 vols. (Madrid, 1954).

Peréz Fernández, Isacio, *Inventario documentado de los escritos de Fray Bartolomé de las Casas* (Bayamon, P.R., 1981).

———. *Cronología documentada de los viajes, estancias y actuaciones de Fray Bartolomé de las Casas* (Bayamon, P.R., 1984).

Pfeilschifter, Georg, ed., *Acta Reformationis Catholicae ecclesiam Germaniae concernentia saeculi XVI*, vols. 1-6 (Regensburg, 1959-74).

Pfnür, Vizenz, *Einig in der Rechtfertigungslehre? Die Rechtfertigungslehre der Confessio Augustana (1530) und die Stellungnahme der katholischen Kontroverstheologie zwischen 1530 und 1535* (Wiesbaden, 1970).

Polman, Pontien, *L'Élément historique dans la controverse religieuse du XVI⁰ siècle* (Gembloux, 1932).

Préclin, Edmond, and Eugène Jarry, *Les luttes politiques et doctrinales aux XVII⁰ et XVIII⁰ siècles*, 2 vols. (Paris, 1955-56).

Pullapilly, Cyriac, *Caesar Baronius, Counter-Reformation Historian* (Notre Dame, 1975).

Queralto Moreno, Ramón-Jesús, *El pensamiento filosófico-político de Bartolomé de las Casas* (Seville, 1976).

Ramos, Demetrio, et al., *Francisco de Vitoria y la escuela de Salamanca. La ética en la conquista de America* (Madrid, 1984).

Reinhardt, Klaus, "Bibelkommentare spanischer Autoren des 16. und 17. Jahrhunderts: Autoren A," *Revista española de teología* 41 (1981), 91-145; "...Autoren B," *Revista española de teología* 43 (1983), 27-55.

Rodríguez, Pedro, and Raúl Lanzetti, *El Catecismo Romano: Fuentes e historia del texto y de la redacción. Bases críticas para el estudio teológico del Catecismo del Concilio de Trento* (Pamplona, 1982).

_____, *El manuscrito original del Catecismo romano* (Pamplona, 1985).

Santos-Escudero, Ceferino, "Bibliografía Suareciana de 1948 a 1980," *Cuadernos salmantinos de filosofía* 7 (1980): 337-75.

Sarmiento, Augusto, *La eclesiología de Mancio*, 2 vols. (Pamplona, 1976).

Schäfer, Philipp, *Eschatologie. Trient und Gegenreformation* (Freiburg/B., 1984).

Schatzgeyer, Kaspar, *Schriften zur Verteidigung der Messe*, ed. Erwin Iserloh and Peter Fabisch (Münster, 1984).

Schmitt, Paul, *La réforme catholique. Le combat de Maldonat (1534-1583)* (Paris, 1985).

Schützeichel, Heribert, *Wesen und Gegenstand der kirchlichen Lehrautorität nach Thomas Stapleton* (Trier, 1966).

Sedgwick, Alexander, *Jansenism in Seventeenth-Century France: Voices from the Wilderness* (Charlottesville, Va., 1977).

Sellier, Philippe, *Pascal et Saint Augustin* (Paris, 1970).

_____. "Jésus-Christ chez Pascal," *Revue des sciences philosophiques et théologiques* 66 (1982): 505-21.

Sepúlveda, Juan Ginés de, and Fray Bartolomé de las Casas, *Apologia*, trans. Angel Losada (Madrid, 1975).

Seybold, Michael, *Glaube und Rechtfertigung bei Thomas Stapleton* (Paderborn, 1967).

Snoeks, Remi, *L'Argument de tradition dans la controverse eucharistique entre catholiques et réformés français au XVIIᵉ siècle* (Louvain, 1951).

Soder, Josef, *Francisco Suárez und das Völkerrecht. Grundgedanken zu Staat, Recht und internationalen Beziehungen* (Frankfurt/M., 1973).

Soto, Domingo de, *De iustitia et iure*, ed. Venancio D. Carro, 5 vols. (Madrid, 1967-68).

Stöhr, Johannes, *Zur Frühgeschichte des Gnadenstreites. Gutachten spanischer Dominikaner in einer bisher unbekannten Handschrift* (Münster, 1980).

Strand, Kenneth A., *Catholic German Bibles of the Reformation Era* (Naples, Fla., 1982).

Suárez, Francisco, *Defensio fidei, III. I, Principatus politicus o la soberanía popular*, ed. Elutério Elorduy and Luciano Pereña (Madrid, 1965).

_____. *Tratado de la leyes y de Dios legislador,* transl. José R. Eguillor Muniozguren, 6 vols. (Madrid, 1967-68).

_____. *De legibus,* ed. Luciano Pereña et al. (Madrid, 1971-).

_____. *De iuramento fidelitatis [Defensio fidei, VI],* eds. Luciano Pereña et al., 2 vols. (Madrid, 1978-79).

Tavard, George H., *La tradition au XVIIᵉ siècle en France et en Angleterre* (Paris, 1969).

_____. *The Seventeenth Century Tradition. A Study in Recusant Thought* (Leiden, 1978).

Tellechea Idígoras, José I., "Credo sanctam ecclesiam. Catequesis de Carranza sobre la Iglesia," *Communio* [Seville] 6 (1973): 33-77.

_____. *Melanchton y Carranza, Préstamos y afinidades* (Salamanca, 1979).

Theiner, Johann, *Die Entwicklung der Moraltheologie zur eigenständingen Disziplin* (Regensburg, 1970).

Vazquez, Isaac, *L'oeuvre de Lucien Ceyssens sur le jansénisme et l'antijansénsime devant la critique* (Rome, 1979).

Vitoria, Francisco de, *Obras de Francisco de Vitoria. Relecciones teológicas,* ed. Teófilo Urdánoz (Madrid, 1960).

_____. *Relectio de Indis o Libertad de los Indios,* eds. Luciano Pereña and José M. Pérez Prendes (Madrid, 1967).

_____. *Relectio de iure belli o Pax Dinamica,* eds. Luciano Pereña et al. (Madrid, 1981).

Wallace, William A., *Galileo and His Sources. The Heritage of the Collegio Romano in Galileo's Science* (Princeton, 1984).

Wetsel, David, *L'Ecriture et le Reste. The "Pensées" of Pascal in the Exegetical Tradition of Port-Royal* (Columbus, Ohio, 1981).

Wicks, Jared, *Cajetan Responds. A Reader in Reformation Controversy* (Washington, D.C., 1978).

_____. "Abuses under Indictment at the Diet of Augsburg 1530," *Theological Studies* 41 (1980): 253-302.

_____. *Cajetan und die Anfänge der Reformation* (Münster, 1983).

_____. "Roman Reactions to Luther: the First Year (1518)," *Catholic Historical Review* 69 (1983): 521-62.

Wilenius, Reijo, *The Social and Political Theory of Francisco Suárez* (Helsinki, 1963).

Willaert, Léopold, *Après le concile de Trient. La Restauration catholique (1563-1648)* (Paris, 1960).

The Inquisition and Inquisitorial Censorship

Agostino Borromeo

OF ALL THE ECCLESIASTICAL INSTITUTIONS of the medieval and modern periods the Inquisition is certainly one of those that has been most closely studied.[1] Anyone examining the ample bibliography on this subject cannot fail to note a further point, namely that in the last three decades or so there has been a marked upturn in research and that this upturn concerns the history of the institution in the modern age and more especially in the period with which this volume is concerned.[2] In that period the Inquisition in some Catholic countries entered a new dynamic phase, with the result that the period ranging from approximately the middle of the sixteenth to the end of the seventeenth century, regardless of the vexed question of the exact chronological limits of the Counter Reformation, is the one for which the greatest amount of inquisitorial documentation is available. It is natural, therefore, that the attention of scholars has been and continues to be focused upon it.

It would appear that at least two factors have principally influenced recent interest in the Inquisition: on the one hand, the greater attention paid by contemporary historiography to questions connected with the history of both lay and ecclesiastical institutions; on the other, the renewed interest in tribunals aroused by the studies of those who, in recent decades, have utilized inquisitorial documentation as the principal source for the study of matters not directly connected with the history of the institution: witchcraft, popular beliefs, and the way of life of certain ethnic minorities.[3]

Whatever the reasons for this extraordinary surge of interest, it is not purely the amount of recent research on the Inquisition that sets it apart from earlier studies, but rather its quality. A new generation of historians has entered the field, with the result that certain preconceived positions that until quite recently caused lively but quite

---

[1]For the general bibliography on the Inquisition, see Vekene (1982).

[2]Some of the most recent publications are listed in the articles of Márquez (1981); Parker (1982); Monter (1983); González Novalín (1985).

[3]Ginzburg's works (1972) and (1976), at least for research done in Italy, have had a stimulating effect from this point of view.

sterile polemics among critics and apologists for the institution have been abandoned. Thus, the influx of new trends that characterize contemporary historiography has made itself felt in this field of studies too. This development has led to a gradual extension of investigations to sources that were once never or little consulted, as well as to a more sophisticated methodology and a broadening of themes and the manner of treating them.

This phenomenon seems destined to grow even more decisively in the future as the results of large-scale programs of research begun by some important institutions become available: for instance, that on the Inquisition in Italy, which the Istituto Storico Italiano per l'età Moderna e Contemporaneà is conducting under the guidance of A. Saitta (Rome); that on the 16,000 processes of the tribunal of Lisbon, directed by R. Rowland as part of the research programs of the Historical Sociology Unit of the Gulbenkian Institute of Science (Lisbon); and that of J. Martínez de Bujanda at the Sherbrooke Renaissance Studies Centre (Canada), with a view to publishing a critical edition of all the Indexes of books prohibited in the sixteenth century. There are, in addition, the scientific and educational activities of two Madrid institutions, the Center of Inquisitorial Studies presided over by J. Pérez Villanueva and the Institute of the History of the Inquisition, recently founded by J. A. Escudero. The data resulting from these programs could perhaps be computer-processed and will in any case provide details on the structure and functioning of the institution that are still little known. Meanwhile, scholars in other fields will have access to material invaluable for the social and cultural history of Catholic Europe in the early modern period.

It must be noted at this point that the research of approximately the last thirty years has not been uniform in either quality or quantity. What must be emphasized, however, is not so much the first deficiency as the second: it is essential to bear in mind that the attention of scholars has not been concentrated evenly over the various geographic areas where the Inquisition was active during the Counter Reformation.

During that period, the Inquisition was active mainly in five geographic areas: Spain and its American dominions, Portugal and its colonial empire, Italy, France, and Spanish Flanders. Though this was the same institution which operated in various parts of Europe in the Middle Ages–that is, an ensemble of ecclesiastical tribunals competent in matters of faith, the heads of which acted as judges delegated by the Holy See–its organization and structures started to diversify, depending on the countries in which it survived, from the end of the fifteenth century. Thus the Spanish Crown, beginning in 1478,[4] and the Portuguese Crown, from 1536 onwards,[5] obtained special concessions from the Holy See that conferred on the Spanish and Portuguese Inquisitions some degree of autonomy, but which also, to some extent at least, placed them under the control of their respective sovereigns. This latter concession concerned particularly the rights of the two sovereigns to appoint the Inquisitor General, the highest official in the two institutions. The Italian tribunals, except for Sicily and Sardinia which came under the Inquisitor General of Spain,[6] were instead subject directly to the authority of the Holy See beginning in 1542. In that year Pope Paul III established the Congregation of the Inquisition with the task of directing, controlling and coordinating the activities of the Inquisitors operating in the Italian States. This institution came to be known as the Roman Inquisition.[7]

The situation was different in France where at the beginning of the sixteenth century the medieval tribunals were still operating. By the middle of the century, anti-heretical repression passed gradually into the hands of secular authorities who exercised this power through the Parlements.[8] The post of Inquisitor continued to survive formally, though in time it came to be a purely honorary title. In the Low Countries, instead, where Lutheran doctrine quickly started to spread, the Inquisition was reorganized by Charles V in 1523. The Emperor, however, did not try to introduce the Spanish Inquisition, but limited himself to placing the activities of the Inquisitors, appointed by him and confirmed by the Holy See, under the control of the Provincial Councils.[9]

As already mentioned, research on the tribunals operating in these five geographic areas has not exhibited the same dynamics. The Spanish and Roman Inquisitions have received closest study. The former, however, has been the object of by far the most numerous and systematic investigations. There are various reasons for this discrepancy,

---

[4] On the origins of the Spanish Inquisition: González Novalín (1980): 126 ff.; Pérez Villanueva and Escandell Bonet (1984): 281 ff.; Kamen (1985): 18 ff.

[5] The latest bibliography on the Portuguese Inquisition, together with the chronology of its most important phases, is to be found in Bethencourt (1984): 43-60.

[6] For the Spanish Inquisition in Sicily and Sardinia, see Borromeo (1977-1978) and (1983-1984).

[7] See Tedeschi (1979).

[8] Mentzer (1984): 10 ff.

[9] Brief bibliographical notices in Valvekens (1949): 171 ff.

but the main one is certainly the diverse status of the source material. While historians of the Roman Inquisition are denied access to the archives of the ancient Roman Congregation of the Inquisition (now kept with those of the Congregation of the Doctrine of the Faith) and are therefore confined almost exclusively to the local archives that survive from some peripheral tribunals, historians concerned with the Spanish Inquisition have at their disposal in the National Historical Archives in Madrid the central archive of the institution, namely that of the Council of the Inquisition. Thus, it is not surprising that there is no comprehensive work on the institution in this period that covers all geographical areas. The very few works of any interest that deal with the Inquisition in general consider for the modern period only the Spanish Inquisition or, at most, the Roman Inquisition in conjunction with it.[10]

Thus, during the last thirty years the only general works in the individual geographic areas have been those concerning the Spanish Inquisition. Of these, the key text, despite its anti-Catholic bias, is still that of the American, H. C. Lea, published in four volumes in 1906-1907. In many ways this work is still of importance today, and, indeed, a Spanish translation has been published recently, complete with a wide-ranging introductory essay by A. Alcalá. Alcalá also oversaw the revision of the critical apparatus, which now provides the present shelf numbers of the archival documents originally consulted by Lea.[11]

But the book that has enjoyed and continues to enjoy deserved and extraordinarily wide diffusion is the manual produced by the Englishman, H. Kamen (1985), now in its second edition after the first had been reprinted many times and translated into various languages. The success of the book is attributable to the clarity of its synthesis and the originality of its approach. This originality stems from the fact that Kamen does not study the various aspects of the Inquisition as an internal history of the institution, but connects them constantly with the social context in which it had to operate. According to Kamen, the fact that the Spanish Inquisition lasted for so many centuries cannot be viewed solely as a phenomenon in the history of intolerance, but rather as a chapter in the history of the social and religious development of Spain. The author emphasizes how, despite the opposition of minority groups and the general fear it aroused, the tribunal enjoyed the support

[10]Testas and Testas (1966) for Spain; Burman (1984) for both.
[11]Lea (1983); the introduction of A. Alcalá is printed in I: XXV-LXXXI.

of the populace as a whole because it was the logical expression of the social prejudices that prevailed all around it–towards heretics in general and towards the descendants of Jews and Muslims in particular.[12]

The image Kamen offers of the Spanish Inquisition is thus radically different from that given previously by some authors, especially Anglo-Saxon, who saw the institution as an instrument of religious fanaticism tyrannically imposed on society. Kamen's interpretation could well be extended to other areas, as the remarkable essay by N. Davidson (1982) on the Venetian Inquisition in the sixteenth century suggests. His article reveals quite plainly the hostile attitude of the civil authorities and also of the citizens as a whole to the phenomenon of heresy, identified as a factor creating not only religious and social disturbances and disintegration, but also leading to political upheaval.

Two other recent general works on the Spanish Inquisition must be mentioned, quite apart from two volumes of congress proceedings edited by Pérez Villanueva (1980) and Alcalá (1984) and an important essay by J. L. González Novalín (1980), whose chronological range however, is limited to the sixteenth century.[13] The first is by B. Bennassar and five collaborators (1979). The book, which has the orientation typical of French historiography, is characterized by the systematic use of quantitative data-processing and by its attention to problems connected with social anthropology and the history of mentalities. The results attained by this team mark a turning point in studies on the Spanish Inquisition. The research establishes as its principle finding that, contrary to what was once believed, the main activity of the Inquisition was not directed so much against the apostasy of those who rejected Catholic doctrine en bloc–"Judaizers," *Moriscos,* or Protestants–but rather against those deviations from the Church's teachings on theological or moral matters of which people who professed themselves to be Catholic were guilty, sometimes unknowingly. The study of processes against blasphemers, bigamists, and sodomites thus led the French team to modify the traditional image of the Inquisition from that of an ecclesiastical tribunal dedicated above all to the repression of formal heresy to that of an apparatus of social control aimed at inculcating in the faithful themselves behavior and beliefs rigorously in conformity with Church doctrine. This is a new point of view that has been immediately welcomed by some specialists

---

[12]Kamen (1985): 250-65.

[13]A further volume of proceedings is to appear shortly: Tedeschi and Henningsen, eds.

in this field. This analysis of the Spanish Inquisition could probably be extended to the Roman Inquisition, too, at least for its activities beginning in the final decades of the sixteenth century, but certainly not to the Portuguese Inquisition, whose repressive action was directed almost exclusively against "Judaizers" or against those suspected of being so.[14]

Bennassar's book, written solely by Frenchmen, is comparable in importance to one written solely by Spaniards, namely the first volume of a history of the Spanish and American Inquisition edited by J. Pérez Villanueva and B. Escandell Bonet (1984). Here the approach is more traditional but also more systematic in pursuing the aim of presenting the institution as a whole in the light of the most recent research. Despite the fact that the division of the work among thirty scholars detracts from the unity of the volume, it is a fundamental contribution because it is both the most up-to-date book available for bibliography and is the only one of a general character that also studies the American projection of the Spanish Inquisition.

No general works like these have been published recently on the other Inquisitions. Only for the Portuguese and Flemish Inquisitions are there a few minor works available, but these represent little more than an introduction to the subjects in question.[15] Though there as yet exists no overall treatment of the Roman Inquisition, owing to the inaccessibility of the main source, attention must be drawn to some articles by John Tedeschi which, because of their general approach and the information they provide, mark the first step towards the history of that institution. In addition to indicating original sources to which scholars have access, Tedeschi deals particularly with the institution's organization and procedures.[16] He has thus cleared the field of some platitudes and prejudices about the Inquisition that are still in circulation even today. Tedeschi highlights the fact that the rights of the accused were perhaps better guaranteed in the inquisitorial process than in the ordinary juridical procedures of the major European countries. Suspects were actually arrested only after careful investigation. The accused was guaranteed the assistance of a defense lawyer, paid for by the tribunal if he was unable to do so on his own

---

[14]Azevedo (1975): 337-38. A similar proportion is obtainable from the condemnations issued by the tribunal of Coimbra in the second half of the the sixteenth century: see Mea (1982): III.

[15]Saraiva (1956²); Valvekens (1949).

[16]Tedeschi (1973, 1979). See also the paper of the same author published in Alcalá, ed. (1984): 185-206.

account. This provision was anything but negligible when it is recalled that in a country like England the right of the accused to be defended was recognized only in 1836. Torture, which was a juridical practice applied in all tribunals, was inflicted only in precisely determined cases, namely when there were good grounds to suspect that the accused was lying or at least hiding part of the truth. Even in these cases, however, he could be tortured only after certain procedures had been followed. These involved, *inter alia,* the favorable vote of the diocesan ordinary or his representative. The death penalty was not inflicted as frequently as was for long believed; for example, of the first one thousand accused who appeared before the Aquileia-Concordia Inquisition between 1551 and 1647, only five were sent to the stake. Similarly, of the more than two hundred sentences of the tribunals throughout Italy issued between 1580 and 1582, only four imposed the death penalty.

The inquisitorial authorities soon came to adopt a skeptical attitude toward the crimes of witchcraft, sorcery, and spell-casting.[17] By the early seventeenth century, Rome had issued special instructions to all tribunals requiring judges to view such accusations circumspectly and duly to weigh all proof. From this time forward the accused received far milder treatment than in civil courts. Indeed, even Paolo Sarpi criticized ecclesiastical justice for not being severe enough in repressing witchcraft.

The points made by Tedeschi are borne out by the research of other scholars. Analysis of the inquisitorial manuals[18] and study of the action taken by the individual tribunals–not just that of Rome, but those of Spain and Portugal as well–confirm that the Inquisition was not that bloody, ruthless tribunal described in some nineteenth-century works. The death penalty, as in Italy, was inflicted in only a very small percentages of cases. The figures supplied by G. Henningsen on the Spanish Inquisition between 1540 and 1700 show that only 1483 out of 49,092 cases (i.e. less than 3 percent) concluded with the death sentence.[19] However, the number of people who were actually burned at the stake was 776, while effigies were burnt in the other 707 cases, as the victim was already either dead or missing. The percentage of death sentences imposed by the Portuguese Inquisition between 1540 and 1732 was somewhat higher, with 1454 out of 24,522 cases (slightly

[17]Tedeschi (1983).
[18]Borromeo (1983): esp. 539-43.
[19]Henningsen (1977): 564.

less than 6 percent, 2 percent as effigies).[20] It was by no means unusual, moreover, for appeals to be lodged against the sentences of the Inquisition, whereas most civil courts provided for no appeal against the sentence for some types of crime.[21] Benassar's investigations on the Spanish Inquisition indicate that only somewhere between 7 and 11 percent of the accused were subjected to torture, depending on the tribunal concerned.[22]

Henningsen, one of the pioneers in the more recent studies on the Spanish Inquisition, has written on the events that led that institution to alter its attitude towards witchcraft, in a similar way to the policies later adopted by the Roman Inquisition. In 1614 the *Suprema* issued a series of rules to be followed by Inquisitors in witchcraft trials. These rules were inspired by suggestions by Inquisitor Alfonso Salazar Rias, who, in the light of experience acquired at the Logroño tribunal, had come to the radical conclusion that witches did not exist. The result was that, following the instructions given in 1614, no one accused of witchcraft was condemned to death in territories under the jurisdiction of the Spanish Inquisitor General.[23]

Even though it has been documented that in some cases the Inquisitors proceeded with surprising mildness,[24] this does not mean that the Inquisition represented a model of moderation and did not instill fear. On the contrary, research confirms that it was highly feared, but not so much because of the procedures it applied, or because it could inflict the death sentence, but rather because of the economic and social consequences stemming from even a light sentence: confiscation of property, banishment, loss of certain rights, and, especially, the infamy heaped on the person condemned and on his descendants.[25]

Another preconceived notion that has been set right by recent studies is that the Spanish Inquisition bears part of the responsibility for the country's economic decline. This idea was supported by Lea,[26] who based his assessment on the confiscation of the accused's property and the fines imposed. Data now available shows this to be completely

---

[20]Azevedo (1975): 489.
[21]Borromeo (1983): 541-43.
[22]Henningsen (1980).
[23]Henningsen (1980).
[24]Santosuosso (1978); Seidel-Menchi (1983-84).
[25]Bennassar (1979): 104 ff.; Borromeo (1983): 543-44.
[26]Lea (1983), II: 259-60.

groundless.[27] While it is true that repression of crypto-judaism reduced to impotency a large group of the urban bourgeoisie–the *conversos*–and that the Inquisition prevented the entry into Spain of foreigners coming from economically more advanced Protestant countries, it is equally true that the institution never had powers to intervene in the making of major economic choices. It did not, moreover, possess enough assets to have an effect on the economic life of Spain, unlike the Church or the land-owning aristocracy.

These conclusions emerge clearly also from a recent study by J. Martínez Millán.[28] This is one of the most original works recently published on the Spanish Inquisition, for it deals with an aspect about which almost nothing has been known–finance. The book examines the specific sources of income and the items of expenditure, which consisted principally in employees' salaries and the costs of holding the *autos de fe*.

Some mention must also be made of the many studies on the various local tribunals, which are quite uneven in their breadth and depth. From Goa to Malta, from Latin America to Friuli, we have a complex range of works providing us with an idea of the organization and actual method of operation of the individual tribunals.[29] Two contributions, however, stand out from this great mass of material for their scope and completeness–the two volumes written by R. García Carcel (1976, 1980) on the tribunal of Valencia and a book by J. Contreras (1983) on the tribunal of Galicia, both part of the Spanish Inquisition. These two studies delve into aspects that are usually ignored, namely structure, organization, and finances. There are similar studies on the tribunal of Toledo by J.-P. Dedieu.[30] There have also been a number of studies on other organs of the inquisitorial apparatus. The most significant contributions in this regard concern especially the Spanish Royal Council of the Inquisition.[31]

Studies on the Inquisition have not focused solely on the institutional aspects. Scholars have also given attention to judges and

---

[27]Kamen (1965); Dedieu (1985).

[28]Notwithstanding the interest of the work, the methodology of the author in elaborating the tables is to be taken with caution; for an example of the correct treatment of data relative to the finance of a particular tribunal, see Birkel (1969) and (1970).

[29]Paschini (1959); Kakba Priolkar (1961); Vella (1964); Greenleaf (1969); Revah (1975): 121-53; Romeo (1976); Siqueira (1978); Esteban Deive (1983); Escandell Bonet (1983-84); Reguera (1984); Del Col (1985).

[30]Dedieu (1977) and (1978). See also the paper of the same author published in Pérez Villanueva, ed. (1983): 893-912.

[31]Escudero (1983); Martínez Millán and Sánchez Revilla (1984).

the accused. As long ago as 1968, J. Caro Baroja insisted on the need to extend research to include a closer study of the figure of the Inquisitor, both in its abstract configuration (training and qualifications) and in its personal individuality.[32] By pure coincidence the first volume of J. L. González Novalín's biography of Inquisitor General Fernando de Valdés was published also in 1968. For its breadth of research and its critical method, this book remains a model. Some smaller, but nonetheless valuable, biographies of Italian, Portuguese, and Flemish Inquisitors must also be noted.[33]

Of much more ample proportions–monographs or editions or processes–are the works on those accused by the Inquisition. Only a few important cases can be signaled here.[34] Among these, however, are three of outstanding importance because of the personality of the accused and the discussion aroused by the proceedings: the case of the Archbishop of Toledo and Primate of Spain, Bartolomé Carranza, that of Cardinal Giovanni Morone, and the celebrated case of Galileo Galilei. The trials of Carranza (1559-1576)[35] and of Morone (1557-1560)[36] seem to mark the decided emergence of the severe approach, which under the pontificate of Paul IV constituted an irreversible change in the struggle of the Counter-Reformation Church against heresy. Quite different was the climate in which the Galileo case was conducted, an event in which scholars continue to show interest.[37]

The Tuscan scientist has always been seen as emblematic of the incompatibility between science and faith. Recently, however, an interpretation of the case has been proffered that locates the process within the confines of strictly theological debate. In a book published in 1983, P. Redondi, on the basis of a hitherto unknown anonymous document, attributed by the author to the Jesuit, Orazio Grassi, proposes that Galileo was not condemned for Copernicanism and problems concerned with biblical exegis but for the incompatibility of his ideas on atomism with the doctrine of Trent on the Eucharist. Despite the undeniable literary quality of his work and the wide diffusion it has achieved, Redondi's thesis has been harshly criticized,

[32]Caro Baroja (1970²).
[33]Caeiro (1961); Beuningen (1966); Santosuosso (1978).
[34]Firpo, L. (1949); Mercati (1955); Llamas Martínez (1972); Pereira (1974); Dias (1975); Lopez (1976); Caponetto (1979); Bozza (1983-84).
[35]Tellechea (1962-81).
[36]Firpo and Marcatto (1981, 1981-84).
[37]D'Addio (1983) and (1984); Wallace (1984).

not least because it is based on only a single document.[38] It should be added, that the author's attribution of the document to Grassi, as indicated by the editor of the trial documents, is anything but convincing.[39]

Research on the Inquisition has received an indirect contribution, as already mentioned, from those who have used inquisitorial sources to study the history of certain religious minorities or certain aspects of popular culture. In some instances the contribution made to the study of the Inquisition has been notable indeed, as when the scholar, though not directly interested in the history of the Inquisition, has published the unabridged text of entire trials. H. Beinart did this for the Castilian "Judaizers" and P. C. Ioly Zorattini for the Venetian. But even when editions of sources are not involved, the numerous studies on converted Jews in other geographic areas have provided a better understanding of the attitudes of some European and American tribunals in their regard,[40] though here, perhaps because of the fewer sources available, the use of inquisitorial documentation has been aimed more decidedly at ascertaining the rites, usages, and customs of the Moorish communities.[41]

Scholars of the religious history of Italy have, rather, been interested principally in the circumstances and doctrines of the Italian reformers, continuing the tradition established by D. Cantimori. Studies like those by A. Stella on Venetian Anabaptism (1967, 1969), C. Ginzburg on Nicodemism (1970), V. Marchetti on Sienese heretical groups (1975), and P. Simoncelli on Italian Evangelism (1979) have helped shed light on the aims and methods of the Roman Inquisition in repressing heresy in various parts of the Peninsula, especially beginning in the 1530s. For the history of heresy, Spanish research has concentrated especially on the *alumbrados*, the followers of that vague heterodox doctrine that exalted individual and direct religious experience, and on the repressive action taken against them by the Inquisition.[42]

[38]For a typical example, see the extended and detailed criticisms of Ferroni and Firpo (1985).
[39]Pagano, ed. (1984).
[40]Salvador (1969); Leibman (1971); Azevedo (1975²); Selke (1980²); Pullan (1983); Saraiva (1985⁵).
[41]Garrad (1960); Dressendörfer (1971); Cardaillac (1977): esp. 87-124; García-Arenal (1978).
[42]Huerga (1978); Márquez (1980²); Llorca (1980).

Studies of magic and witchcraft have also made interesting contributions to the history of the Inquisition. An example is the book Ginzburg has devoted to the *benandanti* (1972[2]), originally followers of a mysterious agrarian fertility-cult dedicated to the defense of the harvest against the evil spells of witches and sorcerers. The *benandanti,* however, themselves became sorcerers. This metamorphosis of the *benandanti* is explained by Ginzburg as the result of the influence exercised on local popular beliefs by the Inquisitors, for whom any form of witchcraft not inspired by the devil was inconceivable. Whether this interpretation is valid or not, Ginzburg has raised the important question of the gap between the culture of the Inquisitors and that of the accused, and of the influence of the former on the latter.[43]

Many recent studies concern the activities of inquisitorial bodies regarding the control of publications. This interest is certainly not new, but while in the past it was the banning of books that interested scholars, especially the Indexes, the latest studies have broadened the field of investigation to the application of these bans and their local influence. At the same time the attention of scholars has been directed towards the local control and prevention systems aimed at inhibiting the penetration and circulation of prohibited works in a given area. There is thus a gradual transition from a history of the Indexes of banned books to a wider history of inquisitorial censorship.

This does not mean that research on the Indexes has been abandoned. Indeed, the most important contribution to the story of censorship has been made only recently by the first two volumes of a series edited by J. M. de Bujanda dedicated to the Indexes of the sixteenth century.[44] Each of the volumes contains, beside an extensive introduction, annotated editions of individual prohibitions, together with bibliography and a facsimile reproduction of the Indexes that are analysed. Scholars have therefore an indispensable research instrument at their disposal, all the more so because in the earliest literature on the subject individual printed works listed in the Indexes had not always been correctly identified. It is justified here to speak of a fundamental contribution to the history of ecclesiastical censorship because the abundance of information provided by the Indexes already published in this series reveals both what materials were most affected and the dates and places of their publication. For example, the analysis of the

[43]See also Ginzburg (1976).
[44]Bujanda (1984); Bujanda, Higman and Farge (1985).

Spanish Index of 1559 reveals that almost all of the Latin works condemned were works published outside Spain (424 out of 431), and that the major preoccupations of the censors seem to have been directed at editions of the Bible and commentaries on it, as well as at pious or devotional literature that proposed a too individualistic spirituality.

While not as exhaustive, studies on the Roman, Spanish, and Portuguese Indexes have appeared in recent years.[45] Apart from a general article about Roman censorship by A. Rotondò (1973), among the most notable recent contributions is the book that V. Pinto Crespo has dedicated to censorship by the Spanish Inquisition in the sixteenth century. His study of the apparatus of censorship and of the actual prohibitions, especially those concerning material not directly connected with faith and morals, induces the author to conform to the definition of the Inquisition as primarily an instrument of control. The Spanish Inquisition therefore is seen as an institution used by the Crown to impose a uniform ideological model.

While Spanish scholars have primarily been interested in inquisitorial censorship as directed from the *Consejo,* the governing body of the institution, scholars of the Roman Inquisition have been interested, rather, in the effect of prohibitions at a local level. There have been a few studies on the activity of the governing bodies of the Roman Inquisition, despite the permanent inaccessibility of the archives of the Congregation of the Index. Some results have been obtained from the study of those documents of the Congregation preserved outside those archives, as evidenced by a recent article by P. Simoncelli, in which some Roman prohibitions have been examined in the wider religious and cultural context of the second half of the sixteenth century.[46]

Research on the records of local tribunals of the Roman Inquisition has produced more substantial results. Among recent studies that of P. Grendler on the control of the press exercised by the Venetian Inquisition as well as that of P. Lopez on the same activity of the Neapolitan Inquisition merit particular consideration.[47] Both books

---

[45]Scaduto (1955); Révah (1960); Pablo Moroto (1976); Martínez Millán (1979); Rêgo (1982). See also the various contributions contained in the congress proceedings by Pérez Villanueva (1980); Alcalá (1984).

[46]Simoncelli (1983-84). See also Rotondò (1963); Tedeschi (1971); Tans and Schmitz du Moulin (1974); Reale Simioli (1981-82).

[47]Lopez (1974); for other contributions on the subject, see Cavazza (1976); Del Col (1980). For the activity of the Italian tribunals under the Spanish Inquisition, see Borromeo (1983-84).

examine the initiatives taken by inquisitorial authorities to prevent the publication of prohibited books or of those considered suspect, as well as the means taken to block the introduction and circulation of the condemned works published abroad. In both cases the efficiency of the inquisitorial action is manifest, even if such efficiency was conditioned by the collaboration of the civil power, which, especially in Venice, was reluctant to support ecclesiastical authorities when political or economic interests of State were concerned.

It is evident that scholars have come to reconsider certain commonplaces also regarding this particular area of study that in the past had been accepted without criticism. Thus A. Márquez has proved the romantic legend of the writer persecuted by the Holy Office to be without foundation, at least for Spanish authors. The Inquisition, in fact, principally concerned itself with prohibiting the publication of works rather than persecuting their authors; writers who between 1506 and 1814 had judicial problems with the Spanish tribunal were not more than twenty-four, and half of these cases were without any consequences.[48] Furthermore, the fishing-nets of inquisitorial censorship now appear as less fine-meshed than has hitherto been thought. Undoubtedly, the action of the Holy Office had a dampening effect on culture, notably in those sectors most closely connected to ecclesiastical studies. Generally speaking, however, the Inquisition did not succeed in impeding totally the circulation of prohibited books, as is evinced by the inventories of a number of private libraries where such works are to be found.[49] Furthermore, doctrines condemned by the Church continued to circulate as a result of the interval between the publication of a book and its prohibition. In Spain, according to calculations made by Pinto Crespo, this interval amounted to an average of approximately five years.[50]

As must be clear by now, considerable advances have been made in studies on the Inquisition in recent years. Much remains to be done. Certainly, the most serious gap concerns the history of the Roman Congregation of the Inquisition, since it impinges upon, in varying degrees, the history of all tribunals. While awaiting the opening of those archives, it is possible to begin studying systematically the documents to be found elsewhere.[51] It is to be hoped, moreover, that

---

[48]Márquez (1970): esp. 245.
[49]Rotondò (1973): 1416; Grendler (1977): 288-89.
[50]Pinto Crespo (1983): 297.
[51]The most important have been listed by Tedeschi (1973). See also Rotondò.

research on other tribunals can be undertaken on the model of the researches already completed in Spain, to produce monographical studies compatible with modern critical standards. Finally, it would be useful to determine with greater precision how deeply rooted the Inquisition was in both the religious and civil society of its day–to study its connections with other ecclesiastical authorities,[52] with civil authorities and, more generally, with the faithful at large. How was it seen and judged? In what varying degrees was it accepted? Research along these lines would contribute greatly to a better evaluation of its effects on the Catholic world.

Bibliography

Alcalá, A., ed., *Inquisición española y mentalidad inquisitorial. Ponencias del Simposio Internacional sobre Inquisición, Neuva York, abril de 1983* (Barcelona, 1984).

Azevedo, J. Lucio de, *História dos Cristaõs Novos portugueses* (Lisboa, 1975²).

Beinart, H., *Records of the Trials of the Spanish Inquisition in Ciudad Real*, 4 vols. (Jerusalem, 1974-85).

Bennassar, B., et al., *L'Inquisition espagnole, XVe-XIXe siècle* (Paris, 1979).

Bethencourt, F., "Campo religioso e inquisição em Portugal no século XVI," *Estudos contemporáneos 6 (1984): 43-60.*

Beuningen, P. T. van, *Wilhelmus Lindanus als inquisiteur en bishop. Bijdrage tot zijn biografie, 1525-1576* (Assen, 1966).

Birkel, M., "Recherches sur la trésorerie inquisitoriale de Lima, 1569-1610," *Mélanges de la Casa de Velázquez* 5 (1969): 223-307; 6 (1907): 309-57.

Borromeo, A., "Contributo allo studio dell'inquisizione e dei suoi rapporti con il potere episcopale nell'Italia spagnola del Cinquecento," *Annuario dell'Istituto Storico Italiano per l'età Moderna e Contemporanea* 29-30 (1977-78): 219-76.

―――, "A proposito del "Directorium inquisitorum" di Nicols Eymerich e delle sue edizioni cinquecentesche," *Critica Storica* 20 (1983): 499-547.

―――, "Inquisizione spagnola e libri proibiti in Sicilia e Sardegna durante il secolo XVI," *Annuario dell'Istituto Storico Italiano per l'età Moderna e Contemporanea* 35-36 (1983-84): 217-71.

Bozza, T., "Introduzione al processo del Carnesecchi," *Annuario dell'Istituto Storico Italiano per l'età Moderna e Contemporanea* 35-36 (1983-84): 79-94.

Bujanda, J. M. de, *Index de l'inquisition espagnole 1551, 1554, 1559* (Sherbrooke, 1984).

―――, F. M. Higman, and J. K. Farge, *Index de l'Université de Paris, 1544, 1545, 1547, 1549, 1551, 1556* (Sherbrooke, 1985).

---

[52]For an initial contribution to the study of a theme which hitherto has been neglected, that is the links between the Inquisition and the diocesan authorities, see Borromeo (1978-1979).

Burman, E., *The Inquisition. The Hammer of Heresy* (Wellingborough, 1984).

Caeiro, F. C., *O arquiduque Alberto de Austria vicerei e inquisidor-mor de Portugal, cardenal legado do papa, governador e depois soberano dos Paises Baixos* (Lisboa, 1961).

Cantimori, C., *Eretici italiani del Cinquecento. Ricerche storiche* (Firenze, 1939).

Cardaillac, L., *Morisques et chrétiens: un affrontement polémique, 1492-1640* (Paris, 1977).

Caponetto, S., *Aonio Paleario (1503-1570) e la Riforma protestante in Toscana* (Torino, 1979).

Caro Baroja, J., *El señor inquisidor y otra vidas por oficio* (Madrid, 1970[2]).

Cavazza, S., "Inquisizione e libri proibiti in Friuli e a Gorizia tra Cinquecento e Seicento," *Studi Goriziani* 43 (1976): 29-80.

Contreras, J., *El Santo Oficio de la Inquisición de Galicia (poder, sociedad y cultura)*, (Madrid, 1982).

D'Addio, M., "Considerazioni sui processi a Galileo," *Rivista di Storia della Chiesa in Italia* 37 (1983): 1-52; 38 (1984): 47-114.

Davidson, N., "Il Sant'Uffizio e la tutela del culto a Venezia nel '500," *Studi Veneziani* n.s.6 (1982): 87-101.

Dedieu, J. P., "Les inquisiteurs de Tolède et la visite du district. La sedentarisation d'un tribunal (1550-1630)," *Mélanges de la Casa de Velázquez* 13 (1977): 235-56.

――――, "Le causes de foi de l'inquisition de Tolède (1483-1820)," *Mélanges de la Casa de Velázquez* 14 (1978): 143-71.

――――, "¿Es responsable la inquisición en el atraso economico de España? Elementos para la respuesta," *Origines del atraso economico español*, ed. B. Bennassar, (Madrid, 1985): 176-87.

Del Col, A., "Il controllo della stampa a Venezia ed i processi di Antonio Bruccioli (1548-1559)," *Critica Storica* 17 (1980): 457-510.

――――, "L'inquisizione," *Società e cultura del Cinquecento nel Friuli Occidentale. Catalogo* (Pordenone, 1985): 181-88.

Dias, J. S. Silva da, *O erasmismo e a inquisicão em Portugal. O processo de fr. Valentim da Luz* (Coimbra, 1975).

Dressendörfer, P., *Islam unter der Inquisition. Die Morisco-Prozesse in Toledo, 1575-1610* (Wiesbaden, 1971).

Escandell Bonet, B., "Caracteres de la inquisición en Indias. Deducciones de un análisis cuantitativo sobre el Santo Oficio peruano del siglo XVI," *Annuario dell'Istituto Storico Italiano per l'età Moderna e Contemporanea* 35-36 (1983-84): 95-114.

Escudero, J. A., "Los origines del Consejo de la Suprema Inquisición," *Anuario de Historia del Derecho Español* 53 (1983): 237-88.

Esteban Dieve, C., *Heterodoxia e inquisición en Santo Domingo, 1492-1822* (Santo Domingo, 1983).

Ferrone, V., and M. Firpo, "Galileo tra inquisitori e microstorici," *Rivista Storica Italiana* 97 (1985): 177-238.

Firpo, L., *Il processo di Giordano Bruno (Napoli, 1949)*.

Firpo, M., and D. Marcatto, "Il primo processo inquisitoriale contro il cardinale Giovanni Morone (1552-1553)," *Rivista Storica Italiana* 93 (1982): 71-142.

————, *Il processo inquisitoriale del cardinale Giovanni Morone,* 3t. in 4 vols. (Roma, 1981-1984).

García-Arenal, M., *Inquisición y moriscos. Los procesos del tribunal de Cuenca* (Madrid, 1978).

García Carcel, R., *Orígines de la inquisición española. El tribunal de Valencia, 1478-1530* (Barcelona, 1976).

————, *Herejía y sociedad en el siglo XVI. La inquisición en Valencia, 1530-1603* (Barcelona, 1980).

Garrad, K., "La inquisición y los moriscos granadinos (1526-1580)," *Miscelánea de estudios àrabes y hebraicos* 9 (1960): 55-72.

Ginzburg, C., *Il nicodemismo. Simulazione e dissimulazione religiosa nell'Europa del '500* (Torino, 1970).

————, *I benandanti. Stregoneria e culti agrari tra Cinquecento e Seicento* (Torino, 1972²).

————, *Il formaggio e i vermi. Il cosmo di un mugnaio del '500* (Torino, 1976).

González Novalín, J. L., *El inquisidor general Fernando de Valdés (1483-1568),* 2 vols. (Oviedo, 1968-1971).

————, "La inquisición española," *Historia de la Iglesia en España,* ed. R. García Villoslada, III (Madrid, 1980): 107-268.

————, "L'inquisizione spagnola. Correnti storiografiche da Llorente (1817) ai giorni nostri," *Rivista di Storia della Chiesa in Italia* 39 (1985): 139-59.

Greenleaf, R. E., *The Mexican Inquisition of the Sixteenth Century* (Albuquerque, N.M., 1969).

Grendler, P. F., *The Roman Inquisition and the Venetian Press, 1540-1605* (Princeton, 1977).

Henningsen, G., "El «Banco de datos» del Santo Oficio. Las relaciones de causas de la inquisición española (1550-1700)," *Boletín de la Real Academia de la Historia* 174 (1977): 547-570.

————, *The Witches' Advocate. Basque Witchcraft and the Spanish Inquisition* (Reno, Nevada, 1980).

Huerga, A., *Historia de los alumbrados: I / Los alumbrados de Extremadura (1570-1582),* (Madrid, 1978); *II / Los alumbrados de la Alta Andalucía (1575-1590),* (Madrid, 1978).

Ioly Zorattini, P. C., *Processi del S. Uffizio di Venezia contro ebrei e giudaizzanti. I / 1548-1560* (Firenze 1980); *II / 1561-1570* (Firenze 1982); *III / 1570-1572 (Firenze 1984); IV / 1571-1580 (Firenze 1985).*

Kakba Priolkar, A., *The Goa Inquisition* (Bombay, 1961).

Kamen, H., "Confiscations in the Economy of the Spanish Inquisition," *The Economic History Review* 18 (1965): 511-525.

————, *Inquisition and Society in Spain in the Sixteenth and Seventeenth Centuries* (London, 1985²).

Liebman, S. B., *Los judios en Mexico y América Central (fé, llamas e inquisición)* (Mexico, 1978).

Llamas Martínez, E., *Santa Teresa de Jesús y la inquisición española* (Madrid, 1972).

Llorca, B., *La inquisición española y los alumbrados (1509-1667)* (Salamanca, 1980).

Lopez, P., *Inquisizione, stampa e censura nel Regno di Napoli tra '500 e '600* (Napoli, 1974).

———, *Il movimento valdesiano a Napoli. Mario Galeota e le sue vicende con il Sant'Uffizio* (Napoli, 1976).

Marchetti, V., *Gruppi ereticali senesi del Cinquecento* (Firenze, 1975).

Márquez, A., *Los alumbrados. Orígenes y filosofía (1525-1559)* (Madrid, 1980[2]).

———, *Literatura e inquisición en España, 1478-1834* (Madrid, 1980).

———, "La inquisición: estado de las investigaciones inquisitoriales," *Revista de Occidente* 6 (1981); 147-56.

Martínez Millán, J., "El catálogo de libros prohibidos de 1559," *Miscelánea Comillas* 37 (1979): 179-217.

———, *La hacienda de la inquisición, 1478-1700* (Madrid, 1984).

———, and T. Sánchez Rivilla, "El Consejo de inquisición (1483-1700)," *Hispania Sacra* 36 (1984): 71-193.

Mea, E. Azevedo, *Senteças da inquisição de Coimbra em metropolitanos de D. Frei Bartolomeu dos Martires (1567-1582)* (Porto, 1982).

Mentzer, R. A., Jr., *Heresy Proceedings in Languedoc, 1500-1560* (Philadelphia, 1984).

Mercati, A., *I costituti di Nicolò Franco (1568-1570) dinanzi l'inquisizione di Roma esistenti nell'Archivo Segreto Vaticano* (Città del Vaticano, 1955).

Monter, E. W., "The New Social History and the Spanish Inquisition," *Journal of Social History* 17 (1983): 705-713.

Pablo Moroto, D. de, "El indice de libros prohibidos en el Concilio de Trento," *Revista española de Teología 36 (1976): 39-64.*

Pagano, Sergio M., ed., *I documenti del processo di Galileo Galilei* (Città del Vaticano, 1984).

Parker, G., "Some Recent Work on the Inquisition in Spain and in Italy," *Journal of Modern History* 54 (1982): 519-32.

Paschini, P., *Venezia e l'inquisizione romana da Giulio II a Pio IV* (Padova 1959).

Pereira, I. da Rosa "O proceso de Damião de Gois na inquisição de Lisboa (4 de abril de 1571-16 de dezembro de 1572)," *Anais da Academia Portuguesa da Historia,* 2d ser., 23, t.1 (1974): 117-56.

Pérez Villanueva, J., ed., *La inquisición española. Nueva visión, nuevos horizontes* (Madrid, 1980).

Pérez Villanueva, J., and B. Escandell Bonet, eds., *Historia de la inquisición en España y America,* I (Madrid, 1984).

Pinto Crespo, V., *Inquisición y control ideológico en la España del siglo XVI* (Madrid, 1983).

Pullan, B., *The Jews of Europe and the Inquisition of Venice, 1550-1670* (Oxford, 1983).

Reale Simioli, C., "Ansaldo Cebà e la Congregazione dell'Indice," *Campania Sacra* 11-12 (1981-1982): 96-212.

Rêgo, R., *Os indices expurgatorios e a inquisição portuguesa* (Lisboa, 1982).

Reguera, I., *La inquisición española en el Pais Vasco. El tribunal de Calahorra, 1513-1570* (San Sebastián, 1984).

Révah, I. S., *La censura inquisitoriale portugaise au XVIe siècle. Etude accompagnée de la reproduction en facsimile des Index,* I (Lisboa, 1960).

———, *Etudes portugaises,* ed. C. Amiel (Paris, 1975).

Romeo, G., "Per la storia del Sant'Ufficio a Napoli tra '500 e '600," *Campania Sacra* 7 (1976): 5-109.

Rotondò, A., "Nuovi documenti per la storia dell' 'Indice dei libri proibiti' (1572-1638)," *Rinascimento,* 2d ser., 3 (1963): 145-211.

———, "La censura ecclesiastica e la cultura," *Storia d'Italia* V (Torino, 1973): 1397-1492.

Salvador, J. Gonçalves, *Cristãos-Novos, jesuitas e inquisição. Aspectos de sua atuação nas capitanias do Sul, 1530-1680* (Sao Paulo, 1969).

Santosuosso, A., "The Moderate Inquisitor: Giovanni della Casa's Venetian Nunciature, 1544-1549," *Studi Veneziani* n.s. 2 (1978): 118-210.

Saraiva, A. J., *A inquisição portuguesa* (Lisboa, 1956²).

———, *Inquisição e cristãos-novos* (Lisboa, 1985⁵).

Scaduto, M., "Laínez e l'Indice del 1559: Lullo, Sabunde, Savonarola, Erasmo," *Archivum Historicum Societatis Jesu* 24 (1958): 237-273.

Seidel Menchi, S., "Inquisizione come repressione o inquisizione come mediazione? Una proposta di periodizzazione," *Annuario dell'Istituto Storico Italiano per l'età Moderna e Contemporanea* 35-36 (1983-84): 51-77.

Selke, A., *Vida y muerte de los chuetas de Mallorco* (Madrid, 1980²).

Simoncelli, P., *Evangelismo italiano del Cinquecento. Questione religiosa e nicodemismo politico* (Roma, 1979).

———, "Documenti interni alla congregazione dell'Indice, 1571-1590. Logica e ideologia dell'intervento censorio," *Annuario dell'Istituto Storico Italiano per l'età Moderna e Contemporanea,* 35-36 (1983-1984): 189-215.

Siqueira, S. A., *A inquisição portuguesa e a sociedade colonial* (Sao Paulo, 1978).

Stella, A., *Dall'anabattismo al socianinesimo nel Cinquecento veneto. Ricerche storiche* (Padova, 1967).

———, *Anabattismo e antitrinitarismo in Italia nel XVI secolo. Nuove ricerche storiche* (Padova, 1969).

Tans, J. A. G., and H. Schmitz du Moulin, *Pasquier Quesnel devant la congrégation de l'Index* (La Haye, 1974).

Tedeschi, J., "Florentine Documents for an History of the 'Index of Prohibited Books,'" *Renaissance Studies in Honor of Hans Baron,* ed. A. Molho and J. Tedeschi (Firenze, 1971).

———, "La dispersion degli archivi dell'inquisizione romana," *Rivista di Storia e Letteratura religiosa* 9 (1973): 298-312.

———, "Preliminary Observations on Writing a History of the Roman Inquisition," in *Continuity and Discontinuity in Church History,* ed. F. F. Church and T. George (Leiden, 1979): 232-49.

————, "The Roman Inquisition and Witchcraft. An Early Seventeenth-Century 'Instruction' on Correct Trial Procedure," *Revue de l'Histoire des Religions* 200 (1983): 163-88.

————, and G. Henningsen, eds., *The Inquisition in Early Modern Europe. Studies on Sources and Methods, (Dekalb, Ill., forthcoming).*

Tellechea Idígoras, J. I., *Fray Bartolomé Carranza. Documentos historicos,* 6 t. in 7 vols. (Madrid, 1962-1981).

Testas, G., and J. Testas, *L'inquisition* (Paris, 1966).

Valvekens, P. E., *De Inquisitie in de Nederlanden der zestiende eeuw* (Brussels-Amsterdam, 1949).

Vekene, E. van der, *Bibliotheca Bibliographica Historiae Sanctae Inquisitionis,* 2 vols. (Vaduz, 1982).

Vella, A. P., *The Tribunal of the Inquisition in Malta* (Valletta, 1964).

Wallace, William A., *Galileo and His Sources. The Heritage of the Collegio Romano in Galileo's Science* (Princeton, 1984).

Liturgy and Liturgical Arts

Niels Krogh Rasmussen, O.P.

MODERN LITURGICAL SCHOLARSHIP has for the most part avoided the period under consideration. The scholarly evidence needed to support the reforms advocated by the contemporary liturgical movement could hardly be found in the very period from which the movement emerged. As a result, the "Tridentine" period was either neglected or presented in negative terms. The most positive statement by previous scholars was that the fixation of the liturgical texts by the Tridentine Canon safeguarded the Roman Catholic Church from even worse disasters, such as plunging into the pits of Rationalism and Pietism, dangers to which the Churches of the Reformation succumbed all too easily.[1]

The reforms of the Second Vatican Council and its aftermath constitute a rupture with Latin and the liturgical tradition of the preceeding four hundred years. Since these reforms are now in place, it is possible to look back and consider the period more objectively and irenically. At the same time, the high level of scholarship that made the reforms possible must be maintained by those who follow the steps of renowned liturgists like Andrieu, Baumstark, Botte, Herwegen, Jungmann, Klauser, and Vogel.[2]

Periodization and Documentation

1. *Periodization*

The period chosen for this *Guide to Research* does not coincide fully with what an examination of the liturgical data would suggest. On the one hand, the codification of the post-Tridentine books must be seen in the light of medieval tendencies to uniformity in the Western liturgy.[3] It is linked as well to the development of printing and its associated economic necessities.[4] Likewise, liturgical reform was on the humanist agenda; some reforms took place long before Trent.[5] These facts alone speak for a more open *terminus ante*. On the other hand, the

---

[1]Jungmann (1951-55): 141.
[2]For bibliographies, see Rasmussen (1969).
[3]Gy (1975).
[4]Martin (1969); Kingdon (1985).
[5]Donner (1976); Rosenthal (1982).

terminus post quem non does not seem cogent in liturgical studies. There is a marked continuity, for example, in the development of scholarly liturgical studies, in the specific evolution in the French Church, and in the accretion of new feasts. These factors warrant a more open-ended chronology than that intended for this volume.

Three contemporary scholars have presented general surveys of the history of Western liturgy. For Anton L. Mayer (d. 1982), the relevant periods are indicated by the titles of his articles: "Renaissance, Humanism and Liturgy" and "Liturgy and Baroque."[6] The weakness of Mayer's work lies in the impressionistic approach inherent in *Geistesgeschichte*, a forerunner of the interdisciplinary history of ideas.

Theodor Klauser (d. 1984) presented a synthesis of liturgical history in *A Short History of the Western Liturgy,* which has enjoyed wide circulation. Klauser divides liturgical history before Vatican Council II into four periods, the third of which is entitled "Dissolution, Elaboration, Reinterpretation, Misinterpretation: From Gregory VII to the Council of Trent." He defined the fourth with the help of a highly qualifying adjective: "Rigid Unification of the Liturgy (*Einheitsliturgie*) and Rubricism: From the Council of Trent to the Second Vatican Council." We note elsewhere Klauser states that "the desire to defend the tradition of the Church against the attacks of the Reformers made the majority of the Fathers [at Trent] blind to medieval liturgical practice and the pressing need for a thorough reform," thus promoting not rupture but continuity.[7]

Enrico Cattaneo has also written a comprehensive history of liturgy, subtitled "Historical Notes," (1984) a work that has its special cogency in dealing with the situation in the Italian states. The treatment of the period from 1500 until 1900 extends over 170 pages, and it is regrettable that the work is largely unknown outside Italy; it is without doubt the best history of the period. The scope of this *Guide* excludes an account of the developments in the churches of the Reformation. There are, however, both direct and indirect influences, cross-fertilizations, and common, non-denominational trends at work. Much needs to be done here.

2. *Documentation*

Printed Books. The fifteenth-century invention and subsequent success of the printing press had immediate effects on liturgical

---

[6]Mayer (1934, 1935, 1971).
[7]Klauser (1969), (1963): 19.

development. The first printed books of a given diocese are precious witnesses to the late-medieval liturgies that they codified. As these books often exist in several copies, they make the liturgical texts of a given diocese accessible. However, even before Trent tendencies towards uniformity can be ascertained from the reduced number of diocesan books in Italy (where Roman books were used instead),[8] while most dioceses and orders in Northern Europe were very keen about procuring printings of their liturgical books.

Studies interrelating the printing press and liturgical history are of paramount importance, but they have only begun to appear.[9] A major problem for these studies is that liturgical books are anonymous and, as such, are poorly treated in major bibliographies. The Library of Congress general heading "Catholic Church . . . Liturgy and Ritual" is a *mare magnum* causing seasickness for those who try to venture into it; the *Catalogue Général* of the Bibliothèque Nationale registers only works by named authors; liturgical works have to be located on large photographic plates reproduced from handwritten index cards from the nineteenth century that endanger the eyesight of the beholder. There is no printed catalogue of the printed books in the Vatican Library. The *General Catalogue* of the British Library, however, is most useful; the entry is "Liturgies."[10]

Some specialized liturgical bibliographies exist for the Missal, the Breviary, the Book of Hours and, most recently, the Ritual and Processional.[11] The liturgical production of the diocese of Lyons, one of the major printing centers of the era, has also been catalogued.[12] But Antiphonaries, Graduals, Pontificals, Ceremonials, Directories, Psalters, Hymnals and other such books still await reliable listings.

Equally necessary are studies of Propers. Printing the texts for specific local or new liturgies and inserting them at the end of a book is the procedure that resolved both the cost of providing complete books (the bulk of which would be identical with all other books of the same category) and making the Roman books truly proper in a given place. The fact that these publications were small and produced as loose leaves suggests that a certain proportion of them are lost. Since those that have survived are bound at the end of a liturgical book, our catalogues

[8]Gy (1975): 609.
[9]Martin (1969); Kingdon (1985).
[10]British Museum (Library) (1962-).
[11]Weale - Bohatta (1938); Bohatta (1909, 1937); Meyer-Baer (1962); Molin and Aussedat-Minivielle (1984); Zanon (1984).
[12]Amiet (1979).

are probably unreliable concerning them; the bibliographer would have been interested in describing the supporting book, not its appendix or appendices. Major tasks of research lie ahead.

Manuscripts. Manuscripts do exist from the period, but study of them is clearly of secondary importance. Calligraphic books, like those used by the pope, or the big *chorali*, which allowed all singers to use a single text, clearly continued. It is mostly with local liturgies that we find Propers added in manuscript, especially when finances or urgency prohibited acquisition of printed texts.

General Works and Bibliography. Besides the works by Klauser, Mayer and Cattaneo already mentioned, some general manuals on liturgy are also partially relevant for our period. For the history of the Tridentine Mass, J. A. Jungmann's work will remain *aere perennis*,[13] to be complemented by the recent French and German introductions to liturgical studies.[14] Although Vogel's *Introduction*, as its full title indicates, and the bibliography by Pfaff deal primarily with medieval liturgies, the close connection between them and the liturgy of our period makes these works useful.[15]

Centers for Study. Doctoral programs in liturgical studies are offered at the University of Notre Dame. In Europe, one must mention the Institut Supérieur de Liturgie of the Institut Catholique, Paris,[16] and the Pontificio Istituto Liturgico of the Pontificio Ateneo S. Anselmo, Rome.[17] Outside these centers, the most important specialized libraries are those of the Liturgisches Institut, Trier,[18] and of the Benedictine Abbeys of Mont César, Leuven,[19] and Maria Laach, West Germany.[20] For liturgical studies the Biblioteca Apostolica Vaticana holds a special place, particularly because of the exceptional quality of the holdings in the reading room.

[13]Jungmann (1951-55); see also Jungmann (1962): 80-89.
[14]Martimort (1983-84); Meyer (1983-).
[15]Vogel (1975); Pfaff (1982).
[16]4, Av. Vavin, F-75006 Paris, France. List of dissertations, see "Mémoires et thèses" (1980).
[17]Piazza dei Cavalieri di Malta, 5, I-00153 Roma, Italy. List of dissertations, see *Tesi di Laurea* (1985).
[18]Jesuitenstrasse 13c, D-5500 Trier, Federal Republic of Germany.
[19]Abdij Keizersberg, Mechelsestraat 202, B-3000 Leuven, Belgium.
[20]Benediktinerabtei, D-5471 Maria Laach, Federal Republic of Germany.

Specific Liturgical Problems

1. *The Liturgy before Trent*

The relatively greater accessibility of the earliest printed liturgical books makes them an easy means of documentation for the medieval liturgies that were to disappear during the sixteenth century. The specifics of that period, however, cannot be forgotten. Reforming tendencies can be discerned long before the decisive activities of the Council. The Benedictine Congregation of Bursfeld simplified its calendar as early as 1468.[21] Jakob Wimpfeling (1450-1528) applied philological criteria to improve the quality of the *textus receptus* of the liturgy.[22] Alberto de Castello (or Castellani, fl. 1490-1523) was instrumental in editing a series of printed liturgical books in Venice.[23]

The renewal of the Latin language also influenced the liturgy. Zaccaria Ferreri (1479-1524) proposed a shortened Breviary and Hymnary *iuxta veram metri et latinitatis normam* (1525).[24] Another project for the Breviary, that of Cardinal Francisco Quiñonez (1475-1540), proved to have greater success. The Breviary was a shortened version of the Office, destined for private recitation (outside choir) by secular priests. Difficulties arose, however, when some religious wished to extend its use to choir. J. A. Jungmann studies its disappearance in a penetrating analysis.[25]

A final aspect of pre-Tridentine liturgy to be considered falls under the heading *Maiestas Pontificia*. The concept, well known in Church history, is linked to the splendor of the papacy in the early Renaissance. Because liturgy was an important component of the life at the papal court, the concept of *Maiestas* is relevant in this context, as has been shown for the liturgical arts by John Shearman (1972) and for liturgical preaching by John O'Malley (1979).

It is beyond the scope of this *Guide* to trace the survival and transformation of the old medieval liturgies in the churches of the Reformation or to study the new forms that emerged as reactions to the inherited liturgy. It is, however, absolutely essential that a correct assessment of the *Nachleben* and of the transformation of the *vetus*

---

[21]Rosenthal (1982).
[22]Donner (1976).
[23]Cattaneo (1967); Dykmans (1985): 134-35.
[24]Cattaneo (1984): 289.
[25]Jungmann (1962): 200-14.

disciplina be undertaken. At the same time, a careful listing of references to liturgical problems, direct or *ex obliquo* in the *corpus* of Reformation literature, Protestant and Catholic, is likewise needed, in order to assess the correspondence of actual reforms to hopes and expectations.

2. Trent and the "Tridentine" Books

Trent dealt specifically with the liturgy. Some of the problems addressed were predominantly doctrinal in character (e.g., the mode of Christ's presence in the Eucharist) and thus pertain more to systematic theology.[26] Others, however, are specifically related to the cultic *praxis* of the Church (e.g., the question of improvement of the liturgical books). Only the latter will be dealt with here.

The critical edition of documents related to the Council (CT), as well as assiduous work by contemporary historians, has brought much information to light. Thus, two of the most important contributions to our topic come from the *Altmeister*, Hubert Jedin himself (1939, 1975). The available material, however, could probably yield even more when examined by professional liturgists.

This is, for example, true of the many pleas for reform contemporaneous with the Council. The German Catholic irenicist, Georg Witzel (1501-73),[27] pleaded as early as 1538 for the abolition of private Masses and Mass stipends; while his work is generally well known, his devotional prayers deserve a scholarly study. This is also true for Jakob Leisentritt (1527-86). Constructive planning for the time ahead was evinced by Tommaso Campeggio (1483-1564), who in 1546 suggested a "Missal common for all the churches, with rejection of what is superfluous, especially several Sequences that contain much unfit material" (CT 5:25).[28] The famous *Deputatio Patrum ad colligendos abusus de sacrificio missae* presented its report (CT 8:916-24) to Cardinal Gonzaga on August 8, 1562, and highlighted an important list of abuses; it showed the keen perception of its authors and is "a mine of information for the scholar of liturgy."[29]

Compared with the reform agendas and the discussions, the specifically liturgical decisions at Trent were few. In most instances where Protestant Reformers had pointed to medieval practices as

[26]Duval (1984).
[27]Pralle (1948); Trusen (1957); Dolan (1957).
[28]Jedin (1957): 39.
[29]Jedin (1966): 520.

deviations, these same practices were affirmed as legitimate and adherence to them became proof not only of orthopraxy but also of orthodoxy. Such is the case, for example, of the defense of private Masses, Masses in which the priest alone receives Communion, the silent recitation of the Canon and the exclusive use of Latin (Session 22; September 17, 1562).[30]

On one point, however, an accomodation was made to the Reformers: the Decree on the concession of the chalice (also 1562) referred this possibility to the pope. Pius IV executed such a decree in 1564 for parts of the Empire, but soon this too was transformed into a test of confessionalism; the concessions and the use did not last beyond the sixteenth century.[31] During the frantic last months of the Council, unfinished agendas were likewise referred to the pope. The last Session (25; December 4, 1563) asked Pius IV to take up the pending questions on indulgences, the Index of Prohibited Books, the catechism and– nearly the last words of Trent–*de missali et breviario* (CT 9: 1106).

The mandate of the Council covered only the Missal and the Breviary. The customary use of the word "Tridentine" to indicate all the liturgical books issued between 1567 and 1614 is therefore inaccurate. We do not know enough about the reform of the Breviary that first appeared in 1568.[32] It contained the new calendar, which was to be used as well for the Missal, thus establishing a strict conformity between celebration of the Hours and celebration of the Eucharist. The calendar was greatly reduced in comparison with the late-medieval calendars and took as its model earlier texts, probably of the eleventh century.[33]

The main work on the Missal of 1570 was done under the direction of the able Cardinal Sirleto (1514-85), who had also been active to some extent in the reform of the Breviary. Much more is known about procedures for the reform of the Missal, thanks to the research of the late A. Frutaz.[34] In both bulls of promulgation, mention is made of the consultation of manuscripts in the Vatican Library that had preceded the publication of these books. The survival of particular liturgies would be tolerated only if they could be proved to be older than two hundred years. The usual stylistic clauses about non-reformability of the new books were included in the bulls as a matter of course.[35]

[30]Schmidt (1950).
[31]Franzen (1955), with indication of broader studies.
[32]Best overview: Denzler (1964): 83-100.
[33]Focke and Heinrichs (1939).
[34]Denzler, ibid.; Frutaz (1960).
[35]Oury (1969).

Succeeding popes did not limit themselves to the two books specifically mentioned by the Council and promulgated under Pius V. In 1583 a new Martyrology was published under Gregory XIII. The text needed improvements, and Baronius (1538-1607) was commissioned to write an authoritative commentary for it, another example of the influence of emerging historical scholarship.[36] As the Martyrology also contains a treatise on *"computus,"* the new Gregorian Calendar (1582) thereby gained an entry into the liturgy.[37]

The Pontifical was reformed in 1596 under Clement VIII.[38] The *Ceremoniale Episcoporum,* the companion to the Pontifical that explains the intricacies of the pontifical liturgy, was issued in 1600. Preliminaries for this undertaking had been done in great part by Charles Borromeo (1538-84), cardinal-nephew of Pius IV.[39] The last book to be released, this time under Paul V in 1614, was the Ritual. The bull did not in this instance impose the new book and suppress the former ones; the new Ritual was only recommended for adoption by the bishops.[40] The specific ceremonial for the papal court, the so-called *Ceremoniale Romanum* now easily accessible in a critical edition, was never revised.[41] This fifteenth-century work by Patrizi Piccolomini continued to be used until our own time.

3. The Congregation of Sacred Rites

The "Tridentine" *corpus* was thus completed by 1614. A way to ensure its imposition and uniform use was needed; the newly organized Roman Curia provided the means. When Sixtus V instituted the permanent Roman Congregations on January 22, 1588, the *Congregation quinta* was defined *pro sacris ritibus et caeremoniis.* While many of the Roman Congregations have had monographs devoted to their function and personnel,[42] the Congregation of Rites has not enjoyed the same attention except for its specifically juridicial aspects.[43] Who were the officials working there? To what extent did scholarly liturgists influence its decisions? These questions remain unanswered.

It was through the decrees issued by this Congregation that "Tridentine" uniformity would be imposed and maintained. Each time

---

[36]Denzler (1964): 109-16.
[37]Denzler (1964): 100-09; Peri (1967); Coyne, Hoskin, and Pedersen (1983).
[38]Dykmans (1985): 149-57.
[39]Borella (1937); Cattaneo (1966).
[40]Löwenberg (1937, 1942); García Alonso (1959); Fischer (1962); Sigler (1964).
[41]Dykmans (1980, 1982).
[42]Del Re (1970) is an excellent guide to the literature on the Roman Curia.
[43]McManus (1954), but see also Gramatowski (1975) for extant sources.

a dispute arose in the local churches, a query (*dubium*) was sent to Rome to be settled. Most requests for alternatives to the text or rubrics of the promulgated books were answered by a refusal. These *decreta* were assembled in collections and had an influence on the liturgical development in the period from 1588 to 1963 that can hardly be overestimated.

The successive editions of the *Decreta* were catalogued anonymously in 1930[44] and by F. McManus in 1954. The collection by Gardellini, supplemented by others up to 1887, contained 5,993 decrees.[45] But to these must be added a further 2,716 decrees from the years 1588-1700 not contained in the official collections but published in *Analecta Iuris Pontificii.*[46] This wealth of material is also important (just as were the pleas for reform at Trent), because they contain many elements relevant for the history of attitudes (*mentalité*) and popular religion. Anyone wishing to work with the *Decreta* will probably be overwhelmed by the tedium, but the results will be worth the effort. The value-laden expression "rubricist," denoting the juridico-liturgical commentators on the liturgical books, likewise needs re-evaluation.

4. *The Liturgy after Trent*

Historians of liturgy and spirituality have generally argued that for our period there seems to have been a definite abandonment of the official corporate worship of the Church as the ordinary vehicle for the faith-life of the believer. What replaced it is called "spirituality" (a term often understood to exclude the liturgy itself and that needs to be submitted to rigorous critique). Nonetheless, the liturgy in many instances continued to be the source of intense spiritual life for the Catholic Christian. A case in point is Pascal, whose biblical reflections in the *Pensées* must be explained by his assiduous daily reading of the Breviary, as has been shown by Phillippe Sellier (1966). The continual quest for better Breviaries in seventeenth- and eighteenth-century France likewise speaks for a living tradition, not meaningless observance.

Liturgy in Rome, Roman Decisions. Ludwig von Pastor's monumental *History of the Popes* contains a wealth of information about the state of the liturgy in Rome and of the activities of the popes in its regard. Although its general perspectives are rather *passé*, Pastor's work may

---

[44]*Bibliophilus* (1930).
[45]McManus (1954): 154.
[46]Decreta (1864); Bibliophilus (1930): 438³.

prove helpful if used with caution, not only in the area of liturgy but also in that of popular religiosity. In his recent *The Popes and the European Revolution* (1981), Owen Chadwick provides useful information in the section entitled "The Church of the Old Regime," which reaches back to the sixteenth century.

The calendar of the saints that had been purified and simplified in 1568 would not remain for long in that state. Pierre Jounel (1960) has shown how feasts were upgraded, older feasts reintegrated and new feasts introduced (a phenomenon familiar from contemporary Roman Catholic practice). The juridical procedure for canonizations was refined, and after 1662 beatification preceded every canonization.[47]

All of this was of course closely related to popular piety, even though political considerations played a part as Pierre Delooz (1969) showed. An interesting account of the process for the canonization of Charles Borromeo in 1610 is given by Angelo Turchini (1984), who analyzes the required miracles as well as the enormous expenses related to the process.

Our period saw a rampant development of Mariological idea-feasts: Rosary, 1571 (extended to the universal Church in 1716); Immaculate Conception, 1661 (extended in 1708); Name of Mary, 1683; Mary Redeemer of Captives, 1696. Mary "became her own cultic center."[48] The attempts of Jean Eudes (1601-80) to have his devotion to the Sacred Heart of Jesus made official by a liturgical celebration was not accepted by the Roman authorities until the following century (1765), supported then by the influence of Margaret Mary Alacoque (1647-90). Another aspect of Christological devotion underwent, however, even greater development in the Eucharist.

As in the cult of Mary and the saints, the cult of the Eucharist soon became an anti-Protestant affirmation and thus characteristic of the "counter" aspect of the Catholic Reform. At the same time, it was rooted in the medieval desire for visualization, "the gaze that saves."[49] Exposition and benediction with the exposed Sacrament developed into an elaborate ritual of "perpetual" adoration, cemented into The "Forty Hours" (*Quarant'ore*).

The Roman style of this devotion was formalized by Clement VIII's instruction *Graves et diuturnae*, November 24, 1592 (later reissued by Clement XI in 1705). This *Instructio clementina* was juridically

---

[47]Veraja (1983), especially 20-111.
[48]Mayer (1935): 136.
[49]Klauser (1969): 135-40.

binding only in Rome but was in fact observed in many other places. Forty Hours Devotion had great success, especially among the Jesuits;[50] great artists were commissioned for the construction of theatrical decorations for the occasion.[51] An engraving by Piranesi of the *Quarant'ore* in the Cappella Paolina in the Apostolic Palace of the Vatican shows the chapel ablaze with thousands of candles and, in the center, the exposed monstrance mystically lit so as to make the host transparent; the papal court lies in prostration before it. "The cult of the Sacrament . . . had swallowed up and subordinated the liturgy to its own purpose."[52]

The intricacies of official papal ceremonies were regulated by the old Ceremonial as applied by the Masters of Ceremonies, who among their obligations had to keep diaries describing exactly what had been done and what had gone wrong. These diaries are important sources for liturgical changes and for other features related to the papal chapel. F. J. McGinnis (1982) used the diaries, for example, to document the preaching before the popes in this period. Unfortunately, these diaries are not widely known; very few extracts have been edited, and no one has yet compiled a catalogue. I would like to produce such a repertory and would be happy to receive suggestions and information concerning it.[53]

Under the culturally rich pontificate of Urban VIII, another attempt was made to revise the hymns of the Breviary by "correcting" the Latin; the same had been attempted the previous century by F. Zaccari. Consequently, the Hymnary of the Roman Breviary was changed, while the Hymnaries of the rites of the religious orders remained in so-called Christian Latin.[54] A scholarly evaluation of the influence of neo-Latin on the liturgy remains to be done.

Liturgy in the Local Churches. What were the actual celebrations in a given parish like? Liturgical scholars usually avoid questions of this kind, probably because they require access to source material outside their field like records of visitations, diaries, and archives of music. This neglect is regrettable, especially when we see how much other historians can draw from these sources.[55] Monographs on diocesan liturgies are often understood as an enterprise in medieval studies. This

[50]Jungmann (1962), 223-38; Weil (1974); Dompnier (1981); Ussia (1982).
[51]Fagiolo dell'Arco and Carandini (1977-78): 138-40, 150-60, 253-55.
[52]Klauser (1969): 139.
[53]Rasmussen (1983): 147-48; Rasmussen (1986).
[54] Springhetti (1968); Lefevre (1970).
[55]e.g. Delumeau (1977 ET): esp. 129-53 and 175-202.

is, however, not the case, especially for the calendar, the Proper of the Saints and the Ritual. It therefore makes sense to undertake such studies, and recent publications demonstrate the success with which they can be done.

An examplary monograph dealing with the diocese of Mainz was published in several parts (1960-72) by Herman Reifenberg. He describes the many changes that the local medieval liturgy underwent during our period, always in the direction of an increasing Romanization (e.g., for the local Breviary: Mainz-Roman rite until 1570, reformed Mainz-Roman rite after 1570, Tridentine-Roman rite after 1655). The same author (1981) has given a useful topo-bibliographical listing of existing liturgical studies in German-speaking and neighboring countries. Similar *instruments de travail* are greatly needed for other regions.[56]

The refusal of Trent to allow the use of modern languages for liturgical texts was circumvented by translations for the faithful and by the introduction of singing in the vernacular while the presiding priest ("celebrant") read the Latin Mass in a low voice in order to guarantee the "validity" and the "licitness" of the celebration. Until recently scholars have not paid much attention to these translations, but they are now being compiled and studied.[57]

Another special problem, long neglected by Roman Catholic scholars for the same reason of their "illegality," arises from what is commonly referred to as "neo-Gallican liturgies." These completely transcend similar evolutions elsewhere and cannot be compared to the liturgical variations discussed above. The development of autonomous and highly original liturgies in France can only be understood in the wider contexts of Gallicanism, the delayed reception of Trent in France and, to some extent, Jansenism.

While the first local French Breviaries, for example, were revised *ad formam tridentini breviarii,* later development became much more independent and, sometimes, contradictory. They were characterized by strong biblicism accompanied by an elaborate, non-biblical hymnology (e.g., by the poet, Jean-Baptiste Santeul [1630-97]) and by numerous Sequences. After the vituperation directed against these liturgies by Prosper Guéranger (1805-75),[58] a more serene approach is

---

[56]Recent publications include García Alonso (1959); Bissig (1979); Kilarski (1981).
[57]Cattaneo (1971); Drapeau (1971); Landotti (1975); Goertz (1977) and Häussling (1984-).
[58]Johnson (1984).

now possible and much research is being done in the field.[59] To study the development of the "neo-Gallican" liturgies, one must include the entire eighteenth century, thus going beyond the limits of our period. *Liturgy Outside Western Europe.* The expansion of Catholicism in our period also has consequences for the development of liturgy. That expansion led, for instance, to closer contact with the churches of the East, both Orthodox and pre-Chalcedonian, and to different attempts at unification and Latinization.[60] The question of how liturgy was performed in the Spanish and Portuguese missions (and, to a lesser extent, in other colonies) is of considerable interest, and few general works on the topic exist.[61] Much remains to be done.

The "Chinese Rites Controversy" originated in the attempts by Jesuit missionaries to use civil Chinese ritual in their ministry. They were opposed in this initiative by Franciscans and Dominicans.[62] This phenomenon is obviously pertinent in contemporary discussions of "inculturation." The Jesuits also fostered prayers sung in community and a sung explanation of the Mass.[63]

Liturgy in Relationship to the Arts

Another reason for the scholarly neglect of this period lies in the lack of adequate tools. A methodology, necessarily interdisciplinary, that will permit a global appreciation of the liturgical fact is as yet not available. Such a methodology must take into account not only the received text but also its articulation into ceremony by various active and passive personnel–in a given space and employing a specific musical setting. This methodological deficiency is characteristic of liturgical studies in general, but it becomes an overwhelming difficulty for our period, defined (by Klauser) in terms of the rigidity of the texts, which were frozen, as it were, by the promulgation of the Tridentine *corpus.* Only with a new method will it be possible to overcome the predominance of the written word and to acknowledge the proper and different character of Tridentine liturgies. American liturgical scholars have been eager to point out the neglect of non-verbal elements, possibly the most important part of liturgy, but no one has as yet

[59]Bremond (1932); Fontaine (1980); Jounel (1980); Ward-Johnson (1982); Brovelli (1982-83); Weaver (1982) Évenou (1983); Johnson (1984); and Johnson-Ward (1984).
[60]Sacra Congregazione . . . (1974); Peri (1975).
[61]E.g., Tsuchiya (1963); López Gay (1970) and Baumgartner (1971, 1972).
[62]Bontinck (1962); Minamiki (1985).
[63]Brunner (1959, 1964).

elaborated a method that can be used for dealing with these phenomena.[64]

1. *Decoration, Architecture, Furnishings*

The limited scope of this chapter prevents any general statements about the art of the Catholic Reformation and of the Baroque. Art historians must be called upon for such an assessment.[65] Our question is more specific: what are the relationships between liturgy and the space and decoration in which the liturgy is acted out? Here the observation by Klauser remains valid: "We still lack a history of church building, viewed as buildings constructed for the liturgy."[66] Lately, however, attempts have been made to fill this lacuna. In an unpublished dissertation from 1960, the late Milton Lewine studies sixteenth-century Roman church interiors and pointed to the many possibilities for effective preaching provided by these spaces. Counter-Reformation ideology was discussed for churches in Florence by Marcia Hall (1979). She noted for the art of the Counter Reformation that "we must also look to periods of decline,"[67] and, reflecting upon the influence of the *Spiritual Exercises,* that "representation of the scene provides useful standpoint for meditation. Church decoration is thus elevated to a role of much greater importance."[68] The increased emphasis on the cult of the reserved Eucharist has been studied in its architectural setting in Venice by Maurice E. Cope (1979).

The most extraordinary document that we have from the period is the work published by Charles Borromeo himself that describes, down to the most minute detail, the interiors of churches and the construction of enclosed monasteries. The *Instructiones fabricae et supellectilis ecclesiasticae* (1577) is now available in a modern translation with commentary by Cecily Voelker (1977).[69]

Some particulars merit consideration in this context, such as the development of the confessional studied by Schlombs (1965), but there are no general histories of the pulpit, organ architecture, the singers' balcony, the baroque altar, liturgical vestments, or liturgical vessels.[70] Much, however, can be learned from the older treatises on these topics

[64]Collins (1975): 90-91.
[65]See however Hautecour (1965) and Prodi (1965).
[66]Klauser (1969): 140.
[67]Hall: viii.
[68]Ibid., 13.
[69]See also Gatti Perer (1980, 1983).
[70]See however Palucci (1980) and Paramenti (1986).

or from catalogues of recent expositions, though access to the latter is not always easy.

A very important aspect of the topic is Jesuit baroque architecture, first and foremost in Rome, then spreading out to the whole Roman Catholic Church. Jesuit architecture in Italy and in France has been repertoried,[71] and the phenomenon has been studied in a collection of essays edited by Wittkower and Jaffe (1972). The predilection of the Baroque for the *ephemeral,* the theatrical construction of a space for a given situation like the changing of a church into a repository for a catafalque, into the setting for a *Quarant'ore* or of Saint Peter's into a *theatrum* for a canonization has been reviewed by Fagiolo dell'Arco and Carandini in their suggestive *L'effimero barocco* (1977-78).[72] With these features we are at the meeting point of the profane and the Christian feast, and recent research on the former can probably be useful for liturgical studies as well.[73]

2. Music

One of the few *abusus* discussed at Trent that actually came to a vote was church music. Trent states: "Composition in which there is an intermingling of the lascivious or impure, whether by instrument or voice, and likewise every secular action, idle and even profane conversation, strolling about, bustle, and shouting must be ousted from the churches" (CT 5:963; Hayburn translation). These few lines were to be repeated in succeeding local reforms, but it is difficult to ascertain to what extent these prescriptions were actually obeyed.[74]

Like the other liturgical books, the books of Gregorian or "plainchant" needed revision in the aftermath of Trent. The influence of Palestrina (1525/6-94) in these revisions seems to have been exaggerated.[75] During the pontificate of Paul V, a new Gradual was prepared and published in 1614-15; as it was produced by the printing press of the Medici, its name is the *Editio Medicaea.*[76]

Specialized works now taught organists how to accompany the originally *a capella* performance of plainchant (e.g., A. Biancherini, *L'organo suonarino,* 1605). The procedure became popular; Alexander VII had to prohibit the use of the organ in Lent, and likewise repeat

---

[71]Moisy (1958); Bösel (1985).

[72]See also: Rasmussen (1986).

[73]E.g. Mitchell (1979); Trexler (1980); Muir (1981).

[74]Schaefer (1985).

[75]*New Grove* (1980), *s.v.* "Palestrina," 423.

[76]Molitor (1899, 1901-02); Hayburn (1979): 33-37.

the earlier prohibitions concerning the organ replacing voices in the alternation of verses (*Piae sollicitudinis,* April 23, 1657).[77]

It is polyphony with its different styles that really differentiates the celebrations in our period. Special care should, therefore, be taken by the liturgist to become familiar with this part of musicology, since it is part of the method we described as appropriate for assessing the Tridentine liturgy. It is clear that the *ethos* of a Mass by Palestrina is widely different from one by Mozart and that the liturgical content of a celebration finds itself highly influenced by the music used.[78]

The development of the role of the organ in churches with bigger and more sophisticated instruments available can be correlated to the introduction of other instruments into church as well, resulting in concerted liturgical music. With these, one is a long way from the "simplicity" attained by Palestrina.[79] The influence of the Jesuit order in architecture is in keeping with the importance given by the Society of Jesus to church music.[80] In music, too, the notion of "the ephemeral" comes into consideration.[81]

While the use of singing in the vernacular languages in church is not well researched outside Germany (e.g., *Deutsches Hochamt*), important works do exist for that country. An analysis of this feature must lead to the conclusion that these songs were truly liturgical and not only, as earlier legalistic approaches would have it, superimpositions upon an "official" (Latin) text. The fact that the phenomenon is most clearly situated in Germany posits the important question of an unnoticed interplay between the Lutheran and Roman Catholic Churches, a topic worthy of careful reexamination.[82]

History of Liturgical Scholarship

This short overview of the Tridentine liturgy must finally take into account the people who have created the discipline of liturgical studies: the scholars. They evolved in much the same way as church historians: products of the Renaissance, used (and misused) in Reformation controversies, and finally establishing themselves as a group, elaborating and respecting the specific methods and procedures of liturgical studies.

---

[77]Hayburn (1979): 76-78.
[78]Overview in Ursprung (1931): 165-239; Weber (1982): 191-99.
[79]Williams (1980); *New Grove* (1980), *s.v.* "Mass."
[80]Culley (1970) and in Wittkower and Jaffe (1972): 118-28; Kennedy (1982).
[81]Stefani (1975).
[82]Nottarp (1933); Fischer (1953); Heine (1975).

Repertory of Liturgists. The learned Italian Jesuit, F. A. Zaccaria (1714-95), published in 1778 the second volume of his *Bibliotheca Ritualis* entitled *De librorum ritualium explanatoribus.* The list of authors he gives there has never been surpassed and has consistently been used by all other scholars.[83]

Scholarly Editions. Many editions of paleochristian and medieval texts were published in the sixteenth and seventeenth centuries. In not a few cases these are the only editions in existence and often even their sources have not survived. Still not superceded are the editions of *De antiquis ecclesiae ritibus* (1700-02), an anthology of liturgical texts with commentary by the great Maurist Benedictine, Dom Edmond Martène (1654-1739). A. G. Martimort has painstakingly researched the provenance of all Martène's texts and has edited a companion to Martène (1978), an indispensable tool for all subsequent use of the work. Nothing similar exists for the important collections by Melchior Hittorp (1564) or Jean Morin (1651, 1655).

The Scholars and their Methods. Behind the texts are the authors. In my opinion, no better biography and presentation of liturgical methodology of a given person exists than *The Life and Work of Edmund Bishop (1846-1917)* by Nigel Abercrombie. Bishop's involvement as a liturgical scholar in both the development of historical studies of the liturgy and in the evolving Modernist crisis and its subsequent repression are vividly described. Many of the liturgists from the two centuries surveyed in this *Guide* deserve similar treatment.[84] This would be true of Cornelius Schulting (1540-1604), Jacques Goar, O.P. (1601-53), Nicolas Letourneux (1640-86), Jean-Baptiste Thiers (1636-1703), and Jean Grancolas (d. 1732), to mention only a few. Bishop himself refers to the learned French Benedictine of Saint Wufram of Abbeville, Dom Claude de Vert (1645-1708), author of the fascinating *Explication simple, littérale, et historique des cérémonies de l'Église* (4 vols., Paris, 1706-13). Of de Vert, Bishop wrote that he was "a writer to whom I must ever feel indebted as introducing me to the study of liturgy and teaching me that it is (or should be) first and foremost a study in life."[85] Research on the scholars active during our period will prove most beneficial to the advancement of liturgical studies and to an understanding of Catholic Reform.

---

[83]Righetti (1964³), 1:86-92; Vogel (1975): 16-18; Cattaneo (1984): 326-28, 353-59.
[84]For our period, see for example Lange (1931) and Scicolone (1981).
[85]Bishop (1918): 316.

Bibliography

CATALOGUES, REPERTORIES, AND BIBLIOGRAPHIES:

Jahrbuch für Liturgiewissenschaft, 1-15 (1921-35); corrected reprint (1973-79). The reprint is accompanied by an indispensable *Registerband* (1982). *Archiv für Liturgiewissenschaft,* 1 ff. (1950-). Provisional *Register* for vols. 1-19 (1950-77). The *Literaturberichten* for our period have been published under various headings, see *Register:* 20-21. Note also that important reviews were published at the end of each volume under the heading *Einzelbesprechungen,* a practice abandoned as of vol. 20-21.

Amiet, R., *Inventaire général des livres liturgiques du diocèse de Lyon* (Paris, 1979).

British Museum, *General Catalogue of Printed Books,* "Liturgies," vols. 138 and 139 (London, 1962), *Tables* vol. 138, after col. 820, then begins separate numbering of columns in vols. 138 and 139: cols. 104-612; *indicia,* cols. 1175-1238; *Ten Year Supplement 1956-65,* vol. 27 (London, 1968): cols. 798-871; *Five Year Supplement 1966-70,* vol. 15 (London, 1972): cols. 292-313; *Five Year Supplement 1971-75,* vol. 8 (London, 1979): cols. 406-34.

Bohatta, H., *Bibliographie der Livres d'Heures des XV. und XVI. Jarhunderts* (Wien, 1909; 1924²).

————, *Bibliographie der Breviere 1501-1850* (Leipzig, 1937).

Meyer-Baer, K., Liturgical Music Incunabula (London, 1962).

Molin, J. B., and A. Aussedat-Minivielle, Répertoire des rituels et processionaux imprimés conservés en France (Paris, 1984).

Pfaff, R. W., *Medieval Latin Liturgy. A Select Bibliography* (Toronto, 1982).

Rasmussen, N. K., "Some Bibliographies of Liturgists," *Archiv für Liturgiewissenschaft* 11 (1969): 214-18, with subsequent supplements 15 (1973): 168-71; 19 (1978): 134-39; 25 (1983): 34-42 (this last with cumulative index).

Salmon, P. *Les manuscrits liturgiques de la Bibliothèque Vaticane,* 5 vols. *(Vatican City, 1968-72).*

Weale, W. H. I., and H. Bohatta, *Bibliographia Liturgica - Catalogus Missalium Ritus Latini ab anno MCCCCLXXIV impressorum* (London, 1938).

Zanon, G., "Catologo di rituali liturgici italiani dell'inizio della stampa al 1614," *Studia Patavina - Rivista di Scienze Religiose* 31 (1984): 496-564.

SECONDARY LITERATURE:

Abercrombie, N., *The Life and Work of Edmond Bishop* (London, 1959).

Baumgartner, J., *Der Gottesdienst in der jungen Kirche Neuspaniens. Mission und Liturgie in Mexico* (Schöneck/Beckenried, 1971).

————, *Die ersten liturgischen Bücher in der neuen Welt* (Schöneck/Beckenried, 1972).

Bibliophilus, "De Sacra Rituum Congregationis Decretorum Collectionibus," *Ephemerides Liturgicae* 44 (1930): 433-48. This is a guide to the existing editions.

Bishop, E., *Liturgica Historica: Papers on the Liturgy and Religious Life of the Western Church* (Oxford, 1918).

Bissig, H., *Das Churer Rituale 1503-1927. Geschichte der Agende - Feier der Sakramente* (Freiburg/Schweiz, 1979).

Bösel, R., *Jesuitenarchitektur in Italien (1540-1773)*, 1- (Vienna, 1985-).

Botinck, F., *La lutte autour de la liturgie chinoise aux XVII et XVIII siècles* (Louvain, 1962).

Borella, P., "De sancto Carlo Borromeo eiusque adiutoribus in caeremoniali episcoporum componendo," *Ephemerides Liturgicae* 51 (1937): 64-80.

Bremond, H., *Histoire littéraire du sentiment religieux en France depuis la fin des guerres de religion jusqu' à nos jours*, 11 vols. (Paris, 1914-33), especially vol. 10, *La prière et les prières de l'Ancien Régime* (Paris, 1932). This classic work is reviewed in a comprehensive way from the point of view of liturgical relevance by [H. H.], *Jahrbuch für Liturgiewissenschaft* 14 (1934): 523-43.

Brovelli, F., "Per uno studio dei Messali francesi del XVIII secolo. Saggi di analisi," *Ephemerides Liturgicae* 96 (1982): 279-406; 97 (1983): 482-84.

Brunner, P., "La Messe chinoise du Père Hinderer," *Neue Zeitschrift für Missonswissenschaft* 15 (1959): 271-84.

———. *L'Euchologe de la Mission de Chine* (Münster, 1964).

Cattaneo, E., "San Carlo Borromeo e la liturgia," *Ambrosius* 42 (1966): [2-42].

———. "Il rituale romano di A. Castellani," *Miscellanea liturgica in onore del Cardinale Giacomo Lercaro*, vol. 2 (Rome, 1967): 629-47.

———, "Le traduzione italiane delle Epistole e dei Vangeli delle Messe nei secoli XV e XVI," *Asprenas* 18 (1971): 484-92.

———, *Il culto cristiano in occidente. Note storiche* (Rome, 1984²).

Chadwick, O., *The Popes and the European Revolution* (Oxford, 1981).

Collins, M., "Liturgical Methodology and the Cultural Evolution of Worship in the United States," *Worship* 49 (1975): 85-102.

Cope, M. E., *The Venetian Chapel of the Sacrament in the Sixteenth Century* (New York, 1979).

Coyne, G. V., M. A. Hoskin, and O. Pedersen, eds., *Gregorian Reform of the Calendar. Proceedings of the Vatican Conference to commemorate its 400th Anniversary 1582-1982* (Vatican City, 1983).

Culley, Th., *Jesuits and Music, I: A Study of the Musicians Connected with the German College in Rome during the Seventeenth Century and of their Activities in Northern Europe* (Rome and St. Louis, 1970).

"Decreta authentica Sacrorum Rituum Congregationis," *Analecta Iuris Pontificii*, 7-8 *(1864-66), fascicles 57-59 and 66-68. Indicia* on the green flyleaves of each fascicle.

Delooz, P., *Sociologie et canonisations (Liège and The Hague, 1969)*.

Delumeau, J., *Le Catholicisme entre Luther et Voltaire* (Paris, 1971); ET: *Catholicism between Luther and Voltaire: A New View of the Counter-Reformation*(London-Philadelphia, 1977).

Denzler, G., *Kardinal Guglielmo Sirleto* (München, 1964).

Dolan, J. P., *The Influence of Erasmus, Witzel and Cassander on the Church Ordinances and Reform Proposals of the United Duchies of Cleve (Münster, 1957)*.

Dompnier, B., "Un aspect de la dévotion eucharistique dans la France du XVII^c siècle: Les prières des Quarante-Heures," *Revue d'histoire de l'Église de France* 67 (1981): 5-31.

Donner, R., *Jakob Wimpfelings Bemühungen um die Verbesserung der liturgischen Texte* (Mainz-Trier, 1976).

Drapeau, B., "Les traductions françaises de l'Ordinaire de la messe jusqu' à la fin du XVII^c siècle" (Unpublished diss., Institut Catholique de Paris, 1971).

Duval, A., *Des sacrements au Concile de Trente* (Paris, 1984).

Dykmans, M., *Le Cérémonial papal de la fin du moyen age à la Renaissance*, 4 vols. (Brussels and Rome, 1977-85).

———, *L'oeuvre de Patrizi Piccolomini ou le cérémonial papal de la première renaissance*, 2 vols. (Vatican City, 1980-82).

———, "Paris de Grassi," *Ephemerides Liturgicae* 96 (1982): 407-82; 99 (1985); 383-417 (to be continued).

———, *Le Pontifical romain. Révisé au XV^c siècle* (Vatican City, 1985).

Évenou, I., "La poesie néo-gallicane," in H. Becker and R. Kaczynski, eds., *Liturgie und Dichtung: Ein interdisciplinares Kompendium* (St. Ottilien, 1983), 1:821-54.

Fagiolo dell'Arco, M., and S. Carandini, *L'effimero barocco, Struttura della festa nel Roma del '600*, 2 vols. (Rome, 1977-78).

Fellerer, K. G., *Geschichte der katholischen Kirchenmusik* (Düsseldorff, 1949²).

Fischer, Balth., "Das 'Deutsche Hochamt'," *Liturgisches Jahrbuch* 3 (1953): 41-53.

———, "Das Originalmanuskript des Rituale Romanum," *Trierer theologische Zeitschrift* 70 (1961): 244-46.

Focke, E., and H. Heinrichs, "Das Kalendarium des Missale Pianum und seine Tendenzen," *Theologische Quartalschrift* 120 (1939): 383-400, 461-69.

Fontaine, G., "Présentation des missels diocésains français du 17e au 19e siècle," *La Maison-Dieu* 141 (1980): 97-166.

Franzen, A., *Die Kelchbewegung am Niederrhein im 16. Jahrhundert* (Münster, 1955).

Frechard, M., "L'année liturgique dans la liturgie de Paris sous Louis XVI," *La Maison-Dieu* 148 (1981): 123-33.

Frutaz, A. P., "Contributo alla storia della riforma del Messale promulgato da san Pio V nel 1570," *Problemi di vita religiosa in Italia nel Cinquecento, Italia sacra*, 2 (Padova, 1960): 187-214.

García Alonso, I., "Edición Tridentina del Manual Toledano y su incorporación al Ritual Romano," *Salmanticenses* 6 (1959): 323-99.

Gatti Perer, M. L., "Prospettive nuove aperte da S. Carlo nelle sue norme per l'arte sacra," *Accademia di San Carlo* 3 (1980): 15-33.

_____. "La manutenzione ordinaria degli edifici sacri e delle lore suppellettili secondo Carlo Borromeo," *Accademia di San Carlo* 5 (1983): 121-47.

Goertz, H., *Deutsche Begriffe der Liturgie im Zeitalter der Reformation: Untersuchungen zum religiösen Wortschatz zwischen 1450 u. 1530* (Berlin, 1977).

Gramatowski, W., "Il fondo liturgico più antico dell'Archivio della S. Congregazione dei Riti (1588-1700)," *Archivium Historiae Pontificiae* 13 (1975): 401-24.

Gy, P. M., "L'unification liturgique de l'occident et la liturgique de la curie romaine," *Revue des sciences philosophiques et théologiques* 59 (1975): 601-12.

Haburn, R. F., *Papal Legislation on Sacred Music* (Collegeville, 1979).

Häussling, A. A., *Das Missale deutsch. Materialien zur Rezeptionsgeschichte der lateinischen Messliturgie im deutschen Sprachgebiet bis zum zweiten Vatikanischen Konzil. Teil 1: Bibliographie der Übersetzungen und Drucken* (Münster, 1984).

Hall, M., *Renovation and Counter-Reformation. Vasari and Duke Cosimo in Sta Maria Novella and Sta Croce, 1565-1577* (Oxford, 1979).

Hautecour, L., "Le Concile de Trente et l'art," Il Concilio di Trento e la riforma tridentina: Atti del Convegno storico internazionale, Trento 2-6 settembre 1963 (Rome, 1965): 345-62.

Heine, H., *Die Melodien der Mainzer Gesangbücher in den ersten Hälfte des 17. Jahrhunderts* (Mainz-Trier, 1975).

Jedin, H., "Das Konzil von Trient und die Reform des römischen Messbuchs," *Liturgisches Leben* 6 (1939): 30-66.

_____. "Das Konzil von Trient und die Reform der Liturgischen Bücher," *Kirche des Glaubens, Kirche der Geschichte; Ausgewählte Aufsätze und Vorträge,* vol. 2 (Freiburg, Basel, Wien, 1966): 499-525.

Johnson, C., *Prosper Guéranger (1805-1875): A Liturgical Theologian. An introduction to his liturgical writings and work* (Rome, 1984), especially ch. 3: "The local liturgies of the French Church,": 147-89.

_____, and A. Ward, "A catalogue of the printed Liturgical Books of the Dioceses of France," *Questions liturgiques* 66 (1985): 53-58.

Jounel, P., "Les développements du sanctoral romain de Grégoire XIII à Jean XXIII," *La Maison-Dieu* 63bis (1960): 74-87.

_____, "Les missels diocésains français du XVIII⁰ siècle," *La Maison-Dieu* 141 (1980): 91-96.

Jungmann, J. A., "The Close of the Middle Ages and the Tridentine Reform" and "The Mass in the Baroque Period, the Enlightenment and the Restoration," chapters in *Missarum Sollemnia. Eine genetische Erklärung der römischen Messe* (Wien, Freiburg, Basel, 1966⁵); English translation, *The Mass of the Roman Rite,* 2 vols. (New York, 1951-1955), 1:127-59. Caution: this is a translation of the second edition of *Missarum Sollemnia* and the original's last edition should always be checked when using it. The abbreviated translation (New York, 1955) is useless.

_____, *Pastoral Liturgy* (London, 1962), a partial (and sometimes faulty) translation of the collection of essays by the author: *Liturgisches Erbe und pastorale Gegenwart* (Innsbruck, 1960).

Kennedy, Th. F., "Jesuits and Music: The European Tradition 1547-1622" (Diss., U. of California, Santa Barbara, 1982).

Kilarski, K., *Die nachtridentinische Messliturgie in Polen im 16. Jahrhundert am Beispiel des liturgischen Schriften des Hieronymus Powodowski* (Frankfurt and Berne, 1981).

Kingdon, R. M., "The Plantin Breviaries: a case study in the sixteenth-century business operations of a publishing house," *Church and Society in Reformation Europe* (London, 1985): Article XIX, 18pp.

Klauser, Th., *The Western Liturgy Today* (London, 1963).

———, *A Short History of the Western Liturgy: An Account and Some Reflections* (New York, 1969). This translation is from the fifth (and latest) German edition (1965).

Labarre, A., "Heures," *Dictionnaire de spiritualité,* vol. 7 (Paris, 1968): cols. 410-31 (fundamental).

Landotti, G., *Le traduzioni del Messale in lingua italiana anteriori al movimento liturgico moderno. Studio storico* (Rome, 1975).

Lefèvre, P., "À propos d'un ouvrage récent sur la réforme de l'hymnodie par le Pape Urbain VIII," *Revue d'histoire ecclésiastique* 65 (1970): 80-86.

Lewine, M. L., "The Roman Church Interior, 1527-1580," (Diss., Columbia, 1960).

Löwenberg, B., *Das Rituale des Kardinals Julius Sanctorius. Eine Beitrag zur Enststehungsgeschichte des Rituale* (München, 1937).

———, "Die Erstausgabe des Rituale Romanum von 1614," *Zeitschrift für katholische Theologie* 66 (1942): 141-47.

Lópes Gay, J., *La liturgia en la missión del Japón del siglo XVI* (Rome, 1970).

Martimort, A. G., (ed.) *L'Église en prière. Introduction à la liturgie,* 4 vols. (Paris, 1983-84); English translation, *The Church at Prayer: Introduction to the Liturgy,* 4 vols. (Collegeville, 1985-).

———, *La documentation liturgique de Dom Edmond Martène. Étude codicologique* (Vatican City, 1978).

Martin, H. J., *Livre, pouvoirs et société à Paris au XVIIe siècle, 1598-1701,* 2 vols. (Genève, 1969). See the important review by J. F. Gilmont, *Revue d'histoire ecclésiastique* 65 (1970): 797-816.

Mayer, A. L., "Renaissance, Humanismus und Liturgie," *Jahrbuch für Liturgiewissenschaft* 14 (1934): 123-70.

———, "Liturgie und Barock," *Jahrbuch für Liturgiewissenschaft* 15 (1935): 67-154.

———, *Die Liturgie in der europäischen Geistesgeschichte. Herausgegeben und eingeleitet von E. von Severus* (Darmstadt, 1971). Contains the two above-mentioned articles with an introduction about the author.

McGinnis, F. J., "Rhetoric and Counter-Reformation Rome: Sacred Oratory and the Construction of the Catholic World View, 1563-1621," (Diss., U. of California, Berkeley, 1982).

McManus, F. *The Congregation of Sacred Rites* (Washington, D.C., 1954). Indispensable tool for reading the technical terms of the decrees.

"Mémoires et thèses présentés à l'Institut Supérieur de Liturgie," *La Maison-Dieu* 149 (1982): 19-25.

Mercati, G., "Vecchi lamenti contro il monopolio dei libri ecclesiastici, specie liturgici," *Opere minori,* vol. 2 (Vatican City, 1937): 482-89.

Meyer, H. B. et al., eds., *Gottesdienst der Kirche. Handbuch der Liturgiewissenschaft,* to be completed in 8 vols., 2 in print (Regensburg, 1983-).

Minamiki, G., *The Chinese Rites Controversy from its Beginning to Modern Times* (Chicago, 1985).

Mitchell, B., *Italian Civic Pageantry in the High Renaissance. A Descriptive Bibliography of Triumphal Entries and Selected Other Festivals for State Occasions.* (Firenze, 1979).

Moisy, P., *Les églises des jésuites de l'ancienne assistance de France* (Rome, 1958).

Molitor, R., "Zur Vorgeschichte der Medicea," *Römische Quartalschrift,* 13 (1899): 365-73.

―――, *Die Nachtridentinische Choralreform zu Rom. Ein Beitrag zur Musikgeschichte des 16. und 17. Jahrhunderts,* 2 vols. (Leipzig, 1901-02).

Muir, E., *Civic Ritual in Renaissance Venice* (Princeton, 1981).

Nabuco, J., "La liturgie papale et les origines du Cérémonial des Évêques," *Miscellanea liturgica in honorem L. Cuniberto Mohlberg* (Rome, 1948): 283-300.

The New Grove Dictionary of Music and Musicians (London, 1980).

Nottarp, H., *Zur communicatio in sacris cum haereticis. Deutsche Rechtszustände im 17. und 18. Jahrhundert* (Halle, 1933).

O'Malley, J. W., *Praise and Blame in Renaissance Rome. Rhetoric, Doctrine and Reform in the Sacred Orators of the Papal Court, ca. 1450-1521* (Durham, 1979).

Oury, G., "Sur le bréviaire: portée de la clause de la bulle de S. Pie V qui interdit toute modification," *Ésprit et Vie* 79 (1969): 536-37.

Palucci, A., "L'arredamento ecclesiale nell'età della Riforma," *Arte e religione nella Firenze de'Medici* (Florence, 1980): 95-110.

Paramenti e arredi sacri nelle contrade di Siena (Siena, 1986; exposition catalogue).

Peri, V., *Due date, un'unica Pasqua. Le origini della moderna disparità liturgica in una trattativa ecumenica tra Roma e Constantinopoli (1582-84)* (Milano, 1967).

―――, *Chiesa Romana e "Rito" Greco. G. A. Santoro e la Congregazione dei Greci (1566-1596)* (Brescia, 1975).

Pralle, L., "Die volksliturgischen Bestrebungen des Georg Witzel (1501-1573)," *Jahrbuch des Bistums Mainz* 3 (1948): 224-42.

Prodi, P., "Sulla teorica delle arti figurative nella riforma cattolica," *Archivio italiano per la storia della pietà* 4 (1965): 121-212.

Rasmussen, N. K., "*Maiestas Pontificia*: A Liturgical Reading of Etienne Dupérac's Engraving of the *Capella Sixtina* from 1578," *Analecta Romana Instituti Danici* (Rome), 12 (1983): 109-48.

―――, "Liturgy and Iconography at the Canonization of Carlo Borromeo, Nov. 1, 1610," *Analecta Romana Instituti Danici* 15 (1986): 119-150.

Re, N. del, *La Curia Romana. Lineamenti storico-giuridici* (Rome, 1970³).

Reifenberg, H., *Messe und Missalien im Bistum Mainz seit dem Zeitalter der Gotik* (Münster, 1960).

———, *Stundengebet und Breviere im Bistum Mainz seit der romanischen Epoche* (Münster, 1964).

———, *Sakramente, Sakramentalien und Ritualien im Bistum Mainz seit dem Spätmittlealter,* 2 vols. (Münster, 1971-72).

———, "Gottesdienst in den Kirchen des deutschen Sprachgebietes. Bestand und Wünsche wissenschaftlicher Bemühungen um die teilkirchliche Liturgie im Laufe eines Jahrhundert," *Archiv für Liturgiewissenschaft* 22 (n.d. [1981]): 30-92.

Righetti, M., *Manuale di storia liturgica,* 4 vols. (Milano, 1964³).

Rosenthal, A., "Eine vortridentinische Reform des Heiligen-Kalenders. Martyrologium (1468) und Festkalender der Bursfelder-Kongregation," *Trierer theologische Zeitschrift* 91 (1982): 327-36.

Sacra Congregazione per le Chiese Orientali, *Oriente Cattolico, Cenni storiche e statistiche* (Vatican City, 1974⁴).

Schaefer, E. E., "The Relationship Between the Liturgy of the Roman Rite and the Italian Organ Literature of the Sixteenth and Seventeenth Centuries" (D.M.A. diss., The Catholic University of America, 1985).

Schlombs, W., *Die Entwicklung des Beichtstuhls in der katholischen Kirche. Grundlagen und Besonderheiten im alten Erzbistum Köln* (Düsseldorff, 1965).

Schmidt, H. A. J., *Liturgie et langue vulgaire. Le problème du langue liturgique chez les premiers réformateurs et au Concile de Trente* (Rome, 1950).

Scicolone, I., *Il cardinale G. Tommasi di Lampedusa e gli inizi della scienza liturgica* (Rome and Palermo, 1981).

Sellier, Ph., *Pascal et la liturgie* (Paris, 1966).

Shearman, J., *Raphael's Cartoons in the Collection of Her Majesty the Queen and the Tapestries for the Sixtine Chapel* (London, 1972).

Sigler, G. J., "The Influence of Charles Borromeo on the Laws of the Roman Ritual," *The Jurist* 24 (1964): 119-68 and 319-34.

Springhetti, A., "Urbanus VIII P.M. poeta latinus et hymnorum Breviarii emendator," *Archivum Historiae Pontificiae* 6 (1968): 163-90.

Stefani, G., *Musica e religione nell'Italia barocca* (Palermo, 1975).

Tesi di laurea edite ed inedite 1962-1984. Pubblicazioni. Pontificio Istituto Liturgico (Rome, 1985).

Theisen, R., *Mass Liturgy and the Council of Trent* (Collegeville, 1965).

Trexler, R., *Public Life in Renaissance Florence* (New York, 1980).

Trusen, W., *Um die Reform und Einheit der Kirche. Zum Leben und Werk Georg Witzels* (Münster, 1957): 55-68.

Tsuchiya, F. X., "Das älteste bekannte Missions-Rituale," *Trierer theologische Zeitschrift* 72 (1963): 221-32.

Turchini, A., *La fabbrica di un santo. Il processo di Carlo Borromeo e la Controriforma* (Casale-Monferrato, 1984).

Ursprung, O., *Die katholische Kirchenmusik* (Potsdam, 1931).

Ussia, S., "La festa delle Quarant'ore nel tardo barocco napoletano," *Rivista di storia e letteratura religiosa* 18 (1982): 253-65.

Veraja, F., *La beatificazione. Storia, problemi, prospettive* (Vatican City, 1983).

Viau, J., "La centralisation romaine et son influence sur le bréviaire et le missel du Concile de Trente à Urbain VIII" (Unpublished diss., Institut Catholique de Paris, 1967).

Vinck, H., "Enquête faite en 1588 sur la nécessité d'une réforme des livres liturgiques," *Questions liturgiques* 56 (1975): 113-25.

Voelker, E. C., "Charles Borromeo's *Instructiones fabricae et suppellectilis ecclesiasticae 1577:* A Translation with Commentary and Analysis" (Diss., Syracuse University, 1977).

Vogel, C., *Introduction aux sources de l'histoire du culte chrétien au moyen âge* (Spoleto, 1975); revised English translation by N. K. Rasmussen and W. G. Storey, *Medieval Liturgy,* (Washington, D.C., 1986).

Ward, A., and C. Johnson, "Où en sont les études sur les liturgies diocésaines en France aux 17ᵉ, 18ᵉ et 19ᵉ siècles?" *Ephemerides Liturgicae* 96 (1982): 265-70.

Weaver, F. E., "Jansenist Bishops and Liturgical-Social Reform," in R. Golden, ed., *Church, State and Society under the Bourbon Kings of France* (Lawrence, KS, 1982): 27-82.

Weber, E., *Le Concile de Trente et la musique. De la Réforme à la Contre-Réforme (Paris, 1982).*

Weil, M. S., "The Devotion of the Forty Hours and Roman Baroque Illusions," *Journal of the Warburg and Courtauld Institutes* 37 (1974): 218-48.

Williams, P., *A New History of the Organ: from the Greeks to the Present Day* (London, 1980).

Wittkower, R., and I. Jaffe, eds., *Baroque Art: The Jesuit Contribution* (New York, 1972).

Zaccaria, F. A., *Bibliotheca ritualis,* 3 vols. (Rome, 1776-78; repr. New York, n.d.).

This chapter was written during a two-months grant from Queen Ingrid's Roman Foundation to the Danish Academy in Rome, and I want to acknowledge my gratitude to this marvelous institution. Professor Balthasar Fischer, Trier, read the manuscript and suggested many invaluable additions and corrections. I am likewise grateful to my graduate assistant at the University of Notre Dame, Mr. John Brooks-Leonard, for revising my English text.

Preaching

Peter Bayley

THE STUDY OF PREACHING stands at the crossroads of several distinct disciplines: Church history (including the history of evangelization), the renaissance of classical rhetoric and its techniques in a Christian rather than a pagan world, the investigation of an early form of printed mass-media, and–perhaps above all–the history of important moments in various major national literatures. Paradoxically, this wealth of possible approaches has held back the development of a coherent and properly comparative research field. Almost every contribution made from one of these perspectives will be found unsatisfactory from another; and least satisfactory of all, perhaps, have been those attempts at general surveys which end up as compilations of out-dated second-hand material and opinions.[1] It may indeed be that a truly comparative overview is an impossible task for a single scholar, requiring as it must an almost unimaginable range of linguistic talent attuned to literary experience, historical learning, and theological acumen. There is, nonetheless, every reason to believe that a much fuller synthesis than we now possess could be achieved collectively. Indeed there are signs that individual researchers are coming to understand the advances that might be made if the dislocated fragments they at present study were, albeit conjecturally and provisionally, pieced together in a more universal map. To explain the progress that is being made, we must first of all understand some of the factors that have held it in check.

Pre-eminent among these, though it is itself a symptom as much as a cause, is the scarcity of easily accessible source-material and the scattered and random nature of much of the material that does exist. Apart from great literary classics such as Bossuet in France or Vieira in Portugal, and with the exception of the field of English preaching (which lies almost wholly beyond the concerns of the present volume), we have virtually nothing comparable to the critically edited corpus of material available to the student of the patristic or the medieval sermon. Migne's *Collection intégrale et universelle des orateurs sacrés*[2] falls lamentably short of being either integral or universal in its selection and reprinting of frequently corrupt texts from this period.

[1] E.g. Schneyer (1968).
[2] 99 vols. (Paris, 1844-66).

The factors behind this are deep and various, to be sought on the one hand in the way the received "canons" of the several national literary histories were laid down by the predominantly rationalist and positivist critical legislators of the later nineteenth century–De Sanctis, Menéndez y Pelayo, Lanson–and on the other in that curious blend of critical timidity and unscholarliness of method which characterized many ecclesiastical amateurs of the period.[3] Only since the rise to favor among the historians of art and taste of what may vaguely be termed "the baroque" has it been fashionable to study post-Tridentine pulpit oratory in the Romance languages. The much earlier acceptance of that notion in Germany and Austria, like the early twentieth-century rehabilitation of the "Metaphysicals" in England, may well explain the much greater strides taken there.[4] The whole subject provides a fascinating laboratory in which to observe how the grandiose but idiosyncratic historical classifications of the different national literary traditions–*"le grand siècle," "classicism," "decadence," "enlightenment," "seicentismo,"* and so forth–have worked to obfuscate the very phenomena they were designed to illuminate. Least helpful of all have been certain unexamined assumptions that underlie a great deal of cultural history: the notion of rise and fall, or again a crude Darwinian evolutionism–the convenient myth that the preceding period is necessarily either "premature" or "in decay" or "in need of reform." These commonplaces are tenacious and widespread: even one of the most modern and thorough contributions to intellectual history based on preaching begins by ludicrously stigmatizing the whole achievement of post-Tridentine preaching in Europe as merely decadent.[5]

Two features in particular of this *damnosa hereditas* have continued to bedevil the study of preaching: a simplistic model of "influence" and a fear of foreigners. They often go hand in hand, and it was perhaps the greatest disservice done to our subject by Croce to suggest that what he saw as the "un-Italian bad taste" of seventeenth-century preachers must have been due purely to a (rather ill-defined) vogue for the corrupt taste of Spain.[6] The scientific study of early modern Italian

---

[3]For an influential work which actually combines these approaches, see Vercesi and Santini (1938). Two crucial decades later, Santini (1960) continues to emphasize the disparity between literary good taste and the study of sermons.

[4]See, for example, Knobloch (1974), chap. 4.

[5]Saugnieux (1976), esp. p. 3: "Il n'est donc pas faux de dire que la rapide décadence de la prédication à laquelle on assista dans les pays catholiques au cours du XVIIe et du XVIIIe siècle fut une conséquence de l'esprit de la Contre-Réforme."

[6]Croce (1899), reprinted many times.

preaching appears as a result to have been blighted for fifty years and has only fitfully begun to recover. On a wider level, it has proved unhelpful to apply to a genre so deeply rooted in scripture and tradition the type of source-hunting that is central to positivist criticism. Here too a survey of the surviving primary sources provides a useful antidote to the dangers of anachronism. For example, because we know that French culture had an important general impact upon German culture in the seventeenth century, we might suppose that the figures whom we now consider important were in vogue then. But we should be wrong, and it is the great merit of one of the most original pieces of major research to appear in the last few years[7] that it dismantles this assumption. Eybl shows that it was not celebrated names like François de Sales or Vincent de Paul, nor even Bossuet himself, but the now relatively unheard-of Pierre de Besse whose works were acquired by the libraries of Austria and Bavaria; and by going on to explore precisely the manner in which those works were exploited, he transforms our ideas of "influence," "originality," and "intertextuality."

Finally, we have to contend with a deep confusion between what one may call the external historical and the internal textual approach. This is especially true of the history of missions. It is disappointing that some of even the latest studies should so decidedly ignore the evidence of the actual texts of sermons, or the fact that these texts are in some cases no longer extant.[8] That is not, of course, to say that much of great value cannot be learned from sources other than printed or manuscript sermons, but it is important to know what the documentary evidence is, and to distinguish between hearsay or secondary opinions and what may legitimately be derived from the originals.[9]

Many of these points have, of course, been made by individual scholars in recent years. A cursory anthology of some of their remarks reveals how striking, despite their isolation, is their agreement. In 1971 Félix Herrero Salgado wrote that the first task of scholars "is to collect materials and study authors."[10] In the same year the Portuguese critic Maria de Lourdes Belchior Pontes lamented that "unfortunately, through a lack of data, through the unconcern of researchers, there is

---

[7]Eybl (1982).

[8]Cf. Lemaître (1983) or Peyrous (1982)–an article in which the description of early seventeenth-century French preaching (p. 574) could have been written a century ago.

[9]The problem is a vexed one and–since my own penchant for the printed texts is so strong–it has led me to omit the very considerable bibliography concerning missions. The field is in any case closer to popular piety and culture.

[10]Herrero Salgado (1971): 3.

still not even a sketch of the panorama of pulpit oratory in Portugal."[11] In 1977 a Polish scholar remarked that "research into Catholic preaching in Poland at this period has barely begun."[12] The remark was echoed a year later by two Italian scholars complaining that "critical studies of seventeenth-century Italian sacred oratory are outdated and few and far between."[13]

This, then, is the background against which advances in knowledge have to be viewed. One should not, however, out of an unduly comparativist zeal, seem to disparage the very considerable contributions made by those working almost exclusively within a single national tradition. The point is that they have produced results that would be fruitful if applied to other national areas, and have in turn strengthened the case (eloquently made out by Jacoebee[14]) for historians of secular literature to take sermons more seriously.

In France, for example, the revival of Bossuet studies in the 1960s[15] has stimulated a veritable school of enquiry into the period that precedes him. Jean Descrains has devoted himself to the most prolific preacher of the period, Jean-Pierre Camus, very properly stressing in those studies to have appeared so far the need for accurate bibliographical information.[16] Jacques Hennequin has thoroughly examined the historical as well as the rhetorical importance of royal funeral orations.[17] He and Truchet have encouraged graduate work in the field. My own work, though obviously indebted to sources of inspiration that are not purely French, continues the task of bibliographical discovery as well as intellectual contextualization and rhetorical analysis.[18] A welcome by-product has been the appearance of accessible modern annotated editions of some of the texts themselves.[19] The wealth of papers on many aspects of the subject given at the colloquium held in 1977 to mark the 350th anniversary of Bossuet's birth demonstrates the vigor of research among specialists of French.[20] It is all the more disappointing that there are so few signs of its extension into the eighteenth century

[11]Belchior Pontes (1971): 173.
[12]Kuc (1977): 134.
[13]Elia and Sensi (1978): 367.
[14]Jacoebee (1982).
[15]The major works are Truchet (1960, 1962), Goyet (1965), Le Brun (1972).
[16]Notably Descrains (1971).
[17]Hennequin (1977, 1978).
[18]Bayley (1980).
[19]Truchet (1961), Descrains (1970), Bayley (1983).
[20]Published by Collinet and Goyet (1980). For examples of other kinds of recent work see Leenhardt (1975); Séguy (1977); Anatole (1978); Landry (1984).

where Candel's magnificent but necessarily old-fashioned classic of eighty years ago remains unrevised, and where more recent contributions[21] hardly represent a significant advance from his general intellectual position, despite timely work being done on the eighteenth-century Church in France.[22]

In Portuguese literature the towering figure of António Vieira continues in a somewhat similar way to inspire studies of high quality, many of them produced outside Portugal. To Cantel's major book must now be added the work of Saraiva (to which I shall return). Books and critical editions (in the series of *Vieira-Texte* und *Vieira-Studien* whose general editor is Hans Flasche) have appeared in Germany under the auspices of the Portugiesisches Institut der Görres-Gesellschaft.[23]

In the German-speaking world,[24] too, there has long existed a distinctive native school of criticism, less concerned with one or two major literary figures (though work on Abraham à Sancta Clara and others continues to appear[25]) than with the evidence sermons, and particularly the *exempla* found in them, supply for the study of folk culture. There are, of course, elements in German preaching which make these attempts to see the daily life of the past reflected in the mirror of extant sermons peculiarly successful, and it may be that they could less easily be reproduced in other countries. Nonetheless, the work of Elfriede Moser-Rath and others[26] has done much to prepare the ground for the rather different sort of research that is beginning to be published.

It is to those new directions of research that we must now turn. I have already suggested that the major renewals in the field have derived from a shift of focus from secondary to primary material: when we lay aside our "received wisdom" about the preaching of the past and instead look closely at the actual material that survives. And a great deal does survive, buried and neglected for the most part in national, institutional, and monastic libraries. The material difficulties of this kind of research are very considerable: many libraries in Europe are difficult of access and possess inadequate catalogues, dating in some cases back to the eighteenth century. Each new discovery requires the researcher to scan

---

[21]E.g. Haillant (1969).
[22]E.g. Viguerie (1981).
[23]Nagel (1972), Wittschier (1973), Leopold (1977).
[24]For help with material in German I am greatly indebted to Professor M. W. Senger of Harvard University.
[25]See Bachleitner (1972) and Knobloch (1974).
[26]Moser-Rath (1964, 1969, 1981, 1983); Intorp (1964).

his field all over again to look for further texts of the author in question or for further copies that might provide some indication of popularity or size of print-run. It is the area in which most is to be hoped for from the computerization of information, slow though that process is likely to be in some countries.

Eventually, the strict accuracy needed for the precise identification of editions (and the consequential statistics concerning reprinting, pirating, dissemination, and so forth) will require full bibliographical descriptions of these texts, preferably along the advanced scientific lines devised by bibliographers in England and America. At the moment we often have to content ourselves with short-title catalogues. A start was made in Spain by Herrero Salgado working through the private library of the great sermon scholar Miguel Herrero García and collating it with seven others. His thoughtfully indexed catalogue runs from 1556 to 1960, but there are 2,090 items up to 1740. Though leaving something to be desired bibliographically, it represents an indispensable checklist and was a useful starting point for the more detailed discoveries of Hilary Smith concerning preaching in the reign of Philip III. My own investigation of thirteen French and English libraries covers the period 1598-1650 and yielded over 300 items (including Protestant sermons).[27] Most recently, Werner Welzig, in collaboration with Franz Eybl, Heinrich Kabas, Robert Pichl, and Roswitha Woytek, has published the first of the promised two volumes of his magnificent catalogue of sermon collections in the conventual libraries of Vienna.[28] The attendant literature already reveals how rich this sort of investigation can be.[29] Research is at a more preliminary stage in Portugal: Aníbal Pinto de Castro made a powerful plea in 1973 for more investigation of sources;[30] meanwhile Belchior Pontes had drawn attention to an invaluable manuscript catalogue of sermons from the second half of the sixteenth century to the beginning of the eighteenth (now MS. 362 of the Biblioteca Nacional in Lisbon).[31] Although remarks about the titles and location of the texts are, of course, to be found scattered in works dealing with Italian preachers (notably in studies of individual religious orders[32]), it is a matter of surprise and

[27]Bayley (1980), Part II.
[28]Welzig (1984).
[29]See Welzig (1979,1980); Pichl (1980); Eybl (1979,1981,1982).
[30]Pinto de Castro (1973): 10.
[31]"A oratória sacra em Portugal no século XVII segundo o manuscrito 362 da Biblioteca Nacional de Lisboa," in Belchior Pontes (1971): 171-82.
[32]E.g. Belluco (1956).

regret that no research of this kind on a major scale appears to be in progress for Italy in the seventeenth and eighteenth centuries. Latin American libraries, too, though overlapping to some extent with the discoveries made in Spain and perhaps especially Portugal (for Vieira preached frequently in Brazil), would be likely to yield a rich harvest. "Sermons did not, however, spring spontaneously to the lips of preachers, and the second area of fundamental research has been the discovery, listing, and, in some cases, publishing of the *artes praedicandi* which appeared in such profusion after the Council of Trent. The major contribution was made long ago by Caplan and King in an indispensable series of articles, though it is not impossible that further research in libraries might modify and amplify their findings. So far such research has largely been the speciality of Spain, where the tradition inaugurated by Fr. Pío Sagüés Azcona's splendid critical edition of Estella's *Modo de predicar* continues to bear recent fruit.[33]

It is in the interpretation of these manuals of preaching, whether by setting them in the wider context of formal rhetoric, by using them as a key to a new understanding of the principles of sermon composition, or by drawing parallels between them and some of the better known early modern treatises on poetics, that the most exciting progress in criticism over the last thirty years has been achieved. It has, of course, been piecemeal and patchy, but surveyed from the present vantage point it nonetheless appears impressive and ripe for a major synthesis.

It has always been known that the Renaissance saw a revival of classical rhetoric. Decades ago Morris Croll began to outline a possible topography of seventeenth-century prose styles based on affiliation to one school of antiquity or another (such as Ciceronianism versus Senecanism).[34] The problem has been that scholars were too hasty in assuming a simple and direct connection between what one may call an author's "school-learning" and his compositional practice, so that if, say, a writer echoed some commonplace of Quintilian it was assumed that his writing would be "classical." The interpretation of some key documents in our subject, such as St. François de Sales's *Lettre à Frémiot,* was long troubled by this confusion. What was needed was a much more complex analysis of the Renaissance debt to antiquity and a set of much subtler distinctions between different kinds of aids to

---

[33]Sagüés Azcona (1951,1979,1982); Robles (1978).
[34]Studies posthumously collected in Croll (1966); the subject has an immense modern bibliography in the history of English literature alone.

composition and declamation. The first of these wants has now been admirably and massively supplied by Marc Fumaroli's authoritative study,[35] which extends well beyond the boundaries of France even though its ultimate concern is to trace the development of a specifically Gallican rhetoric in that country. Its insights and its application to other countries will occupy scholars fruitfully for many years to come.

Preaching, however, occupies only a relatively minor place in Fumaroli's book, which must represent for us a starting point and not a conclusion. Nor is he primarily concerned to highlight links between sermons and the ideas of Trent. Those links, it has now become clear, depend more on practical manuals than on full-dress books of rhetoric. I have sketched out an hypothesis to account for the peculiarity of one French preacher's style in terms of Tridentine injunctions filtered through Borromeo and his disciples in northern Italy.[36] At that time, however, I was not aware of the fascinating work of two Portuguese scholars in tracing the evolution of Renaissance rhetoric into seventeenth-century European "literary theory" and establishing the ways in which these theories might affect (or reflect) prose composition. Pinto de Castro, like Fumaroli, goes beyond preaching, though the centrality of Vieira leads him to give it pride of place. Saraiva's fundamental article, by situating Vieira in a European theoretical context, greatly illuminates that wider context. Both provide important starting points for a reinterpretation of baroque preaching in the light of such "mainstream" literary theorists as Emmanuele Tesauro and Baltasar Gracián.[37] It is in this area, too, that the major contribution of Italian scholars has been made. Already in 1954 Giovanni Pozzi, the leading scholar in a rather sparse field, had invoked Tesauro in order elegantly to disprove Croce's thesis about Spanish influence.[38] Having disposed of that bogeyman, he went on to investigate precisely the role of the thesauruses, commonplace-books (*selve*) and collections of "preachable subjects" (*discorsi or concetti predicabili*) which, it is now clear, stand behind the pulpit oratory of the two centuries after Trent. His illuminating introduction to Marino's *Dicerie sacre* ties these concerns to the mainstream of *seicento* prose

---

[35]Fumaroli (1980), with a very full bibliography pp. 707-836.
[36]Bayley (1977).
[37]For an attempt to situate a French "classic" in this wider European context, see Bayley (1982).
[38]Pozzi (1954), esp. pp. 163-78.

Dicerie sacre ties these concerns to the mainstream of *seicento* prose writing.[39] Giuseppe Cacciatore's two contributions to the introduction to the edition of St. Alfonso de Liguori represent a major extension of this research into the eighteenth century and include the fullest catalogue of *selve* and related material I have seen.[40] More recent studies on individual Jesuit preachers like Giuglaris[41] and Lubrano[42] continue in this line, and there is an obvious need for a series of studies on the leading preachers of the latter part of the period, such as Paolo Segneri the younger (or even his equally celebrated uncle), to match the ongoing work on Tesauro.[43] Indeed, a full-scale study of Italian preaching from Trent to 1740 is now an urgent task.

The ideal model for such research already exists in the form of Hilary Smith's study of Spanish preachers in the reign of Philip III. She has performed the remarkable feat of providing not only a virtual anthology and a thematic study of sermons, but a succinct account of preaching manuals and thesauruses, their relation to contemporary rhetorical theory and practice (which are in turn set in the wider context of Golden Age literary aesthetics as exemplified, for instance, by Gracián's *Arte y agudeza de ingenio*), and a detailed analysis of how *conceptos predicables* actually work. By so doing she has perhaps finally laid the ghost of Fray Gerundio.[44] It is now for the Italians to apply her lessons to their *concetti predicabili* and the Portuguese to their *conceitos predicaveis*. A large number of theoretical works and practical handbooks have been analysed; it is time for a return to the sermons themselves. There could be no better starting point than Smith's remark (in which she anticipates Ebyl's findings about the German exploitation of Pierre

---

[39]Pozzi (1960). The crucial figure in the dissemination of the new preaching style in Italy increasingly appears to be Francesco Panigarola, on whom Pozzi is rumored to have written. I have not found precise references.

[40]Cacciatore (1960), esp. pp. 158-80.

[41]Elia and Sensi (1978).

[42]Sensi (1983).

[43]E.g. Raimondi (1961).

[44]See Padre Isla's *Historia del famoso predicador Fray Gerundio de Campazas*, first published in 1770 and frequently reprinted and translated: the satirical novel that did for post-Tridentine preaching what *Don Quixote* did for chivalric romances. The most recent critical edition is by L. Fernández Martín (2 vols., Madrid, 1978), in whose introduction it is piquant to discover the mirror image of Croce's accusation against Spanish bad taste: "The influence of Italian *seicentismo* introduced the fashion for 'conceits' and 'antithesis' amongst us. Cornelio Musso and Panigarola founded a school whose traits are precisely those of the decadent Spanish oratory of the eighteenth century" (p. 25). But Padre Isla is not to be held responsible for his twentieth-century editor, and this hilarious novel should be required reading for all specialists in our subject.

themselves *artes praedicandi,* containing not only preachable material and model sermons but also rules governing decorum and delivery in the pulpit."[45]

For that to be done, it will be necessary, as I have suggested, to jettison certain national stereotypes. The fruitfulness of "borrowing" the models of other cultures may be clearly seen in the as yet small but convincing flow of work coming from eastern Europe. It is precisely the model of "baroque" Catholic Christendom that has given impetus to the study of Polish preaching[46] and forms the basis of Bitskey's study of one of Hungary's classic preachers.

It seems evident, then, that three areas solicit our research. The foundation on which all else depends is the continued investigation of ancient libraries and, where possible, the publication of new sources. In the nature of things, this is likely to take place within, rather than across, national boundaries, although the older religious orders will no doubt continue to play their traditional and valuable role.[47] The time also seems ripe to coordinate our knowledge of the principles of composition which underlie the writing (and no doubt underlay the delivery) of sermons in the period. We need a proper "theorization" which will take into account the fact that theory follows practice as often as it precedes it, and frequently has more to do with the abstractions of classical school-rhetoric than with actual writing. Following from that, we need a more precise and securely instanced definition of the way, for example, that a "conceit" or "conception" works in a text.

Finally, we need to pool this information and strive for a more comparative perspective (which will not be simply an old-fashioned study of "influences"). The impact of English sermon studies on some students of European preaching shows how fruitful such cross-fertilization can be. Then we shall be in a far better position to assess the truth of what can at present merely be tendered as an hypothesis: that the ideals of Trent, coinciding as they did with the revival of

[45]Smith (1978): vii-ix.

[46]See Kracik (1973); Kuc (1977); Sniegocki (1979); Drob (1981); Zebrowksi (1981).

[47]If I have not discussed as fully as I might the contribution made by the religious orders, it is largely because in recent decades their scholars have tended, in this field, to concentrate on biography and even prosopography rather than on textual or literary criticism. Even detailed studies of preaching orders in individual cities–such as Picard (1980)–yield disappointing results for the seeker after texts; and, in my opinion, we already know enough about the international free circulation of ideas and handbooks in the period to warrant resisting any temptation to chase after the will o' the wisp of distinct "monastic styles."

antique rhetoric, evolved into theories in strong Counter Reformation centers like Borromeo's circle in Milan and, fertilized by contact with cultivated Renaissance minds like Luis de Granada in Spain and disseminated by innumerable handbooks, became by those very methods of dissemination the stuff and texture of the European Catholic sermon for two hundred years.

One of the ways to concentrate a scholar's mind on how his subject should develop is to plan the spending of an imaginary financial windfall. I think the first use I should put it to would be an international conference at which information could be pooled, scholarly friendships forged across the many boundaries that at present obstruct the way forward, and hypotheses—such as the one I have risked above—be tested. The next stage would be a journal—we might call it *Eloquentia sacra*—to maintain those contacts and broadcast fresh information, thereby removing the need for periodic surveys of widely dispersed material such as this. And perhaps, if the author of the windfall were truly munificent, we might even envisage what so many of our colleagues in other fields already possess: a corpus of texts or *Monumenta Concionatorum Catholicorum* which, critically edited and properly indexed, would massively advance our knowledge and our understanding.

Bibliography

Anatole, C., "Réforme tridentine et littérature occitane en pays de Toulouse au XVIIe siècle," *Annals de l'Institut d'Estudis occitans* 5 (1978): 65-76.

Bachleitner, Norbert, *Form und Funktion der deutschsprachigen Gedichteinlagen und Reimsprüche in den Schriften Abraham a Sancta Claras* (Vienna Ph.D., 1981) [summary in *Sprachkunst* 13 (1982): 173].

Bayley, Peter, "Les sermons de Jean-Pierre Camus et l'esthétique borroméenne," *Critique et création littéraires en France au XVIIe siècle*, ed. M. Fumaroli (Paris, 1977): 92-98.

———, *French Pulpit Oratory, 1598-1650: a study in themes and styles, with a Descriptive Catalogue of printed texts* (Cambridge, 1980).

———, "The art of the *pointe* in Bossuet," *The Equilibrium of Wit: Essays for Odette de Mourgues*, ed. P. Bayley and D. Coleman (Lexington, 1982): 262-79.

———, ed., *Selected Sermons of the French Baroque* (New York, (1983)).

Belchior Pontes, Maria de Lourdes, *Os homens e os livros: séculos XVI e XVII* (Lisbon, 1971).

Belluco, Bartolomeo, *De sacra praedicatione in ordine Fratrum Minorum* (Rome, 1956).

Bitskey, Istvan, "Le baroque édifiant dans l'oeuvre d'un archevêque hongrois, Péter Pázmány," *Baroque: revue internationale* 8 (1976): 35-46.

Cacciatore, Giuseppe, "Le maniere letterarie del Seicento religioso" and "La letteratura degli 'exempla,'" in St. Alfonso de Liguori, *Opere ascetiche,* ed. O. Gregorio et al., vol. 1 (Rome, 1960): 157-283.

Candel, Jules, *Les Prédicateurs français dans la première moitié du XVIIIe siècle (1715-1760)* (Paris, 1904).

Cantel, Raymond, *Les Sermons de Vieira, étude du style* (Paris, 1959).

Caplan, H., and H. King, "Latin Tractates on Preaching. A Book-list," *Harvard Theological Review* 42 (1949): 185-206.

———, "Italian Treatises on Preaching. A Book-list," *Speech Monographs* 16 (1949): 243-52.

———, "French Tractates on Preaching. A Book-list," *Quarterly Journal of Speech* 36 (1950): 296-325.

———, "Spanish Treatises on Preaching. A Book-list," *Speech Monographs* 17 (1950): 161-70.

Collinet, Jean-Pierre, and Thérèse Goyet (eds), *Bossuet. La Prédication au XVIIe siècle (Actes du colloque de Dijon, 1977)* (Paris, 1980).

Croce, Benedetto, *I Predicatori italiani del Seicento e il gusto spagnuolo* (Naples, 1899).

Croll, Morris W., *Style, Rhetoric, and Rhythm,* ed. J. Max Patrick et al. (Princeton, 1966).

Descrains, Jean (ed.), *Jean-Pierre Camus: Homélies des États Généraux (1614-1615)* (Paris, 1970).

———, *Bibliographie des oeuvres de Jean-Pierre Camus* (Paris, 1971).

Drob, J., "Model czlowieka wieku XVII w kazaniach Berarda Gutowskiego," *Roczniki Humanistyczne Lublin* 29 (1981): 75-140 [resumé in English].

Elia, P., and C. Sensi, "Per una biografia di Luigi Giuglaris," *Studi piemontesi* 7 (1978): 367-76.

Eybl, Franz M., "Predigt - Sammlung - Literaturprogramm. Zu Florentin Schillings Predigtsammlung 'Amaradulcis,'" *Daphnis* 8 (1979): 299-346.

———, "Jakobus auf dem Dorfe. Eine Festpredigt von Martin Resch, sozialgeschichtlich gelesen," *Daphnis* 10 (1981): 67-93.

———, *Gebrauchsfunktionen barocker Predigtliteratur. Studien zur katholischen Predigtsammlung am Beispiel lateinischen und deutschen Übersetzungen des Pierre de Besse* (Vienna, 1982).

Fumaroli, Marc, *L'Age de l'éloquence. Rhétorique et "res literaria" de la Renaissance au seuil de l'époque classique (Geneva, 1980).*

Goyet, Thérèse, *L'Humanisme de Bossuet,* 2 vols. (Paris, 1965).

Haillant, M., *Fénelon et la prédication* (Paris, 1969).

Hennequin, Jacques, *Henri IV dans ses oraisons funèbres ou la naissance d'une légende* (Paris, 1977).

———, *Les Oraisons funèbres d'Henri IV: les thèmes et la rhétorique,* 2 vols. (Lille, 1978).

Herrero Salgado, Félix, *Aportación bibliográfica a la oratoria sagrada española* (Madrid, 1971).

Intorp, Leonhard, *Westfälische Barockpredigten in volkskundlicher Sicht* (Münster, 1964).

Jacoebee, W. P., "The Classical Sermon and the French Literary Tradition," *Australian Journal of French Studies* 19 (1982): 227-42.

Kracik, J., "Katolicka indoktrynacja doby saskiej w parafiach zachodniej Malopolski," *Roczniki Teologiczno-kanoniczne* 20 (1973): 13-27 [resumé in French].

Landry, J.-P., "Bourdaloue face à la querelle de l'éloquence sacrée," *XVIIͤ Siècle* 36 (1984): 133-40.

Le Brun, Jacques, *La Spiritualité de Bossuet* (Paris, 1972).

Leenhardt, Jacques, "Approche sociologique d'un sermon de Massillon sur Luc 15, 11-13," *Exegesis: Problèmes de méthode et exercices de lecture*, ed. F. Bovon and G. Rouiller (Neuchâtel, 1975): 145-68.

Lemaître, Nicole, "Un prédicateur et son public. Les sermons du Père Lejeune et le Limousin, 1653-1672," *Revue d'histoire moderne et contemporaine* 30 (1983): 33-65.

Leopold, Radegundis (ed.), *Antonio Vieiras Predigt über "Maria Heimsuchung"* [viz. *Sermão da Visitação de nossa Senhora]* (Münster, 1977).

Moser-Rath, Elfriede (ed.), *Predigtmärlein der Barockzeit: Exempel, Sage, Schwank und Fabel in geistlichen Quellen des oberdeutschen Raumes* (Berlin, 1964).

_____, "Volksfrömmigkeit im Spiegel der Barockpredigt," *Zeitschrift für Volkskunde* 65 (1969): 196-206.

_____, "Familienlebe im Spiegel der Barockpredigt," *Daphnis* 10 (1981): 47-65.

_____, "Die Fabel als rhetorisches Element in der katholischen Predigt der Barockzeit," *Die Fabel*, ed. P. Hasubeck (Berlin, 1982): 59-75.

Nagel, Rolf, *Die Antoniuspredigt António Vieiras an die portugiesischen Generalstände von 1642* (Münster, 1972).

O'Malley, John W., "Erasmus and the History of Sacred Rhetoric: The Ecclesiastes of 1535," *Erasmus of Rotterdam Society Yearbook* 5 (1985): 1-29.

_____, "Saint Charles Borromeo and the *Praecipuum Episcoporum Munus*: His Place in the History of Preaching," in *San Carlo Borromeo*, ed. John M. Headley (Washington, 1988).

Peyrous, Bernard, "Saint Vincent de Paul et le renouvellement des missions paroissiales," *Bulletin de la Société de Borda* 107 (1982): 569-84.

Picard, E., "Les Théatins de Sainte-Anne-la-Royale (1644-1790)," *Regnum Dei. Collectanea Theatina* 36 (1980): 99-374.

Pichl, Robert, "Zur Dokumentation der deutschsprachigen Predigtliteratur vom späten 16. bis zum frühen 19. Jahrhundert. Probleme ihrer Durchführung und wissenschaftlicher Auswertbarkeit," *Jahrbuch für Volkskunde* (1980): 166-93.

Pinto de Castro, Aníbal, *Retórica e teorização litterária em Portugal* (Coimbra, 1973).

Pozzi, G. [Giovanni da Locarno], *Saggi sullo stile dell'oratoria sacra nel Seicento esemplificata sul P. Emmanuele Orchi* (Rome, 1954).

———, ed., G. B. Marino: *Dicerie sacre* (Turin, 1960).

Raimondi, Ezio, "Grammatica e Retorica nel Pensiero di Tesauro" and "Ingegno e metafora nella poetica del Tesauro," in *Letteratura barocca: Studi sul Seicento italiano* (Florence, 1961).

Robles, L., "'Reglas para predicar' del obispo Gregorio Gallo," *Revista española de teología* 38 (1978): 359-66.

Sagüés Azcona, Pío, ed., *Diego de Estella [Didacus Stella]: Modo de predicar y Modus concionandi,* 2 vols. (Madrid, 1951).

———, "'Reglas y avisos para predicar' de varios autores del siglo XVI," *Revista española de teología* 39-40 (1979-80): 389-90.

———, "Un sermón sobre San Francisco de Asís del P. Felipe Díez," *Archivo ibero-americano* 42 (1982): 267-92.

Santini, E., "Precisazioni e aggiunte sulla sacra predicazione nel secolo XVII," *Studi Seicenteschi* 1 (1960): 1-14.

Saraiva, A. J., "Les quatre sources du discours ingénieux dans les sermons du padre António Vieira," *Bulletin des études portugaises* 31 (1970): 177-269.

Saugnieux, Joel, *Les Jansénistes et le renouveau de la prédication dans l'Espagne de la seconde moitié du XVIIIᵉ siècle* (Lyons, 1976).

Schneyer, Johann Baptist, *Geschichte der katholischen Predigt* (Freiburg i.B., 1968).

Séguy, J.-B., "Langue, religion et société: Alain de Solminihac et l'application de la réforme tridentine dans le diocèse de Cahors," *Annals de l'Institut d'Estudis occitans* 5 (1977): 79-110.

Sensi, Claudio, "La retorica dell'apoteosi. Arte e artificio nei panegirici del Lubrano," *Studi Seicenteschi* 24 (1983): 69-152.

Shuger, Debora, "The Christian Grand Style in Renaissance Rhetoric," *Viator* 16 (1985), 337-65.

Smith, Hilary D., *Preaching in the Spanish Golden Age. A Study of some Preachers of the Reign of Philip III* (Oxford, 1978).

Sniegocki, Janusz, "Exempla i koncepty barokowe w Kazaniak o swietych Fabiana Birkowskiego," *Roczniki Humnistyczne Lublin* 27 (1979): 109-37 [resumé in English].

Truchet, Jacques, *La Prédication de Bossuet: étude des thèmes,* 2 vols. (Paris, 1960).

———, ed., *Bossuet: Oraisons funèbres* (Paris, 1961).

———, *Bossuet panégyriste* (Paris, 1962).

Vercesi, E., and E. Santini, *L'Eloquenza dal secolo XVII ai giorni nostri* (Milan, 1938).

Viguerie, J. de, "Quelques aspects du catholicisme des Français au XVIIIᵉ siècle," *Revue historique* 538 (1981): 335-70.

Welzig, Werner, "Vom Nutzen der geistlichen Rede. Beobachtungen zu den Funktionsweisen eines literarischen Genres," *Internationales Archiv für Sozialgeschichte der deutschen Literatur* 4 (1979): 1-23.

———, "Allegorese im Dienste einer Titelrhetorik. Beobachtungen zum Titelkupfer einer Barocken Predigtsammlung," *Formen und Funktionen der Allegorie* ed. W. Haug (Stuttgart, 1980): 419-28.

———, *Katalog gedrucker deutschprachiger katholischer Predigtsammlung,* vol. I, Michael Helding (1557) bis Ignaz Sailer (1770) (Vienna, 1984).

Wittschier, Heinz Willi, *António Vieiras Pestpredigt* (Münster, 1973).

Zebrowski, R., "Obraz swiata w kazaniach Aleksandra Lorencowicza," *Roczniki Humanistyczne Lublin* 29 (1981): 5-74 [resumé in English].

Schools, Seminaries,
and Catechetical Instruction

Paul F. Grendler

CATHOLIC EUROPE may have devoted more energy to education than to any other activity in this era. Yet for a long time the study of schools, seminaries, and catechetical instruction has not been part of the mainstream of scholarship but the preserve of local history. Local historians seldom advanced beyond a chronicle of a single person, place, or institution, and usually failed to see their topic within a broader intellectual and societal context. They also tended to exhibit too much *pietas* toward their subject matter. But they accurately and honestly recorded a great deal of useful information. Local history of education flourished in the late nineteenth century and the first twenty years of the twentieth century but then declined. In the 1970s a new generation of historians free of the limitations of their predecessors took up anew the history of education. Social historians in particular have done important work on literacy and the results of basic schooling. They have done less on schools of religious orders, seminaries, the study of curricula, and catechetical instruction. This essay will necessarily concentrate on recent work, but it is written in a spirit of respect for the older local historians who laid the foundations.

The largest amount of research on schooling in both Catholic and Protestant Europe in recent years has focused, first of all, on literacy. Scholars begin with such questions as, what percentage of the population could read, write, or both? Who was literate? Where was literacy highest? They attempt to answer these questions through a broad and relatively neutral source such as signatures on marriage contracts. Having found statistical answers to the above questions, they turn to the conveyer of literacy, the schools. Historians try to determine what social forces brought schools into existence, and how classroom instruction inculcated the moral and social values of society. Finally, such studies often try to study literacy over a period of several centuries in order to detect broad trends.[1]

---

[1] The above comments refer to studies of both Catholic and Protestant Europe and a chronological period of several centuries. Although more research has been done on Protestant Europe and on the eighteenth and nineteenth centuries, this essay will limit itself to Catholicism, c. 1540 to 1700. For excellent surveys of the literature on literacy, see Graff (1981[a], 1981[b], and 1983) and Houston (1983).

The two largest, possibly most influential studies in recent years deal with France and have much in common. Furet and Ozouf (1977) draw on a remarkable nineteenth-century collection of marriage-contract signatures in order to study literacy in the sixteenth through the nineteenth centuries, although the primary focus is the period 1680 through 1860. They conclude that towns began the move toward greater literacy in the sixteenth and seventeenth centuries. Rural areas, in time, also attained greater literacy; by contrast, urban literacy declined somewhat in the eighteenth century. Second, Furet and Ozouf stress, as do most historians, the kaleidoscopic variety of schooling; municipal, church, and private schools, with a good deal of further variation within these three broad categories, existed. Third, they tend to see acquiring the ability to read and write not so much as an intellectual process as an anthropological one, i.e., a transition from oral to written culture.

Chartier, Compère, and Julia (1976) cover much the same chronological ground, but give greater attention to schools than to raw literacy. Again they prove a great deal of statistical information. They see a growth from the fourteenth and fifteenth centuries when schooling was the privilege of a few urban dwellers to the broader schooling of the seventeenth century when the Jesuits, Brothers of the Christian Schools, and other religious orders dominated French education and used the opportunity to transform popular morality into a more amenable Tridentine Catholicism. Signs of educational decadence then appeared in the eighteenth century. Compère and Julia (1984), in the first volume of a projected three, supplement the above with detailed information on individual secondary schools in southern France.

These studies and others like them have focused on the very important social dimension of education.[2] As should be obvious, Furet and Ozouf, Chartier, Compère, and Julia, and the authors of similar studies tend to be *Annalistes* of the strict observance. They provide a wealth of valuable statistical information divided into sexual, regional, and occupational categories, as well as real insight into the social nature of literacy and learning. But they also exhibit the usual *Annaliste* indifference to ideas by refusing to take the content of the curriculum very seriously. Their stress on continuity is valuable, but *la longue durée*

---

[2]See such diverse examples as Kagan (1974) on Spain, Wyczánski (1974) on Poland, and Greer (1978) on Quebec. Although Greer's study deals with a later period, it will have to suffice until research under way on seventeenth-century Quebec is published.

for them means the seventeenth, eighteenth, and sometimes the nineteenth centuries. Why do they ignore the sixteenth century and the educational revolution that Renaissance humanism accomplished? These historians see schooling as social control, "policing the village" through priest and schoolmaster, in Furet and Ozouf's words.[3] They sympathize with an unlettered populace whose natural, free oral culture is threatened by an oppressive academic civilization. This seems a nostalgic judgment and an inadequate perspective on a very complex phenomenon. Finally, looming behind Old Regime schooling is the French Revolution and the searing ideological debates on education in nineteenth- and twentieth-century France; perhaps the issues of the recent past have helped set the agenda for the analysis of the more distant past.

While not all historians share the perspective of French social historians, scholars of literacy and elementary schooling in various parts of Catholic and Protestant Europe and of different chronological periods, do share some conclusions.[4] They agree that the rise and fall of literacy closely paralleled the hierarchies of wealth, occupation, and social status. This is hardly surprising, but perhaps the high degree of correlation is: the bourgeoisie in late sixteenth-century French towns might be over 90 percent literate, but agricultural workers less than 10 percent literate.[5] More men were literate than women; again the difference was enormous and closely linked to social class. Beyond these conclusions, agreement diminishes, largely because of the difficulty of locating enough quantitative data and the complexity of reasons for variation. Research to date seems to indicate that Protestant northern Europe had higher levels of literacy (and, hence, more elementary schooling) than Catholic southern Europe, but the reasons are not clear, and may or may not have much to do with religion. The older assumption that magisterial Protestantism wanted more schools so that the laity could read the Bible is proving hard to substantiate.[6]

Huppert (1984) directs our attention to the earlier phase of French education and corrects an older view accepted by Furet and Ozouf, plus Chartier, Compère, and Julia, that the Jesuits and other religious orders

---

[3]Furet and Ozouf (1982): 62.
[4]Houston (1983): 271-72 for a brief summary.
[5]Chartier, Compère, and Julia (1976): 105.
[6]Gawthrop and Strauss (1984) deny the link between Bible reading and an increase in schools for Lutheran Germany in the sixteenth century. They do assert that a link exists between bible-reading Pietists and an increase in schooling in eighteenth-century Germany.

played the key role in the French *collèges* and thereby set the tone for French education in the Old Regime. As Huppert relates, between 1530 and 1560 city councils dominated by local leaders took control of the schools away from bishops. They established new municipal schools called *collèges* that taught the humanistic curriculum of the Renaissance. City councils hired lay masters of arts from Paris to teach in their schools, which enrolled anywhere from forty to several hundred students each, including a few girls. Most important, the *collèges* did not charge tuition fees to town residents, although those who lived beyond the walls had to pay. These municipal *collèges* flourished for fifty years or more until in the early seventeenth century crown and church opposed them. The crown felt that too much education diverted ordinary folk from useful work, and it also wished to centralize the direction of education. The monarchy encouraged Jesuits and other religious orders to take over the teaching and operation of the *collèges*, which began to charge fees. By the end of the seventeenth century, both enrollment and standards had declined.

Italian city councils, including those of rural hamlets,[7] also sponsored schools, but not so systematically as in France. Probably no unified school system existed anywhere in Catholic Europe; instead, a mix of state, church, and private schools taught Latin and vernacular curricula. Two recent studies briefly describe the primary and secondary schools of Venice in 1587.[8] State schools enrolled 4 percent of the student body, clerical schools 7 percent, and private schools of different kinds the remaining 89 percent. All young Venetians attending state and church schools plus a substantial minority of the students of private schools–about half of the total school enrollment–pursued a Latin classical curriculum. The other half studied vernacular literature and commercial arithmetic, always in private schools.

These studies remind us that schools had different purposes, served more than one constituency, and reflected the diversity of society as a whole. The division of schools into Latin and vernacular, apparently a feature of schooling throughout Europe, split society. Latin schools trained the ruling class of leaders, professionals, and civil servants; vernacular schools trained the merchants, artisans, and others who inhabited the world of work. Although more difficult to study because they attracted less attention, vernacular schools may have been very

---

[7] Pesciatini (1982).
[8] Baldo (1977) and Grendler (1985a). Although the studies rely on the same documents, their approach is somewhat different and the statistics may vary slightly.

widespread. Petrucci (1978) argues that on the basis of a close analysis of the handwriting of Roman tradesmen that most members of the lower ranks of Roman male society possessed basic vernacular literacy in the sixteenth century. More recently, Petrucci (1982) offers a fascinating exhibit of handwritten and printed materials that manifests the richness and variety of popular Roman culture.

The educational structure evolved to meet new needs and to reflect the growth or decline of one kind of school or another. Perhaps the major change occurring in the period of Catholic Reform was the increase in ecclesiastical schools, not medieval cathedral chapter or monastic schools, but those established and staffed by the new religious orders of the Catholic Reformation.

The Jesuits opened their first school in Messina, Sicily, in 1547, and their famous Collegio Romano in 1551. A sign reading "Free School for Grammar, Humanity, and Christian Doctrine" hung over the front door of the latter, signaling the original Jesuit intention of providing free humanistic training and catechetical instruction.[9] But already in the 1550s and early 1560s, the Jesuits changed pedagogical direction: they concentrated on advanced education through seminaries and universities, and on training the governing class of Catholic Europe through fee-paying boarding schools. Much of the story of the early decades of Jesuit schools remains to be told, but a recent documentary publication should help. Four thick volumes of the *Monumenta Paedagogica Societatis Iesu* (1965-1981) print documents from the central Jesuit archive in Rome and other repositories for the period 1540-1580. Jesuit correspondents from Portugal to Poznan reported their successes and failures, giving information on teachers and enrollment. Here also are the curriculum drafts that culminated in the *Ratio studiorum*. Recent studies of Italian Jesuit schools in the sixteenth century point the way. Scaduto (1974) chronicles the establishment of Jesuit schools in Italy, and Donnelly (1982) deals with a conspicuous failure in Padua.[10] The latter study analyzes the volatile mix of educational rivalry, ideological conflict, and political suspicion that Jesuit schools attracted. Fumaroli (1980) provides much information on Jesuit eloquence in France, and the volume edited by Brizzi (1981) discusses Italian Jesuit teaching of rhetoric, cases of conscience, and natural philosophy.

Jesuit boarding schools for the sons of the rich became very important across Europe. Here Renaissance and Catholic Reformation

---

[9]García Villoslada (1954): 19.
[10]Scaduto (1974): 271-467.

met. Modeled on the fifteenth-century humanistic boarding schools of Vittorino da Feltre and Guarino of Verona, the Jesuit boarding schools taught the Latin and Greek classics and theology, plus horsemanship and other gentlemanly arts to the sons of nobles. Brizzi (1976) provides an exemplary study of Jesuit boarding schools in Bologna, Parma, Modena, and Siena. Thanks to comprehensive student records, he analyses the social origins and future careers of the students, many of them non-Italians. He also examines the content of the curriculum. These Jesuit boarding schools became incubators for the ruling class, early modern Catholic versions of the famous English public schools and American prep schools of a later age. It is likely that other scholars will follow Brizzi's lead.[11]

Scholars are aware of Jesuit schools, but other important teaching orders and their schools have not received much recent study. An exception is the Fathers of the Christian Doctrine (*Pères de la Doctrine Chrétienne*) who established their first formal school in 1619. Although founded in 1592 by César de Bus (1544-1607) to provide catechetical instruction, the *"Doctrinaires,"* as they were called, became a major supplier of education in seventeenth- and eighteenth-century France, rivals to the Jesuits, Oratorians, and Brothers of the Christian Schools. A new, model study provides a comprehensive history of the order, including recruitment, finances, and pedagogy.[12]

In 1597, a transplanted Aragonese priest named José da Calasanz (1556-1648) founded in the working-class parish of Santa Dorotea in Trastevere (Rome), a free elementary school to teach poor boys and girls reading, writing, religion, and a trade. Piarist historians sometimes assert the dubious claim that this was the first free "public" school (in the sense of being available to all) in Europe. His school grew, and Calasanz founded the Order of Piarists to operate and staff these "Pious Schools" (*Scuole Pie*) as they were called in Italy. They did not remain elementary vernacular schools limited to the poor, but added Latin grammar and enrolled a cross-section of the population. The "Pious Schools" have received reverent attention from historians of the order, including the publication of basic sources, but they merit broader

---

[11]Frijhoff and Julia (1975) provide a social analysis of the student body of four French *collèges* operated by the *Doctrinaires,* secular priests, Oratorians, and Jesuits. The first three case studies come from the eighteenth century, the last form the period 1598 to 1608.

[12]Viguerie (1976).

study.[13] Liebreich (1982 and 1985) demonstrates what can be done: she offers detailed studies of the Florentine Piarist schools, including finances, enrollment figures, analysis of the social backgrounds, and more.

Similar critical evaluation based on archival material is needed for other schools established by religious orders: the schools of the Barnabites and the Somaschi, the schools of the Oratorians of Pierre de Bérulle (1575-1629), and especially the Institute of the Brothers of the Christian Schools founded in 1680 by Jean-Baptiste de la Salle. The focus of research ought not to be the saintly founder of his or her order, but the practical matters of finances, enrollment, recruitment, and the academic and social roles these schools played. Did all these new religious schools fill a vacuum, i.e., provide schooling where little previously existed? Or did they replace declining state and private schools, so that the global amount of instruction remained about the same?

Curriculum and pedagogical theory have been somewhat neglected in recent years. An exception is Van Egmond's catalogue (1981) of Italian Renaissance mathematical manuscripts and printed books with an introduction describing their pedagogical use. Lucchi (1978) and Grendler (1982) have discussed the elementary texts used in Italian vernacular schools, while Grendler (1985b) lists the elementary Latin grammars used in Italy. Volpicelli (1960) and Secco (1973) offer a great deal of information on pedagogical theory in Italy. The provocative study of Ariès (1960) on the concept of childhood has proved very stimulating to scholars, although much, including his central argument that medieval society had no concept of childhood until seventeenth-century Frenchmen "invented" it, fails to convince.[14]

Various comprehensive studies, such as those of Furet and Ozouf (1977) and Chartier, Compère, and Julia (1976) deal with female literacy on a quantitative basis. But much more research is needed on specific aspects of female education, such as the kinds of schools they attended, why they attended or did not, and the curriculum of these schools. Two recent studies deal with attitudes toward educating women.[15]

---

[13]Sántha, Aguilera, and Centelles (1956); *L'Epistolario di Calasanzio (1950-1956); Sindoni (1971).*

[14]Pollock (1983) disputes this and other theses of Ariès. Although her book is based on English and American sources 1500 to 1900, similar evidence can be found in continental Europe. Also see Mause (1974), Chapters 4, 5, and 6.

[15]Sowards (1982); Labalme (1980), Chapters 5-8.

The female religious orders who taught girls–the Ursuline nuns of Angela Merici, the "Jesuitesses" of Mary Ward, 1585-1645, (suppressed in 1631 but revived as the Institute of Mary), and others–never achieved the quantitative success of the male teaching orders. Why not? Pius V's constitution *Circa pastoralis* (29 May 1566) ordering strict cloistering of all professed nuns meant that female religious could teach only those students who came into the convent. By contrast, professed male religious were not necessarily cloistered and could carry on teaching and other activities outside the monastery. Female religious leaders attempted to work within *Circa pastoralis* or tried to establish teaching communities of women who did not profess solemn vows, but none achieved large-scale success.

Hence, many small, individual, and local convent schools educated a handful of girls. Marcocchi (1974) describes such a school at Cremona, the Collegio della Beata Vergine founded in 1610. This convent school taught ten to twenty noble girls as fee-paying boarding students, and a slightly larger number of day students for free. The girls learned reading, arithmetic, and sewing, but little or no Latin. Marcocchi lists other such convent schools in Italy and beyond, but further research is needed. Eventually, neighborhood schools in which lay women taught girls vernacular reading and writing arose in seventeenth-century Rome (Pelliccia, 1980). Overall, little is known of what appears to have been a fairly dismal picture of female education.

Nor did women attend universities. In 1678, Elena Lucrezia Cornaro Piscopia, a Venetian noblewoman, received a doctorate in philosophy from the University of Padua, the first known example of a woman receiving a degree.[16] Unfortunately, no woman followed her for at least seventy years.

Little space can be given here to the history of universities. In general, prelates and princes in the sixteenth and seventeenth centuries felt uneasy about the traditional academic freedoms enjoyed by the faculty and students of medieval and Renaissance universities and sought to limit them. For example, the Venetian Senate kept a closer eye on the University of Padua, and the Medici Grand Dukes watched over the universities of Pisa and Siena more carefully than their predecessors.[17] But there were limits: neither drove away German Protestant students, despite the pleas of the papacy, because wealthy foreign students contributed a great deal to the economies of university

[16]Maschietto (1978).
[17]De Bernardin (1974) and Cascio Pratilli (1975).

towns. Governments only insisted that heretical foreigners refrain from practicing their own religion openly and avoid insulting Catholic practices. Inserting churchmen into the teaching faculty also tied universities more closely to the Catholic Reformation. Bartolomé Martínez (1983) discusses the successful effort of the Jesuits to establish themselves as teachers of the key subject of Latin grammar in Castilian universities. A new journal, *History of Universities,* should stimulate this fertile if somewhat neglected field. Its first volume (1981) focused on the early modern period with studies of French, Spanish, German, Dutch, and English universities.

In one of its best-known actions, the Council of Trent decreed the establishment of diocesan seminaries to train parish priests. The Council hoped that seminaries would give priests sound theological and pastoral training so that they might become effective leaders of the most important cell in the Catholic Church, the parish. The Collegium Germanicum in Rome (founded 1552) provided seminary training for young Germans, especially nobles, who became leaders of the German Catholic Church (Schmidt 1984). But outside of Rome, founding seminaries and making them work was not easy. Seifert (1978) pursues the long story of the struggle to found and finance seminaries in Bavaria, where the prince, the Jesuits who were to staff them, and the papacy pursued divergent goals.

Eventually seminaries were established.[18] Did they fulfill their intended role of supplying a sound clerical education? We do not really know, but there are hints that the answer may have been mixed. A study of the diocese of Novara in northern Italy, led by a dedicated reforming bishop, shows that only after 1593 did a majority–but not all–priests receive *some* seminary training.[19] In Lyon establishing seminaries began in the sixteenth century, but candidates for the priesthood were not required to attend, even for a few months, until the late seventeenth century.[20] A book on the Spanish church in the eighteenth century reveals that, even then, a minority of priests received no seminary education. Indeed, bypassing the seminary normally led to greater preferment in the Spanish church if the priest attended a university. But those who received only rudimentary education in a local Latin school were doomed to spend their lives in impoverished

---

[18]See, for example, Liberali (1971) for Treviso, Tramontin (1965) for Venice, and Baillargeon (1972) for Quebec.
[19]Deutscher (1981): 305.
[20]Hoffman (1984): 74-79.

country parishes. Spanish seminaries did not always become elevated institutions of learning. Cathedral canons who often directed seminaries sometimes "regarded their students as sources of free labor to arrange chairs, pump organs, and otherwise assist in the liturgical services of the cathedral. . . ."[21] Much research needs to be done on the development of seminaries and their impact on church and society.

The *Catechismus ex decreto Concilii Tridentini ad parochos* (1566), the famous Roman or Tridentine Catechism, a condensed but definitive statement of Catholic doctrine written to instruct parish priests, is synonymous with priestly training. Three new studies have appeared. Rodríguez and Lanzetti (1982) reexamine its composition and establish a greater Thomistic influence by means of the Spanish theologian Domingo de Soto than previously thought. Bellinger (1970) analyzes the ways in which the Roman Catechism responded to the dogmatic points of major Protestant catechisms. Bellinger (1983) publishes a comprehensive bibliography of 521 known Latin printings, 353 printings of translations into nineteen languages, plus 380 printings of variant versions (i.e., edited, abbreviated, adding commentary, etc.). One can assume from this that the Roman Catechism had great influence, but it would be useful to study the pathways and the extent to which it entered the mainstream of Catholic religious life. One approach is to examine the contents of the libraries of parish priests, as Labarre (1971) has done for Amiens, Deutscher (1981) for Novara, and Allegra (1978) for Piedmont.[22] The whole question of the cultural and educational levels of the clergy needs further exploration.

The catechetical movement in both Catholic and Protestant Europe demonstrated the pedagogical originality of the era. Medieval Europeans did not engage in mass religious instruction and wrote very few catechisms for the uneducated. This changed in the sixteenth century, as some clergymen seized on catechetical instruction as the means of teaching religion and morality to the laity. The printing press helped a great deal; for the first time, each child or adult learner could possess his or her own catechism. If students lacked the few coins necessary to buy a catechism, teachers passed them out. A work on German Lutheran catechesis (Strauss (1978) suggests the possibilities of research on catechism schools. Based on an exhaustive analysis of

---

[21]Callahan (1984): 17. On Spanish seminaries, see Martín Hernández (1961 and 1964).
[22]De Maio (1973) studies Italian monastic libraries at the end of the sixteenth century.

Renaissance pedagogical theory, the catechisms themselves, schools and society, and visitation records in which Lutheran pastors meticulously documented their successes and failures, Strauss's work offers a panoramic picture and provocative conclusions: that the Lutheran churches adapted their teaching to serve the needs of a society dominated by the urban upper classes, that obligatory catechism drill produced apathy, and that an appalling ignorance of basic Christian beliefs remained after fifty years of instruction. Strauss also opines that the same conclusions might be applicable to Catholic Bavaria.

Two studies have begun an evaluation of Italian catechism schools.[23] Founded in 1536, the Schools of Christian Doctrine, began as a voluntary, independent, and unauthorized charitable mission to the poor and ignorant that did not come under the bishops' control until the 1580s. Perhaps because the founders and teachers came from the same artisan, working-class world as their pupils, Italian catechism schools seemed more sensitive to their constituency and closer to their roots than Sunday Schools in Lutheran Germany. Italian catechisms also constantly emphasized the importance of good works: if one kept commandments, prayed, and did good works, one would be saved. They dropped the preoccupation with sin characteristic of late medieval catechisms.[24] The Schools of Christian Doctrine also taught rudimentary reading and writing to boys and girls, but separately: men taught boys in one church, women taught girls in another. Catechism schools might be added to the shadowy phenomenon of "informal schooling," that is, instruction occurring outside a formal academic setting: parental and sibling tutoring, autodidacticism, and instruction in the workplace. Lay confraternities of large membership possibly drawn from the same classes as the pupils supported the catechism schools, but they have not been studied.

Spain, Germany, and France also had catechetical movements. In Spain, Blessed Juan de Avila (1500-69) sought to establish catechism schools that, like their Italian counterparts, would teach Christian doctrine as well as elementary reading and writing. He and other Spanish and Portuguese authors drafted catechisms.[25] Catechetical instruction in Catholic Germany is closely identified with Peter

---

[23]Grendler (1984) and Turrini (1982, although not published until 1984). Also see Toscani (1984). The fundamental older work is Tamborini (1939).

[24]See Janz (1982): 29-130, for a translation of *A Fruitful Mirror or Small Handbook for Christians* (1480) of Dietrich Kolde, the most frequently printed German catechism at the end of the Middle Ages.

[25]Huerga (1968).

326 Catholicism in Early Modern History

Canisius (1521-97), who wrote three versions of varying difficulty of his famous catechism.[26]

The organization and approach of the catechetical movement appear to have been the same everywhere.[27] Catechism schools and their books coupled originality of approach with traditional religious content; perhaps only this marriage would attract a Catholic populace generally indifferent to theological innovation. The catechetical movement may offer a means of ascertaining the content and depth of basic religious knowledge of a large part of the population. More important, the appearance of catechetical movements in several countries suggests a grassroots phenomenon. Was this a spontaneous, popularly-based impulse in the Catholic Reformation? Previous generations of historians who have studied popes and princes, bishops and councils, monastic reformers and inquisitors, would surely have denounced this as heresy, but the implications for modifying the traditional view of a hierarchical, clerically-led Catholic Reformation are intriguing. The whole catechetical movement documents an attempt to instruct men intellectually and spiritually typical of the sixteenth and seventeenth centuries. Was there ever an age that took education more seriously?

I wish to thank William J. Callahan, David C. Higgs, Allan Greer, George Huppert, and James M. Weiss.

Bibliography

Allegra, Luciano, *Ricerche sulla cultura del clero in Piemonte. Le biblioteche parrocchiali nell'Arcidiocesi di Torino sec. xvii-xviii* (Turin, 1978).

Ariès, Philippe, *Centuries of Childhood. A Social History of Family Life.* Trans. Robert Baldick (New York, 1962).

Baillargeon, Noël, *Le seminaire de Québec sous l'épiscopat de Monseigneur de Laval* (Québec, 1972).

Baldo, Vittorio, *Alunni, maestri e scuole in Venezia alla fine del XVI secolo* (Como, 1977).

Bartolomé Martínez, Bernabé, "Las cátedras de Gramática de los jesuitas en las universidades de su provincia de Castilla," *Hispania Sacra* 35, fasc. 72 (1983): 449-97.

---

[26]Canisius (1933, 1936). For France, see Dhotel (1967).

[27]Nevertheless, catechetical movements and their catechisms apparently did not cross linguistic and national boundaries to influence one another. For example, although translated into Italian, Canisius' catechisms apparently were little used in Italy and did not influence the organization and content of Italian catechisms. This is a tentative statement because little has been done to locate copies, make comparisons, and compile bibliographies.

Bellinger, Gerhard, *Der Catechismus Romanus und die Reformation* (Paderborn, 1970).

———, *Bibliographie des Catechismus Romanus: Ex Decreto Concilii Tridentini ad Parochos, 1566-1978* (Baden-Baden, 1983).

Brizzi, Gian Paolo, *La formazione della classe dirigente nel Sei-Settecento. I seminaria nobilium nell'Italia centro-settentrionale* (Bologna, 1976).

———, ed., *La "Ratio studiorum." Modelli culturali e pratiche educative dei Gesuiti in Italia tra Cinque e Seicento* (Rome, 1981).

Callahan, William J., *Church, Politics, and Society in Spain, 1750-1874* (Cambridge, Mass., 1984).

Cascio Pratilli, Giovanni, *L'università e il principe. Gli Studi di Siena e di Pisa tra Rinascimento e Controriforma* (Florence, 1975).

Chartier, Roger, Marie-Madeleine Compère, and Dominique Julia, *L'éducation en France du XVIe au XVIIIe siècle* (Paris, 1976).

Compère, Marie-Madeleine, and Dominique Julia, *Les collèges français 16e-18e siècles. Répertoire 1: France du Midi* (Paris, 1984).

Davis, Natalie Z., "Printing and the People," in Davis, *Society and Culture in Early Modern France* (Stanford, Cal., 1975), 189-226.

De Bernardin, Sandro, "La politica culturale della Repubblica di Venezia e l'università di Padova nel XVII secolo," *Studi Veneziani* 16 (1974): 443-502.

De Maio, Romeo, "I modelli culturali della Controriforma. Le biblioteche dei conventi italiani alla fine del Cinquecento," in De Maio, *Riforme e miti nella Chiesa del Cinquecento (Naples, 1973), 365-81.

de Mause, Lloyd, ed., *The History of Childhood* (New York, 1975).

Deutscher, Thomas, "Seminaries and the Education of Novarese Parish Priests, 1593-1627," *Journal of Ecclesiastical History* 32 (1981): 303-19.

Dhotel, Jean-Claude, *Les origines du Catéchisme moderne d'après les premiers manuals imprimés en France* (Paris, 1967).

Donnelly, John Patrick, "The Jesuit College at Padua. Growth, Suppression, Attempts at Restoration: 1552-1606," *Archivum Historicum Societatis Iesu* 51 (1982): 45-78.

L'Epistolario di S. Giuseppe Calasanzio. Ed. Leodegario Picanyol, 8 vols. (Rome, 1950-56).

Frijhoff, Willem, and Dominique Julia, *École et société dans la France d'ancien régime. Quatre exemples Auch, Avallon, Condom et Gisors* (Paris, 1975).

Fumaroli, Marc, *L'Age de l'eloquence. Rhétorique et 'res literaria' de la Renaissance au seuil de l'époque classique* (Genève, 1980).

Furet, François, and Jacques Ozouf, et al., *Lire et écrire. L'alphabétisation des français de Calvin à Jules Ferry. 2 vols.* (Paris, 1977).

———, *Reading and Writing. Literacy in France from Calvin to Jules Ferry* (Cambridge, 1982). English translation of vol. 1.

García Villoslada, Ricardo, *Storia del Collegio Romano dal suo inizio (1551) alla soppressione della Compagnia di Gesù (1773)* (Rome, 1954).

Gawthrop, Richard, and Gerald Strauss, "Protestantism and Literacy in Early Modern Germany," *Past and Present* 104 (August 1984): 31-55.

Graff, Harvey J., ed., *Literacy and Social Development in the West* (Cambridge, 1981). (a)

———, *Literacy in History: An Interdisciplinary Research Bibliography* (New York, 1981).(b)

———, "On Literacy in the Renaissance: Review and reflections," *History of Education* 12 (1983): 69-85.

Greer, Allan, "The Pattern of Literacy in Quebec, 1745-1899," *Histoire Sociale. Social History* 11 (1978): 295-335.

Grendler, Paul F., "What Zuanne Read in School: Vernacular Texts in Sixteenth Century Venetian Schools," *The Sixteenth Century Journal* 13, no. 1 (1982): 41-54.

———, "The Schools of Christian Doctrine in Sixteenth-Century Italy," *Church History* 53 (1984): 319-31.

———, "The Organization of Primary and Secondary Education in the Italian Renaissance," *The Catholic Historical Review* 71 (1985): 185-205.(a)

———, "The Teaching of Latin in Sixteenth-Century Venetian Schools," *Acta Conventus Neo-Latini Bononiensis,* ed. R. J. Schoeck (Binghamton, NY, 1985): 258-76.(b)

History of Universities. Ed. Charles Schmitt. Vol. 1 (Amersham, Bucks, 1981).

Hoffman, Philip T., *Church and Community in the Diocese of Lyon 1500-1789* (New Haven, 1984).

Houston, Rab, "Literacy and Society in the West, 1500-1850," *Social History* 8 (1983), 269-93.

Huerga, Alvaro, "Sobre la Catequesis en España durante los siglos XV-XVI," *Analecta Sacra Tarraconensis* 41 (1968): 299-345.

Huppert, George, *Public Schools in Renaissance France* (Urbana, Ill., 1984).

Janz, Denis, *Three Reformation Catechisms: Catholic, Anabaptist, Lutheran* (New York, 1982).

Kagan, Richard L., *Students and Society in Early Modern Spain* (Baltimore, 1974).

Labalme, Patricia H., ed., *Beyond Their Sex. Learned Women of the European Past* (New York, 1980; reprinted 1984).

Labarre, Albert, *Le livre dans la vie amiénoise du seizième siècle* (Paris, 1971).

Liberali, Giuseppe, *Le origini del seminario diocesano* (Treviso, 1971).

Liebreich, A. K., "The Florentine Piarists," *Archivum Scholarum Piarum* 6, no. 12 (1982): 273-304.

———, "Piarist Education in the Seventeenth Century," *Studi seicenteschi* 26 (1985): 225-77.

Lucchi, Piero, "La Santacroce, il Salterio e il Babuino: libri per imparare a leggere nel primo secolo della stampa," *Quaderni storici* 38 (maggio-agosto 1978): 595-630.

Marcocchi, Massimo, *Le origini del Collegio della Beata Vergine di Cremona, istituzione della Riforma Cattolica (1610)* (Cremona, 1974).

Martín Hernández, Francisco, *La formación clerical en los colegios universitarios españoles (1371-1563)* (Vitoria, 1961).

_____, *Los seminarios españoles. Historia y pedagogía, 1563-1700* (Salamanca, 1964).

Maschietto, Francesco L., *Elena Lucrezia Cornaro Piscopia 1646-84* (Padua, 1978).

Monumenta Paedagogica Societatis Iesu, ed. Ladislaus Lukács. Vol. 1: 1540-56; vols. 2 and 3: 1557-72; vol. 4: 1573-80. (Rome, 1965-81).

Pelliccia, Guerrino, "Scuole di catechismo e scuole rionali per fanciulle nella Roma del Seicento," *Ricerche per la storia religiosa di Roma* 4 (1980): 237-68.

Pesciatini, Daniela, "Maestri, medici, cerusici nella communià rurali pisane nel XVII secolo," *Scienze, Credenze occulte, Livelli di cultura* (Florence, 1982): 121-45.

S. Petri Canisii: Catechismi Latini et Germanici, ed. Fridericus Streicher. 2 vols. (Rome, 1933-36).

Petrucci, Armando, "Scrittura, alfabetismo ed educazione grafica nella Roma del primo Cinquecento. Da un libretto di centi di Maddalena pizzicarola in Trastevere," *Scrittura e Civiltà* 2 (1978): 163-207.

_____, ed., *Scrittura e popolo nella Roma barocca 1585-1721* (Rome, 1982).

Pollock, Linda A., *Forgotten Children. Parent-Child Relations from 1500 to 1900* (Cambridge, 1983).

Rodríguez, Pedro, and "Raúl Lanzetti, *El Catecismo Romano: Fuentes e historia del texto y de la redacción* (Pamplona, 1982).

Sántha, G., C. Aguilera, and J. Centelles, *S. José de Calasanz. Su obra. Escritos* (Madrid, 1956).

Scaduto, Mario, *L'epoca di Giacomo Lainez 1556-1565: L'azione. Storia della Compagnia di Gesù in Italia,* vol. 4 (Rome, 1974).

Schmidt, Peter, *Das Collegium Germanicum in Rom und die Germaniker: Zur Funktion eines römischen Ausländerseminars, 1552-1914* (Tübingen, 1984).

Secco, Luigi, *La pedagogia della Controriforma* (Brescia, 1973).

Seifert, Arno, *Weltlicher Staat und Kirchenreform. Die Seminarpolitik Bayerns im 16. Jahrhundert* (Münster/W., 1978).

Sindoni, Angelo, "Le Scuole Pie in Sicilia. Note sulla storia dell'ordine scolopico dalle origini al secolo XIX," *Rivista di Storia della Chiesa in Italia* 25 (1971), 375-421.

Sowards, J. Kelley, "Erasmus and the Education of Women," *The Sixteenth Century Journal* 13, no. 4 (1982): 77-89.

Tamborini, Alessandro, *La Compagnia e le scuole della dottrina cristiana* (Milan, 1939).

Toscani, Xenio, "Le 'Scuole della Dottrina Cristiana' come fattore di alfabetizzazione," *Società e storia* 7, 26 (ott.-dic. 1984): 757-81.

Tramontin, Silvio, "Gli inizi dei due Seminari di Venezia," *Studi Veneziani* 7 (1965): 363-77.

Turrini, Miriam, "'Riformare il mondo a vera vita christiana': le scuole di catechismo nell'Italia del Cinquecento," *Annali dell'Instituto storico italo-germanico in Trento* 8 (1982) (Bologna, 1984): 407-89.

Van Egmond, Warren, *Practical Mathematics in the Italian Renaissance: A Catalog of Italian Abbacus Manuscripts and Printed Books to 1600* (Florence, 1981).

Viguerie, Jean de, *Une oeuvre d'education sous l'ancien régime. Les Pères de la doctrine chrétienne en France et en Italie 1592-1792* (Paris, 1976).

Wyczánski, Andrzej, "Alpéhabtisation et structure sociale en Pologne au XVIe siècle," *Annales E. S. C.* 29 (1974): 705-13.

Index of Names